MASTERS OF WORLD LITERATURE

PUBLISHED

GEORGE ELIOT	*by Walter Allen*
COLERIDGE	*by Walter Jackson Bate*
T. S. ELIOT	*by Bernard Bergonzi*
MATTHEW ARNOLD	*by Douglas Bush*
JOHN KEATS	*by Douglas Bush*
JOHN MILTON	*by Douglas Bush*
JONATHAN SWIFT	*by Nigel Dennis*
DANTE	*by Francis Fergusson*
STENDHAL	*by Wallace Fowlie*
THOMAS HARDY	*by Irving Howe*
HONORÉ BALZAC	*by E. J. Oliver*
GOLDSMITH	*by Ricardo Quintana*
TENNYSON	*by Christopher Ricks*

IN PREPARATION

PROUST	*by William Barrett*
FLAUBERT	*by Jacques Barzun*
SAMUEL JOHNSON	*by James L. Clifford*
IBSEN	*by Harold Clurman*
EUGENE O'NEILL	*by Harold Clurman*
EMILY DICKINSON	*by J. V. Cunningham*
YEATS	*by F. W. Dupee*
JOYCE	*by Leon Edel*
CONRAD	*by Elizabeth Hardwick*
EMERSON	*by Alfred Kazin*
SHAKESPEARE	*by Frank Kermode*
JANE AUSTEN	*by Louis Kronenberger*
POE	*by Dwight Macdonald*
CHEKHOV	*by Howard Moss*
FIELDING	*by Midge Podhoretz*
HENRY JAMES	*by Richard Poirier*
TOLSTOY	*by Philip Rahv*
MELVILLE	*by Harold Rosenberg*
WORDSWORTH	*by Lionel Trilling*

TENNYSON

MASTERS OF WORLD LITERATURE SERIES
LOUIS KRONENBERGER, GENERAL EDITOR

TENNYSON

Christopher Ricks

Collier Books, New York, New York

Lines from T. S. Eliot's "Burnt Norton" from *Four Quartets* are reprinted by permission of Harcourt Brace Jovanovich, Inc., New York; from Philip Larkin's *The Less Deceived*, by permission of The Marvell Press, England.

The Macmillan Company
866 Third Avenue, New York, N.Y. 10022
Collier-Macmillan Canada Ltd., Toronto, Ontario

Library of Congress Catalog Card Number: 76–165569

Tennyson is also published in a hardcover edition by The Macmillan Company.

FIRST COLLIER BOOKS EDITION 1972

Printed in the United States of America

Contents

Preface

ALFRED TENNYSON HAD a long life, from 1809 to 1892, and he wrote a very great deal—*The Poems of Tennyson*, which I edited for Longman Annotated English Poets (1969), has eighteen hundred pages. Any book which aims to deal with both the life and the work is therefore thrust into drastic decisions. I wished to do three things: to create a sense of what Tennyson in his private life underwent and became; to make an independent exploration of his poetry, seeking to comprehend its special distinction and to establish distinctions; and to suggest some of the relationships between the life and the work, in the spirit of Carlyle's vivid glimpse of Tennyson in 1844: "a man solitary and sad, as certain men are, dwelling in an element of gloom,—carrying a bit of Chaos about him, in short, which he is manufacturing into Cosmos!"

Since a preface is the place for saying what one has not done, it should be made clear what it was that these decisions excluded. First, there is much of Tennyson's poetry which I had no room to mention, let alone to explore; if the poems which figure in these pages are the traditional choices to the point of predictability, that is because in my opinion the traditional sense of what was most creative within Tennyson's achievement is a just one. Second, I have not embarked upon Tennyson's times, upon history or literary history or history of ideas; Tennyson was not a recluse, but his essential life was the private life, and this made me decide, moreover, that a biographical study could without falsification (though with a sad forfeiting of some fine anecdotes) phase itself out. By the 1850s, when Tennyson was married, middle aged, famous, secure, and the Poet Laureate, he had undergone all that truly formed him. Thereafter this book speaks simply of the poems.

A word about the two biographies of Tennyson which matter. *Alfred Lord Tennyson: A Memoir* (1897), by Tennyson's son Hallam Tennyson, is capacious and honorable, at its best in breathing a sense of what it was like in the immediate vicinity of Tennyson during the second half of his life. But the *Memoir* is unfortunately inaccurate, sometimes willfully so, and it is inordinately reticent. The truth about Tennyson's early life was first told by the poet's grandson, Sir Charles Tennyson, in his *Alfred Tennyson* (1949), a biography which is compact, humane, wide ranging, and unsuperseded. Neither of these biographies, however, gives any references; I have tried in the important cases to do what seems necessary at the present stage of Tennyson studies–that is, to go back behind the biographies to their unspecified sources. Such notes are at the end of the present book.

Two other accounts of Tennyson ask mention. R. W. Rader's *Tennyson's "Maud": The Biographical Genesis* (1963) stands as a notably important contribution, revealing, among other things, a love affair the failure of which mattered a great deal to Tennyson. Then, of a very different kind, there is the *Diary* (1907) of Tennyson's friend William Allingham; Allingham establishes, through his innumerable shrewd and exhilarating conversations with and about Tennyson, what seems to me the most living sense of the man Tennyson was.

Acknowledgments

I AM GRATEFUL to Lord Tennyson and Sir Charles Tennyson for permission to quote manuscript and other material. Permission to quote manuscripts has also been kindly granted by Lord Boyne; Mr. Robert Taylor; Major Alfred Tennyson d'Eyncourt; the Beinecke Library, Yale University; the Henry W. and Albert A. Berg Collection, the New York Public Library, Astor, Lenox and Tilden Foundations; the British Museum; the Brotherton Collection, University of Leeds; Duke University Library; the Harvard College Library; the Huntington Library, San Marino; the Library of the University of Texas at Austin; Wellesley College Library. Quotations from the Tennyson manuscripts at Trinity College, Cambridge, are given by permission of Lord Tennyson's Trustees and with the approval of the Master and Fellows of Trinity College, Cambridge. My special thanks are due also to the Tennyson Research Centre, Lincoln, and its director, Mr. F. T. Baker, and to Mrs. N. Campbell; and to the Lincolnshire Archives Committee and Mrs. J. Varley. The British Academy gave permission for me to incorporate, in an amended form, my Chatterton Lecture (1966) on "Tennyson's Methods of Composition"; the *Malahat Review* likewise for an amended form of my essay on "Tennyson as a Love-Poet," published there in October 1969 (number twelve). I am indebted to Professor Cecil Y. Lang, who is editing Tennyson's letters and who most generously shared his knowledge; also to Professor M. A. Epstein, for an opinion on scirrhosis of the liver.

Quotations from the poems are from my edition of *The Poems of Tennyson* (Longman Annotated English Poets, 1969). Remarks by Tennyson, Hallam Tennyson, and Edward FitzGerald for which no source is given will be found in my edition; they derive from the Eversley Edition (1907–8). In quoting from letters, I have made a few minor changes in spelling and punctuation, particularly in expanding casual contractions; similarly in a few cases when quoting from the letters and journals of people other than Tennyson.

Mr. Graham Wicks is at work on a reprint of Hallam Tennyson's *Materials for a Life of A.T.;* this draft of the *Memoir* was printed but not published, and exists in several states at Lincoln; the existence there too of the manuscript draft for the *Materials* makes any reconstruction complicated but rewarding.

Finally, though my particular undertaking made me think it better to use my space to quote from Victorian rather than from twentieth-century critics, I wish to draw attention to two recent essays which I have found especially stimulating and truthful: one by Martin Dodsworth, in *The Major Victorian Poets: Reconsiderations* (edited by Isobel Armstrong, 1969); the other by William E. Fredeman, on "St. Simeon Stylites," in the *University of Toronto Quarterly*, volume xxxviii (1968).

TENNYSON

I

1. Tennyson and his father till 1827

Moreover, always in my mind I hear
A cry from out the dawning of my life,
A mother weeping,
("The Coming of Arthur")

ALFRED TENNYSON HAD SUCH A CRY always in his mind. He was a sixty-year-old smiling (and gruffly scowling) public man when he wrote those lines. He was Poet Laureate. His father would have been proud of him: "My father who was a sort of Poet himself thought so highly of my first essay that he prophesied I should be the greatest Poet of the Time." But could Tennyson feel proud of his father? The cry from out the dawning of his life, the mother weeping: these were the core of his childhood and youth. "In no other English poet of comparable rank," said W. H. Auden, "does the bulk of his work seem so clearly to be inspired by some single and probably very early experience. Tennyson's own description of himself as

An infant crying in the night:
An infant crying for the light:
And with no language but a cry

is extraordinarily acute. If Wordsworth is the great English poet of Nature, then Tennyson is the great English poet of the Nursery." But the early experience was not for Tennyson a single one, and it lasted long past the nursery; it was (as the biography by the poet's grandson, Sir Charles Tennyson, first let the world know) a snarled web of family feud, bitterness, genteel poverty, drunkenness, madness, and violence.

In that same year, 1869, in which the Laureate wrote "The

Coming of Arthur," his wife Emily set down some memories, "Written For My Sons." She told of the fatal misfortune which had ruined the life of Tennyson's father, and which had come near to ruining that of his wife and children: the decision by the poet's grandfather, George Clayton Tennyson, to disinherit his elder son—the poet's father, Dr. George Clayton Tennyson, born 1778—in favor of the younger son Charles.

> You know [Emily wrote for her sons] how owing to some caprice on the part of your great-grandfather [George Clayton Tennyson] your grandfather [Dr. Tennyson] was disinherited and so deprived of a station which he would so greatly have adorned and put into the Church for whose duties he felt no call. This preyed upon his nerves and his health and caused much sorrow in his house. Many a time has your father [the poet] gone out in the dark and cast himself on a grave in the little churchyard near wishing to be beneath it.

Wishing to be dead: the wish—neither simply yielded to, nor simply repudiated—is at the heart of many of Tennyson's best poems. To understand the heart of Tennyson (in both senses) it is necessary to go back to the days before he ever wished he were dead. Would it be too grim to say that this means before he was born? In 1802—three years before marriage and seven years before the birth of Alfred Tennyson—the poet's father was in his early twenties. A family letter from his brother Charles to their father already makes clear which was the favored son; the favored son is somewhat blandly anxious about his unhappy elder brother:

> I hope Dear George reached you safe and *well*, for he was very much the contrary of the latter when at Cambridge; however as he began to get up his looks before he left me, I trust he would not relapse; I think, if I may judge from his appearance when he came, that had he gone on immediately, it would have been little less than suicide.

Suicide: the word about his father was out before Tennyson was born, and the nature of his father's death was later to haunt him. How much was there of metaphor when people saw his father's drinking as suicidal?

It is not clear just when George Clayton Tennyson, "the Old Man of the Wolds," decided to prefer his younger son. Certainly the sons were still young; certainly the Old Man's prophecy that his elder son would not make a fit head of the family was self-fulfilling. And we shall never know whether an elder son more honorably treated would have been more capable thereafter of an honorable life. For George was only twelve when his father arranged that he should go into the church, and that two livings should be kept warm for him till he came of age. For George, the school at York was followed by a mere private tutor; for the younger brother, Charles, the school at York was succeeded by Eton College. By 1796, when George went to St. John's College, Cambridge, the Old Man's preference for Charles seems to have been manifest.

George was put into the Church on December 19, 1802. In 1805 he married Elizabeth Fytche; he had the livings of Somersby and Bag Enderby, and in 1808 the Tennysons occupied Somersby Rectory, twenty-three miles from Lincoln, and sixteen miles from his father's home, Bayons Manor at Tealby. They more than occupied it, they crowded it, since Elizabeth Tennyson gave birth to twelve children in fourteen years: George (who died in infancy) in 1806, Frederick in 1807, Charles in 1808, the poet Alfred in 1809 (August 6), Mary in 1810, Emilia in 1811, Edward in 1813, Arthur in 1814, Septimus in 1815, Matilda in 1816, Cecilia in 1817, and Horatio in 1819. The Rector of Somersby, Dr. Tennyson (as he became in 1813, when he took the degree of Doctor of Civil Law) might on good days have agreed that his stipend—which came at first to about £700 a year, and later to about £1000 a year—was adequate, but it was hardly princely. Certainly the conditions of his life were such as to aggravate rather than soothe his grievance against his brother and father. In 1815, Charles wrote to the Old Man: "George seems to have forgotten me, or to remember me with such bitterness that he will not mention my name or family." The latter, as Charles well knew.

Dr. Tennyson was a man of culture (he played the harp and he wrote poetry) and a man of learning (his library was large, rich, and idiosyncratic). As a man of God he was less satisfactory. And what escape from the pullulating Rectory was there for the young Tennyson? The village school—and then at the age of seven, the school at Louth, where his elder brothers Frederick and

Charles had started the previous year. "How I did hate that school! The only good I ever got from it was the memory of the words, 'sonus desilientis aquae,' and of an old wall covered with wild weeds opposite the school windows." His memories of how miserable he was at school never softened (as they usually do) into rugged sentimentality. "He remembered to his dying day sitting on the stone steps of the school on a cold winter's morning, and crying bitterly after a big lad had brutally cuffed him on the head because he was a new boy." When he was eighty, he spoke "of his hating Louth School so much, that he would not go down the lane where it was, when in later life he was at Louth."

Dr. Tennyson's primogeniture had been slighted; the Doctor was the more insistent that his eldest son, Frederick, should not be slighted. So when Frederick left Louth School in 1818, it was both proper and proud that he should proceed to that great school which the Doctor had been wrongfully denied: Eton. When the next two brothers, Charles and Alfred, left Louth School in 1820, they were to complete the rectification of yesteryear: they were to have a mere private tutor. Mere? Dr. Tennyson himself was to teach them; his motives, the decent one of poverty, the honorable one of pride in his own learning, and the vengeful one of martyring himself. His father and brother would not be kept ignorant of the sacrifices which the aggrieved Doctor was making. From 1820 to 1827, then—from the age of ten to eighteen—Tennyson was plunged back into the intense Rectory. School had not proved to be any kind of freedom, merely a brutal vacancy. Home was the opposite of vacant and yet had its own bitter brutalities. The poet who was to cry "O damnèd vacillating state!" had already tasted a world where one shrank from both of the alternatives. For it was in the 1820s that Dr. Tennyson collapsed into drink and rage.

It was in the very year 1820—when the whole formation of Tennyson, aged ten, was back in the hands of home—that relations between his father and grandfather became morbidly irreparable. "My dear Father," wrote Dr. Tennyson:

I find, to my great disquietude, that you have thought proper to attribute to my suggestion or instigation certain expressions which may or may not have been used by Miss Fytche reflecting upon your conduct as a parent. I utterly disdain to exculpate myself from this charge. I did intend to have visited Tealby, but an accusation so unjust, so frequently reiterated and so totally unsubstantiated has so far oppressed my spirits and irritated my feelings that it is impossible that I can do so with any pleasure. With the sentiments you yet entertain and have entertained for more than twenty years, I cannot wonder you told Mr. Bourne you had not a spark of affection for me. The rude and unprecedented manner in which you first addressed me at Hainton, after a long absence, on your return from York (I quote your own words, "*Now you great awkward booby are you here*") holding me up to utter derision before Mr. Heneage, his sons and Sir Robt. Ainslie, and your language and conduct in innumerable other instances, many of which have made a deep impression upon my mind, sufficiently prove the truth of your own assertion. You have long injured me by your suspicions. I cannot avoid them for the fault is not mine. God judge between you and me. You make and have always made a false estimate of me in every respect. You look and have always looked upon me with a jaundiced eye, and *deeply and experimentally* feeling this, I am sure that my visiting you would not contribute to your satisfaction and at the same time would materially injure my own health and comfort. Conscious also that I am thrown into a situation unworthy my abilities and unbecoming either your fortune or my just pretensions, and resisted in my every wish to promote my own interests or that of my family by removing to a more eligible situation, unaccountably kept in the dark with respect to their future prospects, with broken health and spirits, I find myself little disposed to encounter those unprovoked and sarcastic remarks in which you are so apt to indulge yourself at my expense, remarks, which though they may be outwardly borne, are inwardly resented, and prey upon the mind—the injustice, the inhumanity and the impropriety of which every one can see but yourself, and which in your last visit were levelled against the father of a large family in the very presence of his children and that father between forty and fifty years of age. I should not have proceeded thus far had you not by your unjust aspersions set fire to the mass which was already disposed to ignite. You may forget or pass off as a jest what penetrates and rankles in my heart; you may break what is already bent, but there is a tribunal before which you and I may speedily appear, more speedily perhaps than either of us desire or expect—there it will be seen whether you through life have treated me with that consideration and kindness which a son has a right to expect from a father, and whether (as you have been accustomed to represent me to myself and others) I have been deficient in filial affection and obedience.

It is a letter whose pain, fragility, and dignity are touching. It is the letter of a son whose father had done him the greatest injury of all: making it superhumanly difficult for him to treat his own sons with "that consideration and kindness which a son has a right to expect from a father." The Old Man replied that the letter had been "unkind" and "unjustifiable," but he proceeded to let it be known that he was making a will in which Dr. Tennyson's younger children would have between them £20,000.

Two years later the strain had increased. By 1822 (Tennyson was twelve), the Doctor's health had cracked. He wrote to his mother from Cheltenham: "Eliza and I are both here; she is by no means in a good state of health and I have consulted a Physician with respect to each of our cases. He gives me great hopes that the waters will reestablish my health and says that a scirrhus has not as yet formed upon my liver, but that he could not have answered for the consequences if I had not immediately come here." There is indeed more than one cause of a scirrhus on the liver, but the likelihood is strong that Dr. Tennyson was already the victim of that which sadly clamped together his physical and mental illness: drink. Nine days later, the Old Man of the Wolds wrote to his favored son Charles about Dr. Tennyson and his wife: "It was lucky you left the place before your unbrotherly Brother arrived, I fear he will stir up much strife, I feel for our Dearest Eliza. Burn this letter." Dr. Tennyson was to enter into strife (who first stirred it up is another matter) with most of the family—Mrs. Russell, for example, his sister and later a generous benefactor to her nephew Alfred Tennyson. By January 1824 Dr. Tennyson was quick to resent any such hint at patronage as seemed to him a pretense at restitution.

I did not think that Mrs. Russell had been so ungrateful and so callous . . . But money, I am well persuaded, deadens the feelings, and I suppose Mrs. Russell is not so superior to the rest of mankind as not to feel their paralyzing influence. You would scarcely believe that Mrs. Russell told me, a little before her husband died, that my family could live well and be educated genteelly for £800 a year!!! She would put out my children to school, when in *distress!* This of course I refused . . . Her indifference, and I must say ingratitude, has nettled me to the quick. The only reason which she can allege for this conduct is that when lately she offered to come and see us we had not accommodation. This I suppose is to cancel all former benefits. We are three and twenty in family and sleep five or six in a room. Truly we have great accommodation for Mrs. Russell and her suite. We have not the house at Brighton nor the castle at Brancepeth.

Yet such scorn coexisted with bleak recognition: "The fact is my spirits are very bad and I never set myself about any thing that I can possibly avoid."

Next month the Doctor's body and mind were racked by bitter seizures and bitter envy; he wrote to his brother Charles:

You speak of going to Paris—How happy should I be could I accompany you there.* I think it would give me something like health of which I cannot boast at present. Less application and a change of climate and a removal from the harassing business of instruction would perhaps restore me. But I feel my powers of mind sensibly declining, and the attacks to which I am subject must necessarily injure the intellect. I have had two in the last five days.

* I am so netted in by the instruction of my Family that I cannot.

Could things go on like this? The family, and the Doctor himself, expected his death in July 1825; the Doctor (as his father reported to the favored Charles) "said he hoped everything would be forgotten that had been disagreeable between us and hoped also that I would be a parent to his family. . . My life will not be long of course, but when I am gone I am sure you will supply my place with as much feeling and more ability should your Brother die before me . . . I fear our Dear George cannot regain his strength but Mr. Fytche will write to me if there should be any change for the worse." Two days later, to the patrons of the ecclesiastical livings: "I found him in a very lamentable state, and I entertain very little hope of his recovery. I have to request the favour of you not to dispose of the livings he holds under your Patronage, till I can have the pleasure of personal communication with you."

Something of what this meant to Alfred Tennyson may be seen in the letter, dignified and poignant, which he wrote in August 1825—at the age of sixteen—to his uncle Charles:

It is with great sorrow that I inform you that my poor Father is not any better than before. He had another violent attack of the same nature yesterday. Indeed no one but those who are continually with him can conceive what he suffers, as he is never entirely free from this alarming illness. He is reduced to such a degree of weakness from these repeated attacks, that the slightest shock is sufficient to bring them on again. Perhaps if he could summon resolution enough to get out more, he would be relieved, but the lassitude which the fits leave incapacitates him from undergoing any exertion. He has already had two of these since my Grandfather was here which is not much more than a week ago and some time previous to that had three each night successively.

It was not to be Dr. Tennyson, but his mother, who died in 1825. This sadness may indeed have helped for a time to bring father and son together, but before long it was clear that tension was still what it had been–and Dr. Tennyson and his father were now locked alone in their relationship. The Old Man's daughter Elizabeth, Mrs. Russell, wrote to her father with one severe eye on her brother the Doctor: "Do not my dear and now alas, my *only* Parent encourage the idea that you can be in the way of any of your children, even a *wayward* one must sympathize in your deep sorrow."

Dr. Tennyson regained his wayward strength. It was a damaging strength, and by 1827 things were worse than they had ever been. In October, the eighteen-year-old Tennyson found the strain of life at the Rectory unbearable and went to stay with his grandfather at Bayons Manor. His mother wrote to thank the Old Man, and her letter shows what she was enduring:

I fear we cannot have the pleasure of visiting you at Tealby at the time you proposed as George will not allow any of the children to come with me nor will he let me have the Carriage unless I promise to remain from home half a year, a condition which of course I cannot comply with as I dare not leave the children with him . . . I cannot leave home for any length of time on account of poor George's violence which I fear increases. We had a terrible evening on Sunday.

The day of rest and the man of God did not protect Mrs. Tennyson against terror. But Alfred Tennyson could perhaps escape—to Cambridge. His brother Frederick had started there in 1826, and Charles in October 1827. But Tennyson was thought to need coaching in mathematics, and his aunt Mrs. Russell generously offered to pay for it. So in November 1827, when his father was "extremely ill, and the family in great confusion," Tennyson left for Cambridge. His departure was precipitated by the fact that his sick father was about to visit Bayons; the Old Man of the Wolds wrote to Mrs. Russell: "The day his father came here, Alfred set out for Cambridge, not wishing to meet him, where he proposes to stay till the £100 you kindly promised him is exhausted. What is to be done with him I don't know." Mrs. Russell was perplexed:

> . . . I know not how to direct to Alfred, having heard nothing of him excepting what you tell me, from which I presume he is fixed at college. I thought it had been arranged (as he would not be profited by going thither until he was a better Mathematician) that I should place him with some gentleman for previous instruction. He did not however appear to consider the place fixed upon in Lincolnshire, as one likely to make him happy, therefore just before we separated, I told him if he preferred any other, it was not my wish to fetter him, on *this* probably he has chosen *Cambridge*, but he has not informed me, and I am consequently left in ignorance.

Tennyson had been admitted to Trinity College, Cambridge, on November 9, 1827. Later that month, the family took up the earlier idea that Dr. Tennyson should go to Paris with his brother Charles. Alfred Tennyson, who must have been uneasy at having left his mother and his younger siblings to cope alone, was pleased to be able to share the family optimism; he wrote to his grandfather on December 5, 1827:

> I have received a letter from my Father dated Paris Nov. 30 in which he expresses a great wish to hear from me and I have accordingly written to him to-day—he seems I think to be in much better spirits than when I last saw him and I am almost certain that the constant variation of scene and ideas which occur in travelling will operate as an infallible restorative to his unhinged state of mind.

Mrs. Russell was less optimistic but more emphatic in writing likewise to the Old Man:

> Have you heard often from my Brother George since he went to Paris? I *hope and trust* that diversion from his usual train of thought and study and carking cares, with a change from former injurious habits, narcotics, late hours &c., will be sufficient to recover him.

It looked as though all might yet be well. The closing month of 1827—Tennyson was now eighteen and a Cambridge undergraduate—makes an apt moment for looking back at what he had been through and been about.

2. *Somersby till 1827*

He mastered circumstances, but he was also partly mastered by them, *e.g.* the old calamity of the disinheritance of his father . . .
(Benjamin Jowett, "Notes on Characteristics of Tennyson")

IT MAY BE THOUGHT that so dark a picture of Tennyson's childhood and youth is merely biographer's relish. But though no doubt the brothers and sisters loved and played, and though their mother was good and kind, it was the family feud and the father's "fits of despondency" which told most and which tell most. For however hospitable and generous the old grandfather and the fortunate uncle might intermittently be, any such kindness rankled. And however simply good and long-suffering their mother Eliza might be, nothing could disguise the fact that such goodness was mostly a matter of long suffering; such energy, excitement, and intellectual aspiration as there were in the Rectory were Dr. Tennyson's, and were laced with darker moods. "*Deeply and experimentally* feeling this": if we borrow Dr. Tennyson's poignant italics, and ask what it was that Tennyson–on the verge of manhood and Cambridge–deeply and experimentally felt from his earlier years, the answer is the plight of his father. There was in fact to be a cruel exacerbation of that plight; instead of a release for Tennyson from that which pained him most in his pained childhood, there was to be a prolonged intensification; but in 1827 Tennyson, like the rest of the family, felt hopeful. Yet deeply and experimentally felt (and to be even more so) were the preoccupations of some of his finest poetry: the bond cracked between father and son, madness, the wish to be dead.

Perhaps there were carefree times. But the life of Tennyson (the poems are something else) does not speak of them. The childhood memories which he was to proffer his son Hallam Tennyson are dark. They include his Aunt Bourne, with her fiery Calvinism: Aunt Bourne looking across the street at Spilsby and saying "This reminds me of the great gulf which shall divide the wicked from the blessed"; Aunt Bourne,

> who would weep for hours because God was so infinitely good. "Has he not damned," she cried, "most of my friends? But *me, me* He has picked out for eternal salvation, *me* who am no better than my neighbours." One day she said to her nephew, "Alfred, Alfred, when I look at you, I think of the words of Holy Scripture—'Depart from me, ye cursed, into everlasting fire.' "

Tennyson was never to find such sayings at all comic; he was never to find the doctrine of "everlasting fire" morally tolerable, and he was to return to it again and again; he was never to forget Aunt Bourne. He was in his mid-fifties when she died; he was moved to speak of her kindness, but he was more vividly moved to say that he "knew her to be one of the most wayward and at times violent of human beings." Another characteristically sad memory from childhood combines three of Tennyson's enduring concerns, prophetic fear, memory, and religion: he told his son of his "haunting fear that one day at the Catechism class he would be asked to repeat the Lord's Prayer and would find himself unable to. The day came, the question was asked and the poor boy found that the words had completely vanished from his memory." Ordinary, no doubt, but what was ordinary in Tennyson's childhood seems mostly to have been dispiriting.

Except, of course, for his aspirations and achievements in poetry—and the exception could hardly be larger. To his brother Arthur, Alfred said as a child, "I'm going to be famous." "The Poetry of Tennyson," "The Lyrical Poetry of Tennyson," and "The Prose Writings of Tennyson": the ten-year-old who so deployed his literary works in 1820 (these manuscript writings are in Latin) does of course resemble many a ten-year-old—except that in this case the commitment and gifts were real and were to be realized. Likewise, many a Lincolnshire schoolboy might have inscribed a text of Virgil:

1. A. Tennyson
2. Somersby
3. in Lincolnshire
4. in England
5. in Europe
6. in the world
7. in the air
8. in space

But this particular schoolboy was to develop an imagination which haunted those rippling vistas of space—like "The Mystic,"

> he in the centre fixt,
> Saw far on each side through the grated gates
> Most pale and clear and lovely distances.

Tennyson's father "prophesied I should be the greatest Poet of the Time." Philip Larkin has aimed glum wit at all such prophetic hindsights; "I Remember, I Remember" retails the non-memories which one might have liked to be able to look back upon:

> And, in those offices, my doggerel
> Was not set up in blunt ten-point, nor read
> By a distinguished cousin of the mayor,
>
> Who didn't call and tell my father *There*
> *Before us, had we the gift to see ahead—*

But Tennyson's father apparently had the gift. The grandfather too: "If Alfred die, one of our greatest poets will have gone." Not that the old grandfather was going to be carried away: when Tennyson wrote a poem on the death of his grandmother (1825), the Old Man gave him ten shillings—"There, that is the first money you have ever earned by your poetry, and, take my word for it, it will be the last."

It was the mouthability of poetry, the urge to roll it aloud, which first caught Tennyson. (His detractors might say that he never progressed much beyond a childish delight in such poetic sound.)

The first poetry that moved me was my own at five years old. When I was eight, I remember making a line I thought grander than Campbell, or Byron, or Scott. I rolled it out, it was this: "With slaughterous sons of thunder rolled the flood"—great nonsense of course, but I thought it fine.

Before I could read, I was in the habit on a stormy day of spreading my arms to the wind, and crying out "I hear a voice that's speaking in the wind," and the words "far, far away" had always a strange charm for me.

When I was in my very earliest teens . . . I wrote an epic in three books. It was full of furious battles à la Scott, and descriptions of lake and mountain scenery which I had never looked upon. I never felt so inspired—I used to compose 60 or 70 lines in a breath. I used to shout them about the silent fields, leaping over the hedges in my excitement.

Such excitement is altogether unlike anything which the Rectory housed, and there lay its consolatory power; already the child poet was in a situation where the poetic imagination had the perilous merit of offering something altogether other than the pains of life. But then in 1824 the death of Byron threatened—or promised—to bring into urgent relation the pains of life and the pleasures of imagination; Tennyson brought the news within the saddened auspices of Somersby life. "I was fourteen when I heard of his death. It seemed an awful calamity; I remember I rushed out of doors, sat down by myself, shouted aloud, and wrote on the sandstone: '*Byron is dead!*' " *Awful* was always for Tennyson an awed word; the deep awe, as at some family calamity, can be heard in his other reminiscences of that day, "a day when the whole world seemed to be darkened for me," a day when—because a poet had died—he "thought everything was over and finished for every one—that nothing else mattered." Tennyson was confronting more than the death of Byron.

His mother survives as a gracious silence, at any rate from the years before Tennyson went to Cambridge. The father's pains were alleviated by an optimism about his sons: "I have however some satisfaction in thinking that my boys will turn out to be clever men. Phoenix like, I trust (though I don't think myself a Phoenix) they will spring from my ashes in consequence of the exertions I have bestowed upon them." But that was in 1824, and Dr. Tennyson's relationship with his sons was not to be free of a sour resemblance to his relationship with his father. And the mother's pains? They were alleviated for the time being by her grave piety. Tennyson was to praise her as "the queen of marriage, a most perfect wife" in "Isabel"; more surprisingly, given that "Isabel" was published in 1830 while Dr. Tennyson was still alive, the poem was to describe the marriage of which she was queen:

> The mellowed reflex of a winter moon;
> A clear stream flowing with a muddy one,
> Till in its onward current it absorbs
> With swifter movement and in purer light
> The vexèd eddies of its wayward brother:
> A leaning and upbearing parasite,
> Clothing the stem, which else had fallen quite
> With clustered flower-bells and ambrosial orbs . . .

"Its wayward brother": that particular metaphor may have surfaced for Tennyson because of the circumstances which had muddied his father's clear stream. Was it Dr. Tennyson or the favored brother Charles who had been wayward?*

It was many years before Tennyson was able as a poet to look unflinchingly at his own childhood, and even then the truth about it which he brings himself to utter is most often a piercing parenthesis. His earliest surviving letter was written at the age of twelve; it is a precocious and ostentatious lecturette on literature, but it cares more than it is willing to show. The twelve-year-old quotes from *Samson Agonistes:*

> This passage,
> Restless thoughts, that like a deadly swarm
> Of hornets arm'd, no sooner found alone,
> But rush upon me thronging, and present
> Times past, what once I was, and what am now,
>
> puts me in mind of that in Dante, which Lord Byron has prefixed to his "Corsair." "Nessun maggior dolore, Che ricordarsi del tempo felice, Nella miseria."

Tennyson was later to recollect this sentiment of Dante's, in "Locksley Hall": "this is truth the poet sings, / That a sorrow's crown of sorrow is remembering happier things." But he was never able to stifle the other possibility: that a sorrow's crown of

* See Mrs. Russell's letter, p. 8.

sorrow is not having any happier things to remember. He was a very truthful man, and he had a simple and most honorable conception of what truth consisted in. But he had too a desperate wish to believe that somewhere in his childhood there had been joy.

From the East of life joybeams did strike
On my young brows. Joy rose up like
White Venus, whiter than all stars–
Then uprose trouble, red like Mars.

Joy set: he stayed: as Mars in heaven
Burns by the lonely sisters seven
When Venus having measured all
The arch in western mist doth fall.

Those "joybeams" have rather a determined air. What is deeper in Tennyson, a poignant recognition that happiness may not have been lost but may rather have never been possessed, may be heard in a poem which anticipates "Tears, idle tears" and which he wrote at seventeen: "No More."

Oh sad *No More!* Oh sweet *No More!*
  Oh strange *No More!*
By a mossed brookbank on a stone
I smelt a wildweed-flower alone;
There was a ringing in my ears,
And both my eyes gushed out with tears.
Surely all pleasant things had gone before,
Lowburied fathomdeep beneath with thee, NO MORE!

Had all pleasant things gone before in Tennyson's earlier life, or had they gone before he was ever born?

3. Poems till 1827

IN OCTOBER 1825 (at the age of sixteen), Tennyson adopted rather a grand manner in a letter to that rather grand figure, his uncle Charles Tennyson, M.P.

I have written out, as you desired me, a few more of those Poems, which you were so good as to say you would shew to Moore, but I am afraid that there is too little spirit and originality in them to please the severity and blunt the edge of *Critical acumen* and the Public is a many-headed Monster, which is generally disposed to make little allowance for the sleepy fits observable in an Author. I hope Moore possesses that very Christian and necessary virtue, *Patience*, without which it is utterly impossible to peruse the inclosed trifles, which have nothing in them wherewith they may exalt themselves above the many tadpole and ephemeral productions of the day.

The drawl never came naturally to Tennyson; moreover, his earliest poetic enterprise (apart from a fragment of translation from Claudian) was one of considerable "spirit and originality." At the age of fourteen he wrote a play (or rather, three acts). *The Devil and the Lady*, which Tennyson never published, is an exuberant pastiche of Elizabethan and Jacobean comedy. The old necromancer Magus has a journey to make, and so he conjures up the Devil to guard his wife Amoret against her lovers' importunities; the Devil disguises himself as Amoret, receives the lovers (lawyer, apothecary, sailor, astronomer, soldier, and monk), and embroils them. One tone in the play was not to be frequent in Tennyson's work: an ambivalent zest, an erotic deploring, with negatives acting as positives—as when the Devil admonishes Amoret, "Lie quietly, / Without the movement of one naughty muscle . . ." Most of the play already evidences his lifelong preoccupations. There is the vista of "never-ending space," with its astronomical wonders and metaphysical speculations: "O suns and spheres and stars and belts and systems, / Are ye or are ye not?" There is the visionary nightmare: "dim Phantasies / Came thronging thickly round me." There is the eternal torment of Hell, where time is not the mercy of eternity:

> There is a clock in Pandemonium,
> Hard by the burning throne of my Great Grandsire,
> The slow vibrations of whose pendulum,
> With click-clack alternation to and fro,
> Sound "EVER, NEVER!" through the courts of Hell,
> Piercing the wrung ears of the damned that writhe
> Upon their beds of flame . . .

There is the fascinated anatomizing of old age: Amoret's soliloquy against her old husband, "Thou shrunken, sapless, wizen Grasshopper" with his "mustiness of dry longevity"; and an imagined suitor: "There was no moisture on his fissured lip . . ." There is the grim humor—heard too in another very early poem, "The Coach of Death"—such as was always part of Tennyson's character and conversation but which he too seldom allowed into his poems.* In *The Devil and the Lady* it shows itself in the Devil's vengeful account of how he battered a monk; more importantly, it can be seen in a curiously irrelevant passage full of hatred for the hopes of youth, where the vengefulness seems to be Tennyson's and seems to be self-directed:

> Visions of happiness do float before thee,
> Gay-gilded figures and most eloquent shapes,
> Moulded by Fancy's gentle fingering
> To the appearance of reality,
> With youthful expectations and fond dreams,
> All rendered sunlike by the light of youth,

* "St. Simeon Stylites" and "The Vision of Sin" are important exceptions in the 1830s, and late in his life he was to recover it creatively in his dialect poems, most notably in "Northern Farmer. New Style."

Which glances on them, flit before thine eyes:
But these shall be pinched out of thee—ere morn
There shall be no sound place within thy person;
Thou shalt be all the colours of the rainbow,
With bruises, pinches, weals, ET CETERA . . .

Tennyson's verse, though, is already adept at "eloquent shapes," as in an adroit seascape:

The mighty waste of moaning waters lay
So goldenly in moonlight, whose clear lamp
With its long line of vibratory lustre
Trembled on their dun surface, that my Spirit
Was buoyant with rejoicings. Each hoar wave
With crispèd undulation arching rose . . .

"My Spirit" is the concern of the other notable poem of these early years: "Armageddon," a fragmentary vision of the last great battle, with a Miltonic angel as expositor. The best of "Armageddon" was to be reshaped in 1829 as "Timbuctoo." But its crucially Tennysonian feature is not so much its invocation of prophecy, or its shadowy phantasms, or its mysterious pavilions, or its mystical clarity of vision—rather, its ending. "Armageddon" is the battle that will end battles and will end evil. Tennyson's poem—and this is deeply characteristic—stops short of its own outcome. The poem may envisage, but it does not visualize, the battle of "Armageddon." Instead, it pauses, fraught with expectation. True, it is only a fragment—but that still leaves the question of why Tennyson did not complete it. He was drawn to complete his poems when their completion, their outcome, was less definitive, less final, than that of "Armageddon" would have had to be. Or when their outcome could potently be left unarrived at. "Armageddon," breaking off in mid-line, is an anticipation of such tensions in the later poems. Its ending is a suspending:

There was a beating in the atmosphere,
An indefinable pulsation
Inaudible to outward sense, but felt
Through the deep heart of every living thing,
As if the great soul of the Universe
Heaved with tumultuous throbbings on the vast
Suspense of some grand issue.

That issue never issues forth.

In April 1827, Tennyson and his brother Charles published *Poems by Two Brothers.* (Three brothers, in fact, since Frederick contributed four poems.) It was published anonymously by the booksellers Jackson, of Louth; it earned £20 for the copyright, of which £5 was to be taken in books; it received two brief but blandly favorable notices; and it did little to show that Tennyson either was or would be much of a poet. This is partly because the best of his early work–*The Devil and the Lady*, "Armageddon," and "The Coach of Death"–was not only fragmentary but in any case "omitted from the *Poems by Two Brothers*, being thought too much out of the common for the public taste." Tennyson's contributions were written when he was "between 15 and 17" (1824–26). They have the stilted aspirations suggested by the tone of that letter to his uncle in 1825. Many footnotes parade some genuine, idiosyncratic, but not astonishing, erudition. There are many of the preoccupations that endured for Tennyson, such as the aged speaker; memory and time; prophetic denunciations; the assured simplicities of battle; and "The Grave of a Suicide." But too smoothly rapid a manner, and far too many exclamation marks placed precisely where they are least true to Tennyson's creative temperament: of his forty-five contributions, twenty-nine end with exclamation marks. A further five end with question marks–and yet up till *In Memoriam* (1850) there was to be only one poem ending with a question mark–"Leonine Elegiacs" (1830)–which Tennyson was to retain in his published *oeuvre. In Memoriam* and the later poems do use such an ending, though very infrequently.* But Tennyson, a genuinely questioning poet, was aware of the proclivity of such endings to become mere rhetorical questions. *Poems by Two Brothers* is unaware of such compunctions. Though the knowledgeable admirer of Tennyson will find the stiff book stiff with anticipations, seeds, and nuances, its actual achievement was nugatory. Tennyson was right to think of it as "early rot," and right never to include any of it in his authorized body of work.

* Eight sections of *In Memoriam* end with question marks, as do seven poems from 1865 to 1892.

4. *Somersby 1828–1831*

DR. TENNYSON RETURNED from France in January 1828. Three months later there was a hideous shock when the cook at Somersby was burned to death. Young Charles (on vacation from Cambridge with Alfred) wrote to his grandfather: "I write for my Father whose hand can scarcely pen a line at present as it was burnt so terribly. He desires me to say that he cannot accept your kind invitation as the Cook is in a dying state and he is obliged to superintend the whole arrangements for the poor sufferer." Within months, Dr. Tennyson had relapsed; he was racked by spasms of the chest. In the words of his son Charles, "Last night he suffered very much from the same cause. Tonight it has recurred with great violence. My father is lying for ease on the floor and it is now midnight." It was at this time that Dr. Tennyson and his eldest son Frederick clashed bitterly. Frederick had much of the fierce instability of his father, and in December 1828 he was rusticated for three terms from Trinity College for disobedience and impertinence. Harsh, and probably unjust, such a disgrace exacerbated Dr. Tennyson's resentment at the (so little appreciated?) sacrifices he was making for his sons. Certainly Dr. Tennyson was not alone in thinking that his three eldest sons were far from being improved by their Cambridge education. The old grandfather summed up:

Charles and Alfred left me on Friday. They did not act *dis*respectably to me, but they are so untoward and disorderly and so unlike other people, I don't know what will become of them, or what can be done with, or about them. I tried to impress them with the feeling that they and Frederick was spending or wasting half their Father's income and he had only half to maintain himself [and] his wife, and to educate 4 other boys and 4 girls, and that unless the money expended for their education was to fit them for professions to get their livings, so that they might be out of the way for an expenditure on the education of their brothers and sisters and for putting their brothers in a way of getting their livings, they, Frederick, Charles and Alfred, would be the ruin of them and act most unkindly and dishonourably. Those 3 boys so far from having improved in manner or manners are worse since they went to Cambridge.

Dr. Tennyson's quarrel with his son Frederick shattered his marriage. Separation was the only answer. The Doctor wrote with forcible-feeble authority to the Old Man: "It is impossible that the family should be conducted as it has been hitherto; I have no means to make her a separate establishment, but the children must not be under her care: and I will take care to send all except my two elder daughters from under her superintendence." Dr. Tennyson was casting himself as the injured party, but whose care constituted the graver threat to the children? A long, desperate, and humiliated letter from Mrs. Tennyson in February 1829 to her father-in-law exposes the embittered bankruptcy of the marriage: the hatred, drunkenness, murderousness, and the cruel defection from those Christian standards which Dr. Tennyson was supposed to represent.

My dear Sir
I am sorry to give you, or any one, pain, but it is the extreme necessity of the case that urges me to express my most fixed and final resolution to separate from my husband as the only step that can effectually secure myself and family from the consequences of his ungovernable violence which I solemnly assure you has proceeded to such a length that I do not feel it safe either for myself or my children to remain any longer in the house with him. I understand from him that I have your sanction for this measure which even though it should not meet with your entire approbation, I know it to be absolutely necessary to our future comfort and tranquillity to adopt. Indeed Sir if the welfare of so many human beings is a matter of the smallest consideration, I am sure it can be only want of information

at many points, and misinformation on others that could induce you not to concur most fully in what I am at last determined to carry into effect. Your judgment has been most grossly abused in the representations which we know have been made to you, they are altogether unfounded in truth and therefore in the last degree cruel and insulting. I believe that you have been informed that Frederick said he would murder his Father. The words that Frederick made use of were these "We may thank God that we do not live in a barbarous Country, or we should have murdered each other before this." George did everything to irritate Frederick a few days ago and though Frederick said nothing disrespectful (as I can produce respectable witnesses to prove) he sent for the Constable (Mr. Baumber) and turned him out of doors. He remained with Mr. Baumber three days, he is now with my sister at Louth and is again taken into his father's favour who has allowed him a hundred pounds a year for the present . . . George asserts that he had your authority for turning him out of doors. There is another and perhaps a stronger reason than any I have given for our separation, the impression which his conduct may produce upon the minds of his family, not to mention the perpetual use of such degrading epithets to myself and children as a husband and a Father and above all a person of his sacred profession ought particularly to avoid. A short time since he had a large knife and loaded gun in his room. The latter he took into the kitchen to try before he went to bed and was going to fire it off through the kitchen windows but was dissuaded. With the knife he said he would kill Frederick by stabbing him in the jugular vein and in the heart. I remonstrated with him as having such dangerous weapons and told him he would be killing himself—he said he should not do this but he would kill others and Frederick should be one. I do not say this to impair my poor husband in your opinion but only to convince you that in the state of mind in which he is at times it is not safe for his family to live with him . . . I should be the last person in the world to act as principal in an affair of this kind had it been possible for us to accommodate our differences in any other manner . . . But when insult is aggravated by injury the burthen of such accumulated ills is grievous and insufferable. I shall take lodgings at Louth as soon as possible . . .

Mrs. Tennyson acted at once. Dr. Tennyson was left alone in the Rectory, and his state was abject. A family friend, the Rev. T. H. Rawnsley, felt obliged to write to Charles Tennyson the elder:

I think it prudent, to let you know that my old friend the Dr. is here, under the most deplorable state of mental depression and wretchedness. The scenes we once before lamented, and which I was in hopes would never more return, have been acted again, at Somersby, with the addition of a very unfeeling part, performed by the eldest son. The whole family quitted, and the Dr. was left alone and so ill, that his neighbour sent an express for me, fearing he would sink under his depression, and epileptic tendencies—when I arrived on Monday I found your brother *feeding upon himself*, and most miserable . . . He *must* not return to his family, and the sooner he takes another trip to France, or elsewhere, the better for him and for all concerned for him . . . *alone* he must not be.

So once more Dr. Tennyson toured France. Once more there was some mild optimism, but this time there was a realistic assessment as well. The Old Man wrote to his favored son Charles:

I think things are or may be arranged in such a manner as George might return home, but unless *he will determine* to give up drinking, in a week all will be as bad as ever. I have a Father's affection for him and will do any thing I can to serve him, yet surely he has, with his family, an imperious duty to perform, and it is his duty to do so . . . It is quite discreditable to the family *and the ruin of his* that things should go on as they have done, and as I am sure, that—would he give up drinking all might yet end more to all our credits.

But unfortunately travel proved even less efficacious than last time. This second tour, which lasted a year, seems to have done little to soothe Dr. Tennyson's resentment; the irreparable injury that his father had once done him was being shaped into a sense of injury against the wife whom he had injured: "I shall not write to my Wife at present, nor to any part of my family. They have (the more I consider the subject) treated me in too infamous a manner." Dr. Tennyson himself saw that the cure was not working: "I have endeavoured to dissipate all mental feeling by violent exertion and the inspection of foreign manners and scenery. It will not do. I feel here as an isolated being, an outcast from England and my family." At which point he launched an attack on his wife's family for encouraging the "open rebellion" of his children.

The dismay of his luckier brother is hardly surprising: "Although his Letter is written with steady hand and although his energy in travelling about proves that he abstains from a habit which we have lamented—yet I say I am fearful, *that his mental uneasiness may prey too seriously upon him.*"

One symptom of such mental uneasiness was Dr. Tennyson's preposterous and thrilling fantasizing about his journey. He was nearly swept to death in a carriage that crashed down from a mountain road, but he grasped a pine; at the carnival in Rome a man was stabbed in the Doctor's arms, and the Doctor suspected of the crime; he nearly tumbled from a precipice, and was almost buried by an avalanche. Not much of this is likely to be true, though it seems both that the Doctor was involved in some accident and also that he regretted any embroidering that may have been done. He wrote to his brother during the last stages of his return from France in June 1830: "I hope you have not mentioned any accident which has happened to me . . . every thing might be communicated in a moment to my Wife . . . I must necessarily have been smashed into a thousand pieces, from the exaggerated Accounts which usually are the concomitants of even a trifling report." But Dr. Tennyson seems himself to have been the author of some strikingly untrifling reports, and it may well be that among the strains of Somersby life were those created by a powerful fantasist. For an earlier journey abroad had moved Dr. Tennyson to some rich recollections. Far back in 1801 he had travelled in Russia; Alfred Tennyson was never to forget what he had been told of these adventures, and at the age of sixty-three the Laureate made his companions vibrate with them. But there is good reason to think that these heroic sufferings of Dr. Tennyson were imaginary. The part played by delirium, pennilessness, and drunkenness suggests some strange self-consolation deep in Dr. Tennyson.

Then A. [Tennyson in 1873] told the thrilling story of his father's stay in Russia: how, as a very young man, he was dining with our English Minister, Lord St. Helens, at St. Petersburg, when he said, across a Russian, to Lord St. Helens, "It is perfectly well-known in England who murdered the Emperor Paul: it was Count So and So." Whereat a dead silence fell on the company. After dinner Lord St. Helens called Dr. Tennyson aside and said, "Ride for your life from this city: the man across whom you were speaking to me was the Count So and So, whom you accused of murdering the Emperor Paul."

Dr. Tennyson took horse and rode for weeks and weeks through Russia, till he came to the Crimea where he fell ill. He became delirious, and remembered the wild country-people dancing round his bed with magical incantations. Once in every three months an English courier passed through this village where he lay ill, and as he passed through the village blew a horn. It all depended on Dr. Tennyson's hearing this horn whether he could escape from Russia, for he had no money. In his delirium he would perpetually start up agonized lest he had missed it. At last the courier came, the horn was blown and he heard the sound, and applied to the courier to take him. The courier agreed, and Dr. Tennyson journeyed with him. He was a drunken fellow and dropt all his despatches on the road. Dr. Tennyson picked them up, but did not say that he had done so. The courier was in despair, and at last Dr. Tennyson gave them to him, with a warning that he must not be drunken in future. At one frontier town the sentries had barred the gates, because it was late night. The courier, not to be daunted, shouted out "Le duc de York." An immediate unbarring ensued, and the sentinels all sprang to attention, and saluted him with deference. So, after less drunkenness on the part of the courier, and many adventures, they managed to reach England.

In the summer of 1830, after just over a year away, the prodigal father returned to his wife and children at Somersby. On the brink of his return, his wife had expressed great trepidation: "It appears to me there is but little hope of any permanent tranquillity. I cannot but confess I have the greatest dread of what may happen. May God (as he has mercifully done hitherto) protect my family. You know as well as myself that when under the influence of liquor George is dreadfully violent." And then her thoughts turned at once to Alfred: "Alfred is very ill and went to London to consult an eminent Physician (as he supposed), on a case of life or death. He writes me now that the Physician hopes he is mistaken but desires him to remain in London for a fortnight and then come to him again and has given him some medicine to take." Perhaps Tennyson still preferred to be where his father was not.

Six months after Dr. Tennyson returned, it became clear that God was going to protect the family against him in the only feasible way, though it was a way which would also leave the family unprotected. Dr. Tennyson was about to die. Much of his life had been a long day's dying. In February 1831, Tennyson was called back from Cambridge. The Doctor's pains were hideously similar to those of his earlier wildness and derangement; a nephew darkly speculated upon a possible link:

He is sometimes perfectly sensible—at others, talks wildly and is evidently deranged for the time being. Dr. B [Bousfield] says his disorder is depression of the Brain. My Uncle has been confined to his bed about a week, and I understand, gave way to great excess before his illness.

On March 8, 1831 it was known that he had typhus. One week later, Alfred Tennyson wrote to his uncle Charles:

All shadow of hope with respect to my poor Father's ultimate recovery has vanished. Yesterday he lost the use of one side. It is evident that he cannot last many hours longer. It is a great consolation to us, however, that he is free from all suffering and perfectly mild and tranquil, seeming not to interest himself in anything that passes, which is the effect of pressure on the brain: the strength of his constitution has enabled him to resist his complaint a fortnight longer than his physician expected, during which period we have had many fluctuations of hope and fear: at one time we almost ventured to be confident that he would be restored to us: but that is all over now. We *must* lose him. May my end be as calm as his.

Next day, on March 16, 1831, Dr. Tennyson died.

His wife was able to be candid and forgiving: "His errors were owing to the state of his nerves, which made him view every thing in a gloomy light and deprived him of almost every enjoyment of life." The Doctor's nerves had come near to depriving his wife and children too of almost every enjoyment of life. The Old Man, his father, cannot have been the only one to sense that there was mercy in the death; a week before the Doctor died, the Old Man wrote: "and though his death would hurt and affect me *much*, yet if he should determinately go on as he has done I would rather kiss the rod, I can say no more." Was there some such pained suppression in Alfred's words, "We *must* lose him"? But even before the Doctor's death, the Old Man was shouldering his responsibilities severely: "As to the 3 oldest boys of the family I shall now say no more than that if they expect my countenance and protection they must take a different course of life."

Had it all really been so wild, or is this to see it through the heated haze of family intensities? The cooler perturbation of a Lincolnshire neighbor of the Tennysons, Mrs. Massingberd, confirms it all. In February 1831 she had turned down a house near Somersby: "The house at Enderby would not do, for I should not like to spend my latter days in a place where the Clergyman is so strange a man as Dr. Tennison, and having his strange Family our readiest neighbours would be a great objection." The death of Dr. Tennyson made Mrs. Massingberd shake her head over the whole pack of them:

> As to poor Dr. Tennison I have always felt great compassion for him, though my pity would have been despised, but I think he is as strong a proof as can be that a *warm heart, fine intellect and generous spirit* without good religious principles are rather a hindrance to happiness in this world and the next. I should be very glad to hear his pride of intellect was so far humbled as to induce him to pray to his mediator to intercede for him with the Almighty to pardon his sins: for without that his death to me is quite shocking. Though certainly the searcher of all hearts we may hope would make great allowance for the faults of his Education and being forced to take orders against his inclination. His father has *indeed much* to answer for.

And Tennyson's reaction to the death of his father? "Within a week after his father's death he slept in the dead man's bed, earnestly desiring to see his ghost, but no ghost came. 'You see,' he said, 'ghosts do not come to imaginative people.' "* The action is equivocal and even cool. Perhaps Tennyson remembered this death when the narrator described his absence from a family funeral, in "The Gardener's Daughter" (written 1833–34):

> neither could I go,
> Nor could assimilate peculiar grief:
> Like nature quick to hide the grave with life,
> Grieved that I grieved so little . . .

Those lines he left in manuscript. His published lines on the death of his father are again strangely aloof. The poem, "To J.S.," is for his Cambridge friend James Spedding, whose brother Edward

* "I said long ago, 'A poet never sees a Ghost' " (Allingham's *Diary*, p. 330, August 7, 1884).

had died; it was written eighteen months after Dr. Tennyson's death, on which it touches. The touch is at once wooden and strained:

> In grief I am not all unlearned;
> Once through mine own doors Death did pass;
> One went, who never hath returned.
>
> He will not smile–not speak to me
> Once more. Two years his chair is seen
> Empty before us. That was he
> Without whose life I had not been.
>
> Your loss is rarer; . . .

Is it that Tennyson was too afraid of his feelings, that insofar as they were strong they included strong hostility and fear? There is something oddly weak about "who never hath returned" (do the dead much return?). Was the Doctor given to smiling? And how oblique that empty chair is. And how unfortunate the momentary ambiguity in "Your loss is rarer." True, it is more usual, at Spedding's or Tennyson's age, to lose a father than a brother; and yet "rarer" too much suggests a valuation. We can see the timidity and evasion of Tennyson's lines if we juxtapose them with some lines on the death of Dr. Tennyson by a far lesser poet:

> It hath ceased to feel,
> That heart so tenderfeeble, yet so wild!
> Oh Arm of *God*, what wilt thou bring of this?

Tennyson's friend Arthur Hallam, writing to Tennyson's sister Emily, was to be better able to confront in verse the death of Dr. Tennyson.

5. *Cambridge and Arthur Hallam till "Timbuctoo" 1829*

CAMBRIDGE IN 1827 had not struck Tennyson as vivid or warm. He wrote to his aunt Mrs. Russell:

I am sitting owl-like and solitary in my rooms (nothing between me and the stars but a stratum of tiles). The hoof of the steed, the roll of the wheel, the shouts of drunken Gown, and drunken Town come up from below with a sea-like murmur . . . I know not how it is, but I feel isolated here in the midst of society. The country is so disgustingly level, the revelry of the place so monotonous, the studies of the University so uninteresting, so much matter of fact. None but dry-headed, calculating, angular little gentlemen can take much delight in them.

There is something blasé about such drawling dissatisfaction, but there can be no doubt that Tennyson found more to endure than to enjoy in the university. "There was a want of love in Cambridge then," he was later to say pithily. He was moved to write, though not to publish, a bitter denunciation, "Lines on Cambridge of 1830," which listed the ancient glories of the place but only in order to tell Cambridge that they would avail it nothing, "you that do profess to teach / And teach us nothing, feeding not the heart."* Clearly his first years at Cambridge were much less than the generous liberation for which he had hoped.

* At the age of seventy he was to deplore its unauthorized publication, regretting that "this spirit of undergraduate irritability against the Cambridge of that day ever found its way into print."

Not much is known of Tennyson's time in Cambridge from November 1827 to the spring of 1829. Then within a few months there were three vital flowerings. In about April 1829, Tennyson met Arthur Henry Hallam, whom he was to love and lose. In May 1829, he joined a society of talented undergraduates, the "Apostles." In June 1829, he won the Chancellor's Gold Medal with his prize poem, "Timbuctoo."

Arthur Hallam was eighteen months younger than Tennyson. The son of the distinguished historian Henry Hallam, he had been at Eton (where he knew Frederick Tennyson—and William Ewart Gladstone). After leaving Eton in 1827, he had spent some months in Italy and had become a proficient scholar and even poet in the language. He came to Trinity College in October 1828, and got to know Tennyson in about April 1829. Each stood strongly in need of friendship: Arthur Hallam's former friends were now at Oxford, not Cambridge, and he brooded upon this lack of friendship; Tennyson, who had not yet found much human riches in Cambridge, was all too aware of the spendthrift emotionalism which was racking the family in Somersby. (It was in February 1829 that Tennyson's mother left his father.)

The friendship of Hallam and Tennyson was swift and deep. Together they joined the Apostles, an informal debating society which numbered among its talented members many who were to become eminent (though few—none?—of them preeminent) Victorians: John Kemble, Richard Chenevix Trench, Richard Monckton Milnes, James Spedding . . . It would be easy to exaggerate the intellectual and spiritual influence which the Apostles had upon Tennyson, though much of what they discussed was important, while tinged with self-importance. Tennyson's participation in the group was to be genially torpid—so torpid as to lead to his formal resignation when he failed to deliver his paper on "Ghosts." Thereafter he was "an honorary member extraordinary." The Apostles mattered to him because of their genuine and energetic admiration for his poetry, which they recited, transcribed in commonplace books, circulated to their friends, and urged him to publish.

It was Hallam who proved himself the most urgently and enduringly perceptive admirer of Tennyson's poetry. In December

1828 the subject had been announced for the next prize poem: "Timbuctoo." The year before, Tennyson had made a half-hearted attempt at the prize poem on Napoleon's retreat from Moscow, but his heroic couplets had tailed off, and this probably made him reluctant to try again. On this occasion, though, he was stung. "I fell out with my father," said Tennyson, "for I had no wish to compete for the prize and he insisted on my writing." Dr. Tennyson apparently put it pungently: "You're doing nothing at the university, you might at least get the English poem-prize." In Tennyson's words: "My father said, 'You *must* try for it'—the absurd thing was that I sent in an old poem on 'Armageddon' and, altering the beginning and the end, made it 'Timbuctoo'—I was never so surprised as when I got the prize." The surprise, and not just for Tennyson, was the greater in that the winning poem was, unprecedentedly, in blank verse and not in heroic couplets.

Hallam good-naturedly claimed some credit for Tennyson's victory, as is clear from a letter by J. M. Gaskell, June 25, 1829:

> Have you heard that Alfred Tennyson, a great friend of Hallam's, was successful at Cambridge in the Timbuctoo business? I received a letter this morning from Hallam. He is delighted that Tennyson is successful. He says that Tennyson deserved it, but that he borrowed the pervading idea from him, so that "he is entitled to the honours of a Sancho Panza in the memorable victory gained in the year 1829 over prosaicism and jingle jangle . . ."

Indeed Hallam seized upon this success to issue the boldest of predictions: "I consider Tennyson as promising fair to be the greatest poet of our generation, perhaps of our century." To Hallam, Tennyson was

> A noble being, full of clearest insight—
> A man whom we're beforehand with the time
> In loving and revering; but whose fame
> Is couching now with panther eyes intent . . .

Hallam magnanimously praised the judges' decision when he came to print his own "Timbuctoo" next year. A few years later, Tennyson—embarrassed at these words and not too proud of "poor 'Timbuctoo' "—was to ask Henry Hallam (Arthur's father) not to reprint this prefatory note of Arthur's, whose own "poem is everyway so much better than that wild and unmethodized performance of my own, that even his praise on such a subject would be painful."

It may have been, then, not only Tennyson's shyness, but also his doubts about the poem's worth, which made him ask a friend to read the poem at the ceremony: "I couldn't face the public recitation in the Senate House." He could, though, face his father—except that his father was now abroad for a year; Tennyson sent four copies of the annual prize volume to his uncle Charles, "two of which I shall be obliged to you to transmit to my Father if you know where he is—(I suppose at Paris) with the enclosed Letter." He likewise sent a further two copies to his old grandfather.

Hallam was by no means the only one of Tennyson's Cambridge friends to be delighted. One of them (probably Richard Monckton Milnes, himself an entrant for the prize) praised the poem in the *Athenaeum*, July 22, 1829, as a work of "really first-rate poetical genius, and which would have done honour to any man that ever wrote." Even those who were mystified by the poem were fascinated by it. Charles Wordsworth set out with scornful puzzlement: "If such an exercise had been sent up at Oxford, the author would have had a better chance of being rusticated, with the view of his passing a few months at a Lunatic Asylum, than of obtaining the prize." But he arrived reluctantly at homage: "It is certainly a wonderful production; and if it had come out with Lord Byron's name, it would have been thought as fine as anything he ever wrote."

"Timbuctoo" certainly shows a surprising command of the fluencies, modulations, and mannerisms of blank verse—Miltonic but via the eighteenth century and perhaps Shelley. But the most surprising things about the poem are two—the first is the epigraph:

> Deep in that lion-haunted inland lies
> A mystick city, goal of high emprise.
>
> CHAPMAN

George Chapman? Nobody has ever found the lines there, or indeed anywhere else. Did Tennyson simply make them up? If so, that deft imposture would admirably counteract some of the more grandiose upliftings in which the poem subsequently indulges. The second surprise is the implication of the fact that roughly half of "Timbuctoo" (about 120 lines) was taken over almost verbatim from the earlier fragment, "Armageddon." The fact itself is not surprising; what is surprising is that if one asks what the effect was of totally removing the battle of Armageddon and substituting the legendary splendors of the city Timbuctoo, the answer seems to be virtually none. What had been an immediate prospect adapts itself to a retrospect. The assimilation, so smoothly feasible, is an apt illustration of the puzzling part played by the actual outcome in so many of Tennyson's poems.

"Timbuctoo" is skilled and has much in it to quarry. But two passages especially matter. The first deals with the question of whether myths and legends are consolatory but ultimately false, a question that is to be apt to Tennyson's religious doubts. The immediate simile here for such legends is a revealing one: it tells how, when an earthquake shakes the city,

> At midnight, in the lone Acropolis,
> Before the awful Genius of the place
> Kneels the pale Priestess in deep faith, the while
> Above her head the weak lamp dips and winks
> Unto the fearful summoning without:
> Nathless she ever clasps the marble knees,
> Bathes the cold hand with tears, and gazeth on
> Those eyes which wear no light but that wherewith
> Her phantasy informs them.

The second passage describes a mystical trance, a hypersensitive clarity, such as will frequently in Tennyson provide a momentary assurance that "deep faith" is not self-delusion.

> Each failing sense
> As with a momentary flash of light
> Grew thrillingly distinct and keen. I saw
> The smallest grain that dappled the dark Earth,
> The indistinctest atom in deep air,
> The Moon's white cities, and the opal width
> Of her small glowing lakes, her silver heights
> Unvisited with dew of vagrant cloud,
> And the unsounded, undescended depth

Of her black hollows. . . .
Nay— the hum of men,
Or other things talking in unknown tongues,
And notes of busy life in distant worlds
Beat like a far wave on my anxious ear.

In later life, and in his later poems, Tennyson was to wrestle with the question of what such an experience might mean. But here the poem draws to what is in effect a penultimate ending; the angel says that soon the legendary city Timbuctoo will be revealed by Discovery, and will "Darken, and shrink and shiver into huts." Soon? "The time is well-nigh come / When . . ." Those few words epitomize much that is crucial to Tennyson's poetry. His best poetry is essentially of the "The time is well-nigh come when . . ." kind. Well-nigh come, but seldom well come; in Tennyson the outcome is often, though not always, desolation and loss. Forty years after "Timbuctoo," Tennyson was to end "Pelleas and Ettarre" with a shadowed ending that intimated the end of the Round Table:

The Queen
Looked hard upon her lover, he on her;
And each foresaw the dolorous day to be:
And all talk died, as in a grove all song
Beneath the shadow of some bird of prey;
Then a long silence came upon the hall,
And Modred thought, "The time is hard at hand."

6. *Arthur Hallam 1829–1830*

By the autumn of 1829, Hallam and Tennyson were firm friends. The intensification and deepening of their friendship in December 1829 might never have happened had it not been for a crucial absence: that of Dr. Tennyson, in Europe from about May 1829 to July 1830. For Hallam visited Somersby at about Christmas 1829, and he fell in love with Tennyson's sister Emily. It might seem too much to say that this simply could not have happened if Dr. Tennyson had been there; yet if he *had* been there, would Emily and Mrs. Tennyson have been? The marriage had broken up earlier that year, and it was Dr. Tennyson's removal abroad that brought Mrs. Tennyson and her children back from Louth to Somersby. And even if the household might have been reestablished by Christmas, it is at least unlikely that Tennyson would have pressed an invitation upon Hallam, an invitation to witness the painful pathos of Somersby life; and at least unlikely, too, that Hallam would have been able to see Somersby—and Emily within it—in idyllic terms. Hallam's sonnet to Emily in December 1829 shows that he immediately loved her. His sonnet to Tennyson (written at Somersby, probably in the Easter vacation 1830) shows that he loved Somersby for its soft dim calm—a mood not often precipitated by Dr. Tennyson.

But Hallam's father also was to prove something of an embarrassment. It is important to realize that when in June 1830 Tennyson published his first true volume, *Poems, Chiefly Lyrical*, the publication took quite another form from that which he had hoped. He and Hallam had planned to publish their poems within one volume (as the Wordsworth and Coleridge of their generation proffering a new *Lyrical Ballads*?). Indeed Hallam had drafted the note to his "Timbuctoo," praising "the poem of my friend, whose name is prefixed with mine to this volume." But Henry Hallam had intervened. He disliked some of his son's poems, amatory and otherwise, and he objected to publication, whether independent or joint.

Hallam yielded, but his printed *Poems* were privately circulated from May 1830. He wrote with some sadness to Mrs. Tennyson:

As I have at last the pleasure of sending to Alfred his long-expected book, I take this opportunity of begging that you will accept from me a copy of some poems, which I originally intended to have published in the same volume. To this joint publication, as a sort of seal of our friendship, I had long looked forward with a delight which, I believe, was no-way selfish. But there are reasons which have obliged me to change my intention, and withdraw my own share of the work from the press. One of these was the growing conviction of the exceeding crudeness of style, and in parts morbidness of feeling, which characterised all my earlier attempts.

"Morbidness of feeling": when Tennyson's son came to quote this letter in the *Memoir*, he carefully excised that phrase. It raises vividly the question of what sort of person Hallam was, and so of what it was in their relationship that meant so much to Tennyson.

It is often said that what Tennyson found, needed, and loved in Hallam was some sweet unlikeness to his own darkness of mind.* The black blood of the Tennysons was drawn to the buoyant blood of the Hallams. But in fact Hallam was himself subject, frequently and fiercely, to the darkest feelings. His health, both physical and mental, was not strong. So some important threads in the relationship were dark ones; Tennyson would not have been alone

* *In Memoriam*, LXXIX (Tennyson to his brother Charles): "And so my wealth resembles thine, / But he was rich where I was poor, / And he supplied my want the more / As his unlikeness fitted mine." An understanding of their relationship is thwarted by the fact that Hallam's father destroyed Tennyson's letters to Hallam, and Tennyson's son destroyed Hallam's letters to Tennyson.

in sensing that the dear friendship of Hallam was precarious and mortal. Those who loved Arthur Hallam had some cause for anxiety.

Nine days after Hallam died abroad in September 1833, when the news was not yet known in England, a Cambridge friend was to write to Milnes: "Hallam either is or has been in Germany with his father. He was most absurdly gay last season, a mood and habit so unsuited to his character that I cannot believe the tendency will last long." It is true that by 1833 Hallam will have had to endure a long process of pain and humiliation in his attempt to win consent for his hoped-for marriage to Emily Tennyson, and his spirits were badly battered. But his spirits had never been serene. His father was later to report that serious symptoms of ill health showed themselves in Hallam's first year at Cambridge—and that he experienced "occasionally a considerable depression of spirits, which had been painfully observed at times by those who watched him most, from the time of his leaving Eton, and even before."

Before he ever went to Cambridge, he was despondent about the happy days he had recently spent in love: "They are the brightest days in my life—they were the principal means, under God, of rescuing me from a drooping state of mental misery, a return to which I should look upon as the worst thing that could happen to me." Within months of arriving at Cambridge he confessed his sadness: "I am sick at heart and chill in feeling, and perish without something to invigorate, something to refresh." In May 1829 he was severely ill and had to travel and convalesce before resuming at Cambridge in October.

It was in the summer of 1829 that he confided in Milnes his fears of going mad and of turning atheist: "In my fits of gloom I so often look death, and insanity in the face, that the impulse to leave some trace of my existence on this bulk of atoms gathers strength with the warning that I must be brief." Even the black blood of the Tennysons would not have gone farther than to talk of "this incurable somnambulism we call Life." So the man who declared in March 1830, "I am one of strong passions, irresolute purposes, vacillating opinions," was far from being a bright countercharm to Tennyson's gloom. Tennyson's melancholia (with its relationship to what he had seen of his father's melancholia) found in Hallam the deeper reassurance not of serenity but of similar suffering, doubts, and morbidities which yet were not ignoble. Such morbidity could thus be seen as something other than a uniquely personal weakness or shame; moreover it could be alleviated and humanized by friendship. It is easy to be misled by some of the metaphors which Tennyson was to use in mourning Hallam in *In Memoriam*, into thinking that it was a relationship in which Hallam gave and Tennyson was more blessed to receive. But Tennyson too was blessedly able to give. A draft of "Merlin and the Gleam" (1889) was to speak of Hallam as "The friend who loved me, / And heard my counsel." Whereas the despondency of Dr. Tennyson had apparently been inaccessible to anything that his son might try to do for him, the despondency of Hallam could be soothed and might even be healed by their deep friendship–and likewise Tennyson's despondency in the loving mutuality.

II

Poems, Chiefly Lyrical 1830

"MARIANA," "Supposed Confessions of a Second-Rate Sensitive Mind," "Song: A spirit haunts the year's last hours," and "The Kraken": these are the best of *Poems, Chiefly Lyrical* (1830). Each originates in Tennyson's despondency, and the least successful is the most directly personal: "Supposed Confessions."

"Supposed Confessions of a Sensitive Second-Rate Mind not in Unity with Itself": the last five words of the title were dropped by Tennyson when at last he reprinted the poem toward the end of his life (1884). "Supposed" in order to preclude an autobiographical reading of the poem—as the cleric Richard Crashaw had a poem "Wishes. To his (supposed) Mistresse." A strange poem, desperate but only intermittently candid. To W. J. Fox in his review, Tennyson here personated "a timid sceptic" who evinces "a mixture of self-admiration and self-reproach"—the phrase is a shrewd one, but we have only to think of what Tennyson was to show by way of such a mixture in "St. Simeon Stylites," to sense that the honest doubts in "Supposed Confessions" are not honestly faced. Arthur Hallam indeed intimated as much when he questioned the title as ill-chosen, quaint, and incorrect; he pointed to a fissure within the poem itself:

The mood portrayed in this poem, unless the admirable skill of delineation has deceived us, is rather the clouded season of a strong mind than the habitual condition of one feeble and "second-rate." Ordinary tempers build up fortresses of opinion on one side or another; they will see only what they choose to see. The distant glimpse of such an agony as is here brought out to view is sufficient to keep them for ever in illusions, voluntarily raised at first, but soon trusted in with full reliance as inseparable parts of self.

But among the vacillations is that from candor to self-protection. The poem's first section recognizes frankly that in asking for "a sign," it asks for what its deep doubt would ignore. The second section, too, is frank in its fear and longing.*

How sweet to have a common faith!
To hold a common scorn of death!
And at a burial to hear
The creaking cords which wound and eat
Into my human heart, whene'er
Earth goes to earth, with grief, not fear,
With hopeful grief, were passing sweet!

The repetitions there are not "chiefly lyrical" but wistfully hopeless, as when "sweet" rounds off—with a sigh and a gulp—the precariously unwinding sentence (and yet is chilled by "passing" which, given the funeral context, is not just restrained to "surpassingly"). The off-rhyme *faith / death* clinches nothing; and there is a touching restraint in the poem's manner of asking—it accepts that grief would be inescapable, but how it hopes that grief, not fear, could be its pain.

Yet this delicate tracing (which anticipates effects in *Maud*) is followed at once by the unconvincing retrospect:

Thrice happy state again to be
The trustful infant on the knee!

"The infant's dawning year," happy, free of doubt, is hailed with tinny fervor; the mother's former prayers need to be underlined by the mother's now being dead. Yet the shadow-boxing in the middle of the poem eventually comes up against a real pain—only to follow this, with retreating haste, into mere talk *about* doubt. The juxtaposition thus—

* In 1830, these lines were followed by seventeen lines about hope, of a craven hopefulness; Tennyson's honesty cut them out when next reprinting the poem in 1884.

I am too forlorn,
Too shaken: my own weakness fools
My judgment, and my spirit whirls,
Moved from beneath with doubt and fear.

"Yet," said I, in my morn of youth,
The unsunned freshness of my strength . . .

And so into the false sublime of truth as "An image with profulgent brows," and into an elaborately defensive semi-sequitur about the ox and the lamb (who "raceth freely with his fere") and their not knowing that they will die, and into doubts about the prudence of doubting. All of which is then cut sharply off by a desperate prayer which ends the poem with desolated alternatives that have a click-click alternation like that of Hell's clock:

Oh teach me yet
Somewhat before the heavy clod
Weighs on me, and the busy fret
Of that sharp-headed worm begins
In the gross blackness underneath.

O weary life! O weary death!
O spirit and heart made desolate!
O damnèd vacillating state!

That Tennyson himself remained unwilling to confront the blackness and the whitewashing within the poem is evident in the facile prophylactic narrowness of his comment: "If some kind friend had taken him by the hand and said, 'Come, work' . . . he might have been a happy man, though sensitive."

"Supposed Confessions" splits; the compacted mastery of "Song" is a matter of its perfect integration:

I

A spirit haunts the year's last hours
Dwelling amid these yellowing bowers:
To himself he talks;
For at eventide, listening earnestly,
At his work you may hear him sob and sigh

In the walks;
Earthward he boweth the heavy stalks
Of the mouldering flowers;
Heavily hangs the broad sunflower
Over its grave i' the earth so chilly;
Heavily hangs the hollyhock,
Heavily hangs the tiger-lily.

II

The air is damp, and hushed, and close,
As a sick man's room when he taketh repose
An hour before death;
My very heart faints and my whole soul grieves
At the moist rich smell of the rotting leaves,
And the breath
Of the fading edges of box beneath,
And the year's last rose.
Heavily hangs the broad sunflower
Over its grave i' the earth so chilly;
Heavily hangs the hollyhock,
Heavily hangs the tiger-lily.

The year is dying, and the garden is dying; and the gardener is a "spirit" who "haunts." Age seeps; age talks to himself, and may be heard to sob and sigh at his work, working slowly into the eventide, at the essential work of death–not for him to tie up the flowers, rather "Earthward he boweth the heavy stalks." But there are strangely contrary pulls: the pulls within the stanza, unpredictable and dragging in its line lengths and rhyme scheme, yet intricately patterned–and with the second stanza, by its same pattern, giving to the first stanza a retrospective feeling of something in command. There are the pulls within the rhythm: "Heavily hangs the hollyhock" is a direct challenge to the rhythmical levity of "hollyhock"–in this context the grave's gravity is such as utterly to weigh down the hollyhock. There are the many imperfect rhymes, and the unfecund superfluity by which *flowers* is succeeded by *sunflower* (positioned as rhymes but not with each other). The assonances stretch and mouth a dissolution: "Dwelling amid these yellowing bowers." "Bowers" will find itself, by an autumnal change, becoming "boweth." The second stanza sees—or rather smells—the whole garden as a claustrophobic room—"As a sick man's room when he taketh repose": a momentary pause at the line ending, before "An hour before death." The repose is so much less than the man wants or needs. "An hour before death": such is the characteristic timing of so many of Tennyson's poems,* but here curbed within a comparison. Then "my very heart faints": a surprising and unexplained personal consciousness (*my*), vividly snuffing "the moist rich smell of the rotting leaves" in a way that evidences more than fainting and grieving. "Breath" has dwindled to what we catch a fading breath of (the evergreen shrub box); "the year's last hours" are now all precariously epitomized in "the year's last rose." Yet the repeated four lines of the refrain promise, with their dank monotony, that none of this is for the last time. Unlike Keats's "To Autumn," the poem says nothing of other seasons, and it goes farther toward a longing for death (and not a stoic acceptance of it) than Keats did; but it braces that suicidal slumping, that "moist rich smell," against its patterned harmony, its repetitions that cannot but remind us of the seasons' harmony and repetitions. Every year has its last hours. Tennyson is a poet who persistently denies us an explicit invoking of that which may or will follow the ending of his poems; and yet by using refrains he often points forward along their sequence. The song is not sure that we do really want to live for ever, but it is scrupulous about not insisting that we simply do not.

"The Kraken" is quite other than a science-fiction or Loch Ness fantasy; its depth of feeling comes from Tennyson's pained fascination with the thought of a life which somehow is not life at all.

* "The May Queen" provides a strange instance; when first published in 1832, it was in two parts, the first being happy to be alive, and the second ("New-Year's Eve") being Christianly happy to be about to die. Tennyson was right to think that this would not do, but wrong to plunge on again; in 1842 he added "Conclusion": "I thought to pass away before, and yet alive I am. . ."—a positively last appearance too bravely bright-eyed to moisten our eyes. What was meant to be fortitude comes out as diminutive mawk. And yet "The May Queen" has one truly poignant line: "Wild flowers in the valley for other hands than mine."

His poems contemplate such life in drunkenness, and in madness, and in extreme old age, and in stillbirth, and drugged by the lotos, and paralyzed by Art, and in a world of mirrored shadows like the Lady of Shalott. Indeed the Kraken is like the Lady of Shalott in that he too will awake only to death. For the Kraken's life till then will be only sleep. Tennyson commands another version of his subtle monotony in evoking how little there is of change within this deep world: the rhyme scheme lets "deep" and "sleep" return (the only such return) as inevitable rhymes, chiming with *sea / flee / green / seen;* it chimes *height / light / polypi /lie /die;* and it leaves only *swell / cell* to swell as momentary disturbers of its chiming concordat. The poem awaits the death of its unimaginably alien subject—not, this time, "an hour before death" from a changing garden, but millennia before death from the unchanging deep.

Below the thunders of the upper deep;
Far, far beneath in the abysmal sea,
His ancient, dreamless, uninvaded sleep
The Kraken sleepeth: faintest sunlights flee
About his shadowy sides: above him swell
Huge sponges of millennial growth and height;
And far away into the sickly light,
From many a wondrous grot and secret cell
Unnumbered and enormous polypi
Winnow with giant arms the slumbering green.
There hath he lain for ages and will lie
Battening upon huge seaworms in his sleep,
Until the latter fire shall heat the deep;
Then once by man and angels to be seen,
In roaring he shall rise and on the surface die.

A life which is no life, and which waits for death: this is the core, too, of the finest poem in the 1830 volume, "Mariana."

With blackest moss the flower-plots
  Were thickly crusted, one and all:
The rusted nails fell from the knots
  That held the pear to the gable-wall.
The broken sheds looked sad and strange:
  Unlifted was the clinking latch;

Weeded and worn the ancient thatch
Upon the lonely moated grange.
She only said, "My life is dreary,
He cometh not," she said;
She said, "I am aweary, aweary,
I would that I were dead!"

John Stuart Mill rightly insisted that this is something other than "that rather vapid species of composition usually termed descriptive poetry": it shows "the power of *creating* scenery, in keeping with some state of human feeling; so fitted to it as to be the embodied symbol of it, and to summon up the state of feeling itself, with a force not to be surpassed by anything but reality."*

Mariana lives "without hope of change": yet even within the monotony, desolate and desolating, there is some change. It is a change which clenches into dismay and outcry—heartening as a change at all, disheartening as that change. The refrain is like a ritual to numb pain, but it first undulates and then crystallizes. From "My life is dreary . . . ," through the sluggish to-and-fro of "The night is dreary," "The day is dreary," "My life is dreary," "The night is dreary," "My life is dreary," to the last bleak totality of "I am very dreary." From "He cometh not," tolling six times to the last totality of "He will not come." From "She said, 'I am aweary, aweary,' " tolling six times, to the final inability to quite *say* anything; "She wept, 'I am aweary, aweary.' " From "I would that I were dead!" tolling six times, to the conclusive totality of what is both a prayer and an oath: "Oh God, that I were dead!"

The refrains tell of the passing of time—they kill time. W. J. Fox in 1831 observed that

> The poem takes us through the circuit of four-and-twenty hours of this dreary life. Through all the changes of the night and day she has but one feeling, the variation of which is only by different degrees of acuteness and intensity in the misery it produces; and again and again we feel, before its repetition, the coming of the melancholy burthen.

The burthen both is and bears the burden. Yet time itself does not pace evenly. The first stanza locates time only in the past ("were

* W. J. Fox had said of Tennyson: "He seems to obtain entrance into a mind as he would make his way into a landscape; he climbs the pineal gland as if it were a hill in the centre of the scene."

thickly crusted," "the ancient thatch"); the power of time past has been such as to leave room here now for nothing but place. The second stanza moves through evening, morn, and night; the third, from night to morn. The fourth stanza is once again all place and no time. The fifth is trapped within night, and the sixth is trapped within a day that might as well be night ("All day within the dreamy house . . ."). The last stanza tells of time:

> The sparrow's chirrup on the roof,
> The slow clock ticking,

But though the clock may tick slow, it is Mariana's spirit which turns such a movement into a "slow clock." (The effect is an aural equivalent to the optical one in "Lit with a low large moon," in "The Palace of Art.") Time is time, and once again is not the mercy of eternity. The sudden sketch which shows us that time has passed, the chronographia which in a poet like Milton hearteningly shows us that time has concluded one episode and is about to inaugurate another, has become disheartening, a mere intensification of vacancy, and not a pause between living moments.

> but most she loathed the hour
> When the thick-moted sunbeam lay
> Athwart the chambers, and the day
> Was sloping toward his western bower.

With time as vacancy, movement dwindles and petrifies. The one essential movement is frozen within that iterated negative, "He cometh not." The rusted nails fell from the knots, and her tears fell, and in the moonlight "The shadow of the poplar fell / Upon her bed, across her brow." But such falling is the least of movements; and upon Mariana's bed at night is not the body of a man but the shadow of a tree. At night there may be movement, but it is alien and uncompanionable: "the flitting of the bats." At night, Mariana can move—but only in dreams, and those unhappy: "In sleep she seemed to walk forlorn." The stagnancy is such as to render the vegetable kingdom as a soft-footed reclaiming, a sinister stealth as in that children's game "Grandmother's footsteps" where only unseen movements are permitted:*

* The world of Emily Dickinson's "The Mushroom is the Elf of Plants" and Sylvia Plath's "Mushrooms."

About a stone-cast from the wall
  A sluice with blackened waters slept,
And o'er it many, round and small,
  The clustered marish-mosses crept.

"A stone-cast" powerfully evokes the absence of human energy, by being here the blankest of distances (nobody in this setting will cast a stone); and how perfectly the adjectives edge forward as the marish-mosses take over the water—as their land-cousins have already taken over the flower-plots. The poplar moves, but only as with a nervous disease or old age: "Hard by a poplar shook alway, / All silver-green with gnarlèd bark." With nightfall there is movement again: "And the shrill winds were up and away" (the only instance in the poem of so vigorous a rhythm)—but it means no more to Mariana than that

In the white curtain, to and fro,
  She saw the gusty shadow sway.

Movement is to and fro. Or else it is the creakings, scufflings, and imaginings of the long day:

All day within the dreamy house,
  The doors upon their hinges creaked;
The blue fly sung in the pane; the mouse
  Behind the mouldering wainscot shrieked,
Or from the crevice peered about.

For sounds too have dwindled. Mariana speaks alone. "Unlifted was the clinking latch": it is a cruel turn which at once crushes and raises hope—if it was unlifted it wasn't clinking, though to draw out the phrase (". . . which would have clinked if it had been lifted") is to see how poignant such a paradoxical negative may be. We strain our ears for the unforthcoming sound, for "uplifted," not "unlifted." The moss and the mosses are silent, as are the dews (and the bats would have only a flittermouse squeak); the dawn ("The cock sung out") indeed breaks the silence, but in this love poem it is the opposite of an *aubade* (Mariana wakes to no lovers' parting of pleasurable grief). But the sounds intensify and deepen in the closing stanzas, with the creaking doors, the blue fly, the mouse, the spectral sounds, and finally:

The sparrow's chirrup on the roof,
  The slow clock ticking, and the sound
Which to the wooing wind aloof
  The poplar made, did all confound
Her sense;

The chirrup is desperately sprightly; the wind woos the poplar, but nobody woos Mariana.*

"Mariana" is one of Tennyson's masterpieces in the art of the penultimate. Mariana is consumed in the waiting; and if her lover will not come, she desperately hopes that death will: "Oh God, that I were dead!" (the last words of the poem). Suicide flickers ("Old voices called her from without"), but it asks decision, energy, and movement. And yet to speak of the penultimate is necessarily to think of the ultimate ending, and here the poem abruptly deepens its mystery.

Carlyle was brusque:

If Alfred Tennyson could only make that long wail, like the winter wind, about Mariana in the Moated Grange, and could not get her to throw herself into the ditch, or could not bring her another man to help her ennui, he had much better have left her alone altogether.

But something must be done about an inescapable fact: that before arriving at the poem, a reader meets Tennyson's epigraph: "Mariana in the moated grange" (*Measure for Measure*). Are we or are we not to let *Measure for Measure* color the poem?

She should this Angelo have married: was affianced to her by oath, and the nuptial appointed . . . Left her in her tears, and dried not one of them with his comfort . . . What a merit were it in death to take this poor maid from the world! . . . There, at the moated grange, resides this dejected Mariana.

(III.i.212 ff.)

If we altogether exclude Shakespeare's Mariana, we must find Tennyson's allusion and epigraph irresponsible and ineffectual—mere mood-setting and window-dressing. But if we think that the poem

* Contrast the "us" of "The Lover's Tale" (1832), I.531-5: "The wind / Told a lovetale beside us, how he wooed / The waters, and the waters answering lisped / To kisses of the wind, that, sick with love, / Fainted at intervals. . ."

is a profoundly creative allusion to Shakespeare, our sense of the poem's ultimate ending (off that penultimate ending which Tennyson so often needs) must modify the poem's meaning, our sense of how it asks to be taken. For, on the one hand, the Shakespearean fact is that Mariana does gain Angelo after all, and she ends in a loving marriage. But, on the other hand, this is achieved within a play whose providential considerateness (the Duke's intervening) reminds us, not so much of life's providential kindliness, but rather of life's unassisted exposedness. It is the case therefore that any allusion to the outcome in *Measure for Measure* must be profoundly equivocal–optimistic and a cause for hope, in that Mariana is *not* to pine forever (they will come to her moated grange); pessimistic, in that the world of *Measure for Measure* is patently not the real vulnerable world, whereas the world of "Mariana" may be.

All this may seem un-Tennysonianly circuitous. But a reader must inevitably make some decision about the known outcome in Shakespeare, and an open reader will bear in mind that "Mariana" is only one of innumerable poems by Tennyson in which the final ending is shrouded but magnetic.* "Christopher North" said of "Mariana": "long, long, long indeed is the dreary day, but it will end at last." In what? In death? In marriage? John Stuart Mill was obliged to disintegrate this consummate poem because he refused to consider that what is never mentioned in a poem may yet be potently present, or that the few repeated words "He cometh not" may weigh a hundredfold. So some of Mill's criticism needs to be rotated:

The nominal subject excites anticipations which the poem does not even attempt to fulfil. The humblest poet, who is a poet at all, could make more than is here made of the situation of a maiden abandoned by her lover. But that was not Mr. Tennyson's idea. The love-story is secondary in his mind. The words "he cometh not" are almost the only words which allude to it at all. To place ourselves at the right point of view, we must drop the conception of Shakespeare's Mariana, and retain only that of a "moated grange", and a solitary dweller within it, forgotten by mankind . . . Words surely never excited a

* "Anacaona" (written 1830) speaks much of happiness; its last stanza says "never more," but the known outcome is not mentioned: that the Spaniards kill Anacaona.

more vivid feeling of physical and spiritual dreariness: and not dreariness alone—for that might be felt under many other circumstances of solitude—but the dreariness which speaks not merely of being far from human converse and sympathy, but of being *deserted* by it.

Much was wrong with *Poems, Chiefly Lyrical*—and some of it Tennyson soon realized. He never reprinted twenty-three of its poems, and those he did reprint he listed as "Juvenilia." There were the patriotic ballads ("English Warsong," "National Song"), altogether unthinking about the nature of battle and death. There were the grandiloquent cheer-leadings for poetry which Tennyson never repudiated ("The Poet's Mind," "The Poet"), all hallowed power and haughtiness and capitalizations (Hope, Youth, Freedom, WISDOM) and risky metaphor—"the arrow-seeds of the field flower" (alias dandelion) becoming "the wingèd shafts of truth," a train of non-thought which if taken seriously would leave truth very feebly armed. There was the speculative riddling of "The How and the Why," about which John Stuart Mill was stern. "The questions which a Faust calls upon earth and heaven, and all powers supernal and infernal, to resolve for him, are not the ridiculous ones which Mr. Tennyson asks himself in these verses." Yet the riddles within the poem are real enough: what are time and existence, and dream, and personal identity, and death, and feeling as against knowing—these were so real to Tennyson as to entail recourse to a defensive retreat into the facetious.

> Why the life goes when the blood is spilt?
>   What the life is? where the soul may lie?
> Why a church is with a steeple built;
> And a house with a chimneypot?

Tennyson was later to shed the facetiousness, and at the age of sixty he was to publish the compactly miniature and glinting philosophical poem which would redeem the earlier effort—"Flower in the crannied wall." The pale prettiness of "The Sea-Fairies," its charm such as makes unconvincing its claim that the weary mariners were "Whispering to each other half in fear": this would be sooner redeemed, and consummately, in "The Lotos-Eaters" (1832).

There were the early girly poems which FitzGerald was to deplore ("that stupid Gallery of Beauties")*—"Lilian," "Madeline," "Adeline" and others of 1830 would be joined by "Eleänore," "Rosalind," "Margaret," and "Kate" in 1832. Bulwer-Lytton had some point in his gibe at "School-Miss Alfred." "That ultra-super-exalting spirit" which Leigh Hunt deplored in "Isabel" evaporates most of most of these poems. "All these ladies," said Tennyson engagingly, "were evolved, like the camel, from my own consciousness." This is a traditional gibe at German metaphysics: "The German constructs art as he constructs the camel," said E. S. Dallas, "out of the depths of his moral consciousness." Unfortunately "all these ladies" might indeed as well be camels for all the erotic appeal they have. One might compare such lady-likenesses with the laconic wit of Tennyson's satiric portraiture in "A Character" (1830)—he never wrote another poem like it, mainly because he disapproved of satire, but perhaps also because its sleek enemy, outwardly so "Quiet, dispassionate, and cold," subsequently went mad. The comparison would suggest that at this date Tennyson was simply too ignorant of girls, and too awedly timid of them.

Despite Tennyson's gruff bluntness, there was a timidity there too, as George Gilfillan said in 1847: "His genius is bold, but is waylaid at almost every step by the timidity and weakness of his temperament." What is difficult is to draw the line between a thin evasiveness and a rewarding indirection. Take "A Dirge":

Round thee blow, self-pleachèd deep,
Bramble roses, faint and pale,
And "long purples" of the dale.

Or so it stood in 1830. In 1842, Tennyson removed the quotation marks, which had evoked another dirge (*Hamlet*, IV.vii.168–71):

There with fantastic garlands did she come,
Of crow-flowers, nettles, daisies, and long purples,
That liberal shepherds give a grosser name,
But our cold maids do dead men's fingers call them . . .

Tennyson had another flower than Shakespeare's in mind; but he

* See p. 177; for Bulwer-Lytton, see p. 184.

may have sensed too that the context in *Hamlet* was an embarrassment. However richly apt in its undertone of suicide, the allusion would have to go if there might come with it an undertone of erotic fierceness. Tennyson dwindles into being one of our cold maids.

Elsewhere, though, even if he hardly counts as a liberal shepherd, he elicits an unobtrusive but uncowardly eroticism. Take another Shakespearian allusion in another minor poem of 1830, "Adeline":

> And ye talk together still,
> In the language wherewith Spring
> Letters cowslips on the hill...

Tennyson remarked: "The red spots in the cowslip, as if letters of a fairy alphabet," and he quoted *Cymbeline*, II.ii.39: "like the crimson drops / I' the bottom of a cowslip." But what was it that in *Cymbeline* was "like"?

> On her left breast
> A mole cinque-spotted, like the crimson drops
> I' the bottom of a cowslip.

Tennyson was surely right not to spell it out. Unfortunately in most of these early love poems he did not spell it in. The perfunctorily half-hearted nature of their amorousness is pinpointed in a textual change. The lover of "Madeline" exclaimed:

> If my lips should dare to kiss
> Thy taper fingers three-times-three . . .

Tennyson must suddenly have realized that it sounded as if Madeline were a mutant with nine fingers. Hence the erratum: "*for* three-times-three *read* amorously." It is hardly surprising that in the circumstances "amorously" fails to grip us.

It is not that Tennyson was a prude—"Fatima" in 1832 would prove as much. But *The Christian Teacher*, reviewing the poems of 1842, would have to call on capital letters to manifest its admiration for high-mindedness: "One characteristic of Mr. Tennyson's poetry is a keen and unslumbering perception of the Pure, the Graceful, the Lofty and the Lovely in Womanhood." *Unslumbering* is faintly equivocal. What is unequivocal is the pressure, tentacularly gentle, that such sentiments were to put upon Tennyson—he was supposed to live up to them.

The 1830 volume had too the decorous eroticism-exoticism of "Recollections of the Arabian Nights"—passion and luxury in the best of bad taste. (This Eastern blend of the erotic and the exotic was not redeemed until "Now sleeps the crimson petal, now the white" in *The Princess*, 1847.) John Sterling in his review was to say of "Recollections of the Arabian Nights": "The gold and red arabesque repeats itself, square after square of the pattern, with undeniable splendour, but somewhat wearying monotony." But the splendor is threadbare, despite its "costly doors" and "broidered sofas." The opening lines have buoyancy, but strangely:

> When the breeze of a joyful dawn blew free
> In the silken sail of infancy,
> The tide of time flowed back with me,
> The forward-flowing tide of time . . .

Arthur Hallam liked this: "That happy ductility of childhood returns for the moment." But could it exactly *return* for Tennyson, given that his dawn had not been joyful? The autobiographical wishfulness suggests that the stage is being set for remorseless prettifying. Yet in one respect "Recollections of the Arabian Nights" is very much a Tennyson poem: it ends in the moment before something important is likely to happen. The narrator steals up and sees the Persian girl, and he sees at last the good Haroun Alraschid. "And," we chafe—"and": and the poem ends.

Poems, Chiefly Lyrical adumbrated others of Tennyson's preoccupations. There was the trance of "The Mystic," somewhat too vibratory in manner but responsive to something deep in Tennyson:

> He often lying broad awake, and yet
> Remaining from the body, and apart
> In intellect and power and will, hath heard
> Time flowing in the middle of the night,
> And all things creeping to a day of doom.

There was the baffled skepticism of "All thoughts, all creeds, all dreams are true." There was the revealing title "Dualisms," together with an instance of what dualisms were for Tennyson in the pair of poems, "Nothing Will Die" and "All Things Will Die." (In that order–and in circumstances in which having the first word is less satisfactory than having the last.) Riven as he was by doubt, Tennyson early evolved these "pendants," as he called them: he was enabled at once to do justice and to escape having to judge. Many such pendants may seem only complements, but on reflection the need for such complements can often be both magnanimous and evasive.* "The Merman" will have "The Mermaid"; "Mariana" is other than "Mariana in the South," and "Margaret" than "Adeline"; "Forlorn" is answered by "Happy," and "Despair" by "Faith"; "St. Simeon Stylites" is contrasted with "St. Telemachus," and "Sir Galahad" with "St. Agnes," and "Lady Clara Vere de Vere" with "Lady Clare"; the "Northern Farmer. Old Style" will be matched by "New Style"; "The Charge of the Light Brigade" asks "The Charge of the Heavy Brigade"; "Œnone" must arrive at "The Death of Œnone", "Locksley Hall" will live to see "Locksley Hall Sixty Years After"; "A Welcome to Alexandra" will necessitate "A Welcome to Alexandrovna"; and Tennyson's first poem, "Rape of Proserpine," will find its happy ending in one of his last poems, "Demeter and Persephone."

Such a list does of course scramble together pairings of many different kinds, but it shows how engrained, and even obsessive, pairing was for Tennyson, and it lessens the surprise with which one would otherwise receive his comment on *In Memoriam:*

> I think of adding another [poem] to it, a speculative one, bringing out the thoughts of "The Higher Pantheism", and showing that all the arguments are about as good on one side as the other, and thus throw man back more on the primitive impulses and feelings.

* Divided impulses also underlie Tennyson's ubiquitous recourse to the word "half"; the concordance reveals an extraordinary variety, especially of compounds–some of them very odd ("half-disfame," "half-life," "half-self"). Similarly, for "The Voyage of Maeldune" (1880), Tennyson provided the antithetical islands; the source suggested the Isle of Shouting, but not the Silent Isle; the Isle of Fruits, but not the Isle of Flowers; the Isle under Water, but not the Isle of Fire. "At first I made half the men kill the other half in every fray, and Maildun himself return *alone*."

III

1. The Pyrenees 1830

In sending to Mrs. Tennyson an advance copy of her son's *Poems, Chiefly Lyrical*, Hallam had said that he was going abroad for the summer of 1830, adding: "I earnestly hope Alfred and Frederic will be able to join me then; I think nothing will do the former especially so much good as travelling awhile." Tennyson—who was to spend many hours and many verses in brooding on whether madness and melancholia were hereditary—may have been disconcerted at the way in which the remedy that had twice been proposed for his father was now being proposed for him. Yet the very fact that Dr. Tennyson was returning from the continent that summer probably constituted a good reason for setting out from Somersby. The company of Hallam was itself a cordial, and the more so in that Hallam found the company of Tennyson a cordial. Tennyson was never to forget this summer, free from so much that oppressed him and free to enjoy the friendship of Hallam. The rich landscapes impressed themselves powerfully on him, and were soon to be rendered into creation in "Œnone" and "Mariana in the South"—and long after were to provide the tender elegiac reminiscence of "In the Valley of Cauteretz."

Yet even this radiant summer had its tragic somberness. For Hallam and Tennyson had caught the naïve idealism of those Cambridge freedom-fighters who wished to assist the revolution in Spain of General Torrijos against King Ferdinand. Tennyson's early poems in favor of glorious insurrection and against brutal tyranny show some fervor and no thought. As often, the gap between revolutionary rhetoric and revolutionary feasibility was not to be bridged. Or rather, it was to be bridged by the reactionaries. No harm came to Hallam and Tennyson, who met some of the rebels and gave them money and stirring words. After returning to England, Hallam wrote: "Alfred went, as you know, with me to the south of France, and a wild, bustling time we had of it. I played my part as conspirator in a small way." But there were those who played in a big way. In November 1831 the rising was extirpated; among the fifty-six rebels executed at Malaga was the cousin of John Sterling. Sterling, who had urged the insurrection, was to cry out: "I hear the sound of that musketry; it is as if the bullets were tearing my own brain!"

Did Tennyson hear that sound? He would have been pained at the news, but the débâcle is not likely to have had a profound effect on his political philosophy. His poems may support revolution abroad,* but they are firmly for cautious reform at home. What might be said, though, is that the Torrijos failure—with Tennyson's peripheral embroilment in it—stands as one example of a siege of contraries within Tennyson that never ceased. Tennyson was a poet haunted by the uneasy feeling that actions speak louder than words, and by the feeling that it was the soldier who epitomized action, duty, manliness, and courage. Epitomized or monopolized? Tennyson was never to escape from this tension, and often it was a richly creative one. An unconvincing wishfulness may be sensed whenever he thinks of escaping. As in this flight, which he was to venture upon in his seventies:

And here the Singer for his Art
  Not all in vain may plead
"The song that nerves a nation's heart,
  Is in itself a deed."

* In 1827 he had published "Written During the Convulsions in Spain."

2. *Arthur Hallam and the Tennysons 1831*

THE SAME MONTH, March 1831, which saw the death of Dr. Tennyson, saw a stern move by Henry Hallam against the relationship of his son and Emily Tennyson. He was aware that his son had been passionately in love in 1828 with a Miss Wintour; he was aware, too, that the Somersby Tennysons were not impeccably respectable. Arthur was forbidden to visit Somersby until his coming of age in February 1832 and this was intended to mean that the lovers simply were not to meet. Henry Hallam understood his prohibition to mean that they were not to correspond; perhaps the lovers (and Mrs. Tennyson) misunderstood this, perhaps they merely defied it silently. Either way, the result was that the Tennysons (Alfred to a less extent than Emily) were deprived of Hallam's love just at a time when the family was once again in bitter straits.

Tennyson's hopes had now been grievously disappointed in many a phase. The hopes of childhood had early—perhaps immediately—turned into the disillusionments of the Somersby household. The hopes of Cambridge life, that had at first drawn a blank, had then, it is true, drawn Hallam; but had now drawn Tennyson back to the pains of Somersby. He had left Cambridge with the likelihood that he would not return to take his degree and without any wish to earn a living other than through his poetry. The hopes of a joint publication with Hallam had been thwarted, and in any case Tennyson was already becoming sharply dissatisfied with the poems he had published in 1830. The hopes raised by his friend's love for his sister received the grave setback of Henry Hallam's ban. And although Tennyson cannot simply have enjoyed hopes when his father died, he must have been aware—as others in the family were—that a terrible phase was over and that a new life could perhaps begin for them all. But the new phase offered only different lacerations.

Friction between the Somersby Tennysons and the Old Man of the Wolds was inevitable. Were the three eldest sons willing to face their responsibilities? The Rev. T. H. Rawnsley, the family friend, wrote to the Old Man about Frederick and Alfred the month after Dr. Tennyson died: "They promise to obey your wishes, to proceed with their Degrees *forthwith* and to place themselves in a condition to obtain a competency by their exertions, which *I think, with you* they ought to do, after *such an expensive education.*" Rawnsley pressed the Old Man to accede to Mrs. Tennyson's earnest wish to remain at Somersby (which meant negotiating with the patrons), provided that the young men kept their promise. But already history was in grave danger of repeating itself. Dr. Tennyson's life had been ruined by his being forced into the church—and now the same was being proposed for Frederick. The same crass pressures were likewise put upon Alfred, as is clear from a letter in May 1831, by his uncle Charles to the Old Man:

> We discussed what was to be done with the children. Alfred is at home—but wishes to return to Cambridge to take a degree. I told him it was a useless expense unless he meant to go into the Church. He said he would. I did not think he seemed much to like it—I then suggested Physic or some other profession. He seemed to think the Church the best and has I think finally made up his mind to it. The Tealby living was mentioned and understood to be intended for him.

But at the end of this letter, after speaking of the other brothers, their uncle reverted to Alfred, and made it clear that he could divine Alfred's intentions: "Alfred seems quite ready to go into the Church although I think his mind is fixed on the idea of deriving his great distinction and greatest means from the exercise of his poetic talents."

The younger Charles seems genuinely to have wished to go into the church, and was to do so in 1832. Frederick apparently had no such wish, as is suggested by his uncle's uneasily emphatic underlining: "This is a *choice of his own* and a calling he *seems very desirous of filling*." For Horatio (who was then twelve), his uncle briskly proposed the navy. But it was Edward (aged eighteen) who caused most alarm, and who brings home even at this distance just how oppressive to Alfred was the black blood of the Tennysons.

Edward is understood to be unfit for any *thrift*—and I fear must remain at home—but Alfred says he really fears that his mind will at length so prey upon itself, that he cannot answer for consequences. It is difficult to devise anything for him as an employment with a *real* object. Alfred says he should if possible, for the sake of his mind, go from home and be amused . . . but I fear that if he were sent from home to mix with the world by himself—he would become unhappy from another source as he would find himself unequal to his companions and perhaps be exposed to ridicule which his sensitive mind would not endure. Poor fellow! I feel for him—and will endeavour as far as I can to soften his existence to him—but that existence never, I fear, can be a happy one.

It was of course the financial emergency which necessarily gave the Old Man rights and power. Dr. Tennyson had left debts of nearly nine hundred pounds; if necessary these could be covered by a sale of his books, furniture, plate, etc., valued at over twelve hundred pounds. In fact the Old Man spared the library and personal effects. But it was the university debts which perturbed him: eight hundred pounds (£300 owed by Frederick—and rusticated to boot!, £320 by Charles, and £170 by Alfred). The Old Man—who may have been a beast but was a just beast—disliked the idea that the three eldest sons, already fortunate in their education compared with their siblings, should in effect have more than their fair share of their eventual bequest from him. So he drew up two bonds totalling over £1,400 (formalized in September 1832) which bore upon the three eldest sons and their mother; the bonds were to be realized for the younger children after his death. Mrs. Tennyson was allowed £800 a year, less interest on the bonds and less any expenses which the Old Man incurred on her younger children's behalf. All these long negotiations were humiliating and inescapable for the Tennysons.

3. *Tennyson's brothers and sisters*

In explaining why she was being forced to leave her husband in 1829, Mrs. Tennyson had insisted on "another and perhaps a stronger reason than any I have given for our separation, the impression which his conduct may produce upon the minds of his family." Whether their father was fully responsible for it or not, the minds of most of the Somersby children were not to prove stable. But to show this will entail some glimpses of what had not yet, in 1831, come to pass.

First, Frederick. Frederick, violently irascible, had long done nothing to lessen the friction between Somersby and Bayons Manor, and he had been accused of egregiously misleading his brothers. He had done little for his father but rouse him to fury, and six months after Dr. Tennyson's death he was embroiled in a dispute with his grandfather about a career. He apologized for seeming disrespectful, but louder than the apology was the sound of chafing:

> Again if I said that I believed there were very few just men in the Church, I alluded to the notoriously profligate lives of many of the Bishops and Clergy . . . I never said that I was disinclined to enter into Holy Orders, only it is the consciousness of being no better than other men, that awakens me to the danger of taking them unguardedly . . . You may be sure I am quite as desirous of getting a livelihood myself as any one can be to procure one for me, and Alfred can tell you himself that so far from having used any arguments to dissuade

him from taking a profession, I have invariably urged to him the necessity of doing so, and your desire to that effect.

Second, Charles. Charles (later Charles Tennyson Turner*) seemed the most equably accommodating of them all, and in the end he probably proved so. He was also—apart from Alfred—the most talented; his sonnets were highly, and rightly, praised by Coleridge, and stand among the most delicately satisfying minor verse of the Victorian age. But after leaving Cambridge he was to sink into melancholy and opium, and later into marital fracture; his recovery was to be slow and painful. A letter from Tennyson to James Spedding in February 1833 says: "You inquire after Charles—we see little of him—I believe his spirits are pretty good" —at which point three lines have been indecipherably scratched out and inked out by Hallam Tennyson, in the letter and in the draft *Materials for a Life of A.T.* The offending words seem to be: "though he sometimes . . . by way of refreshment."

Third (omitting Alfred), Mary—but of her, nothing is to the point.

Fourth, Emily. Her health, of body and mind, was by no means good. It was not solely her separation from Hallam in 1831 which caused the pain that can be heard in the letter she wrote to her grandfather that summer:

I am very ill, and have been so a long time, and feel assured, if you knew how I suffer you would immediately furnish me with the means of going to Cheltenham: Dr. Bousfield says, it is the only place for me, the pain in my side evidently increases, and my life is so wretched, that sooner than pass another year as the last, I would be content to follow my poor Father to the grave: now he is gone, who can we look to, my dear Grandfather, but you, as our protector.**

* Charles's inheritance from his uncle Samuel Turner in 1835 necessitated his changing his name to Charles Turner; the convention has grown up of referring to him as Charles Tennyson Turner.

** Cheltenham: there is at Lincoln a copy of a letter from Hallam to Frederick Tennyson; Audrey Tennyson has dated it 1830, but internal evidence points unmistakably to 1831. Hallam says of his week at Cheltenham: "I made up my mind rightly I still think though I confess things may be said on the other side that I ought to take that opportunity of seeing Alfred and Emily." Presumably Hallam observed the letter but not the spirit

Fifth, Edward. The family fears—and Alfred's in particular—that Edward would go mad were to prove sadly justified. In October 1832, the grandfather had to face the news that Edward's "extremely distressing state of mental aberration" was likely to "terminate in hopeless insanity." The doctor's suggestion was that Edward be removed to the asylum at Lincoln: "His present state at home is one of great danger to himself and of anxiety and apprehension to his friends." Edward's uncle Charles proposed a kindly subterfuge by which Edward would be under the doctor's care as a "pupil," and did not agree that Edward was "in that condition which would justify the sending him to you in the distinct character of a Lunatic." But Edward's mother gives a more vividly painful glimpse: "He weeps bitterly sometimes, and says his mind is so unnotched he is scarcely able to endure his existence." For Edward, there was to be no recovery; he was to spend nearly sixty years confined as a lunatic, dying in 1890, only two years before his famous brother.

Sixth, Arthur. His grandfather was not impressed (Arthur was seventeen) in June 1831: "I don't know what Arthur is fit for. He even does not know the multiplication table or indeed anything useful. He could learn if he would but is as idle as a foal. He must be instructed before he can be fit for anything and [his] gestures and twitchings etc. are ridiculous and he would be a subject of ridicule anywhere. They are all strangely brought up." All was not well with Arthur, and in the 1840s he was to collapse for a while into alcoholism.

Seventh, Septimus. Years later, according to a story retailed by Dante Gabriel Rossetti, Septimus rose from the hearth rug on which he had been lying, and advanced with the words: "I am Septimus, the most morbid of the Tennysons." But though the anecdote is comic, Septimus's state of mind was not. Arthur Hallam was already expressing some concern about Septimus's "melancholy" in 1832 or 1833. By 1834, his condition was to become threateningly like that of the deranged Edward. It is worth quoting at length the letter which Alfred was then to send to his

---

of his father's injunction that he should not go to Somersby, and clandestinely met Emily in Cheltenham in 1831.

uncle, since it shows not only the full impact upon Alfred of such a family situation, but also his peculiarly inward understanding of madness and morbidity.

I think it my duty to inform you of Septimus's state of mind. My Grandfather talks of letting him stop at home two or three months longer–if this be acted upon I have very little doubt but that his mind will prove as deranged as Edward's, although I trust that his intellect may yet be preserved by getting him out into some bustling active line of life *remote from the scene of his early connexions.* I have studied the minds of my own family–I know how delicately they are organized–and how much might be done in this instance by suddenly removing Septimus from all those objects and subjects with which he has been familiar and upon which he has been accustomed to brood, into some situation where he might be enabled to form his own friendships with those of his own age and to feel that there is something to live and to care for–but this, if done should be done immediately, because every hour which he wastes at home tends to increase his malady. At present his symptoms are not unlike those with which poor Edward's unhappy derangement began–he is subject to fits of the most gloomy despondency accompanied with tears–or rather, he spends whole days in this manner, complaining that he is neglected by all his relations, and blindly resigning himself to every morbid influence.

For God's sake do not consider these as idle words but use whatever influence you may have with my Grandfather to prevent so miserable a termination. I am sure you will feel with us in this matter. No half measures will do nor ought the saving of a few pounds to be an object here. I repeat it, he should be removed as far as possible from home and into some place where new objects and the example of others might rouse him to energy.

Eighth, ninth, and tenth: but the young Matilda, Cecilia, and Horatio are not to the point. Nevertheless, of the eleven children very few had altogether escaped the black blood of the Tennysons.

4. Tennyson's despondency

In my youth I knew much greater unhappiness than I have known in later life. When I was about twenty, I used to feel moods of misery unutterable! I remember once in London the realization coming over me, of the *whole* of its inhabitants lying horizontal a hundred years hence. The smallness and emptiness of life sometimes overwhelmed me—.

THE MISERY WHICH Tennyson felt was by no means abolished by the friendship of Hallam. But there was also his anxiety about going blind which seems to have been both symptom and cause of his despondency. In July 1829, he told his grandfather about the *muscae volitantes* which floated across his vision and for which he had had to be cupped. Edward FitzGerald later noted that Tennyson was "afraid of blindness," and the fears seem to have been especially severe in 1831. Hallam wrote to him with urgency in July:

I am very much distressed about the condition of your eyes. Surely you owe it to us all not to let yourself carelessly fall into the misery of blindness. It is a hard and a sad thing to barter the "universal light" even for the power of "Tiresias and Phineus prophets old".* Write to me yourself on this subject and speak openly and fully.

Next year, Tennyson was informing his Aunt Russell: "My blindness increases daily."**

* *Paradise Lost*, III. 36.

** Tennyson's sympathy with Aunt Russell's own anxiety about eyesight was one of the things which bound them together. In 1847 (*Memoir*, i. 243) he was to write to her that he "had hoped to have a better account of your eyes. Those 'animals' [*muscae volitantes*] you mention are very distressing and mine increase weekly: in fact I almost look forward with certainty to being blind some of these days." In 1854 too he said he was "grieved to hear about your eyes," and sent her the somber details of "some 15 *new* specks in

In the years of his friendship with Hallam, Tennyson's health—physical and mental—was far from serene. His mother reports in July 1830 that "Alfred is very ill" and has consulted a physician in London. In March 1831, Hallam was issuing kindly adjurations: "Fare thee well. I hope you do fare well, and make head against 'despondency and madness.'"* Hallam clearly thought that Tennyson was despondent, not ill, and he expressed some optimism: "Alfred is, as I expected, not apparently ill: nor can I persuade myself anything real is the matter. His spirits are better: his habits more regular, his condition altogether healthier." But four months later—and with the death of Dr. Tennyson in the interim—Hallam was having to recognize that "anything real" might have to include the morbid: "Poor Alfred has written to me a very melancholy letter. What can be done for him? Do you think he is really very ill *in body?* His mind certainly is in a distressing state." From this point, Tennyson seems somewhat to have curbed his despondency. Hallam was still cautious: "Alfred is in better spirits, I guess, than usual, and apparently not idle; but I have seen no fruits" (August 1831). By March 1832, Hallam was writing to Trench:

> Alfred I was most glad to find better than I had apprehended. I see no ground for thinking he has anything really serious to ail him. His mind is what it always was, or rather brighter, and more vigorous. I regret, with you, that you have never had the opportunity of knowing more of him. His nervous temperament and habits of solitude give an appearance of affectation to his manner, which is no true interpreter of the man, and wears off on further knowledge.

---

my right eye"; it was at this time that he gave up trying to learn Persian (*Memoir*, i. 373). His anxieties were real and to be pitied; but as the years roll by, his dismay starts to look somewhat ludicrous. In 1878 he is writing to Whitman: "As to myself I am pretty well for my time of life—sixty nine on the sixth of this month—but somewhat troubled about my eyes. . . ." Similar glum rumblings were issued every few years, as late as two months before Tennyson died: "I have entered my 84th year. I have entirely lost, as far as reading is concerned, the use of my right eye, and I fear that the left is going in the same way" (August 13, 1892, *Memoir*, ii. 417).

* Wordsworth, "Resolution and Independence": "We Poets in our youth begin in gladness; / But thereof comes in the end despondency and madness."

Yet Tennyson did not simply shake off that despondency which seemed to him a hereditary darkness. There is no affectation in his letter to Aunt Russell, in March 1833, about the new baby: "I hope for his own peace of mind that he will have as little of the Tennyson about him as possible."

5. *Arthur Hallam 1831–1832*

ENFORCED ABSENCE from Emily did not make Hallam's love grow any less fond. Their letters (and perhaps a surreptitious meeting in Cheltenham) kept the love alive. Meanwhile Hallam flung himself into action as an informal literary agent for the poems of Tennyson. In January 1831 he sent to Leigh Hunt (poet, and editor of *The Tatler*) Tennyson's *Poems, Chiefly Lyrical* and Charles Tennyson's *Sonnets and Fugitive Pieces;* Hallam urged Hunt to review them, and praised Tennyson in particular. Two months later, he was able to send Tennyson the review by Hunt. Next he learned that the publisher Edward Moxon now owned the *Englishman's Magazine:* "He wants to start with a flash number if possible; and has already pressed Wordsworth, Southey and Charles Lamb into his service, but he is especially anxious to have something of yours." So Hallam urged Tennyson to send "The Two Maidens" ("The Sisters") or "Rosalind"–or to let Hallam send "The Southern Mariana." Hallam pointed out that Tennyson could become a permanent contributor, and that there was nothing wrong with publishing in magazines, especially in good company–"It will not interfere with your collecting the pieces hereafter into a volume." Eleven days later, Hallam had let the *Englishman's Magazine* have Tennyson's sonnet "Check every outflash": "You will perhaps be angry when I tell you that I sent your sonnet about the 'Sombre Valley' to Moxon, who is charmed with it, and has printed it off. I confess that this is a breach of trust on my part, but I hope for your forgiveness . . ."

Forgiveness was the more likely in that when the sonnet appeared in the *Englishman's Magazine* in August, it was accompanied by Hallam's long, discriminating, and enthusiastic essay "On Some of the Characteristics of Modern Poetry, and on the Lyrical Poems of Alfred Tennyson."

Hallam not only busied himself, most creditably, in Tennyson's service, he also busied their friends. This same month he wrote to Charles Merivale: "Meanwhile, perhaps, I may venture to ask you to take a little trouble for me in London, or rather for Alfred Tennyson, who according to custom has devolved his business on me." Moxon wanted Tennyson to contribute: so would Merivale call on Moxon at 64 New Bond Street,

> introducing yourself under shelter of my name, and Alfred's, and to pop the question to him, "What do you pay your regular contributors? What will you pay Alfred Tennyson for monthly contributions?". Also, while your hand is in, to ask whether, if Alfred was to get a new volume ready to be published next season, Moxon would give him anything for the copyright, and if anything, *what*. You might dexterously throw in, that I have a promise that any article I might write should be admitted either in the *Edinburgh* or *Quarterly*, and that I could therefore vouch for the books being reviewed in one or both. Nevertheless, I know the trade is at present in a most ticklish situation, and I suspect Moxon will fight shy.

A year later, Hallam was to supervise on Tennyson's behalf the printing and publication of *Poems* (which appeared in December 1832, with "1833" on the title page). It is important, then, to realize that what Tennyson gratefully loved in Hallam was not limited to the grandly platonic marriage of true minds, but included the shrewd and generous practicalities with which Hallam furthered the publication and promotion of Tennyson's poems. And, moreover, what Hallam loved in Tennyson was partly the opportunity which all this provided for some energetically disinterested and honorable activity such as Hallam's life would otherwise have lacked.

Tennyson would probably not have brought out a second volume in 1832 (or for some time) had it not been for Hallam's importunity. In March 1832, Hallam was able to write to their friend

Richard Chenevix Trench: "I have persuaded him, I think, to publish without further delay. There is written the amount of a volume rather larger than the former, and certainly, unless the usual illusion of manuscript deceives me, more free from blemishes and more masterly in power."

But the "blemishes" of the early volume were to be deployed and deplored with witty savagery by a powerful reviewer, and Hallam's plans received a setback. "Christopher North" (John Wilson) had emitted some praise and some rumbles in *Blackwood's* magazine in February:

"I have good hopes of Alfred Tennyson. But the Cockneys are doing what they may to spoil him. . . He has a fine ear for melody and harmony too—and rare and rich glimpses of imagination. He has—*genius*."
"Affectations."
"Too many. But I admire Alfred—and hope—nay trust—that one day he will prove himself a poet. If he do not, then am I no prophet."

But three months later the praise was less audible; Wilson's review of *Poems, Chiefly Lyrical* in *Blackwood's* in May was witheringly acerb, not only about Tennyson's weaknesses but especially about Tennyson's publicists. Hallam's recent essay in the *Englishman's Magazine* was held to have been so fatuous as to have been the reason why the magazine had since died.

Tennyson was sensitive to any adverse criticisms*; he was more than sensitive when his friend Hallam, who had ventured much for him, came under attack. Hallam himself was irritated but not perturbed, taking the sensible view that the vivid review was at least good publicity:

Have you seen Wilson's article on Alfred? I have a huge desire to kick

* The matter of Tennyson's alleged deference to reviewers is intricate. Browning was to be amazed: "For Keats and Tennyson to 'go softly all their days' for a gruff word or two is quite inexplicable to me, and always has been. Tennyson reads the 'Quarterly' and does as they bid him, with the most solemn face in the world—out goes this, in goes that, all is changed and ranged . . Oh me!" (to Elizabeth Barrett, February 11, 1845: *The Letters of Robert Browning and Elizabeth Barrett Barrett*, ed. E. Kintner, 1969, i. 19). But Tennyson's own dissatisfactions complicate the issue. See E. F. Shannon, *Tennyson and the Reviewers* (1952), and "The Critical Reception of *Maud*," PMLA, lxviii (1953).

that same Professor—yea, to give him kicks "superhuman, not to say, supernatural." However, all things considered the review will do good rather than harm.

But Tennyson threw off what he himself soon regretted as "a silly squib," "To Christopher North"; it was a pity he ignored Hallam's advice and published it. The refrain, "Crusty Christopher," had originally been different: "One of my sisters when I showed them this version persuaded me that 'Tipsy Kit' was too sharp." Too sharp, and perhaps imprudent, since "Christopher North" was the sort of controversialist who would not have hesitated to point out that the poet's father had often been worse than tipsy.

Certainly this contretemps did not impel Tennyson toward publishing a second volume. But Hallam did not flag, and in June 1832 (he had finished at Cambridge in January) he wrote to Emily:

I was speaking the other day to Moxon about books and the polite publisher touched upon Alfred's, talked of the favourable light with which it was received and asked if Alfred had any views of further publication. I don't doubt that Moxon would publish any volume Alfred might make up for him free of expense. It is worth his considering; a 2nd book just now would set Alfred high in public notice, and afford him the means of putting money in his pocket.

If Hallam was a powerful persuader, so too was money. Not because Tennyson sought comfort, but because he was determined to be independent of the grossly insensitive pressures of his grandfather and uncle. He had no intention of being "put into the Church" as his father had been. But to gain "distinction" from his poetry was not the same as gaining "means" from it. *Poems, Chiefly Lyrical* had apparently left him having to repay Effingham Wilson £11 toward the costs of publication. In Hallam's words:

Alfred, not intending to go into the Church, as the grandfather who has *patria potestas* over him wishes, and not having yet brought himself to cobble shoes for his livelihood, is desirous of putting his wits to profit, and begins to think himself a fool for kindly complying with the daily requests of Annuals without getting anything in return.

Hallam, who lamented the fact that the brother Charles had "entered the Church, and is, I fear, lost to the Muses," believed that Tennyson was rightly staunch: "Alfred has resisted all attempts to force him into a profession, preferring poetry and an honourable poverty." Such confidence in Tennyson's powers, and such acumen in assisting them, made Hallam deeply dear.

Yet even Hallam doubted that he could overcome Tennyson's reluctance. Then in September 1832: "I felt a thrill of pleasure on opening your packet this morning, for, to say the truth, I had begun to despair of your volume getting on, as you seemed so indignant at our endeavours to hasten it." He realized that it was possible to turn to advantage what was usually a nuisance: Tennyson's morbid reluctance to write letters. "If neither Moxon nor I hear from you to the contrary, the printing shall commence next week in the order you specify." The precise contents of the volume were in doubt as late as October, when Tennyson wrote to Moxon: "I scarcely know at present what the size of the volume will be, for I have many poems lying by me with respect to which I cannot make up my mind as to whether they are fit for publication." By November, Hallam was once again alerting Leigh Hunt.

Yet if Tennyson yielded to Hallam's persuasion, he did not abdicate his judgment. The clearest indication is his last-minute decision to withdraw his incomplete long poem "The Lover's Tale." Tennyson wrote to Moxon:

> After mature consideration I have come to a resolution of not publishing the last poem in my little volume, entitled, "Lover's Tale": it is too full of faults and though I think it might conduce towards making me popular, yet, to my eye, it spoils the completeness of the book, and is better away.

Hallam remonstrated: "You must be point-blank mad. . . . Pray—pray—pray—change your mind again." Hallam knew, though, that the voice sent forth can never be recalled, and that no printed poem by Tennyson would blush unseen: "It can't be helped. *Nescit vox missa reverti*. In a selfish point of view I shall gain; for mine is the only printed copy of the 'Tale' and I shall lend it at 5/- a head." Nearly fifty years later, Tennyson—maddened by the way in which his suppressed poem had been "mercilessly pirated"—was to give way and publish the poem himself.

Hallam's disinterested energy was the more admirable in that 1832 was not a happy year for him. He had passionately awaited his coming of age and the right to see Emily again, and yet he had feared too: "I am oppressed with the weight of the future—sometimes I feel as if it would be gain to lie down and die. 'Don't be a fool,' you will say: 'much better get up and be married.' Why so I think too, on the whole." Hallam was markedly liable to speak of death, even when all might have seemed well: "I am now at Somersby, not only as the friend of Alfred Tennyson, but as the lover of his sister. An attachment on my part of near two years' standing, and a mutual engagement of one year, are, I fervently hope, only the commencement of an union which circumstances may not impair and the grave itself not conclude."

The grave, however, was to preclude the union, and circumstances were already thwarting it. For Hallam had no money, and it would be a long time, if ever, before the legal profession would much reward him. Throughout 1832 Hallam was therefore at once excited and dismayed. In April, "the Blue Devils" gripped hard. In May, he wrote of his "very wretched state of mind, and frequent touches of illness." In June, "I am left much to my own thoughts in London, and they are but too apt to follow a gloomy track of their own, unfavourable to sound thinking and courageous living." In August, he wrote to his Cambridge friend Brookfield:

When your first letter reached me, months ago, I was very unwell, and very wretched—not merely hypped, as usual, but suffering the pressure of a severe anxiety, which, although past, has left me much worn in spirit. As I began to get better Alfred came up to town, and persuaded me to go abroad with him. So we went to the Rhine for a month . . . I have been very miserable since I saw you: my hopes grow fainter and fewer, yet I hope on, and will, until the last ray is gone, and then—. . . . I am a very unfortunate being; yet, when I look into Emily's eyes, I sometimes think there is happiness reserved for me. Certainly I am by nature sanguine and hopeful; I was not framed for despondency. If circumstances were as I wish them I hardly think I should moodily seek for new causes of disquiet.

The holiday on the Rhine—with its cholera and corpses—did not do much for Hallam's spirits, or for Tennyson's. Circumstances were too obstructive. The negotiations between Hallam's father and Emily's grandfather were protracted and barren. Henry Hallam deprecated the fact that Emily had not released Hallam from the engagement, and he deplored the fact that they had corresponded during the year (with Mrs. Tennyson's connivance). He declared that he would make his son an allowance of £600 a year but that there was no way of augmenting this to the level at which they might marry—"except what the bounty of Mr. Tennyson may supply." But Emily's grandfather was rigidly determined that his bounty should be justly distributed. The most that he could fairly offer turned out to be fairly nugatory—£70 a year and after his death a share of an estate, the share amounting to about £3,000. Arthur remonstrated with Emily's uncle Charles, but in vain. He urged Emily's brother Frederick either to intercede or himself to advance the money, but in vain. The situation was wretched, and it will not have induced in Tennyson any affection for his grandfather. Hallam groaned:

A negotiation has been going on between my father and the old man whose only good quality is his relationship to the person I love best in the world. The wretch makes most shabby, beggarly offers, which my father considers inadequate; and unless I can by hook or crook induce him to bid higher, I am not likely to be married before the Millennium.

Such was the darkened background against which Tennyson published his *Poems* in December 1832. Darkened, too, by the fact that it seemed the Tennysons would soon have to leave Somersby Rectory. Hallam pleaded tenderly with Emily: "If you set up a 'reg'lar good cry' because it is your *last* Eve at Somersby, how shall I remember it is my *first?*"

With trembling fingers did we weave
  The holly round the Christmas hearth;
  A rainy cloud possessed the earth,
And sadly fell our Christmas-eve.

(*In Memoriam*, XXX)

IV

Poems 1832

TENNYSON SEEMS TO HAVE been spurred into a creative burst by the death of his father, as he was to be by the death of Hallam. Later in 1831 he was moved to both gratitude and thought by Arthur Hallam's essay "On Some of the Characteristics of Modern Poetry, and on the Lyrical Poems of Alfred Tennyson." A powerful and subtle critique of Romantic poetry, it was to be praised by W. B. Yeats as

> criticism which is of the best and rarest sort. If one set aside Shelley's essay on poetry and Browning's essay on Shelley, one does not know where to turn in modern English criticism for anything so philosophic –anything so fundamental and radical–as the first half of Arthur Hallam's [essay].

The exposition of Tennyson's poems is sympathetic without being deferential; Hallam continually penetrated to some fundamental implication of a poem's principle; and he summed up the "five distinctive excellencies" of early Tennyson in a way that has never been bettered:

> First, his luxuriance of imagination, and at the same time his control over it. Secondly his power of embodying himself in ideal characters, or rather moods of character, with such extreme accuracy of adjustment, that the circumstances of the narration seem to have a natural correspondence with the predominant feeling, and, as it were, to be evolved from it by assimilative force. Thirdly his vivid, picturesque

delineation of objects, and the peculiar skill with which he holds all of them *fused*, to borrow a metaphor from science, in a medium of strong emotion. Fourthly, the variety of his lyrical measures, and exquisite modulation of harmonious words and cadences to the swell and fall of the feelings expressed. Fifthly, the elevated habits of thought, implied in these compositions, and imparting a mellow soberness of tone, more impressive, to our minds, than if the author had drawn up a set of opinions in verse, and sought to instruct the understanding rather than to communicate the love of beauty to the heart.

Some of that perhaps craves wary walking, but then so do some of the poems of 1830 toward which Tennyson, as well as Hallam, was too tolerant. "A mellow soberness of tone": the phrase, apt enough to the best of 1830–to "Mariana" and "A spirit haunts the year's last hours"–is at odds with the hectic vacillations of "Supposed Confessions," which have their counterpart in two poems which Tennyson wrote between the volumes of 1830 and 1832 but which he did not publish: "Memory" ("Ay me!") and "Perdidi Diem." "Memory" has its ungainly Gothicisms, but its questions are far more urgent than those of the decorous "Ode to Memory" (1830). For Tennyson's memories are of pain, of a life which seemed sterile as death, of longings that could be expressed only through a violent obliqueness:

Blessèd, cursèd, Memory,
Shadow, Spirit as thou mayst be,
Why hast thou become to me
A conscience dropping tears of fire
On the heart, which vain desire
Vexeth all too bitterly?
When the wand of circumstance
All at once hath bid thee glance,
From the body of the Past,
Like a wandering ghost aghast,
Why wearest thou, mad Memory,
Limb and lip and hair and eye,
Life–life without life or breath,
Death forth issuing from Death?

Tennyson's "moods of misery unutterable" were related to his strange sense of guilt, strange in that—like so many Victorians* and so many Victorian creations (from *Great Expectations* to "Childe Roland to the Dark Tower Came")—it also felt aggrievedly innocent. "Remorse" in 1827 had proclaimed its damnability—but the question "Remorse for what?" stayed unanswerable. The conscience in "Memory" drops tears of fire; they scald like burning lead, as do King Lear's tears, and yet with a deeply neurotic sense that the poet (unlike King Lear) does not know what to reproach himself with—he knows only that he must reproach himself. "Perdidi Diem" expresses this same despondency; true, it tries then to grasp assurance, but its second part—a beatific three-quarter vision—is a shadowy convolution, and ends moreover with a most unwanted ambiguity in the word *last:*

> Our Planets, slumbering in their swiftness, hear
> The last beat of the thunder of God's heart.

Latest, rather than last (too late for religious auscultation). It is the first of part of "Perdidi Diem"** which speaks, and it speaks of Tennyson's morbid guilt, of his fear of death and of a life that is no life.

> And thou hast lost a day! Oh mighty boast!
> Dost thou miss one day only? I have lost
> A life, perchance an immortality;
> I never *lived* a day, but daily die,
>   I have no real breath;
> My being is a vacant worthlessness,
> A carcass in the coffin of this flesh,
>   Pierced through with loathly worms of utter Death.
> My soul is but the eternal mystic lamp,
> Lighting that charnel damp,
> Wounding with dreadful rays that solid gloom,
> And shadowing forth the unutterable tomb,
> Making a "darkness visible"
> Of that which without thee we had not felt

* And, of course, non-Victorians; see Coleridge's "The Pains of Sleep." Mrs. Leavis's essay on *Great Expectations* is to the point (*Dickens the Novelist*, 1970).

** The saying of the Emperor Titus (quoted in Suetonius) when he found at night that he had done no good action that day.

As darkness, dark ourselves and loving night . . .

I must needs pore upon the mysteries
Of my own infinite Nature and torment
My spirit with a fruitless discontent:

And so into a melancholy simile of young ravens, fallen from their nest, and doomed to die before they have ever really lived: "What is the death of life if this be not to die?"

Tennyson was right to exclude "The Lover's Tale" at the last minute from *Poems* (1832). For all its mellifluous skill and scenic artfulness it is centrally unsound: it does not have the powerful personation by which Tennyson makes his fantasies the instrument of truth, but a sicklier and more honeyed fantasy of pretense. Its self-sacrifice is pretense; and so are its "Maydews of childhood," its disencumbered orphandom ("Before he saw my day my father died"), its mythical suicide, its underwrought yearning for death, and its high-minded prurience.

A land of promise flowing with the milk
And honey of delicious memories!

But the false honey of promise in the poem leads all too naturally to the false gall of the lover's disillusionment. The true moment in the poem comes when Tennyson explores that enduring sense of injured guilt:

as an innocent prisoner,
Who, when the woful sentence hath been past,
And all the clearness of his fame hath gone
Beneath the shadow of the curse of man,
First falls asleep in swoon, wherefrom awaked,
And looking round upon his tearful friends,
Forthwith and in his agony conceives
A shameful sense as of a cleaving crime—
For whence without some guilt should such grief be?

The seven poems which matter most in *Poems* (1832) are all concerned in some way with loneliness, guilt, or injustice: "The Lady of Shalott," "Mariana in the South," "Œnone," "The Palace of Art," "The Lotos-Eaters," "A Dream of Fair Women," and "To J.S."

Impatience with "The Lady of Shalott" for being a "tale of magic symbolism" and not that more conclusive thing, an allegory, manifested itself immediately on publication:

The "Lady of Shalott" is a strange ballad, without a perceptible object and as roundabout as

'The yellowleavèd waterlily,
The greensheathèd daffodilly,
Tremble in the water chilly,
Round about Shalott.'

We have said that the author shewed no fear of ludicrous associations; but as there is nothing either romantic or pathetic in this piece, he was safe enough with his Shallot, an onion which could make nobody shed tears.

To tears, perhaps not, but people have been moved by the romance and pathos of "The Lady of Shalott." If an allegorical pointer is needed, the best is still that of R. H. Hutton, who said that the poem

has for its real subject the emptiness of the life of fancy, however rich and brilliant, the utter satiety which compels any true imaginative nature to break through the spell which entrances it in an unreal world or visionary joys . . . The curse, of course, is that she shall be involved in mortal passions, and suffer the fate of mortals, if she looks away from the shadow to the reality. Nevertheless, the time comes when she braves the curse.

The Lady is not seen, but sometimes heard:

Only reapers, reaping early
In among the bearded barley,
Hear a song that echoes cheerly
From the river winding clearly,
Down to towered Camelot:
And by the moon the reaper weary,
Piling sheaves in uplands airy,
Listening, whispers " 'Tis the fairy
Lady of Shalott."

Each of the four parts ends with something said: the reaper's whisper, the Lady's repining: "I am half sick of shadows," the

Lady's cry: "the curse is come upon me," and Lancelot's moment of musing:

He said, "She has a lovely face;
God in his mercy lend her grace,
    The Lady of Shalott."

"She knows not what the curse may be"; simply that it forbids her to look directly at life—she must see life only in her mirror. The mirror is not there simply for the fairy tale; it was set behind the tapestry so that the worker could see the effect from the right side. But what brings the Lady to defy the curse?

And sometimes through the mirror blue
The knights come riding two and two:
She hath no loyal knight and true,
    The Lady of Shalott.

Lancelot is not the first knight that she sees, but he rides alone; nor does he have exactly a "loyal" lover; nor is he exactly a "loyal knight and true" (he is "falsely true" to Guinevere and to Arthur*). It is the sight of "two young lovers lately wed" which wrings from the Lady the cry that mingles weariness and illness: "I am half sick of shadows."

The sight of Lancelot is dazzling:

All in the blue unclouded weather
Thick-jewelled shone the saddle-leather,
The helmet and the helmet-feather
Burned like one burning flame together,
    As he rode down to Camelot.

But the sight of Lancelot is piercingly different from any other sight which the Lady sees in the poem. She sees reflected in her mirror both Lancelot and Lancelot reflected in the river:

From the bank and from the river
He flashed into the crystal mirror,

* Compare "Sir Launcelot and Queen Guinevere" (written 1830–33, published 1842), which Tennyson's friend J. M. Kemble called a "companion to 'The Lady of Shalott.'"

"Tirra lirra," by the river
Sang Sir Lancelot.

At which, "She left the web, she left the loom"—and was done for. The "crystal" mirror suggests the river; for the only time in the poem, a word rhymes with itself—a perfect reflection: *river/river*. Nor is there another reference to the river's reflecting in the poem—notably, given that there is so much about the river and about dazzling light. Her mirror constituted a protection against life for the Lady; it cracks after she sees somebody doubly mirrored—"From the bank and from the river"—within the mirror. It is as if the protection is canceled out: re-re-flection = flection, the impact itself.

The Lady slowly dies as by some mysterious suicide, some consumptive wish not to go on living. The river that had been like a mirror is now a "dim expanse"; and the "glassy countenance" is now the Lady's.

Yet the curse seems at once capricious and deeply apt. Tennyson said that "the new born love for something, for some one in the wide world from which she has been so long secluded, takes her out of the region of shadows into that of realities." She dies in love-birth. But love at such first sight? And are we to think that the reality of love is inherently destructive? Or that it cannot but be destructive once seclusion has long claimed anybody? J. W. Croker, with a wit that is apt as well as hostile, saw the poem basically as a pun on the word *spinster*. But the poem is more of a riddle than that. John Stuart Mill disliked the original 1832 ending, which had quoted the Lady's oracular parchment—"a 'lame and impotent conclusion,' where no conclusion was required." But Tennyson—who was drawn to the right kind of conclusion in which nothing is concluded—did not simply cut out the stanza; he replaced it with Lancelot's musing lines. And in those lines we sense—off the end of the poem again—another destructive love which awaits its catastrophe. When Lancelot says "God in his mercy lend her grace," he speaks as someone to whom God in his mercy will lend grace.

"The Lady of Shalott" is not a perfect poem; it has some Arthurian bric-à-brac and such inattentions as the filler "we see" in: "Like to some branch of stars we see/Hung in the golden

Galaxy." But it creates an intensely memorable myth in which the wish not to face reality and the wish to face it, the impulse toward life and the impulse toward death, an inexplicable guilt and a timorous innocence, shine as from a cracked mirror.

Loneliness and the wish to die throb too in "Mariana in the South." She has her "liquid mirror" but nothing will shatter it. Her curse is of the unshattering kind. The poem was precipitated by Tennyson's visit to the Pyrenees with Hallam, and Hallam plumbed it intelligently:

It is intended, you will perceive, as a kind of pendant to his former poem of "Mariana," the idea of both being the expression of desolate loneliness, but with this distinctive variety in the second, that it paints the forlorn feeling as it would exist under the influence of different impressions of sense . . . You will, I think, agree with me that the essential and distinguishing character of the conception requires in the "Southern Mariana" a greater lingering on the outward circumstances, and a less palpable transition of the poet into Mariana's feelings, than was the case in the former poem.

With one black shadow at its feet,
  The house through all the level shines,
Close-latticed to the brooding heat,
  And silent in its dusty vines . . .

Certainly we sense rather than enter this Mariana's feelings, and far more through the intensities of her environment which go beyond the decaying counterparts of the first Mariana. Here the scene and the climate are less echoic and more punitive:

But day increased from heat to heat,
  On stony drought and steaming salt.

The heat of love and the sterility of drought bring some satisfaction in that they promise to suffocate.

Dreaming, she knew it was a dream:
  She felt he was and was not there.
She woke: the babble of the stream
  Fell, and, without, the steady glare
Shrank one sick willow sere and small.

The river-bed was dusty-white;
And all the furnace of the light
Struck up against the blinding wall.
She whispered, with a stifled moan
More inward than at night or morn,
"Sweet Mother, let me not here alone
Live forgotten and die forlorn."

Yet that last refrain (with its clear suggestion of religious ritual) points to something that crucially distinguishes the two Marianas. Leigh Hunt wittily said that the Southern Mariana "though more Catholic in one sense is less so in another." This one has the Christian religion, in its Catholic intensity, to offer solace, to forbid all thought of suicide and despair. But she gradually and unmistakably quits her religious invocations. In the first stanza, there is "Ave Mary" twice; in the second, "Ave Mary" and "Madonna"; in the third, "Our Lady" and "Mother." But the fourth has nothing. The fifth has "Sweet Mother." From here to the end—stanzas six, seven, and eight—nothing. Lines 61 to 96 are markedly non-Catholic. It might be thought that this is inadvertent; there had been a "Madonna" in the penultimate line of the poem in the original 1832 text, and it might have slipped away with other things when Tennyson revised the last stanza. But in fact the revisions of the last stanza—even if one does not press the view that Tennyson then deliberately cut out a "Madonna" which had once been weightily in—bear notably on Mariana's religious solace.

1832: Ever the low wave seemed to roll
Up to the coast: far on, alone
In the East, large Hesper overshone
The mourning gulf, and on her soul
Poured divine solace, or the rise
Of moonlight from the margin gleamed,
Volcano-like, afar, and streamed
On her white arm, and heavenward eyes.
Not all alone she made her moan,
Yet ever sang she, night and morn,
"Madonna, lo! I am all alone,
Love-forgotten and love-forlorn."

1842:

At eve a dry cicala sung,
  There came a sound as of the sea;
Backward the lattice-blind she flung,
  And leaned upon the balcony.
There all in spaces rosy-bright
  Large Hesper glittered on her tears,
  And deepening through the silent spheres
Heaven over Heaven rose the night.
And weeping then she made her moan,
  "The night comes on that knows not morn,
When I shall cease to be all alone,
  To live forgotten, and love forlorn."

Gone is the divine solace that was poured on her soul; gone her heavenward eyes; gone the assurance that she was not all alone (in that God or the Madonna was with her, presumably); gone the Madonna. Instead there is the beautiful ambiguity of "Heaven over Heaven rose the night," and the very opposite of ambiguity in her cry: "The night comes on that knows not morn." The Christian line would be "The morn comes on that knows not night"—but to Mariana the night of death is devoutly to be wished. Last, there are "her tears," her "weeping." For hitherto her eyes had been

Her melancholy eyes divine,
The home of woe without a tear.

"Divine" is more than a mere approbation; in weeping, does she become less divine and more human? The "image" that has come to her is not a religious image, and its whisper, "But thou shalt be alone no more," is the whisper of death: she will not be alone because she will not *be*. If her lover is not to be embraced, at least death can be. Whether it was indeed embraced cannot be said, for this Mariana does not come clearly under the auspices of *Measure for Measure*, her name being unsupported by an epigraph.

"Dear mother Ida, harken ere I die." That line, or a close variant of it, comes twenty times in "Œnone"—about once every ten lines. For Œnone too has been deserted by her lover, and she too expects (and hopes) to die. "Œnone," though, is not an integrated poem; its three concerns jostle, and each is granted a different manner. Two are successes (though not of the deepest), and the other an imposing failure. The failure is the central scene, the debate between the goddesses Juno, Pallas, and Aphrodite for the golden apple of Paris. Tennyson was already, unfortunately, a master of that thrasonical grandiloquence which was ultimately to mar *Idylls of the King*. Instead of modulated cadence, responsive to the shape of thought, there is the stilted, the unsayable. Jawbreakers like "Whereupon/Rose feud, with question unto whom 'twere due"–which in another poet Tennyson would rightly have deplored as "a line that seems to me hammered up out of old nail-heads." Or the clumsiness of "Sequel of guerdon could not alter me/To fairer"–both cramped and wordy, in that a guerdon (reward) that doesn't come as a sequel isn't really a guerdon at all. There is nothing wrong with the poem's admiration for "Self-reverence, self-knowledge, self-control"; but the poetry too much reverences itself, its knowledge and control are too credulously effortful:

> until endurance grow
> Sinewed with action, and the full-grown will,
> Circled through all experiences, pure law,
> Commeasure perfect freedom.

Such rhetoric too much invites a round of applause.

Dr. Johnson said that, in his Odes, Gray "has a kind of strutting dignity, and is tall by walking on tiptoe." The same goes for the moral muscularity at the center of "Œnone," and it badly damages the poem. The true (though smallish) achievements of the poem are elsewhere: in the love landscapes, and in Œnone's pain.

The opening lines are delicate of echo:

> There lies a vale in Ida, lovelier
> Than all the valleys of Ionian hills.
> The swimming vapour slopes athwart the glen,
> Puts forth an arm, and creeps from pine to pine,
> And loiters, slowly drawn.

But the mood does not loiter. It is as R. H. Horne said, "a fine prelude to love's delirium, which follows it." "For now the noonday quiet holds the hill": the poem is poised, waiting. And this present scene is counterpointed with that earlier noon, when disaster was preluded by the luxuriance through which the goddesses came to Paris's contest:

It was the deep midnoon: one silvery cloud
Had lost his way between the piney sides
Of this long glen. Then to the bower they came,
Naked they came to that smooth-swarded bower,
And at their feet the crocus brake like fire,
Violet, amaracus, and asphodel,
Lotos and lilies: and a wind arose,
And overhead the wandering ivy and vine,
This way and that, in many a wild festoon
Ran riot, garlanding the gnarlèd boughs
With bunch and berry and flower through and through.

J. W. Croker was sure he detected a prudish prurience in this love landscape. In the manner of a pornographer of yesteryear, he slotted in some asterisks: *

Naked they came–

* * * * *

How beautiful they were!

In the place where we have indicated a pause, follows a description, long, rich, and luscious–Of the three naked goddesses? Fye for shame–no–of the "lily flower violet-eyed," and the "singing pine," and the "overwandering ivy and vine," and "festoons," and "gnarled boughs," and "tree tops," and "berries," and "flowers," and all the *inanimate* beauties of the scene. It would be unjust to the *ingenuus pudor* of the author not to observe the art with which he has veiled this ticklish interview behind such luxuriant trellis-work, and it is obvious that it is for our special sakes he has entered into these local details, because if there was one thing which "mother Ida"** knew better than another, it must have been her own bushes and brakes.

Yet Croker has indeed noticed something: that Tennyson relies on "trellis-work" to make his naked goddesses not less but more

* Croker was dealing with the 1832 text (revised 1842), but the point stands.

** The mountain to whom Œnone prays.

appealing. And as Croker details the "luxuriant" natural description, it almost dawns on him too that a luxur is a lecher. That "overwandering ivy and vine"! As Tennyson observed in "Marion":

> Love is a vine, and in the hot
> And southern slopes he takes delight.

What makes the erotic use of landscape so much more effective than other feasible indirect routes to eroticism is the fact that there are two powerful and persistent traditions which bring together love and landscape. It is an ancient commonplace to speak of Nature as a mistress, and so it is to do the opposite: to speak of your mistress as if she were Nature—hence the long vogue for poems which describe lovemaking in topographical terms, as for example in "Venus and Adonis." When Croker speaks of "her own bushes and brakes," he all but stumbles into indelicacy, and he makes manifest the healthy furtiveness of Tennyson's love landscapes in "Œnone."

But the first landscape within Œnone's own words had despaired of love and instead hoped for death, death as quiet (such a quiet as "holds" with an embrace gentler than that of a man), and as rest and as sleep:

> "O mother Ida, many-fountained Ida,
> Dear mother Ida, harken ere I die.
> For now the noonday quiet holds the hill:
> The grasshopper is silent in the grass:
> The lizard, with his shadow on the stone,
> Rests like a shadow, and the winds are dead.
> The purple flower droops: the golden bee
> Is lily-cradled: I alone awake.
> My eyes are full of tears, my heart of love,
> My heart is breaking, and my eyes are dim,
> And I am all aweary of my life."

Yet Œnone strives to resist the pull; her lines can begin, "O happy tears," "O happy Heaven," "O happy earth," and then can momentarily assert a resistance to the hypnotic sequence—not "O happy death," but "O death, death, death." Yet then her cry emerges:

O death, death, death, thou ever-floating cloud,
There are enough unhappy on this earth,
Pass by the happy souls, that love to live:
I pray thee, pass before my light of life,
And shadow all my soul, that I may die.
Thou weighest heavy on the heart within,
Weigh heavy on my eyelids: let me die.

A cry, though? Too calm, calming itself even in the saying, soothed by its repetitions. The verse therefore contains its own prefigurings of the fact that Œnone is not now to die. Croker was moved to a snort:

After such reiterated assurances that she was about to die on the spot, it appears that Œnone thought better of it, and the poem concludes with her taking the wiser course of going to town to consult her swain's sister, Cassandra–whose advice, we presume, prevailed upon her to live, as we can, from other sources, assure our readers she did to a good old age.

But few of Tennyson's people do die on the spot. By making the prophetess Cassandra–with her visions of the burning of Troy–the focus at the end of the poem, Tennyson once more projects his poem into a darkened yet fiery future which encompasses the flames of Troy and of the pyre which Œnone will one day choose as an honorable suicide,* that death which she had claimed too early:

What this may be I know not, but I know
That, wheresoe'er I am by night and day,
All earth and air seem only burning fire.

Burning fire: it has a childlike pathos and incredulity in its slow tautology. The poem was determined not to end, as so many of its lines had ended, with the word *die*. But fire is the far off embraced death of Œnone.

"Give us long rest, or death, dark death, or dreamful ease." The mariners in "The Lotos-Eaters" are drawn toward drug and dream, and away from toil and obligation. Once they have eaten

* See "The Death of Œnone" (written 1889–90).

of the lotos, they prefer its half-life, and they would prefer death to setting forth again. Their weariness is felt in the opening words as a resistance for their commander to overcome:

"Courage!" he said, and pointed toward the land,
"This mounting wave will roll us shoreward soon."
In the afternoon they came unto a land
In which it seemèd always afternoon.
All round the coast the languid air did swoon,
Breathing like one that hath a weary dream.
Full-faced above the valley stood the moon;
And like a downward smoke, the slender stream
Along the cliff to fall and pause and fall did seem.

What will prove to be the most seductively (though equivocally) languorous of Tennyson's poems begins with energetic urging, "Courage!," and gesture, and justified confidence. The second line is an emblem of the proper yielding, the responsible passivity —yielding to the wave so that the wave does the work. (There is no virtue in needless toil.) With the third line, *he* has yielded to *they*, and *land* has rhymed, ominously, with *land*. " 'The strand' was, I think, my first reading, but the no rhyme of 'land' and 'land' was lazier" (Tennyson). The Spenserian stanza had not been better used since Spenser—the repetitions are at once a free lyricism and a menacing pressure; the final alexandrine makes its aural illusion of "pause" into an equivalent of the optical illusion; the archaic expansions ("did swoon," "did seem"—and so into "did go," "did receive," "did seem," "did make") are both precariously wary and having all the time in the world. The five Spenserian stanzas set the scene: the rich landscape, the rosy sunset, and the altogether unthreatening Lotos-eaters (disconcertingly unthreatening):

A land where all things always seemed the same!
And round about the keel with faces pale,
Dark faces pale against that rosy flame,
The mild-eyed melancholy Lotos-eaters came.

"Against" delicately suggests that there is a certain kind of war on —not "the ten years' war in Troy" of which the mariners will sing, but an essential antagonism of the dark faces pale against flame.* And the Lotos-eaters came bearing gifts (*et dona ferentes*), and as the fallen Eve came to Adam: "Branches they bore of that enchanted stem . . ." The mariner eats, and enters upon a life that is an acute form of death:

> and if his fellow spake,
> His voice was thin, as voices from the grave;
> And deep-asleep he seemed, yet all awake,
> And music in his ears his beating heart did make.

Whereupon the music moves outward, via speaking:

> Then some one said, "We will return no more;"
> And all at once they sang, "Our island home
> Is far beyond the wave; we will no longer roam."

"At once"—it is an impressive community of feeling and expressing—there begins the long "Choric Song" from which the poem does not ever return.

The "Choric Song" ebbs and flows, its stanzas alternately evoking deep languor and sharply questioning ("Is there any peace/ In ever climbing up the climbing wave?"). Relaxation never obliterates indignation.

> Death is the end of life; ah, why
> Should life all labour be?

But is death the end of life in being its true aim? All responsibilities can now become dreams; one's parents, all passion spent, can become "Two handfuls of white dust, shut in an urn of brass!" And by a subtle rationalization (subtle enough to be virtually a reason), the counter-duty of *not* returning is discovered:

> Our sons inherit us: our looks are strange:
> And we should come like ghosts to trouble joy.**

The drug is in some respects a truth drug. Yet perilous; we

* The *Odyssey* has its active negative: "So they went straightway and mingled with the Lotus-eaters, and the Lotus-eaters did not plan death for my comrades, but gave them of the lotus to taste."

** The destructive possibilities of such a return were a lifelong preoccupation of Tennyson's, from the early poem "The Coach of Death," through *In Memoriam*, to "Enoch Arden."

should set beside two lines of the poem—"To muse and brood and live again in memory," and "There *is* confusion worse than death"—two sentences from Tennyson's urgent letter of these same years dissuading W. H. Brookfield from opium:

What are you about—musing, and brooding and dreaming and opium-eating yourself out of this life into the next? . . . if you do not ["leave off the aforesaid drug"] I can foresee nothing for you but stupefaction, aneurism, confusion, horror and death.

Yet what of the end of "The Lotos-Eaters"? Tennyson was dissatisfied with the original rhythms, and for 1842 he revised them. But the jaunty was replaced by the galumphing:

We have had enough of action, and of motion we,
Rolled to starboard, rolled to larboard,
  when the surge was seething free,
Where the wallowing monster spouted his
  foam-fountains in the sea.

Unfortunately such rhythms sound as if they couldn't possibly have enough of action, (but this without any subtly apt contrariety), and the last section of the poem remains crudely anti-climactic. And yet the end off the end of the poem greatly matters. The poem had begun with *he* (Odysseus); then to *they* (the Mariners); then to *they* (the Lotos-eaters); and then to *we* (the mariners). The question "who are the Lotos-eaters?" is pertinent; do the mariners become Lotos-eaters by eating the lotos? Do they go native? Does the poem evoke an addiction that nothing can break? E. D. H. Johnson has said that the final change of rhythm is "to express the final troubled moment of decision when the mariners make their choice not to return to the outside world." And certainly the mariners express decision through *will*, not *shall:* "We will return no more," "we will no longer roam," and—concluding the poem—"we will not wander more." Yet is the decision theirs to make? "The Lotos-Eaters" is, among other things, a creative allusion to Homer, and the same question—of a known outcome not mentioned within the poem—arises as with Tennyson's allusion to Shakespeare, "Mariana." For the end of the story in Homer is very definitely not the mariners' drugged wish:

And whosoever of them ate of the honey-sweet fruit of the lotus, had no longer any wish to bring back word or to return, but there they were fain to abide among the Lotus-eaters, feeding on the lotus, and forgetful of their homeward way. These men, therefore, I brought back perforce to the ships, weeping. (*Odyssey*, IX)

In Homer the story ends, not in withdrawal, but in withdrawal symptoms. It ends with Odysseus' assertion of authority. Tennyson's poem, it is true, preserves a potent silence. Yet: "Courage! he said . . ."—the *he* of the first line does not return in the poem, but is he simply dropped? He is assuredly not among those who eat the lotos; perhaps he broods over those who brood. Is the note of command in the first two lines of the poem authoritative enough to command the poem? The poem does not ever return to its narrative from the "Choric Song."* But that is not at all the same as saying that the mariners are not to return from the land of the Lotos-eaters (did Odysseus never complete his journey?). Our wishes—the poem tacitly reminds us—are not necessarily sovereign. Croker, as usual, grasped the right point by the wrong end:

How they got home you must read in Homer:—Mr. Tennyson—himself, we presume, a dreamy lotos-eater, a delirious lotos-eater—leaves them in full song.

The poems of 1832 which most yearn for escape ("Mariana" and "The Lotos-Eaters") are also those which most scrupulously imagine the implications of what it would be to escape. The two poems which strike a stauncher stance are vitiated by flummery: "The Palace of Art" and "A Dream of Fair Women" are important, but unsatisfactory. "Tennyson, we cannot live in Art," his Cambridge friend R. C. Trench had said roundly—but "The Palace of Art" stands too four square. "I send you here a sort of allegory," replied Tennyson in his prefatory poem, of a soul "That did love Beauty only," a soul that did not see the interrelationship of Beauty, Good, and Knowledge. But "The Palace

* The same is true of "The Hesperides" (1832), of which J. W. Croker said laconically that Hanno "appears to have kept on his way without taking any notice of the song. . . ."

of Art" does not explore that interrelationship; it simply asserts that the soul which loves Beauty only, and builds its Palace of Art, will fall into despair and self-loathing.

> I built my soul a lordly pleasure-house,
> Wherein at ease for aye to dwell.

And with the opening words we hear the hollow resonance of strenuous affirmation–that "lordly pleasure-house" is at once so gimcrack in comparison with the "stately pleasure-dome" of Kubla Khan which it recollects. Tennyson was to revise the 1832 text extensively, but he retained too much of this narrative pomposity.

> And high on every peak a statue seemed
> To hang on tiptoe, tossing up
> A cloud of incense of all odour steamed
> From out a golden cup.

This is wordy pretense, with "high" too much overlapping with "peak," and "cloud" with "incense" and "odour" and "steamed"; and with the clumsiness of "To hang on tiptoe,"and the rhyming wastefulness of "up" (incense cannot but rise), and the mock-dignity of "From out." Such preciosity (sadly unmellifluous, incidentally) is endemic in the first half of the poem; it is responsible for the thoughtless vapidity and impotence of such a stanza as this:

> For there was Milton like a seraph strong,
> Beside him Shakespeare bland and mild;
> And there the world-worn Dante grasped his song,
> And somewhat grimly smiled.

This is not percipient portraiture but shallow charade.

Within the first half, "The Spontaneous *Go*" of the poem (FitzGerald's words) is all in the landscapes which set themselves something to capture (a depth of mood at least), though even here the true Tennyson is succeeded by the simulator:

> One seemed all dark and red–a tract of sand,
> And some one pacing there alone,
> Who paced for ever in a glimmering land,
> Lit with a low large moon.

One showed an iron coast and angry waves.
  You seemed to hear them climb and fall
And roar rock-thwarted under bellowing caves,
    Beneath the windy wall.

The second half of the poem—the soul's disillusionment and despair—is more intense. Yet its references to self-destructive madness (lines 203–204), to the complacencies of a false confidence in resurrection (lines 205–207), to a suicidal pride (line 257), are too little trapped and too much trapped out. The horrors—like the architecture—are Gothic (a recurrent protection against real horror in Tennyson): "White-eyed phantasms weeping tears of blood,/And horrible nightmares"—that last phrase openly abdicates. The genuine pain, as so often in Tennyson, is crushed into a simile for the soul's bitter loneliness:

A still salt pool, locked in with bars of sand,
  Left on the shore; that hears all night
The plunging seas draw backward from the land
    Their moon-led waters white.

But the despair—in which the soul hates death and life equally, and finds dreadful both time and eternity, and feels entombed alive—is grimly disproportionate to the soul's error of Aestheticism. John Sterling insisted that "the meaning, the *morality*, is trivial and even mistaken"—he could not see (and perceptively so) that the soul here "is perpetrating some prodigious moral offence for which it is bound to repent in sackcloth and ashes." Even Mill, who found the poem "the most favourable augury for Mr. Tennyson's future achievements"—because "symbolical of spiritual truths"—had to admit that the poem is not "wholly successful." In fact the poem honestly collapses—"honestly" in that at the last minute the soul puts in a plea, but "collapses" in that this should have entailed a total reappraisal:

"Make me a cottage in the vale," she said,
  "Where I may mourn and pray.

"Yet pull not down my palace towers, that are
  So lightly, beautifully built:
Perchance I may return with others there
  When I have purged my guilt."

She did return with others there, in the 1890s. But it makes perhaps the strangest of all Tennyson's conclusions in which nothing is concluded, a bathos that swallows its poem.

"A Dream of Fair Women" does not strikingly disintegrate, but then it never set itself much to integration. Its ostensible purpose—a vision of "Beauty and anguish walking hand in hand/The downward slope to death"—never becomes any kind of inquiry or exploration; it settles for, and into, anecdotes and once again charades. Iphigeneia, Helen, Cleopatra, Jephtha's daughter . . . : the line could as well have stretched out to the crack of doom. But, fragmentary and crude, there are some of the real concerns of Tennyson: the injustice to women (which will be taken more lightheartedly but more seriously in *The Princess*); the sense that it would be better to have died long ago; "Gross darkness of the inner sepulchre," with consciousness buried alive; the destructiveness of a father's love; and above all, the entanglements of self-sacrifice, sacrifice, martyrdom, and suicide—in the stories of Iphigeneia,* Jephtha's daughter, and Cleopatra. These preoccupations were to precipitate some of Tennyson's best poems; here they are too stagey and too brassy. The second stanza should alert us to an unalertness: "Dan Chaucer, the first warbler . . . ," wording which is fatigued in metaphorical condescension and awkward in assonance. The onomatopoeia is too easily satisfied, too battering: "And clattering flints battered with clanging hoofs."

Yet the poem is "A Dream . . . ," and Tennyson's imagination never failed to be ignited by dreams. The two styles of the poem can be seen side by side:

> And once my arm was lifted to hew down
>   A cavalier from off his saddle-bow,
> That bore a lady from a leaguered town;
>   And then, I know not how,

* The 1832 text (Tennyson had the sense to revise it) moved Croker to one of his best exclamations. "One drew a sharp knife through my tender throat—/ Slowly—and *nothing more!*" "What touching simplicity—what pathetic resignation—he cut my throat—'*nothing more!*' One might indeed ask, 'what *more*' she would have?"

All those sharp fancies, by down-lapsing thought
  Streamed onward, lost their edges, and did creep
Rolled on each other, rounded, smoothed, and brought
  Into the gulfs of sleep.

The first stanza is all chivalric posture; the second is an exquisite lacing of the moments between wake and sleep, with the slipping through, all edges lost, mimed in the undulating verbal forms: streamed, lost, rolled, rounded, smoothed, brought, all of them vacillating between past participles and past tenses.

Within a dream, no damaging insincerity was involved in the claim to recall "The times when I remember to have been/Joyful and free from blame." Yet even here such a claim follows at once upon a vista which finds its satisfaction elsewhere than in joy:

I knew the flowers, I knew the leaves, I knew
  The tearful glimmer of the languid dawn
On those long, rank, dark wood-walks drenched in dew,
  Leading from lawn to lawn.

And to end the poem? For once it might seem that Tennyson could not but offer the direct ending: a waking from the dream and a repining:

No memory labours longer from the deep
  Gold-mines of thought to lift the hidden ore
That glimpses, moving up, than I from sleep
  To gather and tell o'er

Each little sound and sight. With what dull pain
  Compassed, how eagerly I sought to strike
Into that wondrous track of dreams again!
  But no two dreams are like.

Yet Tennyson did not tolerate so directly bleak, so final, an ending. He continued for two more stanzas, their bleakness oblique, constituting a belated half-candid admission of the root perplexity: What if one hath not been blest? What if the poet's failure is not "Failing to give the bitter of the sweet" (the bitterness that the sweet is now lost), but a deeper failing to admit that bitterness was all?

As when a soul laments, which hath been blest,
  Desiring what is mingled with past years,
In yearnings that can never be exprest
  By sighs or groans or tears;

Because all words, though culled with choicest art,
  Failing to give the bitter of the sweet,
Wither beneath the palate, and the heart
  Faints, faded by its heat.

The poem had flexed itself to end; at the last moment, it decided instead to faint and fade.

Poems (1832) ended with an elegiac act of friendship, "To J.S." Edward, the brother of Tennyson's friend James Spedding, had died in August 1832; for the opening of "To J.S." Tennyson adapted the opening (all he had written) of part two of a poem which he had already sent to James Spedding. Spedding had quoted this in a letter to Edward, and so the adaptation acts as a kindly private allusion. Something has already been said of "To J.S." and its rather distant dealing with the death of Tennyson's father. Much might be said of its anticipations of *In Memoriam*, in manner and substance. But the poem especially matters for two reasons. The first is the unmelodramatic tranquility with which Tennyson speaks of choosing death in self-sacrifice. The 1832 text has:

Words weaker than your grief would make
  Grief more. 'Twere better I should cease
Although to calm you I would take
  The place of him that sleeps in peace.

FitzGerald thought this too much: "I used to ask if this was not *un peu trop fort*. I think it's altered or omitted in future Editions. It is all rather affected." But FitzGerald underrated Tennyson's fatigued despondency, his wish to sleep in peace. The sentiment was not affected. But it did quietly press self-sacrifice to the point where it could be seen as morbid and suicidal, so Tennyson in 1842 made the protective qualification asked for by good sense:

Although myself could almost take
  The place of him that sleeps in peace.

The second peculiarity of the poem is its frequent ambiguity, most notable in the exquisite concluding stanzas:

Sleep sweetly, tender heart, in peace:
  Sleep, holy spirit, blessèd soul,
While the stars burn, the moons increase,
  And the great ages onward roll.

Sleep till the end, true soul and sweet.
  Nothing comes to thee new or strange.
Sleep full of rest from head to feet;
  Lie still, dry dust, secure of change.

Tennyson has achieved an impersonal serenity, but its source is equivocal. The sequence is from "spirit" to "soul," and from "soul" to "dust." "Sleep," it says five times with gentle admonishment. And to wake? *In Memoriam* was to ponder "If Sleep and Death be truly one"–but there sleep was biding till the Last Judgment. The end of "To J.S." is all sleep and no waking. "Sleep till the end" which may be Judgment Day, or the words may simply mean "till the end." "Nothing comes to thee new or strange"–nothing? "Lie still, dry dust, secure of change": *still* is delicately dual, and how are we to take "secure of change"? Does secure mean "assured of"? In which case the after-life does edge into the poem's conclusion. And yet the whole feeling of these last lines is set against change, is absolute for death. Moreover, the last two lines would seem to recall the innocence in Milton: "asleep secure of harme" (*Paradise Lost*, IV. 791); and in that case "secure of" must mean "secure against." Sleep, not heaven, would stand as the final solace. For all its mildness, the end of "To J.S." is forcefully perplexing. It too is a poem of which the ending may not be the ultimate ending, since we cannot speak of sleeping without wondering about waking.

V

1. Poems between 1832 and Hallam's death

The poems which Tennyson wrote in 1832 but did not then publish, together with those which he wrote between *Poems* (December 1832) and Hallam's sudden death in September 1833, show that serenity was feasible but fitful. It is true that this period saw the lightheartedness of "The Goose" and "Early Spring," and the buoyancy of "Sir Launcelot and Queen Guinevere" ("a companion to 'The Lady of Shalott,'" and a forerunner of Tennyson's Arthurian enterprise). But the glow of such verses is biographically deceptive.

> Yet, by a rule of contraries,
> My spirit in that doleful clime
> Shot herself down beneath the skies
> In rapid rills of merry rhyme.
>
> I was like purple glass, that glows
> Most rich and warm, but if more nigh
> You look through it, it only shows
> A frosted land, a chilly sky.
>
> ("Youth")

The poem at this time which "glows most rich" is "The Gardener's Daughter." Written mostly in 1833, it blends Tennyson's friendship for Hallam (the narrator's for Eustace) with Hallam's love for Tennyson's sister Emily (Eustace's for Juliet)—and with an imaginary lover, the gardener's daughter, for Tennyson himself. (The imaginary was to be tinged by the real in 1834 while Tennyson was polishing the poem.) "The centre of the poem, that passage describing the girl [lines 124–40], must be full and rich," said Tennyson: "The poem is so, to a fault, especially the descriptions of nature, for the lover is an artist, but, this being so, the central picture must hold its place." It is no accident that this should echo Tennyson's comment on his earlier blank verse love-fantasy, "The Lover's Tale" ("I think it is very rich and full—but there are mistakes in it"). He had withdrawn "The Lover's Tale" from publication in 1832, but a modification of its manner persisted in "The Gardener's Daughter," flowered in the best of the "English Idyls" such as "Edwin Morris" later in the 1830s, and was still to be capable of new development in the finest parts of *The Princess* (1847).

Yet in "The Gardener's Daughter" it is the garden, not the girl, that fires the poem. Alfred Austin was right to see an essential aspect of Tennyson in these two lines:

> Not wholly in the busy world, nor quite
> Beyond it, blooms the garden that I love.

"What a mine of confession and suggestiveness there is in those two lines, when we come to consider and accurately measure the genius of their author!" The setting is perfectly attuned to those onomatopoeic liquidities of which Tennyson was proud (but which in a poem like "The Gardener's Daughter" are entrusted with too much): "The mellow ouzel fluted in the elm."*

> The garden stretches southward. In the midst
> A cedar spread his dark-green layers of shade.
> The garden-glasses glanced, and momently
> The twinkling laurel scattered silver lights.

Such a description is consummately unpretentious (as the ensuing one of the girl is not). Mr. Holbrook in Mrs. Gaskell's *Cranford* (1853) was to intone that second line ("Wonderful man!"), and

* The effect is not echoic; what the line evokes is not the sound but the feel of the sound; and there is a kind of wit in the way "mellow" suggests, but does not utter, "melodious." Heard melodies are sweet, but those unheard are sweeter.

was to sense that Tennyson's real interest was less in the two girls than in setting and simile:

> those eyes
> Darker than darkest pansies, and that hair
> More black than ashbuds in the front of March.

Mr. Holbrook: ". . . And I've lived all my life in the country; more shame for me not to know." The accuracy of March does matter (Tennyson originally had "May"); what matters more is the tacit glimpse of the girl's forehead (from those eyes to that hair) in the word "front."

Tennyson was able to write this happy poem only by projecting it far into the future. For the poem ends by unveiling the picture of the girl with whom the narrator has spent his married life,

> My first, last love; the idol of my youth,
> The darling of my manhood, and, alas!
> Now the most blessèd memory of mine age.

In memory and in the distant garden, "She stood, a sight to make an old man young." In fact she possessed for Tennyson a kindlier magic than that: she stood, a sight to make a young man old. Faced with a past that had little serenity and much more bitterness than love, Tennyson would take a soulful bounding leap into an imaginary future from which he could look back upon an imaginary past. The same fiction had been at work in a poem published in 1832, "The Miller's Daughter." It has a tender lyricism, and Tennyson made this possible for himself by telling of a successful young love seen from the vantage point of tranquil old age. In addition to "The Gardener's Daughter" and "The Miller's Daughter" Tennyson wrote in about 1830 "The Doctor's Daughter," and he projected "The Innkeeper's Daughter." They were a release from the intolerably sordid and quarrelsome, and they could be so only because they were "Daughter" poems. Tennyson could not have written a serene sequence of "Son" poems: the shadow of Dr. Tennyson would have fallen too unignorably across them. Even within "The Miller's Daughter," the narrator would be seen to need the kindly status of a classy orphan, unencumbered and secure: "Late-left an orphan of the squire."* And in "The Gardener's Daughter" no parents seem to exist for either the narrator or the girl, to worry about a job, or about social class, or about money. How soaringly different from the actual circumstances of Arthur Hallam's wooing of Emily, and from what would prove to be Tennyson's grim experiences.

In 1832 and 1833, the present was mostly grim, but nevertheless Tennyson also responded with something quite other than "rapid rills of merry rhyme"–the "rule of contraries" did not always operate. "Pierced through with knotted thorns of barren pain" is a fragmentary reworking of "Perdidi Diem," deriving too from the personal pains shrouded in "The Palace of Art." Its second part, a mythic vision, adapts the earliest of Tennyson's poems ("Armageddon" and "The Coach of Death"); but it is the first part which importantly plumbs those "moods of misery unutterable":

Pierced through with knotted thorns of barren pain,
  Deep in forethought of dark calamities,
    Sick of the coming time and coming woe,
As one that tramples some volcanic plain
  And through the yawning rifts and chasms sees
    The scummy sulphur seething far below
And dares not to advance or to retire
  But with a wan discoloured countenance
    Remaining still, lamenteth bitterly
For fear the hidden wells of scorching fire
  Should spout between the clefts and showery glance
    And flicker round his body that he die:
E'en so I lay upon my bed at night:
  All my delight was gone: my hope was fresh
    No longer: and I lay with sobbing breath,
Walled round, shut up, imbarred, moaning for light,
  A carcase in the coffin of this flesh,
    Pierced through with loathly worms of utter death.
And in that spiritual charnel low and damp
  All my past thoughts and actions I did mark
    Thick-thronging to and fro amid the gloom.

* 1842 text; 1832 had "And son and heir unto the squire."

My soul was but the eternal mystic lamp
Wounding with dreadful rays the solid dark
And shadowing out the unutterable tomb.
I closed my eyes and so I kept them tight
And strove to mutter over ancient prayers
And would not look on the phantasmal night
. . . .
my eyelids unawares
Were touched and opened by a finger bright.

The *lacuna* is Tennyson's own, and it poignantly epitomizes that great gulf which he longed to cross, in person and in poetry, from "the phantasmal night" to "a finger bright." But the force of these lines is more documentary and autobiographical than artistic and representative. "The Two Voices" was Tennyson's attempt to shape such feelings into art in 1833.

"When I wrote 'The Two Voices' I was so utterly miserable, a burden to myself and to my family, that I said, 'Is life worth anything?' " But when did Tennyson write the poem? His son's statement is unequivocal but untrue: the poem, "describing the conflict in a soul between Faith and Scepticism, was begun under the cloud of his overwhelming sorrow after the death of Arthur Hallam, which, as my father told me, for a while blotted out all joy from his life, and made him long for death." But Tennyson had longed for death before the death of Hallam, and "The Two Voices" was in circulation three months before Hallam died. In June 1833, J. M. Kemble said in a letter to another Cambridge friend: "Next Sir are some superb meditations on Self destruction called 'Thoughts of a Suicide' wherein he argues the point with his soul and is thoroughly floored. These are amazingly fine and deep, and show a mighty stride in intellect since the 'Second-Rate Sensitive Mind.' " Since this original version ended (or broke off) without the last third of the poem, it is not clear whether Kemble thought that the suicidal voice or the soul was "floored." But Kemble was right to see the lineage from "Supposed Confessions"; one would add the earlier "Remorse," and the recent "Pierced through."*

* Suicide appears, often enacted and sometimes discussed, in "A Dream of Fair Women," "Aylmer's Field," "Charity," "Columbus," "Despair," "Enoch

Yet Arthur Hallam may have influenced the poem, and not just because the last third was probably written after his death. (Which means that despair in the poem antedated his death, and it was the faith in the poem, or aspiration toward it, which followed his death.) "A still small voice spake unto me": it may not be a coincidence that Hallam had written, in his published prize-winning essay on Cicero, that "The voice of the critical conscience is still and small, like that of the moral." It will not have seemed a coincidence, but a hideous premonition, that led Tennyson to draft these lines in a manuscript of the poem:

When thy best friend draws sobbing breath,
Plight thou a compact ere his death
And comprehend the words he saith.

Urge him to swear, distinct and plain,
That out of bliss or out of pain
He will draw nigh thee once again.

Is that his footstep on the floor?
Is this his whisper at the door?
Surely he comes. He comes no more.

The bitter irony of the poem is immediately established–the "still small voice" is not the Lord's:

A still small voice spake unto me,
"Thou art so full of misery,
Were it not better not to be?"

Arden," "Guinevere," "Hero to Leander," "Lady Clara Vere de Vere," "Locksley Hall," "Love and Duty," "Lucretius," *Maud*, "Mithridates Presenting Berenice with the Cup of Poison," "The Captain" (an extraordinary mass-suicide), "The Death of Œnone," "The Grave of a Suicide," "The Lover's Tale," *The Princess,* "The Spinster's Sweet-Arts," "The Two Voices," "The Victim," "The Voyage," "The Voyage of Maeldune," "The Wreck," and "Tiresias." This is to leave aside the martyrs and the military, as well as the suicidal risks (as in "Geraint and Enid," "Semele," "The Ring," and "The Sailor Boy"). As an impulse and a metaphor, suicide comes throughout Tennyson. Mary Gladstone recorded "a plan he had of writing a satire called 'A suicide supper,'" and that he "would commit suicide" if he believed that death was annihilation. The *Memoir* (ii. 35), James Knowles, and William Allingham report Tennyson as saying such a thing.

Martin Dodsworth has commented acutely: "The stuttering formulation (involving repetition) mimes the fall into meaninglessness that suicide, a permanent extinction of the self, would entail." The poem is not simply the feelings but the "Thoughts of a Suicide," and the argument between the voice and the narrator is not merely argufying. Man is not the only thing that is "wonderfully made": you are not uniquely indispensable as a man; human doubts will never clear, since knowledge is infinite; the fear of suicide is the true cowardice–these, and the points that succeed them, are not debating points. Even the narrator's yearning for the moral certainties of battle (lines 124–156), though swathed in phrasing, does constitute a genuine moral affirmation. But one now lost to him.

> Sick art thou–a divided will
> Still heaping on the fear of ill
> The fear of men, a coward still.

Even though the small voice does not always have the best points, it almost always has the most penetrating form for them:

> High up the vapours fold and swim:
> About him broods the twilight dim:
> The place he knew forgetteth him.

One of the oddities of the poem is that the enemy seems to be within the gates, and not just in that the small voice is of course within the narrator's soul. What happens is that the narrator's affirmations betray themselves. Ambiguities that were poised in "To J.S." now topple betrayingly; Tennyson cannot bring himself to permit the narrator to command the situation. The clearest instance is the almost willful invitation to skepticism in the word "forged," in the vicinity as it is of "evidence," at what is meant to be a climactic moment of triumph. The narrator claims that his truth of feeling denies that death is simply a rotting:

> Who forged that other influence,
> That heat of inward evidence,
> By which he doubts against the sense?

The evidence of the senses may be false; but in a discussion of falsity, the word "forged" is so maladroit as to invite the suspicion of some unconscious adroitness deep in Tennyson. There are milder instances throughout the poem. "To flatter me that I may die": this betrays its intended sense (. . . that I am permitted to kill myself) into the hands of the unwanted simpler sense (he not only may die but will). Or the striving souls: "I cannot hide that some have striven"—"I cannot hide"? It sounds like a concession wrung from the voice, rather than an affirmation by the narrator (whose side is he on?). They strove, and

> Saw distant gates of Eden gleam,
> And did not dream it was a dream.

The speaking voice can of course give that last line the stress that makes for a justified hope, but the words of the line are as compatible with credulity as with faith. The very faith of the closing stanzas, when skepticism is supposed to have been defeated, is inadvertently clouded by ambiguity:

> . . . I marvelled how the mind was brought
> To anchor by one gloomy thought;

"Marvelled" is too bland; only "*one* gloomy thought"?; and "brought to anchor"? That the mind should be brought to anchor sounds very healthy; one remembers Tennyson's clergyman complaining of "the general decay of faith . . . there was no anchor, none, / To hold by." Yet here the anchor is to be deplored. A strange business.

But then which are "The Two Voices"? The earlier version had a different title, and it didn't have two voices, in that the "second voice" had not been arrived at. The sense is strong at first in the poem that the two voices are the still small one and the narrator's. When Lewis Carroll parodied it, he postulated "The Three Voices." The poem's triplets prophesy that there will be three, as the good family walking to Church is three.

The final vignette has mostly been deplored, and it is indeed pallid. But it should be noted that its beneficent effect follows upon the narrator's sense that he has defeated the voice not, however, by Christianity but by the very non-Christian belief in transmigration of souls. True, this is put forward as a possibility only

—but one strong enough to render suicide at least imprudent, and to occupy a full thirteen stanzas of the poem.

What animates the final sense of release, then, is at once uncertain and fluctuating. The most memorable moments in the poem remain captured by the first voice. Tennyson's friend Spedding excellently analyzed the state of mind which the poem explores:

The disease is familiar; but where are we to look for the remedy? Many persons would have thought it enough to administer a little religious consolation to the diseased mind; but unfortunately despondency is no more like ignorance than atrophy is like hunger; and as the most nutritious food will not nourish the latter, so the most comfortable doctrine will not refresh the former. Not the want of consoling topics, but the incapacity to receive consolation, constitutes the disease. Others would have been content to give the bad voice the worst of the argument; but, unhappily, all moral reasoning must ultimately rest on the internal evidence of the moral sense; and where this is disordered, the most unquestionable logic can conclude nothing . . .

After so honest an exposition, it is not surprising that Spedding came to an equally honest conclusion: "The dialogue ends, (as such a dialogue, if truly reported, must always do,) leaving every thing unsettled, and nothing concluded." After which is the vignette, in which nothing is concluded. What lingers is what the first voice says twice and two-edgedly: "There is one remedy for all"—a cure for all troubles, available for all people.

"The Two Voices" was a dialogue in which one voice rang more tellingly. In these same months, Tennyson created his first penetrating dramatic monologue, a poem whose force and subtlety stamp it as one of his finest achievements. From its opening words, "St. Simeon Stylites" has an authoritative momentum:

Although I be the basest of mankind,
From scalp to sole one slough and crust of sin,
Unfit for earth, unfit for heaven, scarce meet
For troops of devils, mad with blasphemy,
I will not cease to grasp the hope I hold
Of saintdom, and to clamour, mourn and sob,
Battering the gates of heaven with storms of prayer,
Have mercy, Lord, and take away my sin.

"Grasp" is what the poem both possesses and is about. But in Simeon, the first and most famous of the pillar-hermits, a faith which is held has become a fanaticism which is grasping.

Gerard Manley Hopkins was to say in 1862: "You ask do I admire *St. Simeon Stylites*. Admire! Ha! Of course I do. If you have never heard it spoken of, either you have not attended to conversation or else so much the worse for those who don't speak about it. It is indeed magnificent." For Tennyson had swooped upon a man and a moment which could tap his profoundest concerns—the desolating sense of sin ("those lead-like tons of sin"); of weariness ("Twice ten long weary weary years to this"); of age ("half deaf I am . . . and almost blind"); of illness and decay ("And both my thighs are rotted with the dew"); of isolation ("Then, that I might be more alone with thee . . ."). The fear of hell, and dismay at the belief in it. The living death, a life which is no life. The power of prophecy. The verge of death. The grim humor which was so marked in Tennyson's character and which only here is transmuted into the best of his art. (FitzGerald reported of "St. Simeon Stylites": "This is one of the Poems A.T. would read with grotesque Grimness, especially at such passages as 'Coughs, Aches, Stitches, etc.', laughing aloud at times.") Above all, the poem has at its core that complex of doubts which never ceased to excite Tennyson: the moral ambiguity of self-sacrifice, of saving one's soul and one's self, and—at the heart of it—the intricate evasions by which suicide could rationalize itself as martyrdom.* A lasting consequence of Dr. Tennyson's drinking himself to death, and of Tennyson's "misery unutterable," was the imaginative conceiving of moments in which suicide—like the suicide, was it?, of Samson—might be the

* Arthur Hallam, "Remarks on Professor Rossetti" (1832): "Children were taught to look for models of heroism, not, as heretofore, in the apathetic sublimity of suicidal patriots, but in the virgin martyrs . . ." Martyrdom and self-sacrifice figure substantially—as plot or theme—in "A Dream of Fair Women," "Aylmer's Field," "Demeter and Persephone," "Kapiolani," "Owd Roä," "Sir Galahad," "Sir John Oldcastle," "St. Agnes," "St. Lawrence," "St. Telemachus," "The Dawn," "The Palace of Art," "The Victim," "Tiresias," "Vastness." Tennyson thought too of writing on Bruno, Savonarola, and St. Perpetua; and on two naval stories of self-sacrifice. The metaphor of sacrifice is everywhere in his poems, and he was fascinated by anecdotes about sacrifice and martyrdom.

right course. Or could it only ever *seem* right? Hence the sequence of "Saint" poems: from "St. Lawrence" ("I cannot argue, I can burn") in various versions from 1825 to 1833; "St. Simeon Stylites" and "St. Agnes" (written in the same months of 1833), to "St. Telemachus" (written in the last two years of Tennyson's life). The point is not that Tennyson believed that no distinction could be drawn between suicide and martyrdom ("Sir John Oldcastle" risks death, but does not court it; yet he divines his end: "For I must live to testify by fire"). But his imagination responded most deeply to the doubtful and the dismaying. In "St. Simeon Stylites" he seized a form—a "powerful monodrama"—which permitted the full force of his personal obsessions while yet channelling them by dramatic monologue, history, and psychology. The poem was too much for John Sterling:

> The gift of comprehensive thoughtfulness does not, however, show itself to advantage, in "St. Simeon Stylites," a kind of monological personation of a filthy and mad ascetic. We find exhibited, with the seriousness of bitter poetic irony, his loathsome, yet ridiculous attempts at saintship, all founded on an idea of the Divinity fit only for an African worshipping a scarecrow fetish made of dog's bones, goosefeathers, and dunghill-rags. This is no topic for Poetry: she has better tasks than to wrap her mantle round a sordid, greedy lunatic.

Yet it was just this narrowing conception of Poetry which Tennyson here escaped from; he was often to convert his keen sense of the beautiful into something more penetrating than a cult of Beauty, but he was seldom to cut free of it altogether. R. H. Horne was by and large right in saying of the early monologues and their "faculty of self-absorption in the identity of other idiosyncrasies": "Still, he only selects a peculiar class of characters—those in whom it shall not be requisite to dispossess himself of beauty (Stylites being the only exception)." Right, too, in insisting that "St. Simeon Stylites" is "a work of genius."

Simeon exhibits a ferocious importunity:

> O Jesus, if thou wilt not save my soul,
> Who may be saved? who is it may be saved?
> Who may be made a saint, if I fail here?
> Show me the man hath suffered more than I.
> For did not all thy martyrs die one death?

For either they were stoned, or crucified,
Or burned in fire, or boiled in oil, or sawn
In twain beneath the ribs; but I die here
Today, and whole years long, a life of death.

The swelling indignation of "one death," "crucified," is directed too at the paucity of Christ's martyrdom in comparison with Simeon's own. "A powerfully graphic, and in some respects appalling satire on the pseudo-aspirations of egotistical asceticism and superstition": Leigh Hunt's words are apt but insufficient. For Tennyson it was not so easy to peel the pseudo-aspiration from the real one, or superstition from religion, or martyrdom from suicide. The impurities seem to him more countenanced and even incited by the religion than is comfortable to think. Admittedly critics do well to remind us that poems like "Sir Galahad," "St. Agnes," and "St. Telemachus" manifest "Tennyson's sympathy with a true asceticism." But those three poems are strikingly inferior in weight and penetration to "St. Simeon Stylites"—a judgment which suggests where Tennyson's profoundest sympathies lay, hostile and self-censuring though they partly were. William E. Fredeman, in a first-rate exploration of the poem and its structure, judges that "Simeon is incapable, at this stage of his life, of discerning the contradiction inherent in conscious, premeditated martyrdom." But the poem's dark force comes from the fact that at no stage of his life, and especially not in 1833, was Tennyson free from uneasiness about what seemed to him less a contradiction than a painful and possibly evil paradox: suicide-martyrdom. What would it really be to "*mortify* your flesh"?

When will this life of death end in death?

Now am I feeble grown; my end draws nigh;
I hope my end draws nigh;

Six times, Simeon cries the word, he who is "The watcher on the column till the end": "The end! the end! / Surely the end!" The poem ends before Simeon's end: he asks for "the blessèd sacrament,"

For by the warning of the Holy Ghost,
I prophesy that I shall die tonight,

A quarter before twelve.
                    But thou, O Lord,
Aid all this foolish people; let them take
Example, pattern: lead them to thy light.

It sounds like a firm ending, supported by the rhyme—so crucial in its progression of sense—of *tonight* and *light*. But one recalls a formulation by Professor Fredeman, one of the most acute statements ever made about Tennyson: "Tennyson's poem explores the denouement of that [aberrant] psychology, not the end, but as so often in Tennyson's dramatic monologues and lyrics, the penultimate moment before the end, which is unrevealed." ("A quarter before twelve" is itself a fine epitome of the penultimate moment.) *Unrevealed*, yes, but unknown? For once again a poem by Tennyson sets up a tension between its existing moment and its unmentioned outcome. We may at the time be confident that the masochistic batterer who cries "It cannot be but that I shall be saved" cannot but be heading away from saintdom; we may at the time find the crowd's shout of "St. Simeon Stylites," and Simeon's own adjuration ("Courage, St. Simeon!"), to be pointers away from saintdom; we may, with Sterling, deplore "his loathsome, yet ridiculous attempts at saintship." And yet can the poem simply contradict its own known outcome? Just as "Mariana" or "The Lotos-Eaters" has an outcome unmentioned and therefore baffling but not to be ignored, so "St. Simeon Stylites" does not bear the title "Simeon Stylites." Simeon is indeed now one of those "whose names / Are registered and calendared for saints." The strange tensions within the poem have their counterpart in the tension between the poem and its outcome; their counterpart, too, in the verbal contrarieties of the poem, as in the grim play of "fast" against "slow" in these proud lines in which Simeon may yet be speaking the truth:

Smite, shrink not, spare not. If it may be, fast
Whole Lents, and pray. I hardly, with slow steps,
With slow, faint steps, and much exceeding pain,
Have scrambled past those pits of fire, that still
Sing in mine ears.

The fires sing, not singe.

2. 1833 and Hallam's death

1833 SAW the friction between Somersby and Bayons reaching the point where the Bayons family decided upon an overt act of severance. Tennyson's uncle Charles, now an up-and-coming Member of Parliament, urged his old father to revive the ancient family name of d'Eyncourt, with the long-term hope that the ancient barony might one day return with it. The Old Man of the Wolds protested–the name of Tennyson had always been an honorable one, and they would be derided if they were to "lay aside the name of Tennyson for this Frenchyfied name." But he conceded that d'Eyncourt might be appropriated, "the name of Tennyson to be retained by my late son Dr. Tennyson's family" –though he warned his favored son that this would look partial and discreditable. Charles was determined; the compromise of the double name Tennyson d'Eyncourt was petitioned for and then adopted (though not till 1835). And a further step had been taken: the Old Man had agreed to move from Bayons, handing it over to Charles who set about an elaborate, expensive, and vulgar rebuilding of the whole manor. Bayons was to look like a Tennyson d'Eyncourt home, not a Tennyson one.

The internecine pettiness as well as grander snobbery in all this was to come out explicitly two years later, after the death of the Old Man. The Tennyson d'Eyncourts were shocked at the imprudence of the Tennysons, especially as it reached back to the root grievance, the disinheritance of Dr. Tennyson: "They also say, that *Frederick* ought to have taken the name of d'Eyncourt, as being the eldest of the eldest son!" In fact Frederick (son and grandson as he was of a George Clayton Tennyson) was to toy with the idea of a ridiculing revenge—the Tennyson d'Eyncourts blenched when they heard that he was "determined to take the name of *Clayton forthwith*."

The name may have been Frenchyfied, but the manners were not. The coarse snobbery and hatred were to be clearly heard in a letter of Edwin Tennyson d'Eyncourt:

I am very glad we have changed our name, as it gives us a good position, and if we had not my Father would always have been Mr. Charles Tennyson. Besides which it will keep us in a great measure clear of the Somersby Family who really are quite hogs.

With such feelings built up and building up, it is not surprising that Tennyson felt bitterly alienated from the Bayons family. In March 1833 he expressed something of what he felt in a letter to his aunt Mrs. Russell:

Of my Grandfather I have seen little for the last three years: he has so rooted an antipathy to me from some cause or other, that it is not pleasant to visit him without a special invitation. . . I fear he has little sympathy with any of his numerous descendants, except my Uncle's family, who live with him half the year and never pay us a single visit and yet are so amusing as to wonder that one does not call at 4, Park Street, when in town.

The bitter feelings were reciprocated. As for Tennyson's poems, his uncle Charles knew what he thought of those: "Some of them were good and some rubbish but I had not patience to read scarcely any of them. I do not and never did like his affected and lame style. It is perhaps want of taste—but I felt that the Quarterly Review was scarcely too severe." So the public venom of J. W. Croker (who had published a scabrous but unstupid demolition in the April 1833 *Quarterly Review*) was matched by the private disdain of Tennyson's rich relatives.

Meanwhile the relationship of Hallam and the Tennysons had become less intense and harrowed. Hallam settled to the slow business of earning a legal living and Emily. The friends can be glimpsed in March sightseeing in London—the Zoological Gardens, and then (as Hallam wrote to Emily) "the great microscope and all the horrible lions and tigers which lie 'perdus' in a drop of spring water." Four months later, Hallam wrote to Tennyson who was then in Scotland; the letter shows a mature tenderness:

I feel to-night what I own has been too uncommon with me of late, a strong desire to write to you. I do own I feel the want of you at some times more than at others; a sort of yearning for dear old Alfred comes upon me, and that without any particularly apparent reason.

Hallam was leaving almost at once for Vienna. On September 6, he sent back a long letter to Alfred and Emily.

The gallery is grand and I longed for you: two rooms full of Venetian pictures only; such Giorgiones, Palmas, Bordones, Paul Veroneses! and oh Alfred such Titians! by Heaven, that man could paint! I wish you could see his Danaë. Do you just write as perfect a Danaë!

Four weeks later, Tennyson received the most important letter he ever read. It was addressed "To Alfred Tennyson Esqre / if absent, to be opened by Mrs. Tennyson," and it was written on October 1 by Arthur Hallam's uncle:

My dear Sir,

At the desire of a most afflicted family, I write to you, because they are unequal, from the abyss of grief into which they have fallen, to do it themselves.

Your friend, Sir, and my much loved nephew, Arthur Hallam, is no more–it has pleased God, to remove him from this his first scene of Existence, to that better World, for which he was Created.

He died at Vienna on his return from Buda, by apoplexy–and I believe his Remains come by sea from Trieste.

Mr. Hallam arrived this Morning in 3 Princes Buildings.

May that Great Being, in whose hands are the Destinies of Man–and who has promised to comfort all that Mourn pour the Balm of Consolation on all the Families who are bowed down by this unexpected dispensation!--

I have just seen Mr. Hallam, who begs I will tell you, that he will write himself as soon as his Heart will let him. Poor Arthur had a slight attack of Ague–which he had often had–Ordered his fire to be lighted and talked with as much cheerfulness as usual–He suddenly became insensible and his Spirit departed without Pain–The Physician endeavoured to get any Blood from him—and on Examination it was the General Opinion, that he could not have lived long—This was also Dr. Holland's opinion—The account I have endeavoured to give you, is merely what I have been able to gather; but the family of course are in too great distress to enter into details.

Yet another of Tennyson's profound hopes—and this the profoundest of all—had been offered and then brutally withdrawn.

> Heaven opens inward, chasms yawn,
> Vast images in glimmering dawn,
> Half shown, are broken and withdrawn.
> ("The Two Voices")

Tennyson too was broken and withdrawn. But at least he felt no guilt, unlike Hallam's father, who could not but ponder. To Tennyson he wrote:

I beg you to give my kindest regards to your mother; but especially to assure your poor sister Emily of my heart-felt and lasting affection. All that remains to me now is to cherish his memory, and to love those whom he loved. She above all is ever a sacred object of my thoughts.

Emily was to receive not only his affection but also £300 a year.

That Hallam had been a man of great potentialities—and here Gladstone is one of the many who agreed with Tennyson—is certainly a judgment which plays an important part within *In Memoriam*. But the essential fact is simply that Alfred Tennyson and his sister loved and needed Arthur Hallam and were loved and needed by him. It was integral to that love (as to all love) that they had so much to offer Hallam; here was somebody whom the Somersby Tennysons—so incessantly in need of support—could support, whether in his bitterness of frustration or his energy of involvement. The reciprocity of love enabled Hallam to support them too. In the words of Frederick Tennyson,

We all looked forward to his society and support through life in sorrow and in joy, with the fondest hopes, for never was there a human being better calculated to sympathize with and make allowance for those peculiarities of temperament and those failings to which we are liable.

Or, in the words of Tennyson's later trustful prayer,

Be near us when we climb or fall:
  Ye watch, like God, the rolling hours
  With larger other eyes than ours,
To make allowance for us all.

(*In Memoriam*, LI)

Hallam's death "came as a shock but not a surprise to his friends." To Tennyson it came as a grim corroboration of all he had ever feared. The death of Hallam struck deeply not because he had supposed life to be good, but because he had long known that it was no such thing. The love of Hallam was the last in a series of profound disillusionments. To one Cambridge friend, the death of Hallam was "a loud and terrible stroke from the reality of things upon the faery building of our youth." But Tennyson's youth had never been a fairy building; his poetry may have toyed with such a refuge, but in his life—and increasingly in his art—the reality of things was unignorable. The reality of things had come to threaten even the Christian faith, the faith which his father had represented.

At the end of 1833, a Cambridge friend felt obliged to write to Tennyson about Hallam's death:

Oh my dear Alfred I do trust that this sad loss, which is I believe the greatest affliction that could have befallen you, may work out the end for which I well know that it was sent, and that the sorrow that you must feel yourself, and the still deeper and more sacred grief that you must see, may lead your mind to Him, who has said that "they that sow in tears, shall reap in joy" . . . Depend upon it, it is only in abstract questions that you can have strictly logical proof, and that in practical ones, conviction is wrought in a different way, but is not the less truly and rightly conviction for that. You rely and fearlessly believe in a Mother's and a friend's affection, though you might by applying to these cases the principles of doubt which I have heard you apply to Christianity, doubt the reality of these.

His friends now deplored "that bitterness of spirit" in Tennyson partly because it might not spare the Christian faith.

Nearly thirty years later, Tennyson was to try to console Queen Victoria and her daughter Princess Alice on the death of Prince Albert; he drafted (but did not send) a letter which spoke of how in 1833 he "suffered what seemed to me to shatter all my life so that I desired to die rather than to live." But it did not need the death of Hallam to make Tennyson—or at least some strong part of him—desire to die rather than to live. It was rather that Hallam's life had temporarily eased Tennyson away from "some dark undercurrent woe / That seems to draw—but it shall not be so" (*Maud*, I xviii). Draw where? Tennyson knew what was for him a deep magnetism, the gravity of death.

> And something in the darkness draws
> His forehead earthward, and he dies.
> ("Supposed Confessions")

> Earthward he boweth the heavy stalks
> Of the mouldering flowers:
> Heavily hangs the broad sunflower
> Over its grave i' the earth so chilly;
> Heavily hangs the hollyhock,
> Heavily hangs the tiger-lily.
> ("Song: A spirit haunts")

> 'Twere best at once to sink to peace,
> Like birds the charming serpent draws,
> To drop head-foremost in the jaws
> Of vacant darkness and to cease.
> (*In Memoriam*, XXXIV)

> The dead weight of the dead leaf bore it down.
> ("Enoch Arden")

3. Poems from Hallam's death till the end of 1834

In October 1833, the month after Hallam's death, FitzGerald wrote:

> Tennyson has been in town for some time: he has been making fresh poems, which are finer, they say, than any he has done. But I believe he is chiefly meditating on the purging and subliming of what he has already done: and repents that he has published at all yet. It is fine to see how in each succeeding poem the smaller ornaments and fancies drop away, and leave the grand ideas single.

By December, Tennyson's brother Frederick was reporting that Alfred "will most probably publish again in the Spring." His Cambridge friends were delighted that his spirits were not broken: "Tennyson has, I hear, so far recovered from the catastrophe in which his sister was involved, as to have written some poems, and, they say, fine ones" (January 22, 1834). Yet a more morbid urgency may be heard in the semi-apologetic letter which Tennyson wrote in April 1834 to "Christopher North," repenting of his epigram against the dreaded reviewer, and fearing that "Christopher North" was about to be spurred into a further critique by the polemics of one John Lake.

> I could wish that some of the poems there broken on your critical wheel were deeper than ever plummet sounded. Written as they were before I had attained my nineteenth year they could not but con-

tain as many faults as words. I never wish to see them or hear of them again—much less to find them dragged forward once more on your boards. . . .

The creative revision of his early poems was a major undertaking. A more immediate effect of Hallam's death was a burst of imaginative energy that intensifies and corroborates the achievement of the previous year or so, and makes the years 1833–1834 the most remarkable flowering of Tennyson's genius. Following upon "The Two Voices" and "St. Simeon Stylites" (the distinctive feats of the months before Hallam's death), there came within a year a series of successes: some sections of *In Memoriam*, "Ulysses," "Tithon" (the early version of "Tithonus"), "Morte d'Arthur," "Oh! that 'twere possible," and "Break, break, break." Such achievements ought to make us receive with some skepticism—despite its apt reminder of the faults of his early poems—Tennyson's remark, "I suppose I was nearer thirty than twenty before I was anything of an artist."

A cluster of poems responded at once and directly to Hallam's death. One of them, not published by Tennyson, incorporates a somber ambiguity in the words "Make me live," soliciting not only an animating energy from Nature but also a commanding refusal to permit the suicidal:

> From sorrow sorrow yet is born,
>   Hopes flow like water through a sieve,
> But leave not thou thy son forlorn;
>   Touch me, great Nature, make me live.
>
> As when thy sunlights, a mild heat,
>   Touch some dun mere that sleepeth still;
> As when thy moonlights, dim and sweet,
>   Touch some gray ruin on the hill.

A long series of disillusionments was distilled into the totality of melancholy, the limpid desolation, of that opening antithesis.

A similar tone informs "On a Mourner," written in October 1833 but not published till 1865. In revising it for publication, Tennyson was to make it less directly personal. He veiled and objectified the poem by adding the title; by addressing it to another, changing "my" to "thy";* and by omitting two explicit stanzas about "that friend I loved in vain." The poem sets the essential limits to the consolatory power of the beauties of Nature; real though they are, they are ultimately ineffectual if Nature too is mortal. The poem begins with the delicate softness of Nature and "her airy hill"; it ends with quite other hills of craggy endurance, as the voices of Hope, Memory, Faith and Virtue enter,

> Promising empire; such as those
> Once heard at dead of night to greet
> Troy's wandering prince, so that he rose
> With sacrifice, while all the fleet
> Had rest by stony hills of Crete.

It is a consummate ending, a victory achieved, an empire over oneself, a rest that is beautifully played against the stony. And despite the finality (audible in the concluding hard-edged rhyme), the end is one which—like so many of Tennyson's endings—is poised, waiting.** The fleet will not have rest forever. The Virgilian ending anticipates Tennyson's translation from Homer (1863), where the last fourteen lines form a single sentence, culminating in a fateful pause and poise.

> . . . So many a fire between the ships and stream
> Of Xanthus blazed before the towers of Troy,
> A thousand on the plain; and close by each
> Sat fifty in the blaze of burning fire;
> And eating hoary grain and pulse the steeds,
> Fixt by their cars, waited the golden dawn.

A more histrionic immediacy—grief rather than melancholy—is heard in the unpublished fragment which Tennyson's son was to call the germ of *In Memoriam*, "Hark! the dogs howl! the sleet-winds blow." A visionary flight snatches him up:

* In the late poem "Far-Far-Away" (written 1888), Tennyson was to change the manuscript first person to third person throughout.

** Allingham describes Tennyson reading, "lingering with solemn sweetness on every vowel sound,—a peculiar *incomplete* cadence at the end." (*Diary*, p. 158, August 25, 1867).

I seek the voice I loved—ah where
Is that dear hand that I should press,
Those honoured brows that I would kiss?
Lo! the broad Heavens cold and bare,
The stars that know not my distress.

Tennyson's son, fearing a homosexual misconstruction, preferred not to print that third line, or the cry "I wind my arms for one embrace." Already, as in *In Memoriam* ("like a guilty thing"), there is an unexplained and perhaps inexplicable sense of guilt; the shadow of Hallam "bends his eyes reproachfully." Already there is mingled an awe of Hallam's new grandeur and a fear that such grandeur has outstripped Tennyson:

Larger than human passes by
The shadow of the man I loved.

That awe and that fear were to mingle, too, in *In Memoriam*. Tennyson set to work on the sequence (which was not to be published for seventeen years) in the month in which he heard of Hallam's death. The earliest group (in one of the notebooks now at Trinity College) consists of the following sections: XXX, "With trembling fingers did we weave"; IX, "Fair ship, that from the Italian shore"; XVII, "Thou comest, much wept for"; XVIII, "'Tis well; 'tis something"; a version of XXXI–XXXII, "When Lazarus left his charnel-cave"; LXXXV, "This truth came borne with bier and pall"; and XXVIII, "The time draws near the birth of Christ." The striking thing about this earliest group is that it evinces the less perturbed calm which *In Memoriam* mostly intimates to be an achievement slowly won rather than immediately entered upon. None of these sections shows dismay or dark questioning; already they proffer reassurance:

This truth came borne with bier and pall,
  I felt it, when I sorrowed most,
  'Tis better to have loved and lost,
Than never to have loved at all—

But when Tennyson sorrowed most, he was least able to confront the starkest heart searchings. As the years passed, he brought himself to contemplate more. The point is not about sincerity, but about intensity of meeting. The tender calm manifested so early in this first group (at its best in the two exquisite celebrations of the ship that is bringing Hallam's body) foreshadows the very latest stage of the poem's creation, and makes it unsurprising that at the very last moment in 1850—between the privately printed edition in March and the publication at the end of May—Tennyson added some of the most darkly penetrating sections of the poem. Likewise that he should subsequently have said to a friend, James Knowles, "It's too hopeful, this poem, more than I am myself."

On this same occasion, Tennyson was to compare *In Memoriam* with "Ulysses": "There is more about myself in 'Ulysses,' which was written under the sense of loss and that all had gone by, but that still life must be fought out to the end. It was more written with the feeling of his loss upon me than many poems in *In Memoriam*." Tennyson—and this is not surprising—found himself able to incorporate the direct sense of loss in the poems which by indirections found directions out.

". . . But that still life must be fought out to the end." Yet are the terms of "Ulysses" fighting terms? It opens indeed with a chafing, a clipped impatience:

> It little profits that an idle king,
> By this still hearth, among these barren crags,
> Matched with an agèd wife, I mete and dole
> Unequal laws unto a savage race,
> That hoard, and sleep, and feed, and know not me.

The contempt is pervasive and energizing, with the "barren crags" leading from the "idle king" and leading into the "agèd wife": the marriage match does harsh justice. Yet this stoniness is at once followed by a different kind of affirmation:

> I cannot rest from travel: I will drink
> Life to the lees: all times I have enjoyed
> Greatly, have suffered greatly, both with those
> That loved me, and alone; on shore, and when
> Through scudding drifts the rainy Hyades
> Vext the dim sea. . .

It has amplitude, the affirmation, but a plumped amplitude. "Far on the ringing plains of windy Troy": it rings, but with a strangely unstrange timbre which sounds thin beside that "dim sea." Yet this is not necessarily a failure in the poem, since what it truly aimed at may have been equivocal. "The feeling of his loss upon me" is also in the poem (which Tennyson wrote in the month when he heard of Hallam's death), tempering—or rather the opposite of tempering in the sense of steeling—the poem's staunchness and instead insinuates a deeper wanhope. That the feelings evinced both within and by the poem are ambiguous or paradoxical was noticed by Goldwin Smith in 1855:

> You may trace the hues of this character tinging everything in the poems. Even the Homeric Ulysses, the man of purpose and action, seeking with most definite aim to regain his own home and that of his companions, becomes a "hungry heart," roaming aimlessly to "lands beyond the sunset," in the vain hope of being "washed down by the gulf to the Happy Isles," merely to relieve his *ennui*, and dragging his companions with him. We say he roams aimlessly—we should rather say, he intends to roam, but stands for ever a listless and melancholy figure on the shore.

The point is a telling one: it rightly refuses to believe, simply, what Ulysses tells his mariners. Robert Langbaum explores the paradox further:

> Most characteristic of Tennyson is a certain life-weariness, a longing for rest through oblivion. This emotional bias is all the more powerful because it appears to be subconscious. Not only does it conflict with the poet's often stated desire for personal immortality, but it even conflicts in a poem like "Ulysses" with what seems to be his intent . . . The same weariness and longing for rest is the emotional bias of Tennyson's finest dramatic monologue, "Ulysses"; though here the emotion is couched in the contrasting language of adventure, giving an added complexity of meaning to the poem. To read "Ulysses" as a poem of strenuousness in the manner of Browning, as some critics have done, is to read with the head only and not the sensibility. For its music bears the enervated cadence of "Tithonus" and "The Lotos-Eaters."

There are indeed cadences in the poem which are far from enervated, but are they not sapped and sopped by the insidious enervations ("The long day wanes: the slow moon climbs: the deep /

Moans round with many voices") at the poem's center? The poem's last sentence has its urgency:

> Though much is taken, much abides; and though
> We are not now that strength which in old days
> Moved earth and heaven; that which we are, we are;
> One equal temper of heroic hearts,
> Made weak by time and fate, but strong in will
> To strive, to seek, to find, and not to yield.

It is a beautiful stroke that proffers "in *old* days" for what Tennyson elsewhere speaks of as "our younger days." And rippling underneath that final line, striving to utter itself but battened down by will, is another line, almost identical and yet utterly different: "To strive, to seek, to yield, and not to find."

Ulysses is old; he stands upon the shores of life. The poem conveys a dragging sense of inertia, of *ennui*, strangely matched (but not barrenly) with the vocabulary of adventure and enterprise. Goldwin Smith was right to sense that Ulysses "intends to roam, but stands for ever a listless and melancholy figure on the shore." For though the poem describes the passing of time, it does so with an oily stagnancy of shimmer:

> The lights begin to twinkle from the rocks:
> The long day wanes: the slow moon climbs: the deep
> Moans round with many voices. Come, my friends,
> 'Tis not too late to seek a newer world.

The rhythm and diction (long, slow) are narcotically oppressive. Can the single voice of Ulysses then outdo those "many voices"? Does not the last line poignantly convey a sense that " 'Tis far too late to seek a newer world"? Enterprise draws, but experience drags.

> Yet all experience is an arch wherethrough
> Gleams that untravelled world, whose margin fades
> For ever and for ever when I move.

Matthew Arnold, in one of the most penetrating remarks ever made about Tennyson, observed: "It is no blame to their rhythm, which belongs to another order of movement than Homer's, but it is true that these three lines by themselves take up nearly as much time as a whole book of the *Iliad*."*

Ulysses yearns to believe that his life is not just a past, that it still has a future. But that this is a yearning, and not a confident assurance, comes out in a ubiquitous feature of the poem's language: its reluctance–in a poem of such an adventurous setting forth, so strange as to deserve to be called morbid–to use the future tense. This stylistic tissue of the poem is remarkable–unobtrusive but potent. For this poem, which seizes the chance of a future, rises only at two points into future tenses, neither simple futures. At first, in: "I will drink / Life to the lees," *will*, not *shall:* a determination, not a simple futurity. Near the end, with the future tenses all governed by–and attenuated by–the word *may:*

> It may be that the gulfs will wash us down:
> It may be we shall touch the Happy Isles,
> And see the great Achilles, whom we knew.

But of course the subject of "Ulysses" makes future tenses indispensable; Tennyson can dispense with them only by converting them into equivalents which yet minimize futurity. The characteristic line from "Ulysses" might be "Though much is taken, much abides," or "I am a part of all that I have met": past and present leaving no room for future. The equivalents (not, of course, equivalent to our sensibilities) are persistent, finding a variety of linguistic forms to express and to repress the future:

> . . . Gleams that untravelled world, whose margin fades
> For ever and for ever when I move.

That world to be traveled, whose margin will fade . . . Not "Every hour will bring new things," but "every hour . . . A bringer of new things." "Something . . . may yet be done," not *will be*. "Until I die." And–most richly used of all–the infinitive, such as *to follow*, which is throughout an ambiguous equivalent for the future tense.

* It is true, too, that Arnold managed to misquote five words in these three lines.

And this gray spirit yearning in desire
To follow knowledge like a sinking star . . .

It is not said that Telemachus will fulfill his labor, but that he is "discerning to fulfil" it, and to make mild, and to subdue, and not to fail, and to pay adoration. It is not too late to seek; Ulysses' purpose holds to sail; and the poem ends with a crescendo of such equivalents, which stand in for the future tense but also stand out against it: "but strong in will / To strive, to seek, to find, and not to yield."

Yet one feature of the poem which many critics have found richly equivocal may be poorly so. There is a recurring argument as to how much Ulysses himself is admired or endorsed by the poem. But this uncertainty seems less a matter of a valuable contrariety than of a weakness. The crucial passage is that in which Ulysses hands over the mundane responsibilities to his son Telemachus. But at this point something goes wrong in terms of the poem's addressees. "This is my son, mine own Telemachus": too staged, this invites a demeaning "How do you do." And Tennyson—elsewhere in the poem so subtly meticulous—allows a ruckle of the syntax: Telemachus is

decent not to fail
In offices of tenderness, and pay
Meet adoration to my household gods,
When I am gone. He works his work, I mine.

The sense is of course "decent not to fail . . . and decent to pay. . . . ," but a clumsiness is there. The apparent lordliness of "He works his work, I mine" (as who should say, "We are all doing God's work, you in your way, and we in His") seems therefore more the poet's lapse into misjudgment than Ulysses' lapse into an unattractive and significant hauteur.

The argument is a tricky one. But if the Telemachus lines are faultily wooden rather than dramatically revealing, this might be because of "This is my son. . . ." At this stage of his life (perhaps throughout his life), Tennyson was not able to write with alert conviction about sons and fathers, especially about their mutual respect. Too much from his own life came in the way. St. Simeon Stylites can cry with conviction "O my sons, my sons," but that is because they are not literally his sons. And in "Tiresias," the prophet can address Menœceus throughout with paternal tenderness as "my son" for exactly the same reason.* So the Telemachus passage is neither a fine ambivalence nor a merely technical flaw, but—given Tennyson's shadowing experiences—a recalcitrance deep in the material itself.

"Death closes all." How does the poem close—with the story's outcome? When Tennyson's friend J. M. Kemble sent the poem to another Cambridge friend, he said: "I will fill up my paper with a grand thing of Alfred's, unfinished though it be." But the poem was already finished. For once again there is an interplay between the rich stagnancy of a Tennyson poem (Ulysses standing forever on the shore) and the known outcome of its borrowed story. Ulysses' last voyage is hinted at in the *Odyssey*, but it is related in Dante's *Inferno* (xxvi, 90 ff.). In Dante, Ulysses speaks; Tennyson's indebtedness is open and full.** Cary's Dante gives us "But virtue to pursue and knowledge high" (Tennyson's "To follow knowledge like a sinking star"); within three lines in Cary, "To the dawn / Our poop we turn'd"; and only ten lines later a whirlwind strikes and sinks the ship. "And over us the booming billow closed": so closes the canto of the *Inferno*, a close which follows hard upon Ulysses' speech to his mariners. Tennyson's "Ulysses" ends upon the brink of disaster; Ulysses' future may be real but it is desperately brief. "How dull it is to pause, to make an end." But how strange to use *pause* and *end* virtually as synonyms. The ship of death is poised to set sail. It is this full suspension, this imminence, which underlies Carlyle's very beautiful comment on those poignant lines which the known but silent outcome dooms to stoical wishfulness:

> It may be that the gulfs will wash us down:
> It may be we shall touch the Happy Isles,
> And see the great Achilles, whom we knew.

* In "The Ancient Sage" (written 1885 and—like "Tiresias"—published then), the sage likewise repeatedly calls his young companion "My son." For Tennyson one of the magnetisms of King Arthur was that probably he neither had, nor was, a father.

** "Yes, there is an echo of Dante in it" was Tennyson's understatement (*Memoir*, ii. 70).

"These lines do not make me weep, but there is in me what would fill whole Lachrymatories as I read."

"Ulysses" sought to meet Hallam's death (which it did not exactly confront) by seeking an assurance of the courage of life, life being worth the highest compliment: risk. "Tithonus," which Tennyson spoke of as a "pendant" to "Ulysses," meets Hallam's death at a different angle: by envisaging and envisioning a situation in which immortality is no blessing. Tithonus was granted immortal life but without thought of immortal youth; he is now the ceaselessly withering lover of Aurora, goddess of the dawn. Tennyson wrote the first version of the poem "Tithon," in the closing months of 1833; he did not at first publish it, perhaps because it was too poignant, or not perfected, or too vulnerable in its longing for death. Twenty-six years later, his friend Thackeray badgered Tennyson for a contribution to his new magazine, the *Cornhill;* Tennyson ferreted out "Tithon," transformed it into "Tithonus" (twelve lines longer and revised with supremely creative fitness), and published it in the *Cornhill* in 1860.

"Tithonus" is not, either allegorically or symbolically, a depiction of Tennyson's love of Hallam. But the myth draws upon and is drawn by his mingled fear and love. Perhaps it was fed by the grief of Tennyson's sister Emily, Hallam's betrothed, who was to write to Tennyson: "What is life to me! if I die (which the Tennysons never do). . . ." Probably Tennyson felt as did their Cambridge friend Monteith, who wrote to him in 1833: "Since Hallam's death I almost feel like an old man looking back on many friendships as something bygone." Certainly it grew from the same awed perturbation which Benjamin Jowett felt when years later he visited Hallam's grave; Jowett wrote to the Tennysons: "It is a strange feeling about those who are taken young that while we are getting old and dusty they are as they were."* "Tithonus" embodies a fear as to the *nature* of Hallam's immor-

* This preoccupation was to surface again in the late poem "Tomorrow" (written 1884), where the young lover of long ago is found preserved in the peat-bog: "Thin his Riverence buried thim both in wan grave be the dead boor-tree, / The young man Danny O'Roon wid his ould woman, Molly Magee."

tality, a fear intimated in *In Memoriam*, XLI. His fear, says Tennyson, is rarely "that vague fear implied in death":

Yet oft when sundown skirts the moor
  An inner trouble I behold,
  A spectral doubt which makes me cold,
That I shall be thy mate no more,

Though following with an upward mind
  The wonders that have come to thee,
  Through all the secular to-be,
But evermore a life behind.

Blake said that "Time is the mercy of eternity." To Tithonus, death was the mercy of eternity. The poem is Tennyson's subtlest and most beautiful exploration of the impulse to suicide. From the first words, the poem meets the inexorable with its own inexorability:

The woods decay, the woods decay and fall,
The vapours weep their burthen to the ground,
Man comes and tills the field and lies beneath,
And after many a summer dies the swan.
Me only cruel immortality
Consumes: I wither slowly in thine arms,
Here at the quiet limit of the world,
A white-haired shadow roaming like a dream
The ever-silent spaces of the East,
Far-folded mists, and gleaming halls of morn.

The first four lines breathe peace and equanimity; such a death is breath-less, not breathless. But the fifth line disturbs all this, first by its immediate inversion ("Me only . . ."), unlike anything in the previous lines; next with the epithet "cruel," which springs with further force because the previous lines had not contained a single adjective; and disturbs it finally by its predatory enjambment ("Me only cruel immortality / Consumes"),* whereas

* Yet the predatoriness is doubly paradoxical. First, in that to mortals it is mortality, not immortality, which would be thought of as cruel; so that the first four lines are now heard in the accents not solely of lament but of envy. Second, in that "Consumes," despite its urgent placing, reveals itself as no violent devouring–it consumes as consumption consumes, yet with no release into death: "Consumes: I wither slowly. . . ."

the previous lines had all been self-contained sense-units with terminal punctuation. Tithonus, who is "Here at the quiet limit of the world," is so aged as to be at the limit of life and yet is cruelly denied the chance to cross that limit into grateful death. The sentiment is a desolate counterpart to the retreating limit of aspiration in "Ulysses":

> Yet all experience is an arch wherethrough
> Gleams that untravelled world, whose margin fades
> For ever and for ever when I move.

But Tithonus yearns to reach death, that untraveled world, that undiscovered country from whose bourn no traveler returns. Beauty and promise have become the bitterest of emptiness: the "gleaming halls of morn" can no longer promise any true dawn for Tithonus.

"The ever-silent spaces of the East": one hiding place of the poem's exquisite chill is its evocation of a silence which stands in a triple relation to the poem. It etherealizes the erotic relationship; it tacitly whispers of Tithonus's extreme age; and it is potently contrasted with the superbly mellifluous movements of the verse itself. The opening lines epitomize this ambivalence of silence and sound: the woods which fall evoke no crash; the "burthen" (not just "burden") which the vapors weep "to the gound"–*to* has a double sense–is a silent song, an eternal funereal refrain of silence; and when "After many a summer dies the swan," another silent song–that of the dying swan*–is evoked, the song elicited for us and then rescinded, unmentioned. The limit of the world is quiet; the spaces of the East are ever silent. In the past there was utterance, the only words of speech directly recorded in the poem:

> I asked thee, "Give me immortality."
> Then didst thou grant mine asking with a smile. . .

Not with words, but with a smile; and now that silent smile has been replaced by silent tears:

> Can thy love,
> Thy beauty, make amends, though even now,

* See "The Dying Swan" (1830).

Close over us, the silver star, thy guide,
Shines in those tremulous eyes that fill with tears
To hear me?

We are in a world of impregnated silences: "A soft air fans the cloud apart"—and the air both suggests and denies a musical air. The heartbeat pulses beyond hearing; the hoofs of Aurora's team strike silent sparks from the unimaginable flint of the air, they convert sound into a glory of sight, "And beat the twilight into flakes of fire." Aurora grows beautiful "In silence, then before thine answer given / Departest." From the past of utterance there floats a "saying": "The Gods themselves cannot recall their gifts" (where *recall* superbly suggests not only "call back" but "recollect," an infinite divine forgetfulness of extreme old age). How distant are the "days far-off" when their love was real, its reality attested to by the only moment of uttered audible beauty within the poem:

. . . while I lay,
Mouth, forehead, eyelids, growing dewy-warm
With kisses balmier than half-opening buds
Of April, and could hear the lips that kissed
Whispering I knew not what of wild and sweet,
Like that strange song I heard Apollo sing,
While Ilion like a mist rose into towers.*

No more sounds within the poem—only the final ambivalence (chiming with that of the opening "burthen" and the swan's song) by which the dawn's return is both glidingly silent and "silver," a word traditionally apt to the mellifluous**: "And thee returning on thy silver wheels." In this subtle and persistent paradox of silence and sound, Tennyson found a thrust of relationship with his own fineness of musical verbalism that makes "Tithonus" his most assuredly successful poem, at once quintessentially Tennysonian and yet with its Tennysonian felicities of

* Tennyson's genius in revising his talent is manifest in the fine eroticism of "half-opening buds," rich without prurience; his earlier version had been simply "opening buds."

** *Oxford English Dictionary*, "Silver," 13: 'Of sounds'; from 1526, including Milton and Pope.

sound made stronger and more poignant by its chill of silence, its desolated loss of that "strange song" which had once animated its world. Made stronger, too, by the sudden nakednesses of expression—the word "scare," for instance, so unprotected by mellifluousness, in "Why wilt thou ever scare me with thy tears"; or the total simple urgency of the cry, again unswathed, "Let me go."

The desolation of their love is no consequence of any faithlessness in Tithonus or Aurora. "I" and "me" echo through the poem, but with an impotence that is manifest in the first of them: "I wither slowly in thine arms." The suggestion there is of a passivity that is eternally moribund, an embrace that goes on forever but as a lacerating travesty of lovers' hyperbolical ecstasy: "Yet hold me not for ever in thine East"—the ambiguity there in *hold* (keep me forever, and embrace me forever) does indeed show that what Tithonus gained was loss. The only two occasions—in this love poem—on which *I* governs *thee* epitomize the bitter plot: "I asked thee, 'Give me immortality' "; and the future that ends the poem, "forget . . . thee":

> I earth in earth forget these empty courts,
> And thee returning on thy silver wheels.

Empty of what? The potent absence in the poem, its central emptiness, that which in Tennyson's most pained poems manifests itself as not just emptiness but emptiedness, is the lovers' word *we*. *We* does not come once; *us* comes only once, at the poem's central sadness:

> Can thy love,
> Thy beauty, make amends, though even now,
> Close over us, the silver star, thy guide,
> Shines in those tremulous eyes that fill with tears
> To hear me?

Given the pathos of Tithonus's plight, it invites wonder that the poem staves off self-pity. Again a skill in miniature—a pronoun—effects something not miniature at all. For to the withering Tithonus his past self is another person; the split is painful but free from self-pity because it is virtually unimaginable that so distant a past self is his self. Tennyson nets this by casting "I" as "he":

> Alas! for this gray shadow, once a man–
> So glorious in his beauty and thy choice,
> Who madest him thy chosen, that he seemed
> To his great heart none other than a God! . . .
>
> Ay me! ay me! with what another heart
> In days far-off, and with what other eyes
> I used to watch–if I be he that watched–
> The lucid outline forming round thee . . .

Tithonus seems doomed to the unending. His poem ends:

> Yet hold me not for ever in thine East:
> How can my nature longer mix with thine?
> Coldly thy rosy shadows bathe me, cold
> Are all thy lights, and cold my wrinkled feet
> Upon thy glimmering thresholds, when the steam
> Floats up from those dim fields about the homes
> Of happy men that have the power to die,
> And grassy barrows of the happier dead.
> Release me, and restore me to the ground;
> Thou seëst all things, thou wilt see my grave:
> Thou wilt renew thy beauty morn by morn;
> I earth in earth forget these empty courts,
> And thee returning on thy silver wheels.

An eternal immobility meets the heavenly mobile. The effect is paradoxical, as Henry James remarked in praising this passage for "a purity of tone, an inspiration, a something sublime and exquisite":

> It is poised and stationary, like a bird whose wings have borne him high, but the beauty of whose movement is less in great ethereal sweeps and circles than in the way he hangs motionless in the blue air, with only a vague tremor of his pinions. Even if the idea with Tennyson were more largely dramatic than it usually is, the immobility, as we must call it, of his phrase would always defeat the dramatic intention. When he wishes to represent movement, the phrase always seems to me to pause and slowly pivot upon itself, or at most to move backward.

But is the poem's end its outcome? Tithonus notoriously neither withers endlessly nor is granted "the power to die"—in the words of Tennyson's note, "He grew old and infirm, and as he could not die, according to the legend, was turned into a grasshopper." Unthinkable for *this* poem? Other early poems by Tennyson explicitly use the grasshopper legend, though; and the problem—how can we accommodate such an outcome to such an ending?—recurs in many of Tennyson's best poems. We can neither happily bring in that merciful translation into a grasshopper, nor happily leave it out. "Earth in earth" is, as Tennyson says, Dante's *terra in terra* (*Paradiso*, XXV): "My body is earth in the earth, and it will be there with the rest till our number tallies with the eternal purpose." But the eternal purpose for Tithonus will not leave the body as earth in earth. The contrariety of poem and outcome is here at its most perplexing; neither the tragedy of immortal age nor the tragedy of death will be available to Tithonus, but something much smaller, verging on the kindly ludicrous. Tennyson's poem proffers a world in which the ultimate further alternative to the cruel tragic alternatives is a miraculous but unmagnificent diminution: a grasshopper. What future for Tithonus? Neither of those which he fears. The poem potently eschews the future tense, which surfaces at only one moment, in those closing lines: "thou wilt see my grave: / Thou wilt renew thy beauty"—and then, with a superb elision of the future tense, "I earth in earth forget. . . ." With a profound circularity of return, both "Ulysses"—which yearns to have a future—and "Tithonus"—which yearns to have no future—can find no room for the future tense of hope.

Complementing both "Ulysses" and "Tithonus" is a third poem, "Tiresias." Tennyson began it in late 1833, but did not complete it till 1883 and publish it till 1885. Perhaps he recalled Arthur Hallam's urging in 1831: "Surely you owe it to us all not to let yourself carelessly fall into the misery of blindness. It is a hard and a sad thing to barter the 'universal light' even for the power of 'Tiresias and Phineus prophets old.' " Faced with Hallam's death, Tennyson in "Tiresias" seeks strength and consolation in the deliberate self-sacrifice that redeems death. The poem is a compendium of much that precipitates his best work: the mask of age, sacrifice, death, blindness, a paternal love that can be deep because it is not literally paternal. Yet in this case, the compendium remains just that. Some woodenness encumbers the verse, and the poem's attitudes are struck rather than striking. The skill is patent, too much so:

> . . . smote, and stilled
> Through all its folds the multitudinous beast. . . .

> . . . and what a weight of war
> Rides on those ringing axles! jingle of bits,
> Shouts, arrows, tramp of the hornfooted horse
> That grind the glebe to powder!

What went wrong? A basic timidity renders the poem complacent, and complacency was always fatal to Tennyson. The dire pains and problems are too easily encompassed here. The inactivity of art, its dubious heroism, is too comfortably accommodated within Tiresias's aged blindness: "And these blind hands were useless in their wars . . ." The deep but ambiguous urge to envisage circumstances in which suicide was not merely condonable but honorable—an urge with its roots in Dr. Tennyson's misery, Tennyson's early misery, and now the death of Hallam—is too simply gratified in the story of the ancient curse which can be removed only "if one of these / By his own hand—": as Tiresias urges Menœceus,

> let thine own hand strike
> Thy youthful pulses into rest and quench
> The red God's anger, fearing not to plunge
> Thy torch of life in darkness . . .

Too staunchly unpained and unambiguous. Likewise the aching weariness, the longing for oblivion which animates so much that is truest in Tennyson, is in "Tiresias" too unresistingly at home in a vision of the Elysian fields: "I would that I were gathered to my rest," into Elysian fields too assuredly "golden," too confidently "heroic" an ending for all its shadowy charm:

> while the golden lyre
> Is ever sounding in heroic ears

Heroic hymns, and every way the vales
Wind, clouded with the grateful incense-fume
Of those who mix all odour to the Gods
On one far height in one far-shining fire.

The heroism that is both evoked and embodied in "Ulysses" and "Tithonus" weighs more, is not buoyed up. The ending of "Tiresias"–Menœceus's sacrificial suicide, and Tiresias's waiting for death–is too happily at one with the story's outcome to engage Tennyson's genius.

"Some men yet say in many parts of England that King Arthur is not dead, but by the will of our Lord in another place. And men say that he will come again." Malory's Arthur, mingling loss and hope, called up Tennyson's Arthur. The death of Hallam created "Morte d'Arthur."

Arthur had vanished
I knew not whither,
The king who loved me,
And cannot die . . .
("Merlin and the Gleam")

A great deal of Tennyson went into "Morte d'Arthur"; he wrote it in 1833–34, created a frame for it in about 1837–38 (the prefatory and concluding lines which constitute "The Epic"); and published it in 1842. He later incorporated it in full into *Idylls of the King* as "The Passing of Arthur," where it was preceded by 169 lines, and followed by 29 lines; even so, his "Morte d'Arthur" also retained its place in his published volumes. From the first words, there is a gravity–at once authentic and archaic–that was new in Tennyson:

So all day long the noise of battle rolled
Among the mountains by the winter sea;
Until King Arthur's table, man by man,
Had fallen in Lyonnesse about their Lord,
King Arthur: then, because his wound was deep,
The bold Sir Bedivere uplifted him,
Sir Bedivere, the last of all his knights,
And bore him to a chapel nigh the field,

A broken chancel with a broken cross,
That stood on a dark strait of barren land.
On one side lay the Ocean, and on one
Lay a great water, and the moon was full.

It is fine, yet there is a disconcerting disproportion between the way in which the richly suggestive setting is entered into and the way in which the human figures—Arthur and Bedivere—are held at a distance, are frozen into symbolic attitudes, "Larger than human on the frozen hills." Arthur and Bedivere will both speak much in the poem, but their words have a high sheen that sends back the light of inquiry rather than absorbs it. It is the settings within the poem which capture memory and mystery. There is "the place of tombs" and the sea-wind "Shrill, chill, with flakes of foam." There are the imagined distant icebergs, "the moving isles of winter." There is the stonily alien crag, the limpidly alien lake and moon:

Dry clashed his harness in the icy caves
And barren chasms, and all to left and right
The bare black cliff clanged round him, as he based
His feet on juts of slippery crag that rang
Sharp-smitten with the dint of armèd heels—
And on a sudden, lo! the level lake,
And the long glories of the winter moon.

As in some of the Pre-Raphaelite poems which owe so much to Tennyson, there is the disconcerting play of a sharply visualized setting against a central mist or alienness or vacancy. Disconcerting, or simply ineffectual? From the start "Morte d'Arthur" attracted intelligent criticism at once respectful and dissatisfied. John Sterling's review in 1842 damaged Tennyson's Arthurian ambitions:

The "Morte d'Arthur" . . . seems to us less costly jewel-work, with fewer of the broad flashes of passionate imagery, than some others, and not compensating for this inferiority by any stronger human interest. The miraculous legend of "Excalibur" does not come very near to us, and as reproduced by any modern writer must be a mere ingenious exercise of fancy. The poem, however, is full of distinct and striking description, perfectly expressed; and a tone of mild, dignified sweetness attracts, though it hardly avails to enchant us.

Is the strong human interest in the story itself, in the testing, disobedience and obedience of Bedivere? The question is not rhetorical; but it is not clear what Tennyson intended to make of this central narration. "This way and that dividing the swift mind": the surprising thing about these evocations of Bedivere's dilemma is how little any sense of dilemma presses upon us. Tennyson is supremely a poet of doubt, of a divided mind; yet Bedivere's consciousness is left coldly alien, unentered. Is the point in origin a technical and temperamental one, that Tennyson's sense of loss was not kindled by third-person imaginings but by first-person ones such as those of "St. Simeon Stylites," "Ulysses," "Tithonus," *In Memoriam*, and *Maud*? Certainly there is a quite different depth of entrance in these two passages. Bedivere's future of loneliness is evocative but strangely unbruised:

> "And I, the last, go forth companionless,
> And the days darken round me, and the years,
> Among new men, strange faces, other minds."

The Queens' cry rings less in the ears of Bedivere and Arthur than through an unpeopled landscape; it does not "fuse" a landscape with the mood of a character, as "Mariana" had done, since in this case the insinuations of tone are altogether alien to Bedivere's mood. On the contrary, there is a rupture between the deepest moods within the poem and any moods felt by its human figures.

> —and from them rose
> A cry that shivered to the tingling stars,
> And, as it were one voice, an agony
> Of lamentation, like a wind, that shrills
> All night in a waste land, where no one comes,
> Or hath come, since the making of the world.

It is not just a modern predilection for waste lands which gives those lines a timbre which is more deeply resonant than, and different from, anything felt by Arthur or Bedivere.

Sometimes the disparity of timbre seems a mere failure. Bedivere's way of speaking (honest, simple, cumbrous) is not one that can convincingly incorporate the visionary:

> but were this kept,
> Stored in some treasure-house of mighty kings,

Some one might show it at a joust of arms,
Saying, "King Arthur's sword, Excalibur,
Wrought by the lonely maiden of the Lake.
Nine years she wrought it, sitting in the deeps
Upon the hidden bases of the hills."

"Not bad that, Fitz, is it?": Tennyson to FitzGerald in 1835, about those last two lines. Better than not bad; but strikingly alien to Bedivere's prosy proem.

For "Morte d'Arthur" is divided though Bedivere, by his very nature, could not really be. (Which is why the sense of a test, of a strain, is so markedly absent.) The poem tries to imagine and depict a person left alone after Arthur's death as Tennyson was after his Arthur's. His earlier poems had endued both their protagonist and their setting with both of the contrasting strengths, endurance which can yet so easily harden into induration, and sensitivity which can fray into morbidity. In the case of "Morte d'Arthur," however, Tennyson found that he could face his loss only by a severe dissociation: by giving to Bedivere, his human protagonist and surrogate, a staunchness of endurance, and to the settings and vista'd comparisons the sensitivity or morbidity. R. H. Hutton said in 1888 that "Tennyson is never so great as when he has a mystic dread to paint, when Tithonus is shivering at the prospect of an immortal burden, or Arthur asking himself on the edge of the hereafter, whether there had been anything of true eternity in his life here." True—and yet how different is Tithonus's shivering from anything in "Morte d'Arthur," where it is less a human being than "A cry that shivered to the tingling stars." Staunchness *or* sensitivity? The poem hoped itself to effect a creative healing union that is presented *within* the poem as impossible. Arthur sails "To the island-valley of Avilion": "Where I will heal me of my grievous wound." For one of the paradoxes of this apparently equable elegiac poem is that one has to ask whether Arthur is *mort.* The outcome of the poem may be death, but even death can be shrouded in mystery and in hope ("King Arthur is not dead").

Long stood Sir Bedivere
Revolving many memories, till the hull
Looked one black dot against the verge of dawn,
And on the mere the wailing died away.

The verge is the dawn of death or of life; the black dot is not a full stop to bring the poem to an end; the sound effect is of a fading echoic truncation, with "away" as a thinning dying ripple from "the wailing": "And on the mere the wailing died away." Martin Dodsworth has pointed out the syntactic ambiguity of the last line—is it a main clause, or subordinate ("Bedivere stood until the wailing died away")?

The uncertain status of the final clause softens its conclusiveness greatly. When Tennyson decided to continue the poem further for the *Idylls of the King*, and to give it a more optimistic ending ("And the new sun rose bringing the new year") he had no very difficult task, because the old ending had always left room for a continuation.

This is excellently said. Moreover the old ending had itself had a continuation: the frame of "The Epic."

"The Epic" is important evidence of an uneasiness deep in Tennyson. For it tells of how the poet "burnt / His epic, his King Arthur, some twelve books"; and yet one book, the eleventh, had been picked from the hearth; so the poet, "with some prelude of disparagement," agreed to read it, "mouthing out his hollow oes and aes." "The Epic" has charm, but a betraying charm. Leigh Hunt was acutely severe:

A certain air of literary dandyism, or fine-gentlemanism, or fastidiousness, or whatever he may *not* be pleased to call it, which leads him to usher in his compositions with such exordiums as those to "Morte d'Arthur," and "Godiva". . . We suspect that these poems of "Morte d'Arthur" and "Godiva" are among those which Mr. Tennyson thinks his best, and is most anxious that others should regard as he does; and therefore it is that he would affect to make trifles of them. The reader's opinion is at once to be of great importance to him, and yet none at all. . .

Leigh Hunt is shrewd about "this involuntary exhibition of uneasiness," but the crucial thing is not so much that Tennyson thought "Morte d'Arthur" one of his best poems as that he felt it to be one which he could least bear to have ridiculed or despised. Hence his wish to protect it by "a kind of unpoetical nonchalance or indifferent superiority to himself over his own performances." A fatal move, of course, since "The Epic" inanely suggests that

Prince Albert can be seen as Arthur come again ("Come again, and thrice as fair"), nakedly inviting Swinburne's unforgettable thrust, "Morte d'Albert."* In fact "Morte d'Arthur" is remarkably free of any such mawkishness, the only instance being this: "And looking wistfully with wide blue eyes / As in a picture." That offers Arthur too totally as what James Joyce called a "bleaueyedeal." But "The Epic" invited the contempt which it sought to anticipate, to prevent. There is nothing like armor for offering your adversary a chink. But the strangest chink is that casual detail: in "The Epic" the "Morte d'Arthur" was the eleventh book of twelve. How was the Arthurian epic to end? Not, apparently, with "The Passing of Arthur." It is a mysterious little matter, and a perfect emblem for Tennyson's art of the penultimate.

Oh! that 'twere possible,
After long grief and pain,
To find the arms of my true-love
Round me once again!

That too is a new note in Tennyson, poignantly direct, a deep blankness that is "the real thing strange." Tennyson later assented to Jowett's opinion that these were his most touching lines. He wrote two drafts of the poem in 1833–34 after Hallam's death; in 1837 he was pestered by Milnes for a poem, and he therefore added forty lines which purported to give the poem an arc. But he did not include the poem in his 1842 volumes; eventually "Oh! that 'twere possible" was to form the core of *Maud* (1855). So the poem's poignancy in 1837 hung in a strange vacuum; it is not surprising that the *Edinburgh Review* (October 1837) said: "We do not profess perfectly to understand the somewhat mysterious contribution of Mr. Alfred Tennyson, entitled 'Stanzas.' "

"Oh! that 'twere possible": but why isn't it possible? The poem does not at first say that the loved one is dead. In line 11, "A shadow flits before me": and the shadow becomes a ghost.

* There is a revealing clumsiness in the unwanted but intrusive nauticality of "port": "There came a bark that, blowing forward, bore / King Arthur, like a modern gentleman / Of stateliest port."

The dead Hallam becomes a dead girl, which leads to a few softnesses of phrasing ("Do I hear the pleasant ditty, / That I heard her chant of old?") and to some of the feebler stanzas of 1837. But this transformation is manifestly irrelevant to the poem's reattainment of its center: a desperate loneliness which is felt as shameful (shamefully unmanly, shamefully self-centred, shamefully unwilling to accept the will of God), a loneliness exacerbated by the cityscape:*

Then I rise: the eave-drops fall
  And the yellow-vapours choke
    The great city sounding wide;
The day comes—a dull red ball,
  Wrapt in drifts of lurid smoke,
    On the misty river-tide.

Through the hubbub of the market
  I steal, a wasted frame;
It crosseth here, it crosseth there—
Through all that crowd, confused and loud,
  The shadow still the same;
And on my heavy eyelids
    My anguish hangs like shame. . . .

Then the broad light glares and beats,
  And the sunk eye flits and fleets,
And will not let me be.
  I loathe the squares and streets,
And the faces that one meets,
  Hearts with no love for me;
Always I long to creep
To some still cavern deep,
And to weep, and weep and weep
  My whole soul out to thee.

* Reviewing Alexander Smith in 1853, A. H. Clough said: "There is a charm, for example, in finding, as we do, continual images drawn from the busy seats of industry; it seems to satisfy a want that we have long been conscious of, when we see the black streams that welter out of factories, the dreary lengths of urban and suburban dustiness,

The squares and streets,
And the faces that one meets,

irradiated with a gleam of divine purity."

Let go by the paraphernalia of the two ghosts, and the heavenly hopes, and the wishful insubstantiality of the eroticism; one need make no conscious effort to remember what is here effortlessly memorable: a broken cry, a suicidal wish for oblivion, for dissolution, for dissolving into tears. An insufficient attitude, no doubt, in the face of loss; but the attitude which would feel simply superior to such human insufficiency is worse than insufficient. There is something more than a mere succumbing to morbidity in verses such as these which come so shapedly into mind on utterly nonliterary occasions, occasions when one is thinking, not about shame and loss in literature, but about shame and loss.*

The pain in "Oh! that 'twere possible" is masterly, but precariously mastered. In "Break, break, break" (probably written in early 1834), there is an equanimity, a transparency, strangely matched with a puzzling obliqueness of logic or argument. In a sense, the poem's sense is plain enough; yet–like most of the best poems–it has a riddling quality too. For it is hard to grasp by what thread of thought we are to swing across the gulf from the injunction "Break, break, break" to the *And* of line 3; from the "O well for the fisherman's boy" (lines 5–10) to the *But* of line 11; from the injunction again to the final *But* of line 15. The poem's juxtapositions and conjunctions tantalizingly suggest a progression of thought which yet remains elusive. The heartbreak of which the poem knows–(when the poem begins, we do not know what it is that is being urged to "Break, break, break": the heart is heard as a flickering suggestion)–is not something of which it can bring itself openly to speak. The dissociative gulf between the outer scene and the inner pain is one which the sturdy words of reason like *And* and *But* can ultimately only pretend to bridge.

Break, break, break,
  On thy cold gray stones, O Sea!
And I would that my tongue could utter
  The thoughts that arise in me.

* Allingham to Tennyson: " 'One believes in a poet,' I said, 'whose lines are perpetually coming into one's mind. Yours do with me.' " Tennyson's endearing refusal to be ingratiated comes out in his immediate retort: "Repeat a line." (Allingham's *Diary*, p. 327, July 27, 1884.)

O well for the fisherman's boy,
  That he shouts with his sister at play!
O well for the sailor lad,
  That he sings in his boat on the bay!

And the stately ships go on
  To their haven under the hill;
But O for the touch of a vanished hand,
  And the sound of a voice that is still!

Break, break, break,
  At the foot of thy crags, O Sea!
But the tender grace of a day that is dead
  Will never come back to me.

"No poet ever made the dumb speak so effectually": the words are R. H. Hutton's, introducing the best critical account we have of this masterpiece of puzzling plainness:

Observe how the wash of the sea on the cold gray stones is used to prepare the mind for the feeling of helplessness with which the deeper emotions break against the hard and rigid element of human speech; how the picture is then widened out till you see the bay with children laughing on its shore, and the sailor-boy singing on its surface, and the stately ships passing on in the offing to their unseen haven, all with the view of helping us to feel the contrast between the satisfied and the unsatisfied yearnings of the human heart. Tennyson, like every true poet, has the strongest feeling of the spiritual and almost mystic character of the associations attaching to the distant sail which takes the ship on its lonely journey to an invisible port, and has more than once used it to lift the mind into the attitude of hope or trust. But then the song returns again to the helpless breaking of the sea at the foot of crags it cannot climb, not this time to express the inadequacy of human speech to express human yearnings, but the defeat of those very yearnings themselves. Thus does Lord Tennyson turn an ordinary sea-shore landscape into a means of finding a voice indescribably sweet for the dumb spirit of human loss.

By the summer of 1834, Tennyson was entering upon the more serene manner, the levity even, that would characterize the poems of 1835–37. He had published "The Sleeping Beauty" in 1830;

"Life and death," said "Christopher North," "meet in the stillness of that sleep—so profound that it is felt as if it were immortal." The paradox of a life that is not life; the sense of time heavy with waiting; the happy outcome altogether unmentioned in the poem itself: these are quintessentially Tennysonian. Tennyson then incorporated "The Sleeping Beauty" into the sequence "The Day-Dream," which he completed about June 1834. The outcome now comes in; "the fated fairy Prince" arrives, and all is well. Not that all is so well with the poem, since even the felicities of phrasing now lack the tautness, the tension, which the isolated sleeping beauty created. Tennyson was uneasy about how to end the poem; the section "Moral" was at first called "Epilogue," with "L'Envoi" concluding the poem. As it stands, "The Departure" is followed by "Moral" and then by "L'Envoi" and then by "Epilogue." No wonder that Tennyson at one stage in manuscript thought of having to invoke, with bantering self-deprecation, "a lady's postscript." No wonder that in his closing lines, he invoked the legendary "long-tailed birds of Paradise" which never alight. The dilemma—ending versus outcome—is one which often richly teased him into thought; here it teased him into teasing. He could not find it in him to joke convincingly on such a subject; he had too darkly imagined

> a weary bird on wing
> Cursed never to alight, no restingplace,
> No stay—no shrouding of the weary head
> Beneath the weary plume...
>
> ("The Lover's Tale," manuscript)

VI

1. 1834–1837

In January 1834, Arthur Hallam was buried at Clevedon in Somerset. Next month Henry Hallam wrote to Tennyson about the projected volume of Arthur's *Remains*, a cautious selection from the prose and poetry to be privately printed and circulated. Would Tennyson like to communicate anything that might figure in the short memoir? "I should desire," said Henry Hallam, "to have the character of his mind, his favourite studies and pursuits, his habits and views, delineated." Tennyson urged the inclusion of Arthur's religious exploration into evil, *Theodicaea Novissima*, and this was reluctantly granted. (Henry Hallam later suppressed the piece.) But the poet who had already written some of the sections of *In Memoriam* was yet too painfully close. His reply to Henry Hallam has a poignant dignity and hope:

> I attempted to draw up a memoir of his life and character, but I failed to do him justice. I failed even to please myself. I could scarcely have pleased you. I hope to be able at a future period to concentrate whatever powers I may possess on the construction of some tribute to those high speculative endowments and comprehensive sympathies which I ever loved to contemplate; but at present, though somewhat ashamed at my own weakness, I find the object yet is too near me to permit of any very accurate delineation. You, with your clear insight into human nature, may perhaps not wonder that in the dearest service I could have been employed in, I should be found most deficient.

"At that time my heart seemed too crushed and all my energies too paralysed."

But 1834 was to prove a strange blend of old fears and new hopes. What was old surfaced with the melancholia of Tennyson's brother Septimus, and then soon after with the collapse of his brother Charles. A letter within the Tennyson d'Eyncourts gives a sharp glimpse of the tensions and embarrassments:

I pity poor Charles who is almost killing himself with laudanum and suffering so much from lowness of spirits—but it would be very disagreeable in many respects to have a tribe of Somersby people so near us, as of course Mary would expect to go every where we did.

Once again it must have seemed that history was repeating itself, that the sins of the fathers were reenacted by the sons. Two years later, the Tennyson d'Eyncourts were still commiserating over the dissipated clergyman who was a son of the dissipated clergyman, and saying of Charles: "I cannot help pitying him poor fellow, for he is the most good-natured fellow in the world, and I think he will kill himself soon."

Kill himself: that was ominous both as memory and threat. Indeed Frederick feared that even Alfred might succumb as their father and their brother Charles had done:

Alfred will probably publish again in the Spring but his health is very indifferent, and his spirits very variable. He too if he does not mind will be obliged when he has lost the plumage of his Imagination, to fledge it with Tobacco leaves, if he does not take to some stronger or more fatal stimulant.

Yet despite the family morbidities, and despite the death of Hallam, 1834 was an invigorating year for Tennyson. He fell in love. It was to be a brief and frustrated love, but it was never to fade from his memory. Rosa Baring lived at Harrington Hall, two miles from Somersby; she was rich—she was indeed a Baring; and she was to prove both beyond his reach and beneath his love. He probably first met her in about 1825; in 1834 he fell in love; by 1835–36 he had become disillusioned with her socially conventional coquetry. And in 1838 she married Robert Shafto.

The facts are soon told; the influence was deep and abiding. Not in the early poems about Rosa, which express a commonplace love and a commonplace disillusionment. But it was the disappointment with Rosa—yet another in a long series of deep disappointments, this time at shallowness–which was to animate his many poems which tell of "marriage-hindering Mammon" and "The rentroll Cupid of our rainy isles."* Family pride, social snobbery, money pressures: Tennyson already knew what these were from the feud within the Tennyson family and from the thwarting of Arthur Hallam and Emily Tennyson. But he knew them all the better, all the worse, after Rosa Baring, and in his poems he showed what he knew: in such poor poems as "The Flight," "The Wreck," and "Charity," and in such diversely good poems as "Locksley Hall," "Edwin Morris," "Aylmer's Field," "Northern Farmer. New Style," and above all *Maud*.**

Tennyson came to pardon Rosa, and by the end of his life he even came to despise her no longer. When he was eighty and she was about seventy-five, by a tender fiction he blended his proud terrace at Aldworth with her proud terrace at Harrington Hall, and so–through a benevolent revenge–re-lived his finest feelings for her:

Rose, on this terrace fifty years ago,
  When I was in my June, you in your May,
Two words, "*My* Rose" set all your face aglow,
  And now that I am white, and you are gray,
That blush of fifty years ago, my dear,
  Blooms in the Past, but close to me today
As this red rose, which on our terrace here
  Glows in the blue of fifty miles away.

"Fifty years ago," in 1836, he had fallen in love with Emily Sellwood.

In February 1835 Tennyson was badly short of money, and he sold his Cambridge gold medal for £15. Then, in July, the Old Man of the Wolds died, in his mid-eighties. Would his bequests at last make possible that independence, that new phase of life, which the Tennysons so hoped for? Yet another dawning came

* "I used to rage against the social conditions that made marriage so difficult" (Allingham's *Diary*, p. 158, August 25, 1867).

** A passage not in the end adopted in *Maud* imagines her

Lying a splendid whoredom to full-fed heirs at the Ball,
"Buy me, O buy me and have me, for I am here to be sold."

and went, a false dawn. For though they were by no means forgotten, they were not sufficiently remembered. To Frederick, property at Grimsby. The younger Charles already had the Grasby living. For the deranged Edward, £3,000 in trust. To Alfred, a property at Grasby worth about £3,000. For the seven younger children, an estate to be sold, worth fifteen or twenty thousand pounds. The trouble was not that the grandfather was too ungenerous to the Somersby Tennysons, but that he was too generous to his favored son, who received the remainder of the landed estates. Epitomizing the resented discrimination was the matter of the bonds entered into by Mrs. Tennyson and the three eldest sons. The bonds were now to be realized for the residuary estate. As Charles Tennyson Turner indignantly put it, "they want the treacherous bond money paying, you perceive, and as quickly as possible."

None of the Somersby Tennysons came to the Old Man's funeral. This was unmagnanimous of them, but then apparently neither the Old Man nor his favored son had come to Dr. Tennyson's funeral. Their aunt (Charles Tennyson d'Eyncourt's wife) was waspish: "I hear the family at Somersby are one and all, much disappointed, at their *handsome* increase of Property—but they expected more, and the girls very handsome fortunes besides. Some people are never satisfied!!"

Uncle Charles professed to be puzzled and was certainly shocked:

> I know no reason why any of that family should be dissatisfied—my Father has done what he always said he would do, and this was well known to them all—and is the same as he would have done if my Brother had lived except that he has been *a Father* to the Younger Children. Alfred I find has been so violent (though he gets the Manor of Grasby and an Estate there) that Mr. and Mrs. Bourne sent him away from Margate where he was with them.

Uncle Charles did at least preserve the decorums; cousin Edwin was less refined:

> Your letter to my Aunt which she received last night has convinced me what *a hog* that Alfred is and what can you expect from a pig but a grunt. However I would not trouble myself by thinking about it. It

is too contemptible a subject. As to his not seeing me, I can assure him that I feel excessively grateful for his decision on that point, because I would rather be excused meeting a bloated ploughman.

The "bloated ploughman" would eventually have the last word. And two years after the Old Man died, the Tennysons ceased to be a local embarrassment to the Tennyson d'Eyncourts. They had to leave Somersby Rectory—the patrons, the Burtons, wanted it.

Unwatched, the garden bough shall sway,
The tender blossom flutter down,
Unloved, that beech will gather brown,
This maple burn itself away . . .
(*In Memoriam*, CI)*

At High Beech, Epping, a new phase might begin for them all.

* See too "A Farewell."

2. *Poems 1835–1837*

The poems of 1835 to 1837 are mostly temperate and undistinguished; the pains of Tennyson's life were now debilitating vexations rather than anguish, and few of the poems greatly command either pain or pleasure. Tennyson's disillusionment with Rosa Baring was to be succeeded by his love for Emily Sellwood; at this date, neither was an urgent prompting to his art. His main effort, a truly creative one, was bent upon revising the poems published in 1830 and 1832. Some shrinking of nerve is evident, but a letter to Spedding in the spring of 1835 shows that Tennyson possessed a reason and not just a rationalization:

John Heath writes me word that Mill is going to review me in a new Magazine to be called the London Review–and favourably. But it is the last thing I wish for and I would that you or some other who may be friends of Mill would hint as much to him: I do not wish to be dragged forward again in any shape before the reading public at present, particularly on the score of my old poems most of which I have so corrected (particularly "Œnone") as to make them much less imperfect . . .

At the same period, Tennyson was also attempting a new mode: a Wordsworthian simplicity, such as that of "Michael." The *Memoir* (i. 265) reports (but without giving an authority, and without plausibility) that Wordsworth said: "Mr Tennyson, I have been endeavouring all my life to write a pastoral like your

'Dora' and have not succeeded." But Tennyson's achieved only a strained pastiche. According to him, " 'Dora,' being the tale of a nobly simple country girl, had to be told in the simplest possible poetical language, and therefore was one of the poems which gave most trouble." Matthew Arnold was to proffer a definitive comparison of the opening of "Michael" with that of "Dora":

So true is this, that when a genius essentially subtle, or a genius which, from whatever cause, is in its essence not truly and broadly simple, determines not to admit a shade of subtlety or curiosity into its expression, it cannot even then attain real simplicity; it can only attain a semblance of simplicity . . . The real quality it [French criticism] calls *simplicité*, the semblance *simplesse*. The one is natural simplicity, the other is artificial simplicity.

The inorganic nature of Tennyson's rhythms here (alien to his own nature, as Arnold intimates) is suggested by a comparison of the 1842 text and its revision:

1842: "Consider: take a month to think, and give
An answer to my wish; or by the Lord
That made me, you shall pack, and nevermore
Darken my doors again." And William heard,
And answered something madly . . .

1843: "Consider, William: take a month to think,
And let me have an answer to my wish;
Or, by the Lord that made me, you shall pack,
And never more darken my doors again."
But William answered madly . . .

The alteration of the line endings, slid along, suggests an arbitrariness of rhythms—the lines measured out like cloth. A pity, because the subject of the poem—a father's stubbornness that kills his son and desolates his own life—was one that was real to Tennyson. Too real, perhaps, for him to contemplate except through the rosy spectacles of this tamed pastoral. Coleridge's daughter, Sara, was right:

This "Dora" is a poet's dream. Crabbe's people say strong things—not just what the poet would have them say. Tennyson's Farmer becomes very soft all at once—and William says on his death-bed just what dying men . . . seldom say—but what people imagine in such a case, when they make it all very fine for their own edification and amusement.

A poet's dream: but on this subject, at this date, the only true Tennyson poem would have had to be a nightmare.

Nevertheless, 1836 was to show that Tennyson could strike a note of deep tranquility provided that life would only provide a glimpse of deep tranquility. At the wedding of his brother Charles to Louisa Sellwood, he met once again Emily Sellwood; he was to capture this minute in "The Bridesmaid." His tender hopes live in an epithalamium which was probably precipitated by Charles's marriage. "Move eastward, happy earth" is Tennyson's first creative celebration of happiness, something very different from those "rapid rills of merry rhyme."

Move eastward, happy earth, and leave
  Yon orange sunset waning slow:
From fringes of the faded eve,
  O, happy planet, eastward go;
Till over thy dark shoulder glow
  Thy silver sister-world, and rise
  To glass herself in dewy eyes
That watch me from the glen below.

Ah, bear me with thee, smoothly borne,
  Dip forward under starry light,
And move me to my marriage-morn,
  And round again to happy night.

The limpid delicacy is achieved by patterning and diversity of repetition. Lines 1 and 2 are wound back, with meticulous gravity, in lines 3 and 4 (the effect of chiasmus: *a b b a*): "Move" first, "go" last, and so on, and so closing in and then widening out. "Go" is taken rhymingly up into "glow"; "sister-world" alerts us to all such pairs and patterns; "silver" crystallizes against "orange"; "glass" is the mirror of her "eyes," and with "*dewy* eyes" gently prophesying "morn." "Ah" remembers "O"; "bear me" continues the other awed imperatives ("Move," "go") and is then affectionately subsumed within "borne"; "Dip forward" is yet another unimperious imperative (with "forward" advancing from "eastward"); "starry light" succeeds the "sunset" and the silver moon; "move me" (a step forward from that first intransitive "Move"). "And round again to happy night"–*again*, indeed, and from "happy earth" and "happy planet." Night–which had figured earlier–is explicitly mentioned for the first time as the poem's climax and consummation. One line–that which unobtrusively insists upon the presence not far away of his loved one –stands out as uniquely neither giving nor receiving the filaments: "That watch me from the glen below." Or rather, as giving only "me" to the rest of the poem. The lyrical interweaving is controlled yet supple, as inexorable and as fresh as the revolutions of night and day. The same tact which modulates the repetitions tempers the hyperboles: the tone which tells the earth to "move eastward" needs to be perfectly judged if it is not to sound arrogant or insane. The earth will move without the telling–which is why it matters that the tone thrills with a conscious luxuriance of needlessness, the happiest act of supererogatory speech that a man happily, confidently, waiting can imagine. For once, a poem by Tennyson which ends before its outcome awaits a happy outcome; the penultimate moment openly awaits an ultimate happiness.

The nature of Tennyson's happy success in "Move eastward" is the clearer in that these years also engendered that perplexing burst of unconvincing merriment, "Will Waterproof's Lyrical Monologue." What wins credence in the poem is its dislike of critics ("I grow in worth, and wit, and sense, / Unboding critic-pen") and its envy of the old days before literary gossip plagued the poet, "Ere days, that deal in ana, swarmed / His literary leeches." What neither fetches nor carries any conviction is the bluff conviviality.

> For I am of a numerous house,
>   With many kinsmen gay,
> Where long and largely we carouse
>   As who shall say me nay:
> Each month, a birth-day coming on,
>   We drink defying trouble,
> Or sometimes two would meet in one,
>   And then we drank it double.

Well, I shall say you nay. The grim ghost of Dr. Tennyson could not be exorcised by such uneasy levity. Not for the first time, there was to be more truth—both autobiographical truth and poetic truth—in one of those dialect poems in which the old Tennyson was to revisit his young self. "The Northern Cobbler" is the story of a fight against alcoholism. No talk of how "we carouse":

> 'Sottin' thy braäins
> Guzzlin' an' soäkin' an' smoäkin' an' hawmin' about i' the
> laänes,
> Soä sow-droonk that tha doesn not touch thy 'at to the Squire';
> An I looöked cock-eyed at my noäse an' I seeäd 'im a-gittin'
> o' fire . . .

In 1835 Tennyson had said unequivocally that he did "not wish to be dragged forward again in any shape before the reading public at present." But two of his Cambridge friends managed to drag him. First, W. H. Brookfield persuaded Tennyson, despite his having "a sort of instinctive hatred towards annuals each and all," to contribute to *The Keepsake* for 1837 (published November 1836); Tennyson sent "St. Agnes." Second, and more important, Richard Monckton Milnes was encouraged by this to press Tennyson for a contribution to *The Tribute*. Tennyson wrote back a bantering letter, regretting that he had ever broken his earlier oath, and offering nothing. Milnes was either genuinely hurt by some of the jokes, or cunningly pretended to be; at any rate, was indignant at Tennyson's "insulting Irony," and threatened to let *The Tribute* have Tennyson's early poem "Anacaona." Tennyson capitulated, and eventually sent "Oh! that 'twere possible," the passionate poem of 1833–34 to which he now proceeded to add forty lines and which he was to incorporate in a revised form in *Maud*. Nevertheless Tennyson was hurt at Milnes's being hurt, and he offered a vivid sketch of his own situation as he saw it in comparison to Milnes's:

> What has so jaundiced your good natured eyes as to make them mistake harmless banter for *insulting Irony* . . . Had I been writing to a nervous, morbidly-irritable man, down in the world, stark spoiled with the staggers of a mis-managed imagination and equally oppress by

Fortune and by the Reviews, it is possible that I might have halted to find expressions more suitable to his case—but that you, who seem, at least, to take the world as it comes, to doff it and let it pass—that you a man everyway prosperous and talented should have taken pet at my unhappy badinage made me———lay down my pipe and stare at the fire for ten minutes till the stranger fluttered up the chimney.

3. 1837–1840

"His two elder brothers being away" (Frederick in Corfu and then Florence—for good; and Charles settled at Grasby), it was upon Tennyson that there "devolved the care of the family and of choosing a new home." High Beech served them from late in 1837 till 1840. Mrs. Tennyson, though, was "in such a nervous state that he did not like to leave her." "My mother," he wrote, "is afraid if I go to town even for a night; how could they go on without me for months?" The letter was to Emily Sellwood, whom he loved.

She was the daughter of Henry Sellwood, a solicitor in Horncastle (five miles from Somersby). Tennyson had first met her in 1830 at Somersby, when Hallam was there. In the words of her reminiscences,

> Next morning we some of us went to Holywell. Arthur Hallam kindly walked with me . . . While we were there Alfred made his appearance wrapt in a cloak and sportively said: "Are you a Naiad or a Dryad or what are you?"

The next visit to Somersby which she remembered was after Hallam's death in 1833, when Tennyson's bereaved sister appeared "with one white rose in her black hair as her Arthur had loved to see her." Then in May 1836 there had occurred the event which was to precipitate their love and also later to jeopardize it: the marriage of her sister Louisa to Tennyson's brother Charles. Emily was a bridesmaid, and she and Tennyson fell in love. He celebrated the moment in "The Bridesmaid," with its affectionately double use of the saying "A happy bridesmaid makes a happy bride." By July he was announcing to a friend: "I am much better in health than when I saw you and altogether more cheerful." In November 1836 the poet George Darley put a good question to Tennyson's friend Milnes: "But what can T. have to drown him in the slough of despond, as you tell me, if he retain the free use of his faculties?" But Darley couched his final question in quite the wrong terms: "But what can be the worm at Tennyson's heart? Is he in the flames, furies, and tortures, agonies and excruciations of the 'tender passion'?"

In 1838 the engagement of Emily and Alfred was recognized by Emily's family. Deep among Tennyson's feelings must have been the sense, *at last*. In 1840 the engagement was broken off. Yet another possibility of life had been shown and then withdrawn.

The *Memoir* (i. 150) by Tennyson's son speaks in clipped accents: "My mother and he were then quasi-engaged but were not able to marry owing to want of funds."

> On that day
> Two lovers parted by no scurrilous tale—
> Mere want of gold—and still for twenty years
> Bound by the golden cord of their first love—
> Had asked us to their marriage.
>
> ("The Ring")

By 1887 Tennyson could look back with some equanimity. But it was not "mere want of gold" alone which now obstructed the marriage. For one thing, it later became clear that Emily was gravely anxious about Tennyson's religious beliefs. For another, she and her father could not but doubt whether it was wise to marry into the Tennyson family. For the marriage of Tennyson's brother to her sister was in pieces by 1839; Charles had relapsed into his earlier bondage to opium, Louisa's health had broken down, and she had now separated from him. The sufferings of Mrs. Tennyson in 1829 were being reenacted by the next generation's Mrs. Tennyson (married to a Tennyson in holy orders) in 1839.

Tennyson himself had come to feel fearful and unworthy of his engagement to Emily. ("I bless thee who am not worthy to bless thee, for I know thy worth.") His son was to say baldly: "After this date all correspondence between Alfred Tennyson and Emily Sellwood was forbidden; since there seemed to be no prospect of their ever being married"—because of money. Tennyson will have had distressing memories of Arthur Hallam's thwarted engagement to his Emily—thwarted by lack of money, and obstructed by the decision of the girl's father to forbid correspondence between the lovers.

But though it was Henry Sellwood who forbad any correspondence, it was the lovers—indeed, it was Alfred—who broke off the engagement. " 'Tis true, I fly thee for my good, perhaps for thine, at any rate for thine if mine is thine. If thou knewest why I fly thee there is nothing thou wouldst more wish for than that I should fly thee." His brother Charles, whose example had been both creative and destructive, was to report that their love "continued unshaken, and that but for an overstrained, morbid scrupulousness as to what was conceived to be duty, they might have been contented to wait (an engaged couple) and so both might have been spared much suffering." In "Love and Duty" (1840, published 1842) Tennyson tried to blend the bitter moment and his distant optimism. The poem somberly accepts that even madness ("The set gray life, and apathetic end") would be better than the knowledge that love can fail, and it sees the lovers' parting as a suicide-pact:

> O then like those, who clench their nerves to rush
> Upon their dissolution, we two rose...

It ends with a dawn-scene which was to dawn for him—but not till 1850.

> ... till thou wake refreshed
> Then when the first low matin-chirp hath grown
> Full quire, and morning driven her plow of pearl
> Far furrowing into light the mounded rack,
> Beyond the fair green field and eastern sea.

The years 1838 to 1840 saw great pressure on Tennyson to

publish a volume. He had thought of doing so in the spring of 1834; since then, his friends had inveigled him into publishing two short poems, "St. Agnes" (1836) and "Oh! that 'twere possible" (1837). They now tripled their efforts. In March 1838 one Cambridge friend, Trench, wrote to another, Milnes: "Do you ever see Tennyson? and if so, could you not urge him to take the field?" Milnes believed that "Tennyson composes every day, but nothing will persuade him to print, or even write it down." Another Cambridge friend, G. S. Venables, wrote with urgent shrewdness:

Do not continue to be so careless of fame and of influence. You have abundant materials ready for a new publication, and you start as a well-known man with the certainty that you can not be overlooked and that by many you will be appreciated. If you do not publish now when will you publish? If you do not ever publish do not you think you will have even that which you have published taken out of its napkin and given to him who has published ten volumes?

In 1839, FitzGerald—who was to play the part in the publication of the 1842 volumes that Arthur Hallam had played ten years earlier—deplored the situation: "I want A.T. to publish another volume: as all his friends do . . . but he is too lazy and wayward to put his hand to the business—He has got fine things in a large Butcher's Account Book that now lies in my room."

Wayward, perhaps; but lazy, no. For Tennyson's reluctance went deeper than that. His dismay and disillusionment at the prospect of publication (even though he had written some of his most successfully serene poems in 1838 and 1839) are manifest in a fragmentary poem of 1839 which he never published. His hatred for biographical prying* and for the literary world is

* Notable among the many poems which rebuke biographical intrusion are "To—, After Reading a Life and Letters," and "The Dead Prophet." Tennyson said some swingeing things, of which the best was reported, with some irony, by Henry Taylor (*Autobiography*, 1885, ii. 193): "He was very violent with the girls on the subject of the rage for autographs. He said he believed every crime and every vice in the world were connected with the passion for autographs and anecdotes and records, —that the desiring anecdotes and acquaintance with the lives of great men was treating them like pigs to be ripped open for the public; that he knew he himself should be

heard in these bitter unfinished cogitations which constitute one of the most directly personal poems that Tennyson ever wrote:

Wherefore, in these dark ages of the Press
(As that old Teuton christened them) should I,
Sane mind and body, wish to print my rhyme,
Fame's millionth heir-apparent? why desire
(If like a man that hath his sense compact
I write a clean fair hand) the public thumb
Of our good pamphlet-pampered age to fret
And sweat upon mine honest thoughts in type,
The children of the silence? I today
Lord of myself and of my ways, the next
A popular property, nauseate, when my name
Shot like a racketball from mouth to mouth
And bandied in the barren lips of fools
May yield my feeling organism pain
Thrice keener than delight from duest praise?
   And if I be, as truecast Poets are,
Half woman-natured, typing all mankind;
So must I triple-man myself and case
My humours as the caddisworm in stone,
Or doing violence to my modest worth
With one long-lasting hope chain-cable-strong
Self-fixt, immoor in patience, till I die.
   Am I so hopeful—(now I take my glass,
Walk in and out and laugh or sulk at ease)
So strong, that I should lay the nerve of self

---

ripped open like a pig; that he thanked God Almighty with his whole heart and soul that he knew nothing, and that the world knew nothing, of Shakespeare but his writings; and that he thanked God Almighty that he knew nothing of Jane Austen, and that there were no letters preserved either of Shakespeare's or of Jane Austen's, that they had not been ripped open like pigs. Then he said that the post for two days had brought *him* no letters, and that he thought there was a sort of syncope in the world as to him and to his fame." It is to the point that Tennyson's two most famous growls (as to Bessie Langton's tittle-tattle about Dr. Johnson; and a proposal to "raise an altar" to the old lady, shocked by Froude on Carlyle, who burned her letters from the great men of her time) are both explicitly connected with his deploring any gossip about Arthur Hallam (*Memoir* i.202, i.184, ii.301, where the *Memoir* omits remarks about Hallam which survive in Lincoln notes and in the relevant letter).

Bare to the slurs of shallow cleverness,
The blame of stumblingblocks that trip the good,
The wordy misapplauses of the weak,
The careless misconception of the strong
Too grievous to be borne? for who could brook,
What flesh and blood—but for a doubt—to be
So bellowsblown with puffs of heated friends,
So hustled, and so clapt upon the back,
So plastered with the gossip and the slang—
Or that his warmth should shine upon the world
But to bring out its vermin? who endure
To breed that human sorrow to himself,
That he should reverence mighty minds the less
For those mean jealousies in mighty minds—
Bats in the sunlight. Oh my friend be wise,
My fame, if just, is a peculiar fame,
And cannot butt for masterdom with thine,
And be that pith within me, which should last,
Thy dictum could not quash it: be there not,
The God of truth forbid my life should run
Yoked with a hackneyed thought and curbed with shame
Until the scandal of my leanness turn
To bywords with the market and the muse.
   And if I win no praise the want is mine,
And if I win false praise the shame is mine;
The grain of reputation which accrues
Will rot into the sapless blade, that bears
No ear but loathing: when my sense of Art,
From shame of contrast, gathers triple strength
And clear as conscience to the moral man
Points where I fail and works me bitterness.
What this Art-Conscience preaches I to that
Lend credit, not to him or him and least
The general throat. All ages, sample-rife,
Have preacht a truism, that nine-tithes of times
Too rathe a harvest of the public voice
Foregoes the latter Lammas of a name.
Should I be pleased then, though my verse should head
Some chapter in the three-tomed prodigies
Of half a June? or tickled, though my name
On paper drafts of notoriety

Betwixt this sabbath and the next, should float
With rumour, current from the chalky spikes [. . .]

It was something more profound than laziness, then, that Fitz-Gerald and his friends had to overcome. Tennyson's pitiable insecurity is evident from a letter by James Spedding to the editor of the *Edinburgh Review* in February 1840:

His bookseller as well as his friends are urgent with him to publish another edition of the old ones [now out of print], and a volume of new—but from some doubt as to the value or the probable reception of them he will not be persuaded. He would be willing, however, to publish, *if I could undertake to review him.*

4. *Poems 1837–1840*

"LOCKSLEY HALL" was Tennyson's first attempt to face as a poet some of the most painful of his experiences. It was also the first of his poems to manifest a stridency. (This was to evolve into something less histrionic and more resonantly grating in *Maud*.) The poem was written in 1837–38, its effort being to shape Tennyson's disillusionment with Rosa Baring and his contempt for the moneyed snobbery of the Tennyson d'Eyncourts into an art independent of the merely personal. Effort, though, is too patent. Tennyson, as so often, was to insist that it was "an imaginary place and imaginary hero": "The whole poem represents young life, its good side, its deficiencies, and its yearnings." But the poem makes it specially (and perhaps not accidentally) difficult to tell which of the speaker's outbursts are offered as a fierce freedom from hypocrisy and which are self-indulgent or deranged. The speaker lashes out, and then lashes out at himself—but is the latter supposed to cancel the former? The dramatic monologue in this midway flux has neither the mysterious alienness of the monologue at its purest ("Tithonus," or Browning's "My Last Duchess"), nor the controlling specificity of drama. A form particularly well suited to the exploration of evasion also lends itself particularly to evasion. There is no way of interpreting the speaker's self-contempt: "Well—'tis well that I should bluster!" or "Fool, again the dream, the fancy! but I *know* my words are wild." But such knowing can be indiscriminate.

Venturing as he was on these painful privacies, Tennyson was the more determined to be secretive; the ceaseless clang of judgments being passed in the poem is to smother the central silence, the fear of judgment, at the heart of the poem. Moreover, Tennyson had deliberately excluded the truly painful experience which fed his distaste for Bayons Manor and so for Locksley Hall: his father. The speaker has the unlucky luck that his father fell in battle in India—"I was left a trampled orphan, and a selfish uncle's ward." (He never knew his mother either.) This is both too close to, and too free with, his own experiences (the selfish uncle) for him to control it. The result is that a reader feels that R. H. Hutton had a point in speaking of "the smarting and not very deeply wounded heart of a grandiose and somewhat bumptious lover," and likewise G. W. Foote in finding the hero "a selfish cad who poses through every line of faultless eloquence, until at last we suspect that 'cousin Amy' has not met the worst fate which could befall her." Whitman saw a "finding fault with everything." But what Hutton and Foote and Whitman find is manifestly what Tennyson proffered for the finding.

Hopkins's friend R. W. Dixon was to say of the versification: "It had the effect of being artificial and *light:* most unfit for intense passion, of which indeed there is nothing in it, but only a man making an unpleasant and rather ungentlemanly row." The artificiality and lightness—we might compare a line like "In the Spring a young man's fancy lightly turns to thoughts of love," with *Maud*'s "And dream of her beauty with tender dread"—is a consequence of the poem's blustering timidity. Suicide dwindles to a lovers' fantasy ("Rolled in one another's arms, and silent in a last embrace") or to an understatement: "I had been content to perish, falling on the foeman's ground," where the thinness of the imagined battle is a mere yearning for moral certainties, and where "I had been content" is a euphemism for "I yearned." But the most revealing evasion concerns childhood and youth, and it is signaled—as so often, since Tennyson was betrayingly honest—by ambiguities of wording. The speaker looks back upon his "youth sublime": "When I clung to all the present for the promise that it closed." *Enclosed*, of course—but "ended" presses in, perfectly against the grain of the official sentiment. Or see how the superb simile, at once excited and uneasy (itself "like a dreary dawn"), disrupts and shrivels the affirmations, past and future:

> Yearning for the large excitement that the coming years
> would yield,
> Eager-hearted as a boy when first he leaves his father's field,
>
> And at night along the dusky highway near and nearer drawn,
> Sees in heaven the light of London flaring like a dreary dawn;
>
> And his spirit leaps within him to be gone before him then,
> Underneath the light he looks at, in among the throngs of men:
>
> Men, my brothers, men the workers, ever reaping something
> new . . .

For action is the only savior ("I myself must mix with action, lest I wither by despair"*), and yet the poem cannot imagine what form such action could take: "What is that which I should do?" Hence the vigorous vacuity with which the poem ends:

> Let it fall on Locksley Hall, with rain or hail, or fire or snow;
> For the mighty wind arises, roaring seaward, and I go.

Go? Where, and to what? And to say, "To join his comrades who have sounded their horn," would be to succumb to the poem's thinnest pretense. Waiting for a lover to come, or for a leader to assert his authority, or for death: these Tennyson can imagine and render into art. But waiting for one's own decision is something which he cannot. "Locksley Hall" itself is unable to mix with action, and it withers by despair.

Tennyson in these years was to achieve more in the less torrid mode of some poems which he grouped in the "English Idyls." Of these, "Walking to the Mail" is the slightest; its charm is genuine, but insufficient in the face of its concerns, which are rather too evidently made light of: the impossibility of escaping from one's poltergeist, and the fear of bloody revolution. The nub of the poem is a state of mind which it then gracefully flinches from

* The wording—"I myself must mix with action"—is worm-eaten with inaction; whatever it may be to mix with action, it is less decisive than "I myself must act."

exploring (and which, cunningly, it would not have been apt to chat much about while "Walking to the Mail"):

> Vexed with a morbid devil in his blood . . .
> He lost the sense that handles daily life–
> That keeps us all in order more or less– . . .

The serenity of "Audley Court," "Edwin Morris," and "The Golden Year" (1838 and 1839) reflects the mood of these two years when Tennyson and Emily not only loved but were recognized as engaged. "Audley Court," with its affectionate banter, does much to contradict FitzGerald's stern warning about Tennyson's sternness:

> Alfred, whatever he may think, cannot trifle–many are the disputes we have had about his powers of badinage, compliment, waltzing, etc. His smile is rather a grim one.

For "Audley Court" Tennyson recollected a pastoral tradition, the song-contest, which could both give free play to, and good-naturedly control, his deep need always to express a counterview. Francis sings a tenderly cynical song, altogether without bitterness; the narrator replies with a lovesong that is "The pilot of the darkness and the dream." But it is Francis's that tells most, both as a poem and as a document; its manner is one that Tennyson was seldom to command, and its freedom from anything like morbidity argues a deep, though temporary, release:

> "Oh! who would fight and march and countermarch,
> Be shot for sixpence in a battle-field,
> And shovelled up into some bloody trench
> Where no one knows? but let me live my life.
> "Oh! who would cast and balance at a desk,
> Perched like a crow upon a three-legged stool,
> Till all his juice is dried, and all his joints
> Are full of chalk? but let me live my life.
> "Who'd serve the state? for if I carved my name
> Upon the cliffs that guard my native land,
> I might as well have traced it in the sands;
> The sea wastes all: but let me live my life.
> "Oh! who would love? I wooed a woman once,
> But she was sharper than an eastern wind,

And all my heart turned from her, as a thorn
Turns from the sea; but let me live my life."

"Let me live my life": in these years it seemed to Tennyson that such might indeed be going to happen. So strong is the confidence within the poem that the narrator can even imagine himself as somebody with money and with "fallow leisure." The last sentence of the poem unwinds with tranquil dignity through sixteen lines, ending with an end that is—perhaps for the first time in Tennyson—not a curtailment or an expectation but a fully contented pause:

So sang we each to either, Francis Hale,
The farmer's son, who lived across the bay,
My friend; and I, that having wherewithal,
And in the fallow leisure of my life
A rolling stone of here and everywhere,
Did what I would; but ere the night we rose
And sauntered home beneath a moon, that, just
In crescent, dimly rained about the leaf
Twilights of airy silver, till we reached
The limit of the hills; and as we sank
From rock to rock upon the glooming quay,
The town was hushed beneath us: lower down
The bay was oily calm; the harbour-buoy,
Sole star of phosphorescence in the calm,
With one green sparkle ever and anon
Dipt by itself, and we were glad at heart.

In "Edwin Morris," Tennyson did more than exorcise Rosa Baring, he forgave her. (His love for Emily made this possible.) The speaker remembers his rambles by the lake with the poet Edwin Morris and the curate Edward Bull, and how they used to talk about love. The speaker's own love affair with Letty Hill came to nothing—he simply was not rich enough.

She went—and in one month
They wedded her to sixty thousand pounds,
To lands in Kent and messuages in York,
And slight Sir Robert with his watery smile
And educated whisker.

Tennyson here did not so much indict as deprecate "The rentroll Cupid of our rainy isles," and he hit precisely the right note, neither soft nor bitter. In the perfect conclusion of the poem, unwinding once more through one sentence, it is the word "smoulders" which does full justice to the fact that there had indeed been resentment and which also draws together the landscape and the erotic memory. And yet the poem can end firmly, not with the cloud but with the crag—an enduring strength which yet is delicately tempered by the epithet "summer":

> Nor cared to hear? perhaps: yet long ago
> I have pardoned little Letty; not indeed,
> It may be, for her own dear sake but this,
> She seems a part of those fresh days to me;
> For in the dust and drouth of London life
> She moves among my visions of the lake,
> While the prime swallow dips his wing, or then
> While the gold-lily blows, and overhead
> The light cloud smoulders on the summer crag.

Elsewhere in the poem, in the character of Edwin Morris the poet, Tennyson wrote one of his most lucid and attractive pieces of self-criticism; he stood back from his own "Parnassian"* mannerisms, and treated them with ironical affection. Into the mouth of Edwin, Tennyson puts the words of early Tennyson, self-borrowing but with self-criticism. He did not just make up lines of plangent self-indulgence (they might have become too much like parodies), he quoted his young self.

> And once I asked him of his early life,
> And his first passion; and he answered me;
> And well his words became him: was he not
> A full-celled honeycomb of eloquence
> Stored from all flowers? Poet-like he spoke.

We should not miss the irony in "poet-like" and "well his words became him"; and the self-regarding simile ("a full-celled honeycomb of eloquence / Stored from all flowers") was an indulgence which Tennyson had permitted himself in an early draft of "The Gardener's Daughter."

* See p. 279.

Then Edwin speaks; of these ten lines, all but two are from the manuscripts of "The Gardener's Daughter," so that if we feel the effect is sonorously Tennysonian, Tennyson would have agreed:

> "My love for Nature and my love for her,
> Of different ages, like twin-sisters grew,
> [Twin-sisters differently beautiful.
> To some full music rose and sank the sun,]
> And some full music seemed to move and change
> With all the varied changes of the dark,
> And either twilight and the day between;
> For daily hope fulfilled, to rise again
> Revolving toward fulfilment, made it sweet
> To walk, to sit, to sleep, to wake, to breathe."

As Parnassian verse (lovely, incidentally, in its feeling for time), this is exquisite. But by this date Tennyson was dissatisfied with the Parnassian.

For Edwin's second speech, too, Tennyson found no need to create plangencies; once again he culled them from drafts of "The Gardener's Daughter." So here too is self-quotation:

> "I would have hid her needle in my heart,
> To save her little finger from a scratch
> No deeper than the skin: my ears could hear
> Her lightest breath; her least remark was worth
> The experience of the wise. I went and came;
> Her voice fled always through the summer land;
> I spoke her name alone."

But the poet Edwin was not allowed to rest satisfied; in a remarkable passage of self-criticism, the speaker bridles at the mannerisms:

> Were not his words delicious, I a beast
> To take them as I did? but something jarred;
> Whether he spoke too largely; that there seemed
> A touch of something false, some self-conceit,
> Or over-smoothness: howsoe'er it was,
> He scarcely hit my humour, and I said:
> "Friend Edwin, do not think yourself alone
> Of all men happy . . ."

The poem "Edwin Morris" is one of Tennyson's best on the power of time (seen here by him confidently, not tragically); it is also a poem which has at its heart his perennial habit of self-quotation, used here with a different kind of awareness and with humor.

"The Golden Year" is another poem that has enough serenity to engage in a self-criticism that is not self-contempt:

> for I bantered him, and swore
> They said he lived shut up within himself,
> A tongue-tied Poet in the feverous days . . .

Once again, Tennyson lets two voices have their say. Leonard, the poet within the poem, has his song of sober prophetic pleasure:

> "We sleep and wake and sleep, but all things move;
> The Sun flies forward to his brother Sun;
> The dark Earth follows wheeled in her ellipse;
> And human things returning on themselves
> Move onward, leading up the golden year."

But within this poem the other voice is not to be a song: James, the gruff Carlylean figure, says his say—and is then, in the moment of the poem's ending, corroborated by the outside world:

> ". . . but well I know
> That unto him who works, and feels he works,
> This same grand year is ever at the doors."
>
> He spoke; and, high above, I heard them blast
> The steep slate-quarry, and the great echo flap
> And buffet round the hills, from bluff to bluff.

It is a consummate ending, a consummation of the poem. "I heard them": *them* is perfectly chosen, the unknown men who unbeknownst are at work while Leonard and James talk about work and prosperity. The echoic vignette is more than just a skill of linguistic mimicry, with "blast" broadening and loosening into "flap" and then into "buffet," and with "buffet" echoing into "bluff to bluff" ("blast"–"buffet"–"bluff"). More than just mimicry, because it brings together modern man and the ancient slate; because it presents, without any prior warning, an activity nearby that is oblivious but impinging; and because it is an emblem of destructive force that is nevertheless controlled, a beneficent explosion. "The Golden Year," like "Audley Court" and "Edwin Morris," and unlike "Locksley Hall," can contemplate a rewarding conclusion.

"The Vision of Sin" is an uneasy mixture, the unease being in the poem and not just in the reader. Much of it is too overtly allegorical—Tennyson sometimes lapsed into allegory which is then disconcertingly unmysterious (a bad misjudgment in a poet most urged by a sense of mystery), too openly proffering itself for translation:

He rode a horse with wings, that would have flown,
But that his heavy rider kept him down.

Tennyson's comment on the poem inadvertently suggests such a diagram.

This describes the soul of a youth who has given himself up to pleasure and Epicureanism. He at length is worn out and wrapt in the mists of satiety. Afterwards he grows into a cynical old man afflicted with the "curse of nature," and joining in the Feast of Death. Then we see the landscape which symbolizes God, Law and the future life.

The first section ("the soul of a youth") is too composed, and the second ("pleasure and Epicureanism") simply shows that the clergyman's son, quite properly, could not imagine an orgy, especially a psychedelic one ("Purple gauzes, golden hazes, liquid mazes"). But with the third section, "the mists of satiety," something more mysterious—more insidiously misty—detaches, fold by fold:

And then I looked up toward a mountain-tract,
That girt the region with high cliff and lawn:
I saw that every morning, far withdrawn
Beyond the darkness and the cataract,
God made Himself an awful rose of dawn,
Unheeded: and detaching, fold by fold,
From those still heights, and, slowly drawing near,
A vapour heavy, hueless, formless, cold,

Came floating on for many a month and year,
Unheeded: and I thought I would have spoken,
And warned that madman ere it grew too late:
But as in dreams, I could not. Mine was broken,
When that cold vapour touched the palace gate,
And linked again. I saw within my head
A gray and gap-toothed man as lean as death,
Who slowly rode across a withered heath,
And lighted at a ruined inn, and said:

What he said forms the fourth section. Its general reflections, whether political, religious or moral, express a shallow cynicism which cannot be artistically exculpated by saying that they dramatically represent the shallowness of cynicism. For in his personal spurts, the sinner is altogether more penetrating and lacerating. E. D. H. Johnson has said that "the old rake's song in section four is a masterpiece of grotesque and mordant humour of a kind infrequently met in Victorian poetry and almost never in Tennyson's subsequent work." For "almost never," one might say "too seldom"—and for "a masterpiece," perhaps "intermittently a masterpiece." The sinner is phosphorescently alive when his fierce monologue envisages an audience, and is not generalized reflection; alive, therefore, in hailing those at the inn: "Wrinkled ostler, grim and thin!," "Bitter barmaid, waning fast!," "Slipshod waiter, lank and sour." Alive, too, at the dance of death, since the skeletons are there to be treated with a contempt which speaks much of nakedness but itself half-masks fear:

Death is king, and Vivat Rex!
  Tread a measure on the stones,
Madam—if I know your sex
  From the fashion of your bones . . .

Lo! God's likeness—the ground-plan—
  Neither modelled, glazed, nor framed:
Buss me, thou rough sketch of man,
  Far too naked to be shamed!

Yet it is the final section which goes deepest, which justifies Tennyson's own predilection for the poem, and which rebukes James Thomson ("B.V.") as inordinate when he drafted "A

Real Vision of Sin," "in disgust at Tennyson's which is very pretty and clever and silly and truthless." Pretty?

> The voice grew faint: there came a further change:
> Once more uprose the mystic mountain-range:
> Below were men and horses pierced with worms,
> And slowly quickening into lower forms;
> By shards and scurf of salt, and scum of dross,
> Old plash of rains, and refuse patched with moss.

The vision is indeed controlled, but it is a hideous glimpse of a perverted evolution that runs backward, the paradox bitterly trapped in "slowly quickening" (Tennyson had originally put "festering"). The end to such a vision is a question, not an answer; or rather, the answer is itself newly disconcerting.

> At last I heard a voice upon the slope
> Cry to the summit, "Is there any hope?"
> To which an answer pealed from that high land,
> But in a tongue no man could understand;
> And on the glimmering limit far withdrawn
> God made Himself an awful rose of dawn.

The limit of the poem glimmers and is far withdrawn. God creates beauty out of Himself and for Himself ("God made Himself an awful rose" is an awed ambiguity). The poem ends with dawn. But it is not for a religious poem to hope presumptuously for anything that might be called "so quick, so clean an ending"; the outcome of such a poem as this is not in the creator's but in the Creator's hands. Dawn dawns at the end, but—as often in Tennyson—it is not exactly dayspring. ". . . Sees in heaven the light of London flaring like a dreary dawn" ("Locksley Hall").

> And ghastly through the drizzling rain
> On the bald street breaks the blank day.
>
> (*In Memoriam*, VII)

It was A. C. Bradley who remarked with subtle acumen that, in *In Memoriam*, LXXII ("Risest thou thus, dim dawn, again"), the word *day* finds its impulse reversed: "The word is repeated throughout the poem almost as if it were a term of reproach."

5. 1840–1847

TENNYSON PUBLISHED no volume of poems between December 1832 and May 1842, and much has often been made of "the ten years' silence." But although there was indeed some important failure of nerve and some morbidity in his reluctance to publish, the years from 1833 to 1840 had been richly creative. He had written a great deal, including some of his finest poems–sections of *In Memoriam*, and "Ulysses," "Tithon," "Tiresias," "Morte d'Arthur," "Oh! that 'twere possible," "Break, break, break," "Locksley Hall," "Edwin Morris." The ten years' silence, then, had its secretly profound consolations and achievements–Tennyson knew he was biding his time. The years from 1840 to 1845 constitute the most wretched phase of his life: he knew he was losing his time. With the possible (but unlikely) exception of two small poems, all the poems published in the 1842 volumes had been written by 1840. In 1845 Tennyson was to set seriously to work upon *The Princess*, to be published in 1847. Between 1840 and 1845, he probably wrote some further sections–though not all that many–for *In Memoriam*. Otherwise, nothing.

The sequence which led to the publication of *Poems* (1842) should first be separately traced, though it involves sidling ahead. Tennyson was to put the matter bluntly in conversation with William Allingham: "I hate publishing! The Americans forced me into it again. I had my things nice and right, but when I found they were going to publish the old forms I said, By Jove, that won't do!" Tennyson had received a letter in 1838 from C. C. Little and Co. (Boston), saying they intended to reprint his volumes of 1830 and 1832. Nothing came of this, perhaps because of protests from Tennyson. But by 1841 the American threat had surfaced again; Tennyson wrote to the importunate FitzGerald:

You bore me about my book; so does a letter just received from America, threatening, though in the civilest terms, that, if I will not publish in England, they will do it for me in that land of freemen. Damn! I *may* curse, knowing what they will bring forth. But I don't care.

Nevertheless he did care. To the publisher C. S. Wheeler (of Little, Brown), after remarking "What a high privilege it is for a writer to be born into a language common to two great peoples," Tennyson wrote:

I am conscious of many things so exceedingly crude in those two volumes that it would certainly be productive of no slight annoyance to me, to see them republisht as they stand at present, either here or in America. But I will tell you what I will do, for when I was wavering before, your letter has decided me. I have corrected copies of most that was worth correction in those two volumes and I will in the course of a few months republish these in England with several new poems and transmit copies to Little & Brown and also to yourself (if you will accept one) and you can then of course do as you choose with them.

That was in February 1841. In October, Tennyson was reported as preparing for publication. By March 1842, FitzGerald felt obliged to act; "I carried him off to the auction: and then with violence to Moxon: who is to call on him to-morrow, and settle the publishing of a new volume." Two weeks later:

Poor Tennyson has got home some of his proof sheets: and, now that his verses are in hard print, thinks them detestable–There is much I had always told him of–his great fault of being too full and complicated–which he now sees, or fancies he sees, and wishes he had never been persuaded to print. But with all his faults, he will publish such a volume as has not been published since the time of Keats: and which, once published, will never be suffered to die. This is my prophecy: for I live before Posterity.

FitzGerald was perceptive about those faults which Tennyson condoned when reprinting:

It is a pity he did not publish the new volume separately. The other will drag it down. And why reprint the Merman, the Mermaid, and those everlasting Eleanores, Isabels,—which always were, and are, and must be, a nuisance, though Mrs. Butler (who recognised herself in the portrait, of course) said that Eleanore (what a bore) was the finest thing he ever wrote. She has sat for it ever since, I believe. Every woman thinks herself the original of one of that stupid Gallery of Beauties.

Not that Tennyson was undiscriminating. *Poems, Chiefly Lyrical* had included twenty-three poems which Tennyson did not subsequently reprint, as well as seven poems which were not reprinted in 1842 but were later. Likewise, *Poems* (1832) had included seven poems never to be reprinted, as well as seven not reprinted in 1842. The first of the two 1842 volumes, then, was a careful selection (and on the whole a very perceptive one) from the earlier books; moreover Tennyson had creatively revised the texts (most notably, of "The Lady of Shalott," "Mariana in the South," "Œnone," "The Palace of Art," and "The Lotos-Eaters"). The second volume consisted of newly published poems, all of the very important work written between 1833 and 1840 with three exceptions: sections of *In Memoriam* (not completed till 1850), "Oh! that 'twere possible" (published in 1837 but not reprinted till it formed part of *Maud* in 1855), and "Tithonus" (written in 1833–34, revised and published in 1860).

As FitzGerald prophesied, the 1842 volumes established Tennyson as the foremost poet of his generation, that which succeeded Keats, Shelley, and Byron. But to Tennyson in 1842 the publication was mostly an occasion for glumness; he wrote to FitzGerald:

Don't abuse my book. You can't hate it worse than I do, but it does me no good to hear it abused; if it is bad you and others are to blame who continually urged me to publish. Not for my sake but for yours did I consent to submit my papers to the herd, damn 'em, and all reproach comes too late.

The years from 1840 to 1845 were barren for Tennyson, but his sufferings did not center in poetry; rather, in his loss of Emily, his financial nightmares, his ill-health and melancholia. Yet in his earlier sufferings he had never lost his creative impulse; indeed the death of Hallam had precipitated an extraordinary creative moment. Now not only could he not write, his not writing became for him a further anguish not ameliorated by the fact that at this period when he could hardly create he could publish instead.

In February 1840, Edward FitzGerald saw him:

When I got to my lodgings, I found A. Tennyson installed in them: he has been here ever since in a very uneasy state: being really ill, in a nervous way: what with an hereditary tenderness of nerve, and having spoiled what strength he had by incessant smoking &c. —I have also made him very out of sorts by desiring a truce from complaints and complainings—Poor fellow: he is quite magnanimous, and noble natured, with no meanness or vanity or affectation of any kind whatever —but very perverse, according to the nature of his illness.

"Poor fellow": the very words which had been applied to Tennyson's brother Edward as he drifted toward madness.

Madness in fact precipitated the next catastrophe in Tennyson's life. In 1840 he got to know Dr. Matthew Allen, who ran an asylum near High Beech. A friend reported the news of Tennyson: "He has been on a visit to a madhouse for the last fortnight (not as a patient), and has been delighted with the mad people, whom he reports the most agreeable and the most reasonable persons he has met with." Unfortunately Dr. Allen had a bright idea: wood-carving by machinery. "This philanthropic undertaking . . . oak panels and oak furniture carved by machinery, thus brought by its cheapness within the reach of the multitude": a service to the community (the name "Pyroglyph" was toyed with), it would also constitute a service to those prepared to invest in it.

Tennyson had his grandfather's bequest and also one of £500 from Arthur Hallam's aunt. This sum of £3,000 had not been enough to win the hand of Emily Sellwood. Half desperate and wholly credulous, he entrusted it to Dr. Allen. The other Tennysons, too, liked the idea—and Dr. Allen especially liked the idea of inveigling the richest of the brothers, Frederick. Then in 1841 Dr. Allen was himself duped by an agent, and the undertaking took on an increasingly hectic air. Dr. Allen fired off a series of letters to Frederick, trying in vain to cajole him out of his three or four thousand pounds ("I have others with money ready—but" etc.), and hugely promising: "Yesterday it was the decided opinion of my Bankers and Solicitors that in twelve months your share would be worth Ten thousand Pounds, and that in five years it ought to give you that yearly."

But in less than twelve months the crash was looming. Tennyson in September 1842 could report that his newly published *Poems* had made a sensation—"I wish the wood-works would make a sensation! I expect they will"—but by the end of the letter his expectations sounded less than great: "What with ruin in the distance and hypochondriacs in the foreground I feel very crazy. God help all."

Hypochondriacs? One of the Tennysons was certainly hypped. Once again a Tennyson son was re-living Dr. Tennyson's pains. By March 1843, Arthur's drinking and debts had become such as to force his mother to tell the news to Charles Tennyson d'Eyncourt: "Arthur has voluntarily placed himself (to conquer the ruinous and destructive habit of drinking) in the Crichton, an institution nobly endowed for the insane and others who like to place themselves there in order to conquer any evil propensity." Drinking—Dr. Tennyson; the insane Edward Tennyson: the omens were not good. Later that year, Arthur went abroad with Frederick. "God help all."

But by 1843 ruin was no longer in the distance. The scheme had collapsed, and Tennyson's money was gone. Poor Dr. Allen was hysterically broken, flinging himself on Frederick's unforthcoming mercy: "I have done all that is possible for man to do to save your family, and I have *utterly ruined myself* in the attempt . . . Every stick and stave is to be sold to pay A. T. *this day*—and yet people boast! I ail! and I suffer! and I die!—*Come up!*—you must save something." And Tennyson?

> So severe a hypochondria set in upon him that his friends despaired of his life. "I have," he writes, "drunk one of those most bitter draughts out of the cup of life, which go near to make men hate the world they move in."

These two years had also seen a surprise at once saddening and heartening. Tennyson's sister Emily, after eight years of quasi-widowed fidelity to Arthur Hallam, became engaged in the autumn of 1841 to Richard Jesse, and married him in 1842. Jane Elton (a cousin of Hallam's) was moved to virulent indignation, on Julia Hallam's behalf and on Henry Hallam's: "I feel so distressed about this, really it quite *hurts* me, I had such a romantic admiration for her, looked at her with such pity, and now all my feeling about her is bouleversĕd—and Alfred Tennyson falls headlong into the abyss with her—but I cannot think he would like her to marry." And the annuity of £300 from Henry Hallam? "The Tennyson's are reckoned *proud*, and I suppose Emily felt twinges in having to say 'I must leave it, of course, entirely to you whether or not you continue the annuity you have so generously allowed me.' " Henry Hallam did the gentlemanly thing. Alfred Tennyson, one supposes, was also distressed—it is unlikely that he would have wished Emily to marry. Possibly her marriage may have been one of the factors which delayed the publication of *In Memoriam* for another eight years; some of the moments in which the poem presented Hallam's Emily may have seemed too vulnerable to coarse ridicule in the immediate wake of her marrying—or "marrying again (it is just the same thing as marrying again)," in the fierce words of Jane Elton. But Tennyson preserved, it seems, an honorable silence. He had suffered a great deal in three years.

In December 1843, FitzGerald reported of Tennyson that he had "never seen him so hopeless." The hopelessness can be heard in a letter (February 2, 1844) which Tennyson wrote to FitzGerald from Cheltenham, where his father and his sister Emily had each sought health and peace of mind (was there no end to these rending reenactments?):

It is very kind of you to think of such a poor forlorn body as myself. The perpetual panic and horror of the last two years had steeped my nerves in poison: now I am left a beggar but I am or shall be shortly somewhat better off in nerves. I am in an Hydropathy Establishment near Cheltenham (the only one in England conducted on pure Priessnitzan principles). I have had four crisises (one larger than had been seen for two or three years in Gräfenberg—indeed I believe the largest but one that has been seen). Much poison has come out of me, which no physic ever would have brought to light. Albert Priessnitz (the nephew of the great man) officiates at this establishment, and very quick and clever he is and he gives me hopes of a cure in March: I have been here already upwards of two months: of all the uncomfortable ways of living sure an hydropathical is the worst: no reading by candlelight, no going near a fire, no tea, no coffee, perpetual wet sheet and cold bath and alternation from hot to cold: however I have much faith in it—

My dear Fitz, my nerves were so bad six weeks ago that I could not have written this and to have to write a letter on that accursed business threw me into a kind of convulsion. I went through Hell. Thank you for enquiring after me. I am such a poor devil now I am afraid I shall very rarely see you. No more trips to London and living in lodgings, hard penury and battle with my lot . . . You are the only one of my friends who has asked after me and I really feel obliged to you.

At such a time, it is not surprising that Tennyson refused to contribute to Mrs. Anna Maria Hall's magazine; it is perhaps surprising that he was so frank: "I am at present in such a deranged state of health that my medical man forbids the excitement of composition, forbids me to read, even to think." A cure was effected, but it proved temporary; by August 1844 Elizabeth Barrett was reporting that Tennyson "has since relapsed, and been very unwell indeed."

Yet a shrewd act of kindness was to do much for Tennyson. His friend Edmund Lushington had married Tennyson's sister Cecilia in 1842; Lushington now had the excellent idea of insuring Dr. Allen's life in Tennyson's favor. By December 1844, Tennyson's sister Cecilia was speaking darkly in a way that might have attracted the attention of the police:

Old Allen still lives—it is a sad thing one is obliged to wish for the death of any man—I suppose thou knowest that Alfred will get most of his money back when that desirable event takes place—to secure this Edmund pays some eighty pounds a year for him.

Next month, Dr. Allen died. A stroke. A stroke of good fortune.

FitzGerald was pleased and fanciful after a visit from Tennyson:

Last night he came: looking much better: but a valetudinarian almost: —not in the effeminate way; but yet in as bad a man's way. Alas for it,

> that great thoughts are to be lapped in such weakness—Dr. Allen, who had half swindled his money, is dead: and A. T. having a Life insurance, and Policy, on him, will now, I hope, retrieve the greater part of his fortune again. Apollo certainly did this: shooting one of his swift arrows at the heart of the Doctor; whose perfectly heartless conduct certainly upset A. T.'s nerves in the first instance.

Carlyle more sombrely reported that Tennyson, "the fiery Son of Gloom," would now get £2,000 back—"I wish he would straightway buy himself an annuity with it."

It was a long time before Tennyson came to forgive Dr. Allen. Dying earned him some forgiveness, and the insurance inadvertently earned him some more. But it is doubtful if Tennyson ever forgave Dr. Allen for being both wildly untrustworthy and the devout author of *On the Temper and Spirit of the Christian Religion* (1820; second edition as *On the Graces of the Christian Character . . . and Christian Forbearance*). Twelve years after Dr. Allen died, Tennyson exercised both a serene judgment and a Christian forbearance; his poem "Sea Dreams" describes an investment swindle perpetrated by a religiose scoundrel—the scoundrel has suddenly died, and now: "I do forgive him!" An unconvincing poem, too timid for an exorcism.

Yet the financial recuperation did not lead straight to an emotional recuperation. True, by June 1845 he had set to work on *The Princess*, and FitzGerald was right to divine that this new poem was both a symptom and a cause of Tennyson's improved state of mind: "He was looking well, and in good spirits; and had got two hundred lines of a new poem in a butcher's book." Yet next month Aubrey de Vere found Tennyson in a fierily despondent state:

> On my way in, paid a visit to Tennyson, who seemed much out of spirits, and said that he could no longer bear to be knocked about the world, and that he must marry and find love and peace or die. He was very angry about a very favourable review of him. Said that he could not stand the chattering and conceit of clever men, or the worry of society, or the meanness of tuft-hunters, or the trouble of poverty, or the labour of a place, or the preying of the heart on itself. . . He complained much about growing old, and said he cared nothing for fame, and that his life was all thrown away for want of a competence and

retirement. Said that no one had been so much harassed by anxiety and trouble as himself. I told him he wanted occupation, a wife, and orthodox principles, which he took well.

Carlyle had mentioned that Tennyson ought to buy an annuity and later that year came the best kind of annuity: a pension. In fact it was Carlyle who mentioned the idea to FitzGerald the previous year: "It has struck me as a distinctly necessary Act of Legislation, that Alfred should have a Pension of £150 a year. They have £1,200 every year to give away. A hundred and fifty to Alfred, I say; *he* is worth that sum to England! It should be done and must."

A grander move, but a premature one, had been made in 1843 by "Barry Cornwall" (B. W. Procter); when the Poet Laureate Southey died, an approach was made on Tennyson's behalf. But the Laureateship had already been offered to Wordsworth. As an alternative, "a palliative of Mr. Tennyson's complaint" was mentioned in a courtly manner, but Tennyson apparently refused such an act of alms-giving.

It was Henry Hallam who obtained the pension for Tennyson in 1845. He was in touch with the poet about it in January, a hindrance being that Gladstone had just resigned. Next month, Henry Hallam wrote to Sir Robert Peel, pointing out that Tennyson "is considered by many as the very first among the younger class of living poets. He is at least a man of a fertile and thoughtful mind, and few would hesitate to ascribe to him the high praise of genius." Samuel Rogers, Henry Taylor, and Richard Monckton Milnes were suggested as likely to sponsor Tennyson. Sir Robert Peel read some of Tennyson's poems, said he had "formed *a very high estimate* of his powers," and offered the single sum of £200, there being no pension-money available. Gladstone then weighed in; he cited Rogers's high praise, adding: "Still it appears established that, though a true and even a great poet, he can hardly become a popular, and is much more likely to be a starving one." In September 1845, Peel proposed recommending to Queen Victoria "that a pension of £200 per annum should be granted to him for his life." Jane Welsh Carlyle was wittily gleeful, and cited the revolutionary slogan, *À chaqu'un selon sa capacité!*. Moreover, she knew what Tennyson really wanted money for, and knew too that £200 per annum was not going to be enough.

Lady Harriet told me that he wanted to marry; "must have a woman to live beside; would *prefer a lady*, but–cannot afford one; and so must marry a maid-servant." Mrs. Henry Taylor said she was about to write him on behalf of their housemaid, who was quite a superior character in her way.

A year later, Tennyson's friends were to be shocked at the use to which he was putting the royal largesse, as is clear from a letter to Henry Hallam's son:

Mr. Moxon said Alfred one day while travelling said to him, "Moxon, you have made me very unhappy by something you said to me at Lucerne," the unfortunate speech having been "Why Tennyson you will be as bald as Spedding before long." Poor Alfred brooded over this till on his return to England he put himself under a Mrs. Parker (or some such name) who rubs his head and pulls out dead hairs an hour a visit, and ten shillings an hour, besides cosmetics *ad libitum*. Your father's hair would bristle up at the idea of the Queen's pension being spent in this manner, but really his hair is such an integral part of his appearance it would be a great pity he should lose it–and they say this woman does really restore hair, and she is patronised by Royalty itself! Can I say more in her favour or in extenuation for A.T.

This was genial enough; a sourer view of Tennyson's pension came from Edward Bulwer-Lytton, in Part II of his anonymous satire *The New Timon* (January 1846):

Not mine, not mine, (O Muse forbid!) the boon
Of borrowed notes, the mock-bird's modish tune,
The jingling medley of purloin'd conceits,
Outbabying Wordsworth, and outglittering Keates,
Where all the airs of patchwork-pastoral chime
To drowsy ears in Tennysonian rhyme!

. . . . . .

Let School-Miss Alfred vent her chaste delight
On "darling little rooms so warm and bright!"
Chaunt, "I'm aweary," in infectious strain,
And catch her "blue fly singing i' the pane."
Tho' praised by Critics, tho' adored by Blues,
Tho' Peel with pudding plump the puling Muse,

Tho' Theban taste the Saxon's purse controuls,
And pensions Tennyson, while starves a Knowles,
Rather, be thou, my poor Pierian Maid,
Decent at least, in Hayley's weeds array'd,
Than patch with frippery every tinsel line,
And flaunt, admired, the Rag Fair of the Nine!

Tennyson had long deplored Bulwer-Lytton, whom he had described in 1837 as one "who, big as he is, sits to all posterity astride upon the nipple of Literary Dandyism and 'takes her milk for gall.'" Tennyson probably suspected (and probably rightly) that Bulwer-Lytton had written the vicious anonymous review of *Poems* (1832) in the *New Monthly Magazine.* More immediately exasperating, though, even than the "very weak lines" of *The New Timon* were the circumstances, involving as they did the ancient grievance:

At the very time he was writing or had written these, he was visiting my cousins, the d'Eyncourts, and said to them, "How much I should like to know your cousin Alfred" . . . Moreover, he stated in a note that I belonged to a very rich family. The younger son, his friend, who had inherited was rich enough, but the older branch was shut out in the cold, and at that time I had scarce anything.

Stung by all this, Tennyson threw off some elegantly bitter lines against the dandiacal Bulwer-Lytton, "The New Timon, and the Poets." His friend John Forster sent them to *Punch,* where they appeared on February 28, 1846. A week later, there appeared Tennyson's "After-Thought" (later entitled "Literary Squabbles"), deploring all such wrangling. Bulwer-Lytton removed his offensive lines from his next printing, and thirty years later Tennyson (not without a memory of the Tennyson d'Eyncourts, and not without a mild revenge) dedicated his play *Harold* to Bulwer-Lytton's son: "Your father dedicated his *Harold* to my father's brother; allow me to dedicate my *Harold* to yourself." This, it seems, was "to obliterate the memory of the old literary passage-of-arms." In fact Tennyson did not cease to despise both Bulwer-Lytton and his son.

Elizabeth Barrett had news of Tennyson in the month of *The New Timon;* her letter to Robert Browning might point to a relationship (paradoxical yet unsurprising) between his chained state of mind and his escaping poem *The Princess:*

But the really bad news is of poor Tennyson. . . He is seriously ill with an internal complaint and confined to his bed. . . Which does not prevent his writing a new poem—he has finished the second book of it—and it is in blank verse and a fairy tale, and called the "University," the university-members being all females. . . I don't know what to think—it makes me open my eyes. Now isn't the world too old and fond of steam, for blank verse poems, in ever so many books, to be written on the fairies?

Carlyle, who believed that people should pull themselves together, was soon exasperated: "Alfred looks haggard, dire, and languid: they *have* got him however to go and *draw* his Pension; that is reckoned a great achievement on the part of his friends! Surely no man has a right to be so lazy in this world;—and none that is so lazy will ever make much way in it, I think!"

Some such irritation was natural enough, since at this period of his life Tennyson was in real danger of capitulating to "complaints and complainings." Even the trip to Switzerland which he took with his publisher in August 1846 did not greatly resuscitate him. He was indeed moved by some of the natural beauties ("the stateliest bits of landskip I ever saw"), and they were to fire his imagination in the fine lines of *The Princess,* "Come down, O maid, from yonder mountain height." But even here his lugubriousness was fed too: "I was satisfied with the size of crags: but mountains, great mountains, disappointed me. I couldn't take them in, I suppose, crags I could. The Swiss people—no words can describe their lowness in the scale of man, gain greedy, goitred, miserable-looking poor devils." The mingling of contempt and pity there could slide easily into a mingling of self-contempt and self-pity. An immense slackening ache is sensed when he writes to Mrs. Burton at Somersby in March 1847: "Call your child Alfred if you will—he was born in the same house, perhaps the same chamber as myself and I trust he is destined to a far happier life than mine has been—poor little fellow!" The commiseration is only pretending to be for the baby.

Yet our commiseration is still in order, for Tennyson in 1847 had again to undergo the water-cure. He wrote to his aunt Mrs. Russell:

They tell me not to read, not to think: but they might as well tell me not to live. I lack something of the woman's long-enduring patience in these matters. It is a terribly long process, but then what price is too high for health, and health of mind is so involved with health of body.

By December 1847 the strains, the doubts, and the high gifts of Tennyson were presenting a strange picture to the world, a picture which Carlyle sketched with fierce sympathy:

A truly interesting Son of Earth, and Son of Heaven, –who has almost lost his way, among the will-o' wisps, I doubt; and may flounder ever deeper, over neck and nose at last, among the quagmires that abound! I like him well, but can do next to nothing for him. Milnes, with general cooperation, got him a Pension; and he has bread and tobacco: but that is a poor outfit for such a soul. He wants a *task;* and, alas, that of spinning rhymes, and naming it "Art" and "high Art" in a Time like ours, will never furnish him.

VII

1. The Princess 1847

FitzGerald thought *The Princess* "a wretched waste of power at a time of life when a man ought to be doing his best." Carlyle was even less kind: "very gorgeous, fervid, luxuriant, but indolent, somnolent, almost imbecile." Yet a poem which incorporates three of Tennyson's finest lyrics—"Tears, idle tears," "Now sleeps the crimson petal, now the white," and "Come down, O maid, from yonder mountain height"—is patently not negligible. *The Princess* has not been neglected by Tennysonians, by those who enter on the poem with keen convictions about Tennyson's work and character. But for all its skill and idiosyncracy, it is a profoundly unsatisfactory poem in that its intricate failure goes to much that is deepest in Tennyson.

The Prologue presents a group of friends at a country-house fête, a charitable-cum-educational occasion. Earnestly and banteringly, they speak of women's rights—and agree to tell a communal tale, each taking it up in turn. The tale is of a Princess who founds a university for women; her plans are broken by an irruption of men and then by an eruption of love. A medieval tournament mingles with modern politics—politics to which the Conclusion returns us. *The Princess: A Medley*—Tennyson's subtitle has that defensiveness, at once ingenuous and disingenuous, which he reserved for the enterprises to which he most committed himself. *The Princess* comes armored in those good-humored self-incriminations which act as self-exculpations. Its unity? But remember that this is "a sevenfold story," and anyway the circumstances were, you must admit, so oddly heterogeneous—"This *were* a medley!" It is the Conclusion which with sly self-depreciation, and knowing that it is found guilty, asks like a wheedling criminal for its other cases to be taken into consideration:

So closed our tale, of which I give you all
The random scheme as wildly as it rose . . .

For the men wanted the banter of "mock-heroic gigantesque," whereas the women "wished for something real," "true-heroic—true-sublime":

Which yet with such a framework scarce could be.
Then rose a little feud betwixt the two,
Betwixt the mockers and the realists:
And I, betwixt them both, to please them both,
And yet to give the story as it rose,
I moved as in a strange diagonal,
And maybe neither pleased myself nor them.

Something, despite the candor, is false there. "To please them both," or rather to pain neither of them? *The Princess*, for all its manly talk, would like to pretend that nobody feels any pain. That Tennyson himself is uneasy comes out—not in the explicit assurances of unease, which are smooth—but in the tiny syntactical wrinkle in that last line, "And maybe neither pleased myself nor them." Surely, either "pleased neither myself nor them," or "neither pleased myself nor pleased them"—the clumsy misplacing of "neither" is in its small way a hint that all is far from well. The "diagonal," as Tennyson himself acknowledged, is that of the parallelogram of forces; all his life, buffeted by severely contrarious forces, he hoped that there would somehow be a crisp clear diagonal which could reconcile them and could be his line, direct, unbroken, unwavering. Yet for creation, Tennyson's truthful hopes needed to meet his truthful fears, in another parallelogram of forces, and it was exactly this which in the years of *The Princess*, 1845–47, he could not bring himself to do. What is wrong with *The Princess* stems from its innumerable evasions.

What is wrong was summed up by J. W. Marston in 1848:

> The grand error of the story is the incoherency of its characteristics. Its different parts refuse to amalgamate. They are derived from standards foreign to each other. The familiar and conventional impair the earnestness of the ideal:—and what might else have been appreciated as genial satire loses its force from its juxtaposition to tragic emotion. Nor are these opposite elements used as contrasts to each other. It is sought to identify them; but in the attempt to fuse both, each parts with its distinctiveness . . . It is true that the author has anticipated our exceptions. His very title-page declares *The Princess* to be a "Medley." In the Prologue we have this avowal in detail . . . But this consciousness of an eccentric plan can scarcely excuse it. We fancy that the Prologue is in reality an apologetic supplement.

To Marston, all this was simply "unskilful." Yet *The Princess* manifests great skill—directed, though, not to poetic achievement but to a therapy of evasion. Tennyson wrote it after the worst five years of his life, and he created a complicated series of evasions such as could temporarily stave off his dilemmas and disasters. *The Princess* does not ignore all these, both artistic and human; it ingeniously (the ingenuity is ultimately barren) evades them. It evades the artistic problems of the long poem, of narrative, drama, and lyric, by proffering a "Medley." Similarly, the moral issues of women's education are invoked and evaded by a "strange diagonal"; the tone, the story, the outcome are at once earnest and flippant, and the crucial question—"What's to be done?"—is left where it was found. In fact the phrase "moral *issues*" is misleading, since it is precisely an issue—a way out or forward—which ceases to be sought, let alone found. Tennyson thereby ministers to both of the forces which racked him in the 1840s: he at once assuages and intensifies his feelings of guilt by both opening and closing an issue. Likewise with the political concerns, which the poem both expresses and belittles. The rick-burning of the 1830s (which Tennyson did care about) is indeed brought within the poem's compass (women's rights are an intensely political matter, after all), but—equally "indeed"—the rick-burning appears there as a Homeric, or mock-Homeric, simile for the angry flush on the Princess's face. Similarly the political excesses of France—"Revolts, republics, revolutions"—which again Tennyson cared deeply about: these are brought explicitly within the poem but are then—by a cunning but sterilizing hygiene—attributed as sentiments to "the Tory member's eldest son." Then there is geology, with its intimidating vistas of time and its stony stare at religion. Three years later, in *In Memoriam*, Tennyson was to confront the terror of geology. In *The Princess*, he converts it into an exquisite miniature, one of the few moments when an artistic success is created from his wish simultaneously to switch on the fearful and to de-fuse it:

> Many a little hand
> Glanced like a touch of sunshine on the rocks,
> Many a light foot shone like a jewel set
> In the dark crag: and then we turned, we wound
> About the cliffs, the copses, out and in,
> Hammering and clinking, chattering stony names
> Of shale and hornblende, rag and trap and tuff,
> Amygdaloid and trachyte, till the Sun
> Grew broader toward his death and fell, and all
> The rosy heights came out above the lawns.

How delicately Tennyson's unobtrusive puns on "light" and "set" soften the scene, soften even the word "stony." How peaceful the death of the sun, and how rich the rosy glow of its death. How calmly does geological time take its place in this chronographia (or picture of the passing of time—a traditional literary figure, as here, to end a section of a poem)—as calmly as that everyday marking of a span of time, a sunset. Such a poetic achievement is a reminder that the point made about Tennyson's calmative strategy in *The Princess* is not in itself an accusation—though it often does have to be one.

There are the more directly personal forces incorporated and evaded: Arthur Hallam is to be present (Florian, "my other heart, / And almost my half-self"), but is to be faded and blanched. The catastrophe is to be caused by drunkenness, but is to turn out—as it mostly did not in Tennyson's vicinity—not really to be a catastrophe after all. Then there is madness: the hero, wounded in the tournament and now nursed by the Princess, reports that "still she feared that I should lose my mind." But the poem itself evidently fears no such thing; indeed, the poem is in its odd way a triumph of bringing the fearful within its purlieus and then tranquilizing everything. Madness is mentioned in order that it may be (all too perfunctorily from the artistic point of view) tamed; the same with hereditary melancholia, which did indeed haunt Tennyson's mind but which here his mind adroitly evades. A sorcerer had foretold "that none of all our blood should know / The shadow from the substance":

> And, truly, waking dreams were, more or less,
> An old and strange affection of the house.
> Myself too had weird seizures, Heaven knows what:
> On a sudden in the midst of men and day,
> And while I walked and talked as heretofore,
> I seemed to move among a world of ghosts,
> And feel myself the shadow of a dream.

The house of Tennyson had indeed lived through "waking dreams"—those of madness, alcohol, drugs, and even art. But this is no strenuous exorcism; rather, it is a varnishing. The Prince's seizures are deeply equivocal: on the one hand, they suggest spiritual insight and resemble those trance-like moments which Tennyson valued so highly, in his life and in his poems; on the other hand, they are a curse and even perhaps a hereditary disease, and they threaten the Prince as with epilepsy. Either way, it is difficult to be convinced by the Prince's final assurance that the Princess's reciprocating his love has forever cured him of these seizures. As so often in Tennyson, the wishful and the wistful are near allied.

The parental-filial relationships in the poem are, again, at once present and evaded. The Prince's mother is especially important, and yet it is never clear whether she is alive or dead. The Prince's father—burly to the point of brutality—is no less important. "At last I spoke. 'My father, let me go' ": we might wish to apply the line to much in Tennyson. "But 'No!' / Roared the rough king, 'you shall not.' " They steal away by night,

> half in dread
> To hear my father's clamour at our backs
> With Ho! from some bay-window shake the night.

Fortunately the king is later at their backs in a more helpful sense; when the Prince is captured, his father takes hostage the Princess's father. The young men may slink like schoolboys from the father, but the poem then takes a silent pleasure in his being "belaboured" on rib and cheek by the eight rustic amazons who protect the Princess. It all makes odd and ambivalent reading, as with the half-unwanted (wholly unwanted?) ambiguity in the direction of the word "foes" when the Princess and the Prince's father meet over the wounded Prince:

> So those two foes above my fallen life,
> With brow to brow like night and evening mixt
> Their dark and gray.

It is hard to know what to make of the relationship of the Prince to his father, so crucial to the poem. But it is not hard to hear things left unsaid. When the Princess exclaims,

> there is nothing upon earth
> More miserable than she that has a son
> And sees him err:

there is a tacit sense of something in some respects yet more miserable: he that has a father and sees him err.

In the falsely, ingeniously, consolatory world of *The Princess*, manliness becomes compatible with prolonged disguise as a woman. "And if I be, as truecast Poets are, / Half woman-natured. . . ."* Martial valor becomes compatible with the cushioning of a tournament ("I trust that there is no one hurt to death"). Love and marriage become both a royal and ancient precontract and a new-awakened passion (neither of which were they for Tennyson and Emily)—with the actual exigencies of marriage safely off the end of the poem, safely and very beautifully:

> Approach and fear not; breathe upon my brows;
> In that fine air I tremble, all the past
> Melts mist-like into this bright hour, and this
> Is morn to more, and all the rich to-come
> Reels, as the golden Autumn woodland reels
> Athwart the smoke of burning weeds.

Death becomes above all a precipitator of love. "I shall die tonight": the Prince's words are the very same ones that had been

* See p. 161.

used by Tennyson's St. Simeon Stylites, but whereas with St. Simeon we know that the words mean that he will surely die, with the Prince we know they mean that he will surely not. Instead,

> She stooped; and out of languor leapt a cry;
> Leapt fiery Passion from the brinks of death . . .

But those brinks had never been truly perilous.

Yet the most telling sign of the poem's central evasion is that it possesses a villain, or perhaps one should say villainess. It is usually a marked characteristic of Tennyson's work that, in an age when villains were ubiquitous and unconvincing, he had so little play with them. Apart from *Idylls of the King* (and even there the villain, Modred, and the villainess, Vivien, stand unsatisfactorily in relation to those erring non-villains, Lancelot and Guinevere), Tennyson's work is strikingly free from any recourse to villainy as a problem-dissolver whether in literature or in life. But in *The Princess*, poor Lady Blanche is made physically and morally unprepossessing; she is rendered as a petty villain, demeaned to a scapegoat. There is not much of her, but in what there is, the unsavoriness is rather the poem's than hers. She furnishes the most important evasion of all: the evasion of blame. Fortunately and unfortunately, blame was one of the things which Tennyson could least happily evade, and the shallow inconsequence of so much in *The Princess* is a healthy unsatisfactory result. Tennyson attempted in 1850 to strengthen the poem's structure by inserting songs between the sections, these songs mostly invoking a child,* and thus consolidating that aspect of the story which showed the child Aglaïa, and so motherhood, to be the Princess's fatal miscalculation. But the attempt was belated,

* Tennyson said: "The child is the link through the parts, as shown in the Songs (inserted 1850), which are the best interpreters of the poem." Of these six songs, all but two explicitly mention children; and in "The splendour falls on castle walls," the line "Our echoes roll from soul to soul" is partly an invoking of one's posterity. This leaves only the final intercalated song, "Ask me no more," which makes one think of, but which may not present, a child; it depicts the moment of yielding to passionate love. Such a yielding is to precede marriage and children, and here it inaugurates the love and marriage within the final section of the narrative.

one more admission of the fact that *The Princess* as a whole sought evasion and defeat. "He talked of *The Princess* with something of regret, of its fine blank verse, and the many good things in it: 'but,' said he, 'though truly original, it is, after all, only a medley.' "

Yet there are indeed many good things in *The Princess*. The poem glitters with those phrases which it ringingly praises, those

> jewels five-words-long
> That on the stretched forefinger of all Time
> Sparkle for ever.

There is a range of immediately striking skill, bent sometimes to small purposes but commanding them fully. The shapes and sounds of words are cunningly held and rotated, in evoking "Light coin, the tinsel clink of compliment," or a deeper pulse: "The summer of the vine in all his veins." Of an effect such as this:

> and overhead
> The broad ambrosial aisles of lofty lime
> Made noise with bees and breeze from end to end.

we may feel that it is too easy. But we should concede that the effect aims at and gains ease, that it is markedly unpretentious, and –lastly–that when we say "easy" we mean for Tennyson rather than for the rest of us. The beauty of the sound-links in the following passage is partly a matter of sensing an audacity vindicated by true tact. The pattern ("Ida," "leader," "breaker," "murmured," "Ida") actually incorporates the sound "clang" while yet ringing insinuatingly and not just clangingly:

> at eve and dawn
> With Ida, Ida, Ida, rang the woods;
> The leader wildswan in among the stars
> Would clang it, and lapt in wreaths of glowworm light
> The mellow breaker murmured Ida.

The finest verbalism of *The Princess* is certainly something much smaller than the best of his previous poems, but the penetration and gravity that were to inform *In Memoriam* and *Maud* owe a great deal to the resourcefulness and resources which Tennyson discovered in writing his medley. The artistic–as distinct from the therapeutic–achievement of *The Princess* is mainly that of the landscapes and of the integral lyrics.

Landscape is not altogether the word, since the poem offers such a rich variety of -scapes. There are the two superb stormscapes, both masquerading as similes but both outstripping their occasion in a way that is cause for immediate delight and for an ultimate disappointment. The "pillar of electric cloud" is felt in its rendings–in many senses, a *tour de force*. The melancholia that overtakes the Princess is seen as a stormscape–magnificent as vignette but lopsided as simile, in that Tennyson was far more interested in the storm and in melancholia in general than in the Princess:

> And she as one that climbs a peak to gaze
> O'er land and main, and sees a great black cloud
> Drag inward from the deeps, a wall of night,
> Blot out the slope of sea from verge to shore,
> And suck the blinding splendour from the sand,
> And quenching lake by lake and tarn by tarn
> Expunge the world:

There is the glancing starscape, again smuggled in as simile, which sets as jewels

> those three stars of the airy Giant's zone,
> That glitter burnished by the frosty dark . . .

There is an unforgettable riverscape (III.272-78); there is the infinite skyscape or nightscape which paradoxically concludes the poem, with a limpid regret (Conclusion 106-118); there is the seascape which ends section I, and which conveys with the utmost power and delicacy what underlies the sense that sleep and dreams are a sea:

> I gave the letter to be sent with dawn;
> And then to bed, where half in doze I seemed
> To float about a glimmering night, and watch
> A full sea glazed with muffled moonlight, swell
> On some dark shore just seen that it was rich.

They are the very words needed for Tennyson's landscapes of

mood. Such poetry does swell; it is full, glazed, and muffled, its darkness the condition of its richness.

Yet a critic must try to elucidate such darkness, without casting too inappropriately stark a light. What needs to be said is that the evasive (and ultimately illusory) freedom of *The Princess* enabled Tennyson—as *Endymion* had enabled Keats—to experiment and widen his ideas of linguistic propriety. *The Princess* is full of covert puns, suggestions glimpsed between the interstices. "And watch / A full sea glazed . . .": "glazed" seems to be precipitated by "watch," out of "gazed." There are the alternating shifts ("cracked," "wrinkling," "water") into the epithet "dry" after describing King Gama's smile:

> His name was Gama; cracked and small his voice,
> But bland the smile that like a wrinkling wind
> On glassy water drove his cheek in lines;
> A little dry old man . . .

There is the suggestion, at once erotic and maternal, within the girls' lecture hall:

> There sat along the forms, like morning doves
> That sun their milky bosoms on the thatch,
> A patient range of pupils.

There is the suggestion of "sank down" in "There leaning deep in broidered down we sank / Our elbows"; the hint of both the color and the flower "rose" (with its scent, too) in the verb here:

> A fragrant flame rose, and before us glowed
> Fruit, blossom, viand, amber wine, and gold.

A great many more instances might be given of this liberated, almost sportive, quality in the style of *The Princess*, but one passage must suffice.

> So saying from the court we paced, and gained
> The terrace ranged along the Northern front,
> And leaning there on those balusters, high
> Above the empurpled champaign, drank the gale
> That blown about the foliage underneath,
> And sated with the innumerable rose,
> Beat balm upon our eyelids.

The lines are an extraordinary tissue of linguistic relations, with a subsidiary sense of "ranged" (roved) at once precipitated and held off by "paced"; a subsidiary sense of "front" (forehead) likewise in tension with "eyelids"; of "champaign" (the fields) in tension with "drank"; of "blown" in tension with "rose." Some of these interplays may be wayward, but they evince a linguistic confidence and leisure which Tennyson gained for himself within the (otherwise inordinately) protected and protecting confines of *The Princess.*

The linguistic confidence is at its finest in the integral lyrics. All of them are notable. There is the exquisitely rotatory movement of "O Swallow, Swallow, flying, flying South," with the syntax turning like a delighting mobile, confident that time and space are on its side:

> Why lingereth she to clothe her heart with love,
> Delaying as the tender ash delays
> To clothe herself, when all the woods are green?

There is the exultant prophetic fury of "Our enemies have fallen, have fallen," a song that rings with political evolutionary hope. Preeminently, there are "Tears, idle tears," "Now sleeps the crimson petal, now the white," and "Come down, O maid, from yonder mountain height."

> Tears, idle tears, I know not what they mean,
> Tears from the depth of some divine despair
> Rise in the heart, and gather to the eyes,
> In looking on the happy Autumn-fields,
> And thinking of the days that are no more.
>
> Fresh as the first beam glittering on a sail,
> That brings our friends up from the underworld,
> Sad as the last which reddens over one
> That sinks with all we love below the verge;
> So sad, so fresh, the days that are no more.
>
> Ah, sad and strange as in dark summer dawns
> The earliest pipe of half-awakened birds
> To dying ears, when unto dying eyes
> The casement slowly grows a glimmering square;
> So sad, so strange, the days that are no more.

Dear as remembered kisses after death,
And sweet as those by hopeless fancy feigned
On lips that are for others; deep as love,
Deep as first love, and wild with all regret;
O Death in Life, the days that are no more.

No poem of Tennyson compacts more of his deepest feelings with a more graceful fluency. The intricate relationship of pain to pleasure; the essential ambiguity of memory; the moment that waits for death; the sense of "Death in Life": these were abiding concerns which knew about transience. "This song came to me on the yellowing autumn-tide at Tintern Abbey, full for me of its bygone memories. It is the sense of the abiding in the transient." No lyrical poem in English gives so powerful a feeling of moving upon effortless rhyming while in fact being unrhymed; the poem is about the most potent of absences, and it conveys this groundswell by making us sense what in a poem of this kind, with this stanza and movement, is a most potent absence: the absence of rhyme. T. S. Eliot's lovely lines about daylight in "Burnt Norton" might be applied to the stylistic and experiential movement of "Tears, idle tears":

Investing form with lucid stillness
Turning shadow into transient beauty
With slow rotation suggesting permanence . . .

Tennyson's own comments are unusually important:

He told me that he was moved to write "Tears, idle tears" at Tintern Abbey; and that it was not real woe, as some people might suppose; "it was rather the yearning that young people occasionally experience for that which seems to have passed away from them for ever."

"It is in a way like St. Paul's "groanings which cannot be uttered . . . It is what I have always felt even from a boy, and what as a boy I called the 'passion of the past.'* And it is so always with me now; it is

* Nearly forty years after "Tears, idle tears," Tennyson tried once more to elucidate these feelings, in "The Ancient Sage" (written 1885):

Today? but what of yesterday? for oft
On me, when boy, there came what then I called,
Who knew no books and no philosophies,
In my boy-phrase "The Passion of the Past."

the distance that charms me in the landscape, the picture and the past, and not the immediate to-day in which I move."

Yet, as F. W. Bateson has pointed out in what is the best discussion of the poem, "Tears, idle tears" manifests a deep fissure. "*Either* the days that are no more are the objective past of kings and monasteries, *or* they are the subjective past of the poet's and reader's own earlier life. They cannot be both together." Yet it is precisely *both* that the poem seeks to encompass; it is a poem about the wish to find a congruence between the public past and a private past. The wish, but not the fulfillment; the poem is, in Mr. Bateson's words, "the authentic expression of an unintegrated personality." The five years that preceded the writing of *The Princess* had cruelly deepened the fissure within Tennyson. His poem gazes with self-command at this fissure, but does not collapse into it. Tennyson saw that regret is something other than half-hearted tragedy, and that the quintessence of regret–regret at the loss of what has never really been possessed–might precipitate a poem whose manner and movement had no predecessor in English poetry.

Now sleeps the crimson petal, now the white;
Nor waves the cypress in the palace walk;
Nor winks the gold fin in the porphyry font:
The fire-fly wakens: waken thou with me.

Now droops the milkwhite peacock like a ghost,
And like a ghost she glimmers on to me.

Now lies the Earth all Danaë to the stars,
And all thy heart lies open unto me.

The first gray streak of earliest summer-dawn,
The last long stripe of waning crimson gloom,
As if the late and early were but one–
A height, a broken grange, a grove, a flower
Had murmurs "Lost and gone and lost and gone!"
A breath, a whisper–some divine farewell–
Desolate sweetness–far and far away–
What had he loved, what had he lost, the boy?
I know not and I speak of what has been.

Now slides the silent meteor on, and leaves
A shining furrow, as thy thoughts in me.

Now folds the lily all her sweetness up,
And slips into the bosom of the lake:
So fold thyself, my dearest, thou, and slip
Into my bosom and be lost in me.

The poem has an exquisite poise and reciprocity. It takes the darkest feelings and finds that they can be sources of light and delight: the downward impulse here (drowning, oblivion, lost) finds its identity as the gravity of love. There is a mysterious interpenetration; "Now" loses any sense of the precipitate, the fleeting, and becomes—through its steady throbbing—a calm enduring state, a mood and a love out of time. "Nor," which stands in such complete parallelism to "Now" as to seem at first almost a misprint for it ("Now sleeps," "Nor waves," "Nor winks")—"Nor" loses its sense of negation and privation. What we sense instead is a pause, a poise—waiting within the unstirred cypress is the impulse to wave, waiting within the sleeping fish is the impulse to wink a gold fin. There is a crystallized contrariety: you cannot employ the English language to say "Nor winks the gold fin in the porphyry font" without our glimpsing—through the interstices of the negative—the winking fin.* The poem is about the deep suspensions of sleep; its sources are akin to those that animated "The Sleeping Beauty," though as art it far outdoes the earlier poem. Sleep is seen as a deeply restorative and recuperative activity, a rich future suspended and brooding warm ("Lay hidden as the music of the moon / Sleeps in the plain eggs of the nightingale," "Aylmer's Field"). The poem is framed by imperatives which are yet gentle; the first quatrain urges "waken thou with me," but the wakening is into a world of serene dreaming; of a ghost that causes no fear; of a rape-story (Danaë and the shower of gold) that is somehow free of fear, treachery, and mercenariness; of the heavy earth become as easy to plough as the air (the

* This dream-poem bears upon Freud's remarks: "The way in which dreams treat the category of contraries and contradictories is highly remarkable. It is simply disregarded. 'No' seems not to exist so far as dreams are concerned" (*The Interpretation of Dreams,* VI (tr. 1954), p. 318).

"shining furrow" points down to the soil as well as up to the night-sky); of a drowning, a loss of identity, that creates the mutuality of love. The sobriety of waking is matched by the wonder of dreaming; the urgency of a moment, by a tranquility of enduring love which is inheritance not conquest; the delicate pleasures of patterning, by a supple variety and unpredictability. What is striking in the poem's modulations is not solely sensibility but intelligence, transmuting and protecting but without falsifying or sentimentalizing. To lie all Danaë to the stars is to give Danaë the force of an adjective, some such epithet as "wide-open"; "open" at once surfaces in the next line, as if from the poem's dreaming subconscious, and "heart" therefore becomes—well, not a euphemism, but not all that the lover yearns for. It was not Danaë's heart that was open to Jupiter. And yet to put it like that is to encourage the snigger which Tennyson totally excluded. By presenting the golden shower as starlight (emanating not from lecherous Jupiter but from the chaste stars), Tennyson succeeds in the hardest task of all: distinguishing love from lust in erotic poetry. That Tennyson developed, rather than stumbled upon, such central tact, comes out in a simple comparison.

> Now folds the lily all her sweetness up,
> And slips into the bosom of the lake.

Tennyson in 1847. Tennyson in 1827 could offer such a line as "And the lake's gloomy bosom is full to the brim," where the metaphor in bosom had better stay altogether dead.

The next poem which the Princess reads from "a volume of the Poets of her land" is "a small / Sweet Idyl": "Come down, O maid, from yonder mountain height." The poem's conclusion is justly famous as a triumph of Tennyson's melopoeic art:

> and sweet is every sound,
> Sweeter thy voice, but every sound is sweet;
> Myriads of rivulets hurrying through the lawn,
> The moan of doves in immemorial elms,
> And murmuring of innumerable bees.

Superb in its way—but the way has caused some unease, some sense that such mellifluousness is too gratified, too limited, a skill.

But the poem is conscious of this—not with a bad self-consciousness, but with a deliberate playing of this concluding seduction (placing all its values within a delighted and delighting satisfaction of the ear) against other values pictured within the poem. For "Come down, O maid" is—just as much as Marvell's "To His Coy Mistress"—a poem of courteous seduction.

> What pleasure lives in height (the shepherd sang)
> In height and cold, the splendour of the hills?

But the poem itself incorporates a recognition that there are values other than pleasure; that height and cold create a splendor. "Love is of the valley"—*come*, the poem urges three times in two lines. Love is indeed richly suggestive—

> Or hand in hand with Plenty in the maize,
> Or red with spirted purple of the vats,
> Or foxlike in the vine—

Suggestive but irresponsible, insinuating, certainly not monopolizing the poem's values. To Love (and to the urgent lover), the heights are sterile. But Tennyson conveys their dignity and their potent reminder. Before we reach the finally proffered rivulets, we see the Alpine torrent; before we hear "the moan of doves," we hear the "lean-headed Eagles yelp"; before the "immemorial elms," "the blasted Pine." Ruskin was redressing a balance (a balance which, as with the best of Spenser, is a matter of values and not just of expertise) when he singled out the seen mountain, not the heard valley: "Perhaps one of the most wonderful pieces of sight in all literature is—Nay, that's just it; I was doing to say a bit of Tennyson—the piece of Alp in the 'Princess.' " Love is of the valley—

> nor cares to walk
> With Death and Morning on the silver horns,
> Nor wilt thou snare him in the white ravine,
> Nor find him dropt upon the firths of ice,
> That huddling slant in furrow-cloven falls
> To roll the torrent out of dusky doors:
> But follow; let the torrent dance thee down
> To find him in the valley; let the wild

Lean-headed Eagles yelp alone, and leave
The monstrous ledges there to slope, and spill
Their thousand wreaths of dangling water-smoke,
That like a broken purpose waste in air:
So waste not thou; but come . . .

And so into the last seductive sounds–sounds which do not, however, simply comprise the poem's values, but which are judged, with affectionate unsentimentality, against the dignity and mystery of the mountain height. "So waste not thou": the lover's adjuration has all the traditional cunning that is needed to win a coy mistress, but the poem's deeper cunning outdoes the shepherd's–and has outdone those critics who have too simple a view of the status of Tennysonian mellifluousness in Tennyson's poems.

2. *Emily and marriage 1848–1850*

It was now eight years since the breaking of Tennyson's engagement. Emily had suffered ill-health, and they had met only once and that by accident. Tennyson was thought to be in Italy, and Emily visited his sister Cecilia and her husband; Tennyson unexpectedly turned up, and Emily felt obliged to leave. But by 1848 things must have looked better: there had been the success of *Poems* (1842) and now the publication of *The Princess*, and there was the pension, which was at once money, recognition, and royal respectability. Aubrey de Vere said of Tennyson in 1848, "He is all in favour of marriage, and indeed will not be right till he has some one to love him exclusively." It was at this time that Tennyson nerved himself to propose to Emily. He was refused. She had come to believe that they "moved in worlds of religious thought so different that the two would not 'make one music' as they moved."

Tennyson was shattered. He spent the autumn of 1848 back yet again at a water-cure.

> Of love that never found his earthly close,
> What sequel? Streaming eyes and breaking hearts?
> Or all the same as if he had not been?

In 1840 Tennyson had been able at once to answer his questions about "Love and Duty" with a resounding "Not so." In 1848, rejected and for profounder reasons than "that eternal want of pence," it was not only his heart that was in danger of breaking. FitzGerald now all but despaired of him:

Tennyson is emerged half-cured, or half-destroyed, from a water establishment: has gone to a new Doctor who gives him iron pills; and altogether this really great man thinks more about his bowels and nerves than about the Laureate wreath he was born to inherit. Not but he meditates new poems; and now the Princess is done, he turns to King Arthur—a worthy subject indeed—and has consulted some histories of him, and spent some time in visiting his traditionary haunts in Cornwall. But I believe the trumpet can wake Tennyson no longer to do great deeds; I may mistake and prove myself an owl; which I hope may be the case. But how are we to expect heroic poems from a valetudinary? I have told him he should fly from England and go among savages.

It was not to be his Arthurian plans, though, which brought about his winning Emily, but the elegies for Arthur Hallam which he had begun in 1833 and which in the 1840s he had been augmenting and arranging. In 1849 Tennyson asked Emily for her opinion about the two versions of "Sweet and low," a song which he was going to introduce into the next edition of *The Princess*—a small matter. A larger matter was the reconciliation of Tennyson's brother Charles and Emily's sister Louisa; their broken marriage healed itself in 1849* (as the marriage of Dr. Tennyson had never done). Then in 1850 Emily Sellwood was given the chance to read the work by Tennyson which would persuade her that his world of religious thought was not alien from hers. Her cousin lent her a manuscript of *In Memoriam*, and in April 1850 Emily found herself wishing to thank Tennyson in these terms:

Katie told me the poems might be kept until Saturday. I hope I shall not have occasioned any inconvenience by keeping them to the limit of time; and if I have I must be forgiven, for I cannot willingly part from what is so precious. The thanks I would say for them and for the faith in me which has trusted them to me must be thought for me, I

* There were still to be relapses; Emily wrote to Tennyson in 1859: "Poor Charles. Perhaps we shall be able to do something towards convincing Louy but I fear not because she is fully aware of what has been so often said by others that abstinence is easier than moderation."

cannot write them. I have read the poems through and through and through and to me they were and they are ever more and more a spirit monument grand and beautiful, in whose presence I feel admiration and delight, not unmixed with awe. The happiest possible end to this labour of love! But think not its fruits shall so soon perish, for they are life in life, and they shall live, and as years go on be only the more fully known and loved and reverenced for what they are.

So says a true seer. Can anyone guess the name of this seer? After such big words shall I put anything about my own little I? —that I am the happier for having seen these poems and that I hope I shall be the better too.

The "true seer" was apparently Charles Kingsley, famous and very Christian, who now "strenuously" urged Emily to marriage. In the words of her reminiscences, "In all these years she said that she had lost courage and she did not know whether she should ever, feeling the great responsibility, have ventured to become Alfred's wife had not Kingsley . . . not only encouraged but urged her to do so." With the publisher Moxon now offering an advance and a yearly royalty on *In Memoriam* (to be published at the end of May), all obstacles were removed.

Except the obstacle of Tennyson's self-distrust. All was not well with him; on May 7, he wrote to his cousin: "Pray dearest Lewis forgive me. I throw myself on your mercy. I took I know not what absurd fancies into my head and I have had enough perplexity and vexation this week to drive most men crazy." The marriage license is dated May 15—at which point Tennyson, who "was just then suffering from one of his fits of depression," found himself unable to fix a date and stick to it. His sister Mary complained in June that "Alfred maintains a cruel silence about his engagement, which I think is not fair towards his family, especially as the Rawnsleys know it." But one reason why Tennyson did not let his family know of his forthcoming marriage—he did not tell even his mother until afterward—was that he still was not convinced that the marriage would take place. At last he steeled himself and settled upon June 13. It all recalls the reluctant steps of Byron toward his disastrous marriage ("The bridegroom more and more *less* impatient"), and in the circumstances it is not surprising that Tennyson's sister Mary saw the probabilities as grim: "Poor thing, I dare say he is miserable enough at times, thinking of what he is about to do."

On June 13, he did it. Tennyson, with that gruff naïveté of his, said, "to the amusement of those around, 'it was the nicest wedding he had ever been at.'" Mary Tennyson had her doubts: "Well, all is over. Alfred was married to Emily Sellwood last Friday—*Friday, and raining*, about which I feel very superstitious . . . Emily looked bright, they say . . . I hope they will be happy, but I feel very doubtful about it." The day after the wedding, Tennyson sent a bluff two-sentence letter to Sophy Rawnsley: "We seem to get on very well together. I have not beaten her yet." Tennyson's brother Charles sent them affectionate greetings: "Dear double sister and long-single brother. . . ."

It had been Arthur Hallam—through the manuscript pages of *In Memoriam*—who had from the grave reached out dead hands to comfort them. So Emily and Tennyson went at once to Clevedon where Hallam was buried; neither had been there before, and —in Emily's words—"It seemed a kind of consecration to go there."

The next stage of the honeymoon was sharply different. "Great was my horror," wrote Emily, "when some injury to one of his nails making a painful little operation necessary, the doctors gave him chloroform—then a new thing. I was turned out of the room and heard him shout as if hallooing the hounds. His poor mouth was blistered for the chloroform was not of the best but no other evil came of it." No other evil, but Tennyson never forgot the experience.

Soon after, Carlyle offered a characteristically vivid glimpse of the new couple:

> Alfred looks really improved, I should say; cheerful in what he talks, and looking forward to a future less "detached" than the past has been. Poor fellow, a *good* soul, find him where or how situated you may! Mrs. T. also pleased me; the first glance of her is the least favourable. A freckly *round*-faced woman, rather tallish and without shape, a slight lisp too.

She was to prove devoted—and indefatigable—despite the gradual failure of her health from as early as 1859. She was to prove a firm and kindly mother to her two sons, a thoughtful encourager of her husband's poetic projects, and—since Tennyson loathed writing letters—a tireless secretary.* Edward Lear thought her incomparable: "I should think computing moderately that 15 angels, several hundreds of ordinary women, many philosophers, a heap of truly wise and kind mothers, 3 or 4 minor prophets, and a lot of doctors and school-mistresses, might all be boiled down, and yet their combined essence fall short of what Emily Tennyson really is." Could she be all that and not the right wife for Tennyson? FitzGerald was to see Tennyson as "sunk in coterie worship, and (I tremble to say it) in the sympathy of his most lady-like, gentle wife." (FitzGerald was to grant—but two-edgedly—that she was "a Lady of a Shakespearian type, as I think A.T. once said of her: that is, of the Imogen sort, far more agreeable to me than the sharp-witted Beatrices, Rosalinds, etc. I do not think she has been (on this very account perhaps) so good a helpmate to A.T.'s Poetry as to himself." The distinction between Tennyson's poetry and his self is a fair one, and it is true that words such as Nathaniel Hawthorne was to use—"capable of appreciating him and fit to make him comfortable"—have themselves too comfortable an air. There are kinds of comfort inimical to the creation of great poetry. But then there are kinds of discomfort no less inimical, and those who think that Emily too much tamed and calmed Tennyson will need to ask themselves whether the wild melancholia of the 1840s would not probably otherwise have ended in madness or inertia.

Emily perhaps saved Tennyson from madness and inertia. But her immediate hope (as Aubrey de Vere noted in October 1850) was to save Tennyson for religion:

* Tennyson: "You know that I would any day as soon kill a pig as write a letter." Emily was to have so much to do that it is hardly surprising she sometimes erred. February 4, 1859: "Mr. Alfred Tennyson presents his compliments to Mr. Whing and begs to thank him for his 'Earnest Pilgrim' and for the kind words which accompany it. Mr. Tennyson hopes Mr. Burnard Neville is well and prosperous." The reply, February 6: "Madam, The name on the Title-page of my book is J: W: King. The title of the book 'Ernest *the* Pilgrim,' and the gentleman named in my note Neville Burnard not Burnard Neville. I am, Madam, Yours very sincerely, John: W: King." To a friend, Emily deplored "the man's impertinence."

Her great and constant desire is to make her husband more religious, or at least to conduce, as far as she may, to his growth in the spiritual life. In this she will doubtless succeed, for piety like hers is infectious, especially where there is an atmosphere of affection to serve as a conducting medium. Indeed I already observe a great improvement in Alfred. His nature is a religious one, and he is remarkably free from vanity and sciolism. Such a nature gravitates towards Christianity, especially when it is in harmony with itself.

VIII

In Memoriam 1850

TENNYSON HAD BEGUN *In Memoriam* during the month when he heard of Arthur Hallam's death, October 1833; and four months later he had indicated to Henry Hallam that he hoped in the future to concentrate his powers on the construction of a tribute to his dead friend. By 1841, "the number of the memorial poems had rapidly increased," and by 1845 FitzGerald was reporting Spedding's pressure on Tennyson to publish the elegies:

A.T. has near a volume of poems–elegiac–in memory of Arthur Hallam. Don't you think the world wants other notes than elegiac now? "Lycidas" is the utmost length an elegiac should reach. But Spedding praises: and I suppose the elegiacs will see daylight, public daylight, one day.

But Tennyson's uncertainties ran deep. In 1847 he wrote to Aunt Russell:

With respect to the non-publication of those poems which you mention, it is partly occasioned by the considerations you speak of, and partly by my sense of their present imperfectness; perhaps they will not see the light till I have ceased to be. I cannot tell but I have no wish to send them out yet.

By January 1849, he had promised Aubrey de Vere "to *print* at least his exquisite Elegies, and let his friends have a few copies." This private issue, or trial edition, seems to have been printed in March 1850; Tennyson then made some important last-minute revisions, and *In Memoriam A.H.H.* was published anonymously at the end of May 1850. The title *In Memoriam A.H.H.* had been either suggested or preferred by Emily Sellwood, whom Tennyson married in June 1850.

The title *In Memoriam A.H.H.* directs attention firmly to one focus, despite Tennyson's injunction: "It must be remembered that this is a poem, *not* an actual biography." Another title which Tennyson had considered would direct attention rather differently: *The Way of the Soul.* Yet a third would suggest, with frankness and probably with truth, that the poem as a whole does not possess a firm focus: *Fragments of an Elegy*. For the most important critical question about *In Memoriam* remains the first and most obvious one: in what sense do the 133 separate sections, ranging in length from 12 lines to 144 lines, constitute a whole, a poetic unity, a poem?

The sections were written at many different places, and as the phases of our intercourse came to my memory and suggested them. I did not write them with any view of weaving them into a whole, or for publication, until I found that I had written so many. The different moods of sorrow as in a drama are dramatically given, and my conviction that fear, doubts, and suffering will find answer and relief only through Faith in a God of Love. "I" is not always the author speaking of himself, but the voice of the human race speaking through him. After the Death of A. H. H., the divisions of the poem are made by First Xmas Eve (Section XXVIII), Second Xmas (LXXVIII), Third Xmas Eve (CIV and CV etc.).

More informally, Tennyson told his friend James Knowles that "the general way of its being written was so queer that if there were a blank space I would put in a poem." He also explained to Knowles that there were nine natural groups or divisions in the poem: I-VIII, IX-XX, XXI-XXVII, XXVIII-XLIX, L-LVIII, LIX-LXXI, LXXII-XCVIII, XCIX-CIII, CIV-CXXXI.

Literary criticism since Tennyson's time has become more aptly flexible in its ideas as to artistic unity, less committed to a narrow or mechanical idea of such unity. But it has also become more skilled at imagining some such unity where it may not exist, and (a natural consequence of professional academicism) more skilled at exculpating works of art which in fact deserve the higher compliment of not being whisked away into the irreproachable. Tennyson himself did not make large claims for *In Memoriam* as a unity; his sense that the Christmases provided an apt and serviceable division of the poem should not be taken as warrant for believing that a poem on the scale of *In Memoriam*, and with such large concerns, could be adequately unified by such links and cross-connections as modern criticism rightly delights in and wrongly pretends can be structurally crucial. The Christmases, or the imagery of dark and light, of water and of the human hand: these do much in the way of "weaving them into a whole," but it remains weaving, not growing or building. Unifying principles which would be adequate to a short poem, and which might be adequate to a poem on the scale of *Four Quartets* (though even here there has been a great deal of special pleading), cannot take the strain they are asked to bear if we press them to take responsibility for the unity of a poem as long, various, ranging, and uneven as *In Memoriam*. Admirers of the poem should be convincing as well as convinced, and should not protest too much. Charles Kingsley in 1850 was right in thinking that he could afford an important concession: "Not that there runs throughout the book a conscious or organic method. The poems seem often merely to be united by the identity of their metre. . . ." There is something likewise refreshing about Humphry House's asseverations, which are not so stiff-necked as to be uncompromising but which are rightly uncompromised:

It is impossible to apprehend it as a unified whole; for it is not a whole; and it fluctuates waywardly. . . . The poem then was never planned as a whole, and its composition was spread over a long period; and also its theme was never properly *apprehended* as a whole. I say its theme; but part of the problem is to be sure whether there was a single theme. Is the theme the personal sorrow for Arthur Hallam's death? Is the theme the whole question of human immortality? Is the theme the interplay of the personal sorrow with the general doubt about survival?

House argues persuasively that no convincing case for unity can be made. Nor does the charting of Tennyson's doubts and hopes within the poem provide such a unity of apprehended theme;

"The Way of the Soul" would indeed provide a graph, but a graph is not the same as an artistic unity. Moreover, such a claim would play into FitzGerald's unsentimental hands (he was writing in 1845, five years before Tennyson published the poem):

> We have surely had enough of men reporting their sorrows: especially when one is aware all the time that the poet wilfully protracts what he complains of, magnifies it in the Imagination, puts it into all the shapes of Fancy: and yet we are to condole with him, and be taught to ruminate our losses and sorrows in the same way. I felt that if Tennyson had got on a horse and ridden 20 miles, instead of moaning over his pipe, he would have been cured of his sorrows in half the time. As it is, it is about 3 years before the Poetic Soul walks itself out of darkness and Despair into Common Sense.

Although Tennyson did not ordinarily permit the reprinting of selected sections from *In Memoriam*, he did let his friend F. T. Palgrave print such a selection in his volume of *Lyrical Poems* from Tennyson (1885), with the sections moreover in a different order. A remark by Palgrave is especially apt; he reported that his selections "from *In Memoriam* (peculiarly difficult to frame, from the reasons which I have noted above in regard to Shakespeare's Sonnets) follow a list which he gave me." Shakespeare's *Sonnets* are not only an important source for *In Memoriam*, they are its most important analogue. Not that the question of unity simply dissolves if we invoke the authority of the sonnet sequence–no authority attaches as such to the sonnet sequence, which even in Shakespeare's day was less often a creative whole than an inordinately convenient means of gaining some of the advantages of the long poem without having to face its proper responsibilities and difficulties. Nevertheless, the precedent is an illuminating one: separate poems, occasionally and loosely linked into groups, engaging with a multiplicity of themes, and achieving the inner interrelationships of a *congeries* rather than of a single poem.* From

* For the affinities between *In Memoriam* and John Berryman's *Dream Songs* (both are theodicies, are on the death of friends, and are modern equivalents of the sonnet sequence), see an essay by the present writer in the *Massachusetts Review*, XI.ii, Spring 1970. Arthur Hallam had written a theodicy.

the start, it was seen too that the love of Tennyson for Hallam had a precedent in the *Sonnets*. Charles Kingsley, with some recklessness, exulted in finding a successor to "the old tales of David and Jonathan, Damon and Pythias, Socrates and Alcibiades, Shakespeare and his nameless friend, of 'love passing the love of woman' "; he was drawn twice to that rather perilous phrase, praising *In Memoriam* for "a depth and vehemence of affection 'passing the love of woman' . . . altogether rivalling the sonnets of Shakespeare."

It is not only a post-Freudian world which finds some cause for anxiety here. Benjamin Jowett remarked of Tennyson:

> Once again, perhaps in his weaker moments, he had thought of Shakespeare as happier in having the power to draw himself for his fellow men, and used to think Shakespeare greater in his sonnets than in his plays. But he soon returned to the thought which is indeed the thought of all the world. He would have seemed to me to be reverting for a moment to the great sorrow of his own mind. It would not have been manly or natural to have lived in it always. But in that peculiar phase of mind he found the sonnets a deeper expression of the never to be forgotten love which he felt more than any of the many moods of many minds which appear among his dramas. The love of the sonnets which he so strikingly expressed was a sort of sympathy with Hellenism.

Fearing a homosexual misconstruction, Tennyson's son cut this for the *Memoir*, removing the last sentence and that which begins "It would not have been manly. . . ."

Arthur Hallam had worshipped Shakespeare's *Sonnets*. It is likely that Arthur's father, Henry Hallam, was remembering the opinions of Arthur and of Tennyson when he influentially deplored the ardor of the *Sonnets* in 1839, between the death of Arthur and the publication of *In Memoriam*, insisting: "It is impossible not to wish that Shakspeare had never written them." Tennyson was to speak bluntly: "Henry Hallam made a great mistake about them: they are noble."

But do we too need to speak bluntly? Is Tennyson's love for Hallam a homosexual love? The crucial acts of definition will have to be left to the psychologists and psychiatrists, though it should be said that the literary historians usually vitiate their arguments by conveniently jumbling the old severely differentiating view with the newer "something of it in everybody" one. Was Tennyson, so to speak, abnormally abnormal? A new anthology entitled *Sexual Heretics: Male Homosexuality in English Literature from 1850 to 1900* does not hesitate to quote extensively from ten sections of *In Memoriam;* its editor, anxious to enlist or if necessary pressgang Tennyson, quaintly says that "the fact that Tennyson evolved an emphatically heterosexual image in later life does nothing to disqualify him as homosexual when he wrote *In Memoriam.*"

The vehemence of Tennyson's love for Hallam is certainly remarkable, but then a powerful and original poem is likely to be remarkable. Perhaps it is rather some particular turns of speech which disconcert.

> A spectral doubt which makes me cold,
> That I shall be thy mate no more. . . .
> (XLI)

Is the metaphor in "mate" (even allowing for the variety of the word's other uses) an inadvertently revealing one? And what of the manuscript lines which cry to Hallam's spirit?

> Stoop soul and touch me: wed me: hear
> The wish too strong for words to name. . . .
> (XCIII)

But then manuscript readings lend themselves all too easily to a "heads I win, tails you lose" argument; if the manuscript reading is the same as the final reading, then we can claim that from the start the poet's conception did not waver and is unquestionably such-and-such. And if the manuscript reading differs (as here; what Tennyson published was "Descend, and touch, and enter," which is in some ways even more disconcerting), we can claim that his original, his truest, conception was subsequently suppressed. Even so, the anxiety about *In Memoriam*, whether moralistic or critical, is a real one. Anybody who believes that Tennyson's feelings for Hallam were not homosexual should try to say why.

First, there is the fact that the reiterated metaphor of man and wife in the poem is sufficiently explicable in the simplest terms:

that Hallam had been about to marry Tennyson's sister Emily. The frustration by death of such a marriage is an explicit concern of the poem, which speaks often of Emily and of Tennyson's own hopes from the marriage. Moreover, the poem ends with an epilogue in which the happy wedding of another of Tennyson's sisters to another of his dear friends provides both an instance and an augury of joy and aspiration. It is of course true that the transference of such metaphors so that they include not only Emily but also Tennyson is an extension which could mask other feelings in the poet. But it need not do so, and the family tragedy is sufficiently represented in the poem for it to be clear that there is a strong sense of the word *too* whenever Tennyson speaks of himself as a widowed heart, or a widower, or no longer Hallam's "mate"; it is as if such moments invoke the community of feeling by saying to Emily "I too am widowed." It may still be strange to cry "wed me," but at least a critic will need to grant that part of the point of the cry is that it is addressed to someone who had hoped to wed a Tennyson while alive but could not. Moreover, it is relevant that Tennyson's relationship with his sisters within the poem is presented (and this too is faithful to the family situation) as one in which Tennyson had to be father as well as brother.* His paternal relationship to his sisters again modifies the metaphors of marriage. Also the metaphors themselves have often been misread, as with XCVII.**

Second, there is the fact that Tennyson is both conscious and unselfconscious in ways that work against his being a "sexual heretic." His gruff lack of self-consciousness is evident in his comment on CXXII: "Oh, wast thou with me, dearest, then. . .": "If anybody thinks I ever called him 'dearest' in his life they are much mistaken, for I never even called him 'dear.'" Naïve, perhaps, but not tonally suggestive of homosexuality. There is the

* Epilogue: "Nor have I felt so much of bliss / Since first he told me that he loved / A daughter of our house"; "For I that danced her on my knee, / That watched her on her nurse's arm, / That shielded all her life from harm / At last must part with her to thee." As elsewhere in Tennyson, a brother makes a good father.

** Tennyson: "The spirit yet in the flesh but united in love with the spirit out of the flesh resembles the wife of a great man of science."

same directness, altogether unmisgiving and altogether unsinister, in Tennyson's story of the dream which he had the night before he received the letter offering him the Laureateship: "That night he had had a dream that the Queen and the Prince had called on him at his Mother's and been very gracious, the Prince kissing him which made him think 'very kind but very German.' " Yet Tennyson combined this unselfconsciousness with an intelligent consciousness in just this area. When he praised Hallam for "manhood fused with female grace," he was willing to make unembarrassedly explicit the likeness to Christ, "that union of man and woman." He saw such a union as morally and religiously desirable, not sexually so. But he was careful (and again explicit) in distinguishing this ideal from anything tawdry, as in his epigram "On One Who Affected an Effeminate Manner," or in his remark that "Men should be androgynous and women gynandrous, but men should not be gynandrous nor women androgynous." Moreover, like his friend Aubrey de Vere he was aware of the traditional truth about the poet's sexual empathy; de Vere did not giggle when asked if his devotion was to a lady: "Certainly, if, as old Coleridge said, every true Poet is inclusively woman, but not the worse man on that account–Alfred Tennyson." Man must grow more like woman, and vice versa, said Tennyson: "More as the double-natured Poet each." He will not have been dismayed at Swinburne's fine praise of the lines about the mother and her son's bones in Tennyson's late poem "Rizpah": "But six words of them . . . 'they had moved in my side'–give perfect proof once more of the deep truth that great poets are bisexual."

But if Tennyson was not self-conscious, his son was–and by the 1890s, when he was writing the *Memoir*, misconstruction and suspicion must have seemed threatening. Hallam Tennyson therefore made the great mistake of censoring just exactly those things in Tennyson which are jubilantly straight. A letter from Tennyson to James Spedding in February 1833, for instance, with its jokes about Arthur Hallam; Tennyson mockingly deplored Spedding's remarks about Hallam:

Ironical sidehits at a person under the same roof with myself and filling more than a just half of the sheet–(i.e. not the person–but the sidehits–it looks as though I meant that the person in question slept with me and I assure you that we have a spare bed and the bed is not so spare either, but a bed both plump and pulpy and fit for your domeship. . .

And so, banteringly, on. The banter does not sound strained or anxious.

The one argument in defense (so to speak) of Tennyson which does not effect much is precisely the one that is usually reached for: the general claim that it is somehow unhistorical, naïvely post-Freudian, to imagine any such thing. Thus Gordon Haight has said:

The Victorians' conception of love between those of the same sex cannot be understood fairly by an age steeped in Freud. Where they saw only pure friendship, the modern reader assumes perversion. . . . Even *In Memoriam*, for some, now has a troubling overtone.

But, as so often, the position of the historical purist is itself unhistorical. "*Now* has a troubling overtone"? Some Victorians, who found Shakespeare's *Sonnets* troubling, found *In Memoriam* troubling.* The reviewer who attributed the poem to "a female hand" may be dismissed as a joke, albeit a disconcerting one, but the reviewer in *The Times* was no joke. He deplored "the tone of . . . amatory tenderness," and after quoting from LXXIV he asked piercingly: "Very sweet and plaintive these verses are, but who would not give them a feminine application?"

But does it matter? Even the least biographical of critics would have to admit that the last two lines of the following poignant section (never published by Tennyson) will have slightly different meanings according to our differing biographical judgments as to Tennyson's love:

Speak to me from the stormy sky!
  The wind is loud in holt and hill.
  It is not kind to be so still.
Speak to me, dearest, lest I die.

* Arthur Hallam had discussed Plato's "frequent commendation of a more lively sentiment than has existed in other times between man and man, the misunderstanding of which has repelled several from the deep tenderness and splendid imaginations of the Phaedrus and the Symposium . . ." ("Essay on Cicero," 1831).

Speak to me: let me hear or see!
  Alas my life is frail and weak.
  Seest thou my faults and wilt not speak?
They are not want of love for thee.

T. S. Eliot said of *In Memoriam:* "It is a long poem made by putting together lyrics, which have only the unity and continuity of a diary, the concentrated diary of a man confessing himself. It is a diary of which we have to read every word." The analogy is a suggestive one, but as with the sonnet sequence the claim for this as an artistic unity should not be pressed; a diary is an ambiguous thing. Moreover the parallel will have to include all those personal references which both set limits to the kind of success achieved by the poem and are the conditions of that success. Unobtrusively but persistently, Tennyson incorporated details of Hallam's life and writings; the wording of the poem incorporates reminiscences which then modify a reader's response.

'Tis well; 'tis something; we may stand
  Where he in English earth is laid,
  And from his ashes may be made
The violet of his native land.

(XVIII)

With quiet grace and with a deeper timbre (this is no affectionate hyperbole), Tennyson is returning the compliment which Hallam had paid him: in his essay on Tennyson's poems, Hallam had quoted Persius, *Nunc non e tumulo fortunataque favilla / nascentur violae*, remarking: "When this Poet dies, will not the Graces and the Loves mourn over him?" Such reminiscences might create a stylistic analogy to the moral fact

That men may rise on stepping-stones
Of their dead selves to higher things.

(I)

The phrase "their dead selves" recalls Tennyson's earlier self, and those of his Cambridge friends, which may yet live as part of a moral evolution: the phrase had formed part of a poem by one of Tennyson's Cambridge friends in 1829 written to another. It is true that such allusions utter their confidences so quietly as to be virtually confidential, and this privacy limits the nature of *In Memoriam*—but it also provides some of its sources of energy. Something of this paradox—*In Memoriam* is anonymous but confessional, private but naked—is caught in a fine sentence of R. H. Hutton's, which pits "magnifying" against "secret" in a delicate discussion of effects of scale within the poem: "*In Memoriam* is full of such magnifying-glasses for secret feelings, and doubts, and fears, and hopes, and trusts."

"Yet art thou oft as God to me": that exclamation (which Tennyson did not permit to emerge from manuscript) lends warrant to George Eliot's remark: "Whatever was the immediate prompting of *In Memoriam*, whatever the form under which the author represented his aim to himself, the deepest significance of the poem is the sanctification of human love as a religion." Yet here too there is the paradox in Tennyson which George Gilfillan noticed a few years before *In Memoriam* was published: "His genius is bold, but is waylaid at almost every step by the timidity and weakness of his temperament." But we need to distinguish two areas where this does apply from two where it does not. It does not, for example, justify the famous epigram of Verlaine's which Yeats reports: "M. Verlaine talked . . . of 'In Memoriam,' which he had tried to translate and could not, because 'Tennyson was too noble, too *Anglais*, and when he should have been broken-hearted had many reminiscences.' " Despite the insouciance, it is a torrid sentimentality, too *français*, which takes for granted that a broken heart and reminiscences must necessarily exist on different planes. Despite Verlaine, hearts may break with different causes and with different effects, and reminiscences may be precisely those memories which are not softened but made even more poignant by being humanized and localized.

Nor does the accusation of timidity properly indict the religious position of *In Memoriam* as a whole. Certain expectations will be false ones; we should heed Tennyson's complaint that "they are always speaking of me as if I were a writer of philosophical treatises," and we should receive with some skepticism articles on Tennyson and Teilhard de Chardin. But the important thing is that the poem is explicit in not claiming to be able to arrive at religious truth by argument. This might be deplored on two quite different grounds: some believers might argue that Tennyson sells Christianity short in underrating the degree to which its beliefs are susceptible of substantiation by argument; or unbelievers might argue that it is bad for people to believe things which are not susceptible of argument. But it is possible to think that Tennyson's poem offers almost all that can hereabouts be honestly offered by the Christian, and that it is hearteningly free of the heartlessness which comes from the conviction that the problems of pain, death, and evil can be dealt with by arguments. Dr. Johnson rebuked such high-minded heartlessness in Soame Jenyns:

> I do not mean to reproach this author for not knowing what is equally hidden from learning and from ignorance. The shame is to impose words for ideas upon ourselves or others. To imagine that we are going forward when we are only turning round.

In Memoriam does not impose words for ideas; it does not much claim—in argument, as distinct from mood and feelings—to be going forward but rather is turning round. Indeed, the *In Memoriam* stanza (*abba*) is especially suited to turning round rather than going forward. To speak personally for a moment: as an atheist, I should greatly prefer Tennyson to agree with me; but I find it hard to understand the view that somehow he is stuck there in a half-complacent, half-morbid tangle from which we know—know so uncomplacently—that we have escaped.

Nevertheless, the accusation of timidity does hold in two ways. First, there are Tennyson's disclaimers, which go beyond the prudently modest and become abjectly and disingenuously disarming.

> If these brief lays, of Sorrow born,
> Were taken to be such as closed
> Grave doubts and answers here proposed,
> Then these were such as men might scorn:
> (XLVIII)

Swinburne was rightly indignant about the "incompatible incoherences of meditation and profession":

> To say that these effusions of natural sorrow make no pretence, and would be worthy of contempt if they pretended, to solve or satisfy men's doubts—and then to renew the appearance of an incessant or even

a fitful endeavour after some such satisfaction or solution–is surely so incongruous as to sound almost insincere.

Second, there are the local failures of nerve.

> But brooding on the dear one dead,
> And all he said of things divine,
> (And dear as sacramental wine
> To dying lips is all he said)...
> (XXXVII)

But *The Times* (November 28, 1851) found this shocking: "Can the writer satisfy his own conscience with respect to these verses? ... For our part, we should consider no confession of regret too strong for the hardihood that indicted them." The offending words were changed:

> (And dear to me as sacred wine
> To dying lips is all he said)...

That "to me" introduces an enfeebling tone of doubt or of the apologetically personal; there is now a disconcerting swaying ("to me ... to dying lips"). And Tennyson had meant what he had written: sacramental, not sacred–the emphasis was on a solemn ceremony not only sacred in itself but having the power to make sacred. Tennyson would have done better to stand by his fiercely truthful hyperbole.

A similar thing happens with the prepublication history of *In Memoriam*. In the first edition, CXXIX ended:

> Strange friend, past, present, and to be;
> Loved deeplier, darklier understood;
> Behold, I dream a dream of good,
> And mingle all the world with thee.

The first two lines are superb; the suggestion of paradox in "Strange friend" (the dead friend cannot but be almost a stranger) is beautifully taken up in "Loved deeplier, darklier understood"– when you love someone deeply, you do indeed understand them more and yet the understanding is not a simple illumination–love makes you more aware of the mysteriousness of another, makes you understand "darklier" the person you understandingly love. It is not only the grave which darkens the relationship in such understanding (though that is of course Tennyson's starting point); to be loved deeplier even on earth would still be to be darklier understood. Yet the final two lines of the stanza are merely skillful, swathed in the Tennysonian. To FitzGerald, *In Memoriam* "is full of finest things, but it is monotonous, and has that air of being evolved by a Poetical Machine of the highest order." "Behold," "dream a dream," "mingle": these here have something of the plangent tremulousness which comes when Tennyson is writing "Parnassian" verse. But if Tennyson is remarkable at perfecting his own poetry, how is it that in the trial edition of *In Memoriam* this stanza is so much better? Because Tennyson became concerned, not to consummate his wording, but to retreat from a possibly offensive notion.

Strange friend, past, present, and to be;
  Loved deeplier, darklier understood;
  Let me not lose my faith in good
Lest I make less my love for thee.

Instead of Parnassian or Tennysonianisms, there is an austere confession that for Tennyson what counted supremely was not his faith in good but his love for Hallam. Because of the very mildness of tone, the effect is sharp to the point of paradox, and Tennyson must suddenly have realized that he had virtually said: "I could not love Honour so much, loved I not Hallam more." Hence his retreat into the ripe fluency of Parnassian verse. His wording was always considered; sometimes it was too considerate.

There is much in *In Memoriam* that does not carry conviction. Its language falters or coarsens whenever Tennyson pretends that his life until the death of Hallam had been a happy one; whenever he swings into politics ("The blind hysterics of the Celt" is a line not without blindness and hysteria); whenever he refuses to admit that he cannot imagine heaven, let alone activity and energy in heaven; whenever he remembers his father; whenever he tries to feel that his love must daunt time, whereas it is time which does the daunting; whenever he makes any lordly claim about his attitude to death; whenever he has patent recourse to allegory (as in CIII); most of all, whenever he offers hopes which deep down he knows are hopeless.

"No, like a child in doubt and fear. . . ." For it is the lack of conviction which carries the deepest conviction. "It's too hopeful, this poem, more than I am myself." At the last minute, he changed from the trial edition; he added the profound sincerity of VII: "Dark house, by which once more I stand"; and LVI, with its bitter awareness of "Nature, red in tooth and claw / With ravine"; and XCVI, in defense of "honest doubt." "I should reproach Tennyson not for mildness, or tepidity, but rather for lack of serenity," said a poet whose deepest subject was his lack of serenity, T. S. Eliot: *In Memoriam* "is not religious because of the quality of its faith, but because of the quality of its doubt. Its faith is a poor thing, but its doubt is a very intense experience."

Where then should the stress fall? Preeminently on the poems of most intense feeling, and these tend to be the darkest. Tennyson was not simply "a morbid and unhappy mystic" (in Harold Nicolson's words), since he was many things; but such is here the profoundest of his writing. II, "Old Yew, which graspest at the stones"; VII, "Dark house"; XV, "Tonight the winds begin to rise"; L,

> Be near me when my light is low,
> When the blood creeps, and the nerves prick
> And tingle; and the heart is sick,
> And all the wheels of Being slow.

There are not many such sections, even when we add the supreme evocations of geological time, such as CXXIII, "There rolls the deep where grew the tree." Yet we should not underrate the very different evocations of "tender gloom," the sections which have a Horatian elegiac serenity. Such sections—which constitute, not the poem's faith, but its hope—do not evade the perplexity and questioning. They accommodate them within a world of imagined peace (that it is imagined is not disguised, so that the effect is at once calmative and tense), a world in which "perplex" becomes a matter of the ship's gentle passage: "All night no ruder air perplex / Thy sliding keel" (IX); a world in which the answers to our direst questions, to our sense that we are in a mist, might be as forthcoming, as hearteningly resonant, as the Christmas bells: "The Christmas bells from hill to hill / Answer each other in the mist" (XXVIII). One thinks of such sections as IX, "Fair ship, that from the Italian shore"; XI, "Calm is the morn without a sound"; XVII, "Thou comest, much wept for"; XLIII, "If Sleep and Death be truly one"; LXXXIII, "Dip down upon the northern shore"; LXXXVI, "Sweet after showers, ambrosial air"; XCV, "By night we lingered on the lawn"; CXV, "Now fades the last long streak of snow"; CXXI, "Sad Hesper o'er the buried sun"; and the magnificent moonlit landscape in the epilogue. The modern sentimentality of darkness is disconcerted by the truthful optimism (an optimism justified and sensitively circumscribed) such as is appropriate at the end of this epithalamium which imagines the future offspring of a happy union as an augury of a happier future.

Hopkins was perturbed in 1864 when he realized Tennyson's imperfections. But he saw that there was now more danger of being "fooled" into underrating Tennyson than into overrating him:

He is, one must see it, what we used to call Tennysonian. But the discovery of this must not make too much difference. When puzzled by one's doubts it is well to turn to a passage like this. Surely your maturest judgment will never be fooled out of saying that this is divine, terribly beautiful—the stanza of *In Memoriam*, beginning with the quatrain

O [Sad] Hesper o'er the buried sun
And ready, thou, to die with him,
Thou watchest all things ever dim
And dimmer, and a glory done.

"And ready, thou, to die with him": muted and tender, distant but immediate, it is one of Tennyson's finest evocations of what a mature act of self-sacrifice should aspire to resemble. It does not speak of Christ's sacrifice, but it hints at the mystery of the Trinity, for "Sad Hesper" and "Bright Phosphor" are even better than one and the same, they are also two and the same. The division within Tennyson, especially the division between present and past, is here healed:

Sweet Hesper-Phosphor, double name
For what is one, the first, the last,
Thou, like my present and my past,
Thy place is changed; thou art the same.

In Memoriam, like so many of Tennyson's poems, stands strangely to its ending. As a sequence of poems, it is involved constantly in ending and then again beginning. Its prologue, "Strong Son of God, immortal Love" which precedes section I, has been described as "a conclusion more truly than an opening to *In Memoriam*. Insofar as it is a prologue, it is one not so much to the poems it precedes as to the new way of life Tennyson was about to enter." Mrs. Mattes notes too that the trial edition had this prologue before, and not after, the title *In Memoriam A.H.H. Obiit MDCCCXXXIII*, which made a considerable break and gave a different impression of the prologue's relationship to the succeeding poems.

In Memoriam both yearns for and fears an end. "O last regret, regret can die!" (LXXVIII): can the immediate rebuke, "No–," cancel such a fear?

And saying; "Comes he thus, my friend?
Is this the end of all my care?"
And circle moaning in the air:
"Is this the end? Is this the end?"
(XII)

For the moaning fear is that the end (finis) may be something quite other than an end as a purpose or goal.* "What end is here to my complaint?" He wishes not to be in pain, but it is his pain which is the living witness to his love.**

Oh, if indeed that eye foresee
Or see (in Him is no before)
In more of life true life no more
And Love the indifference to be. . . .
(XXVI)

* The manuscript of "Ulysses" had included the strange line, "As though to live were all the end of life."

** Sometimes Love vindicates itself, as in the beautifully paradoxical placing of "fail" at the end of CXXV, where the rhythm and the buoyant persistence insist on a feeling of triumph not of life's failing:

Abiding with me till I sail
To seek thee on the mystic deeps,
And this electric force, that keeps
A thousand pulses dancing, fail.

—then welcome death. What Tennyson most wants in all the world is to exorcise this fear about Hallam: that he is in his grave, and oh the indifference to be.

On such a quest, to travel hopelessly is better than to arrive. Hence the exquisite aptness of Tennyson's choice of stanza for *In Memoriam: abba*, which can "circle moaning in the air," returning to its setting out, and with fertile circularity staving off its deepest terror of arrival at desolation and indifference. It is a stanza which rises to a momentary chime and then fades—but does not fade into despair or vacuity, only into dimness and regret, since after all (after all its lines) there is indeed the distant rhyme. It is the perfect embodiment of the true relationship of faith to faintness in the poem:

> I stretch lame hands of faith, and grope,
> And gather dust and chaff, and call
> To what I feel is Lord of all,
> And faintly trust the larger hope.
>
> (LV)

Faith, trust, and hope are there, but they are framed within something fainter, a fainter rhyme scheme. The very reasons which make the stanza so utterly unsuitable for sustained argument (and whose pressures help to make such sections of argument in *In Memoriam* so feeble and ill judged)—its continual receding from its affirmations, from what it momentarily clinches, so unlike the disputatious sequences of the heroic couplet: these very reasons make it the emblem as well as the instrument for poems in which moods ebb and flow ("There twice a day the Severn fills"), in which hopes are recurrent but always then dimmed—though never shattered. R. H. Hutton remarked that it was a feature of Tennyson's style, this "air of moving through a resisting medium"; Henry James likewise saw the style as "poised and stationary": "the phrase always seems to me to pause and slowly pivot upon itself, or at most to move backward." On the *In Memoriam* stanza itself, a most perceptive comment was made by Kingsley in 1850:

> . . . their metre, so exquisitely chosen, that while the major rhyme in the second and third lines of each stanza gives the solidity and self-restraint required by such deep themes, the mournful minor rhyme of each first and fourth line always leads the ear to expect something beyond . . .

Tennyson most imaginatively senses what such a shape can do.

> Bring in great logs and let them lie,
>   To make a solid core of heat;
>   Be cheerful-minded, talk and treat
> Of all things even as he were by;
>
> (CVII)

—where the birthday festivity for Hallam, the solid core of heat and of warm cheerfulness, is the solid core of the stanza itself.* Or the Christmas bells:

> Four voices of four hamlets round,
>   From far and near, on mead and moor,
>   Swell out and fail, as if a door
> Were shut between me and the sound:
>
> (XXVIII)

—where the sense that the bells "swell out and fail" is evoked through the stanza's own pattern of sounds.

The *In Memoriam* stanza is a fine instance of what Geoffrey Hartman has subtly explored as a relationship of ends to middles in the language of poetry. He quoted Milton's line, "Sonorous metal blowing martial sounds," suggesting that we look at it

> as generated from a redundant concept, "sonorous sounds," which we recover by collapsing the ends. The verse, from this perspective, is the separating out of "sonorous sounds"; a refusal, by inserting a verbal space between adjective and noun, to let them converge too soon.

The *In Memoriam* stanza, though it permits convergence, does so on the strict condition that it be temporary—that it not be, in the strictest sense, final. It is not surprising that the poem contains lines which lend themselves well to Hartman's suggestions.

> And bless thee, for thy lips are bland,
>   And bright the friendship of thine eye;
>   And in my thoughts with scarce a sigh
> I take the pressure of thine hand.
>
> (CXIX)

* Such festivity exists now only in the imagination, and pain is being staved off. Emily's journal, August 6, 1871: "I think Alfred has a happy birthday though we do not mention it to him."

That last line has its tension and force–indeed, its pressure–from the way in which it declines to hurry or economize itself into "I take thine hand." So *take* gains a gravity, a sense of endurance, and "take the pressure" has something of taking a weight or a strain or a responsibility; the pressure is at once gently affectionate and also pressing. At which point one notices that the last two lines themselves reenact the form of the stanza, *abba;* set within the stanza with unobtrusive delicacy, the pattern refines itself to a conclusion:

> *And* in my thoughts with scarce a *sigh*
> *I* take the pressure of thine *hand.*

And the poem's ending? It hated to contemplate the short-term eventuality, so to speak, but it could trust in the eventual, the "event" of all time:

> That friend of mine who lives in God,
>
> That God, which ever lives and loves,
> One God, one law, one element,
> And one far-off divine event,
> To which the whole creation moves.

It is the distance which lends enchantment and might never ask for it back; one day the creation would arrive at the time "when there should be time no longer" (*Revelation*, X.6-7). In the meantime, *E pur si muove.* Again in the meantime, "that friend of mine" receives his last tribute, for it was Hallam himself whose sonnet on the Three Fates had spoken of "The Love / Toward which all being solemnly doth move."

IX

1. 1850–1855

WILLIAM WORDSWORTH, Poet Laureate, died on April 23, 1850. Shortly afterward, Tennyson wrote to his friend John Forster: "I see that the Spectator mentions two candidates for the Laureateship basking in the sunshine of royal favour. Does he mean already enjoying pensions? If so, does he mean L. Hunt and myself? I sincerely hope Hunt will get it rather than myself."* It will be remembered that Tennyson's name had been mooted, and a move made on his behalf, seven years earlier when Southey died; indeed, Henry Crabb Robinson had written to Wordsworth himself, somewhat unthinkingly, "Who is to be the new Laureat . . . There is one old and there is one young poet . . . These are Campbell and Alfred Tennison—As we hear nothing about it, there is a possibility that the office may be abolished."

In 1850 there was once again an old poet, Samuel Rogers, aged eighty-six; Rogers was officially offered the honor in May, but declined it because of "his great age." In September, the prime minister wrote to the Queen, suggesting that "there are three or four authors of nearly equal merit, such as Henry Taylor, Sheridan Knowles, Professor Wilson, and Mr. Tennyson, who are qualified for the office." (Tennyson would hardly have relished the honor's going to Professor Wilson, his old adversary "Christopher

* Hunt was to send Tennyson a characteristically generous letter of congratulation in November.

North.") By October, the Queen was expressing a preference for Tennyson, and inquiring into his character as well as his literary merits. Assured as to both, she offered him the post in November. Tennyson was later to tell his friend James Knowles:

> The night before I was asked to take the Laureateship, which was offered to me through Prince Albert's liking for my *In Memoriam*, I dreamed that he came to me and kissed me on the cheek. I said, in my dream, "Very kind, but very German." In the morning the letter about the Laureateship was brought to me and laid upon my bed. I thought about it through the day, but could not make up my mind whether to take it or refuse it, and at the last I wrote two letters, one accepting and one declining, and threw them on the table, and settled to decide which I would send after my dinner and bottle of port.

He was appointed on November 19.

Perhaps he did not much need to persuade himself, but he was able to point to a genuine reason for accepting: "I was even told that being already in receipt of a pension I could not gracefully refuse it: but I wish more and more that somebody else had it. I have no passion for courts but a great love of privacy: nor do I count having the office as any particular feather in my cap." It was not an honor about which he ever became self-important. Sometimes he was sympathetically childlike about it, as when, traveling incognito in Cornwall in 1860, he noted: "Mr. Poelaur would be a good name to direct to me by." Sometimes he was shrewdly unsentimental, as in conversation with William Allingham in 1866:

> A.–"He [Byron] was the one English writer who disparaged Shakepeare. He was a Lord, and talked about, and he wrote vulgarly, therefore he was popular."
>
> T.–"Why am I popular? I don't write very vulgarly."
>
> A.–"I have often wondered that you are, and Browning wonders."
>
> T.–"I believe it's because I'm Poet-Laureate. It's something like being a lord."

As for the Tennyson d'Eyncourts, they gnashed their teeth. Tennyson's uncle Charles was to be exasperated by the statement in a magazine that Tennyson had spent his boyhood at Bayons ("it is not true. He was a Somersbyite altogether"), and was to deplore the "rubbish" in *Maud, and Other Poems* (1855): "What a strange thing that such a writer should be so generally admired and crowned with laurels by the Queen! Perhaps it is our want of taste which blinds us to his merits!" A week later, his pique had still not cooled:

Horrid rubbish indeed! What a discredit it is that British taste and Poetry should have such a representative before the Nations of the Earth and Posterity! for a Laureate will so appear. Posterity will, it is hoped, have a sound judgment on such matters, and if so what an age *this* must appear when such trash can be tolerated and not only tolerated but enthusiastically admired!! However I do not wish to have my opinion circulated as to my Nephew's talents—for it would only appear to many that I was either without taste or spiteful and he hearing of it would deem it ungracious &c.

As to the Laureate's duties, Tennyson underrated the extent to which they would prove apt to his talent. "The taskwork ode has ever failed," he was rightly to observe, and to Sophy Rawnsley he wrote: "As for writing court odes except upon express command from Headquarters, that I shall not do. Pretty things they are likely to be." In fact he was to find a great deal that was very congenial (not taskwork at all) in the Queen's hopes from him, and it is worth remembering that it was an integral part of his creative temperament that he should receive—and even solicit—suggestions for poems from his friends and family. The Queen herself he was to thank with dignity—"Revered, beloved"—in his first publication as Poet Laureate, "To the Queen" which he dated "March 1851" and published as the dedication of the seventh edition of his *Poems* in 1851.*

In April 1851, a sad blow: Emily was delivered of a still-born baby boy. Tennyson was deeply touched, both by personal sorrow and by the profound mystery of this life that perhaps had never become a life.

Dead as he was I felt proud of him. To-day when I write this down, the remembrance of it rather overcomes me; but I am glad that I have

* Yet Max Beerbohm's cartoon, "Mr. Tennyson, reading 'In Memoriam' to his Sovereign," retains its pungency. Hallam Tennyson, at the age of ten, recorded that "you must stand until the Queen asks you to sit down. Her Majesty does not *often* tell you to sit down."

seen him, dear little nameless one that hast lived though thou hast never breathed, I, thy father, love thee and weep over thee, though thou hast no place in the Universe. Who knows? It may be that thou hast . . . God's Will be done.

Tennyson did not forget this "great grief." Eight years later it can be sensed beneath the memories of "The Grandmother." But in 1851 Tennyson desired only to set down the experience for Emily and himself, in a simple poem which he never published:

> Little bosom not yet cold,
> Noble forehead made for thought,
> Little hands of mighty mould
> Clenched as in the fight which they had fought.
> He had done battle to be born,
> But some brute force of Nature had prevailed
> And the little warrior failed.
> Whate'er thou wert, whate'er thou art,
> Whose life was ended ere thy breath begun,
> Thou nine-months neighbour of my dear one's heart,
> And howsoe'er thou liest blind and mute,
> Thou lookest bold and resolute,
> God bless thee dearest son.

To recuperate, Emily and Tennyson took a holiday in Italy. They enjoyed it, but on their return Emily had to admit that he "looks thin and is not, I fear, the better for his journey . . . So we are come back, I am sorry to say to rather a melancholy house." The melancholy did not altogether lift until the birth of Hallam Tennyson in August 1852. (The second son, Lionel, was born in March 1854.) In November 1853 the Tennysons were to move to a spacious and dignified home: Farringford in the Isle of Wight, which they were to buy in 1856 and which was their home for the rest of their lives.*

Not that Tennyson simply entered bliss. His anxieties were never to leave him, as is clear from a letter to Coventry Patmore in April 1854 after the birth of Lionel:

Many thanks for your congratulations, if the births of babes to poor

* In 1868 they were to build a second home, Aldworth, at Blackdown, Haslemere. Tennyson's mother died in 1865.

men are matters of congratulation. When you call me such a happy man you err: I have had vexations enough since I came here to break my back. These I will not transfer to paper, though I can yet scarcely repeat with satisfaction the proverb of let bygones be bygones; for most of these troubles have not gone by . . . Happy, I certainly have not been. I entirely disagree with the saying you quote of happy men not writing poetry. Vexations (particularly long vexations of a petty kind) are much more destructive of the "gay science," as the Troubadours (I believe) called it.

Nevertheless Aubrey de Vere was judging aright when in September 1854 he said that Tennyson "is much happier and proportionately less morbid than he used to be."

There would still be some of the old shuddering. "I'm black-blooded like all the Tennysons."* Even Emily feared the "hereditary tenderness of nerve"; she was to write to Elizabeth Barrett Browning about her sons' playfulness (aged five and three): "I feel it should at present be indulged that they may have what chance we can give them of gaining strength to bear the weight of over–very, I will not say over–sensitive nerves that may have descended to them and that many signs make me believe have descended and I cannot wish it otherwise." It was to be such shocks as that of Hallam Tennyson's serious illness at school in 1867 that would make Tennyson relapse into self-doubt: "God will take him pure and good, straight from his mother's lessons. Surely it would be better for him than to grow up such a one as I am."

It is with the years 1850–1855 that the alternating exposition of Tennyson's life and his work comes naturally to an end. True, one might say that the story of Tennyson's life until the publication of *Maud* in 1855 is *essentially* the story of his poetry, if by "essentially" one means that it is after all simply Tennyson's poetry which secures attention for his life. Pressed by an anthologist for a biographical paragraph in 1837, Tennyson would send only the "dry dates": "I have no life to give–for mine has been one of feelings not of actions–can he not miss me out altogether?" But from 1855 his life is essentially his work in another sense. By 1855 he

* Aunt Bourne to George Tennyson d'Eyncourt, May 29, 1837: "May God bless you with health and nerves more than ever a Tennyson or d'Eyncourt yet possessed."

was, in important respects, all he was ever to be as a man: his greatest achievements were behind him, though fine ones to come too; he was successful, famous, secure,* and the Poet Laureate; he was a husband and a father. The past had done its worst (and its best), and from 1855 the few things within the story of his life which are importantly new need to be subsumed within an account of his works.

Two observers excellently catch the strange combination of the smouldering and the craggy in the Alfred Tennyson who now had years and honor. The first observer is Nathaniel Hawthorne in 1857:

Tennyson is the most picturesque figure, without affectation, that I ever saw; of middle-size, rather slouching, dressed entirely in black, and with nothing white about him except the collar of his shirt, which methought might have been clean the day before. He had on a black wide-awake hat, with round crown and wide, irregular brim, beneath which came down his long black hair, looking terribly tangled; he had a long, pointed beard, too, a little browner than the hair, and not so abundant as to incumber any of the expression of his face. His frock coat was buttoned across the breast, though the afternoon was warm. His face was very dark, and not exactly a smooth face, but worn, and expressing great sensitiveness, though not, at that moment, the pain and sorrow which is seen in his bust. His eyes were black; but I know little of them, as they did not rest on me, nor on anything but the pictures. He seemed as if he did not see the crowd nor think of them, but as if he defended himself from them by ignoring them altogether. . . As it happened, an acquaintance had met him, an elderly gentleman and lady, and he was talking to them as we approached. I heard his voice; a bass voice, but not of a resounding depth; a voice rather broken, as it were, and ragged about the edges, but pleasant to the ear. His manner, while conversing with these people, was not in the least that of an awkward man, unaccustomed to society; but he shook hands and parted with them, evidently as soon as he courteously could, and shuffled away quicker than before. He betrayed his shy and secluded

* Tennyson's financial rewards, his sales, and his relations with his publishers would be matter for a book in themselves; the material exists at Lincoln for a full study. It should be added that Aunt Russell continued her generosity to Tennyson into the 1850s. In 1892 Tennyson left £57,206.13s.9d.

habits more in this, than in anything else that I observed; though, indeed, in his whole presence, I was indescribably sensible of a morbid painfulness in him, a something not to be meddled with. Very soon, he left the saloon, shuffling along the floor with short irregular steps, a very queer gait, as if he were walking in slippers too loose for him. I had observed that he seemed to turn his feet slightly inward, after the fashion of Indians. . . He is exceedingly nervous, and altogether as un-English as possible; indeed, an Englishman of genius usually lacks the national characteristics, and is great abnormally, and through disease.

The other observer is Sir Henry Taylor, Tennyson's neighbor on the Isle of Wight. Taylor sketched Tennyson in 1860:

And in the midst of all this beauty and comfort stands Alfred Tennyson, grand, but very gloomy, whom it is a sadness to see, and one has to think of his works to believe that he can escape from himself and escape into regions of light and glory. . . With all his shattered nerves and uneasy gloom, he seems to have some sorts of strength and hardihood.

2. *Poems 1852–1854*

TENNYSON'S FIRST SEPARATE publication as Poet Laureate was his "Ode on the Death of the Duke of Wellington." Wellington had died in September 1852; the poem was written in some haste for November, and was extensively revised and reprinted three months later. The reviews were mostly hostile, and Tennyson's distinguished acquaintances were not impressed. Thackeray remarked that "Perhaps the most remarkable thing about the few lines is, that Moxon has given £200 for it," and T. H. Huxley was even colder: "I send Tennyson's ode by way of packing–it is not worth much more." Yet the poem has a sober dignity from its opening command, modulating at once, with apt discretion–the great commander is dead–into authoritative injunction:

> Bury the Great Duke
>   With an empire's lamentation,
> Let us bury the Great Duke
>   To the noise of the mourning of a mighty nation. . .

There is admittedly something stiff about such dignity; its admiration for Wellington rings entirely true, but despite those moments in the poem when Tennyson rightly–and secretly–hopes that he himself may have some sympathetic affinities with Wellington–

> Rich in saving common-sense,
> And, as the greatest only are,
> In his simplicity sublime–

despite these, Wellington is humanly too remote from Tennyson, too alien in his decisiveness, for the poet to be able to enter far. The poem appropriately has recourse to noble reticence. "The last great Englishman is low": this is better than anybody was able to do on the death of Churchill–indeed, found itself quoted on that occasion. But the poem has two flaws, failures of conviction which lead to failures of impression. "Whose life was work": this is honorably to the point, but the trouble is that Tennyson then simply cannot imagine what work in Heaven could be like. So he proffers that dire invitation to doubt, "we doubt not":

> Until we doubt not that for one so true
> There must be other nobler work to do
> Than when he fought at Waterloo,
> And Victor he must ever be.

No doubt. The effect is even less convincing, given that Wellington certainly had done a life's work, than that in *In Memoriam*, where Arthur Hallam "doubtless" is at full stretch in Heaven:

> And, doubtless, unto thee is given
> A life that bears immortal fruit
> In those great offices that suit
> The full-grown energies of heaven.
> (*In Memoriam*, XL)

Like "doubtless," "those" is sheer bluff (oh, *those*). What an honest poet cannot imagine, he had better not write of; his honesty will let him down.*

The same goes for everything that the "Ode" says about Wellington's "eternal honour," his "ever-echoing avenues" of fame. For Tennyson did not, as he perhaps once had, really believe in the eternity of such honor. Fame, he had come to realize, is lost and emptied in the great vistas of geological and astronomical time. Which explains why the "Ode" most strongly asserts itself at the very end, when it sets itself aside:

> Speak no more of his renown,
> Lay your earthly fancies down,

* Carlyle said: "Browning has far more ideas than Tennyson, but is not so truthful. Tennyson means what he says, poor fellow!" (William Allingham's *Diary*, p. 205, June 28, 1871).

And in the vast cathedral leave him.
God accept him, Christ receive him.

Part of the trouble with the "Ode" was that Tennyson was unable to imagine what for a man like Wellington constituted the difficulties of life. Tennyson liked the idea of battles because they seemed simple, not difficult. Such a poem as "Will," of this same date (Tennyson seems to have thought of incorporating it in the "Ode"), gives a sense of what the human difficulties were that did energize his imagination. The optimistic first stanza—"O well for him whose will is strong!"—is too orotund. But the second stanza, about fatigue of will, ends with an apocalyptic intensity which yet is horrified by an outcome, a destination, never to be reached:

He seems as one whose footsteps halt,
Toiling in immeasurable sand,
And o'er a weary sultry land,
Far beneath a blazing vault,
Sown in a wrinkle of the monstrous hill,
The city sparkles like a grain of salt.

The horror of the last line is exacerbated, not diminished, by its lyrical glinting finality. "Grain" impinges as it does because of "sand" earlier, strikingly different and yet desolatingly alike in that both sand and salt are sterile. So that *sown* is seen as the bitterest perversion—salt is sown to make the land barren—which is the counterpart to the perversion of the will. It was perhaps not only the piercing sight of that last line but also its moral imagination which made Ruskin say that "he would sacrifice nearly all his books to have written one of Tennyson's lines—the last line of 'Will': 'The city sparkles like a grain of salt.' "

The new security of these years, 1852–54, was by no means a pure serenity, but it did hearten Tennyson to transmute into poetry the affection, respect, and love which he felt for some who still lived and not only for those, like Hallam and Wellington, who had died. Three poems especially stand out as finer than anything he had earlier written about his Cambridge friends. "To E.L., on His Travels in Greece" is grateful praise to Edward Lear for his *Journals of a Landscape Painter in Albania and Illyria* (1851);

Tennyson pays tribute to a fellow writer without either condescension or mock-modesty, and the poem's symmetry represents the true symmetry of the relationship between writer and reader: two sentences only, each encompassing three stanzas, with the first sentence reviewing—as it were—the book, and with the second letting the book efface itself into the transparency of art, leaving personal response and a redolent landscape:

> For me the torrent ever poured
>   And glistened—here and there alone
>   The broad-limbed Gods at random thrown
> By fountain-urns;—and Naiads oared
>
> A glimmering shoulder under gloom
>   Of cavern pillars. . .

A similar courtesy informs "To the Rev. F. D. Maurice." In October 1853 Maurice was forced to resign from his professorship for arguing that the popular belief in the endlessness of future punishment was superstitious. Tennyson abhorred the belief in eternal punishment; and he had already asked Maurice (who had agreed) to be godfather to Hallam Tennyson, born in August 1852. Tennyson's verse-invitation glowingly revives the Horatian epistle, and bears comparison with such classics of the kind as Ben Jonson's "Inviting a Friend to Supper." The opening—which welcomes Maurice and dismisses the "college-councils" which "Thunder 'Anathema,' friend, at you"—is excellently judged, in that it can provide a living instance of what magnanimity is, without having to praise itself (thanks to the unmagnanimity of Maurice's Christian opponents). A weakness in the poem is its confidence that it could absorb the Crimean War; the pictorial effect from Farringford too much eclipses the politico-moral matter, as is clear in this transition:

> Where, if below the milky steep
> Some ship of battle slowly creep,
>   And on through zones of light and shadow
> Glimmer away to the lonely deep,
>
> We might discuss the Northern sin
> Which made a selfish war begin. . .

Goldwin Smith in 1855 was right to feel some distaste at the picture of the poet "chatting of the war over his wine, while the men-of-war sailing outwards lend another charm to the beautiful sea view." But the poem's core is altogether sound; its evocation of a hospitality that is deep but buoyant, creating, as F. W. Bateson has imaginatively said, "a poetry of the might-have-been in which a Horace collaborates with a Marvell":

> You'll have no scandal while you dine,
> But honest talk and wholesome wine,
> And only hear the magpie gossip
> Garrulous under a roof of pine:
>
> For groves of pine on either hand,
> To break the blast of winter, stand;
> And further on, the hoary Channel
> Tumbles a billow on chalk and sand. . .

In such a setting, human and poetic, what need of an ending? The poem, truly hospitable, can open into a vista that does not forebode but promise, in urging Maurice to pay Farringford a visit:

> Nor pay but one, but come for many,
> Many and many a happy year.

There the prospect is delight; in "The Daisy," delight is the retrospect, and the poem can end with *again*: "My fancy fled to the South again." "The Daisy" is to Tennyson's wife, remembering their Italian tour of 1851, "in a metre which I invented, representing in some measure the grandest of metres, the Horatian Alcaic." It rings and sings at once with the reciprocity of love:

> O love, what hours were thine and mine,
> In lands of palm and southern pine;
> In lands of palm, of orange-blossom,
> Of olive, aloe, and maize and vine.

The affectionate suggestions are truly aligned: the flicker of doubt as to whether it is love itself or a person loved who is being spoken to; the evolution of "hours" into "thine and mine" so that it tacitly incorporates "ours" (they rhyme in lines 41–42); the repetitions which rotate a memory with slow delight and with new wonder, as if saying "lands of palm . . . think of it! . . . lands of palm," culminating in the awed surprised delight of the newly unfolding *and:* "Of olive, aloe, and maize *and* vine"; the marriage memories symbolized in the orange-blossom.*

From the start, the poem is built upon *what* and *how:* what hours, what Roman strength; how like a gem, how richly. Yet despite this persistent shaping, of exclaimed memories, the poem firmly controls its exclamations; it knows that the exclamatory is the enemy of the true exclamation, and it allows only two exclamation marks to be wrung from it, a consequence of the central artistic grandeur of Milan and of the involuntary cry "O":

O Milan, O the chanting quires,
The giant windows' blazoned fires,
  The height, the space, the gloom, the glory!
A mount of marble, a hundred spires!

The only question-mark within the poem (a rarity likewise in tension against "what" and "how") is the wondering and musing of "What more?"

The poem is truly a love poem in its assurance throughout of "we" and "ours," yet never extinguishing the individualities which enter the poem too as "you" and "I." It evokes reciprocity through its visualizing:

What Roman strength Turbia showed
In ruin, by the mountain road;
  How like a gem, beneath, the city
Of little Monaco, basking, glowed.

Basking receives what *glowed* gives forth. "What slender campanili grew . . .": grew, with a natural spontaneity that belongs to these bell-towers as much as to the assonantally chiming plant, "A milky-belled amaryllis," in the same vignette. The daisy of the title was plucked in Italy; it evoked England then, and now—"though crushed to hard and dry"—it speaks tenderly of Italy:

Still in the little book you lent me,
And where you tenderly laid it by.

The reticence of the poem is altogether acute—not till line 50 does it call upon the word "Remember" which has so been waiting to

* On her honeymoon Emily had written to Charles and Louisa, June 17, 1850: "The smell and sight of real orange flowers was almost the only sign of a wedding."

enter the poem, and even then the memory is a rueful one: "Remember what a plague of rain . . ." It is the poem in which Tennyson most deeply expressed all that he owed to Emily, and there is no sentimentality in our feeling gratitude to her as well as to him for one of the finest poetic evocations of gratitude.

In 1854, Tennyson was spurred by a report in *The Times* ("some hideous blunder") into one of his most famous poems, "The Charge of the Light Brigade." "Not a poem on which I pique myself," he said, and at one stage he intended to omit it from the third edition of *Maud, and Other Poems*. Was Milnes right about it?—"A real gallop in verse, and only good as such." Yet it is a stirring poem, the more so for anyone who has heard the recording of Tennyson reading it:

"Forward, the Light Brigade!"
Was there a man dismayed?
Not though the soldier knew
Some one had blundered:
Their's not to make reply,
Their's not to reason why,
Their's but to do and die:
Into the valley of Death
Rode the six hundred.

Tennyson's voice swoops upon *knew* with an emphasis at once awed, exasperated, and half-incredulous at the immediately culpable folly of *some one* (the effect in the recording is riveting). Yet the force of the poem is in its own envious yearning, its knowledge that it was "their's," but is not Tennyson's, "not to make reply," and "not to reason why," and "but to do and die." For Tennyson such an assured simplicity is to be envied. In the heroic futility of the Charge of the Light Brigade, he found a perfect emblem of something which his father's death and his own early misery led him always to envisage: a situation in which it was not merely condonable but actually honorable to commit suicide.*

* Dan Jacobson has said of Edward Thomas and the First World War: "Even the directly suicidal impulses he had from time to time been afflicted with were now given some kind of external direction or sanction" (*The Review*, June 1970).

How characteristic, not only of the movements of Tennyson's mind but also of the movements of his verse, this thrusting forward which then wheels back. The repetitions in the poem (there within the opening line, "Half a league, half a league") epitomize the outward-homeward curve; "Cannon in front of them," then "Cannon behind them"; "Into the mouth of Hell," then "Back from the mouth of Hell." Like the sword Excalibur, rising from the lake and at last returning to it; like the coming and the passing of Arthur, "From the great deep to the great deep he goes"; like "The Golden Year,"

> The dark Earth follows wheeled in her ellipse;
> And human things returning on themselves. . .

–like these, "The Charge of the Light Brigade" advances and wheels. At the very end of his life, Tennyson was to envisage such a curve more truly, as something other than a heroically fatuous reversal:

> But such a tide as moving seems asleep,
> Too full for sound and foam,
> When that which drew from out the boundless deep
> Turns again home.

X
Maud 1855

Tennyson in the 1840s had been so beset by misery that his mildly defiant creation took the shape of banter, fantasy, and evasion: *The Princess*. In the 1850s he was fortified by marriage, financial security, and the Laureateship; he could now afford a more audacious exorcism: *Maud*. *Maud* was an intense and precarious attempt—compacted and impacted—to encompass the bitter experiences of four decades of a life in which many of the formative influences had also been deformative. *Maud* is a story of hereditary melancholia and madness; of a father's bankruptcy and suicide; of family feud; of a love which unexpectedly flowers in spite of snobbery and opposition, but which then, expectedly and grimly, is shattered; of death and loss; of brutal Mammonism. It is a story which gave fierce play to all the central griefs and grievances of Tennyson's life. His dismay at his father's ravings, financial degradations, and suicidal proclivities. His ache at his mother's loneliness. His distaste for the Old Man of the Wolds, aloofly machinating, and for the vulgar pretensions and political posturings of the Tennyson d'Eyncourts ("Seeing his gewgaw castle shine, / New as his title, built last year"). His profound exasperation at being torn by "the feud, / The household Fury." His horror at the madness of his brother Edward and the derangement of his brother Septimus. His contempt for the contemptuous power of Mammon—his Aunt Russell, who had long been so generous to him, was appalled at *Maud*'s attack on the coalmine-owner (her husband's money had come from coal), and Tennyson was then reassuringly sure that he had not been in any way thinking of the Russells. Yet even the sincerest gratitude has its darker pangs and prongs. Still, the fraudulent Dr. Allen had also had his investments in coal; Tennyson's feelings about that squalid débâcle could likewise be channelled into this story of how "a vast speculation had failed," as could Dr. Allen's madhouse. Then there was the love of Tennyson for Rosa Baring, a love condemned by social snobbery; the love of Tennyson for Emily Sellwood, a love impeded by disreputability and respectability; further in the past, the love of Arthur Hallam for Tennyson's sister Emily, a love that had been frustrated forever by pride, bickering, ham-handedness, and tight-fistedness. Beneath and behind these three loves there lurked for Tennyson that series of injustices perpetrated and perpetuated by the Old Man of the Wolds. The loss of Arthur Hallam, too, is at work in the poem—less directly and more controlledly; the germ of *Maud*, "Oh! that 'twere possible," had been written in the year after Hallam's death, but Tennyson had subsequently converted and diverted the poem so that it evinces a genuine maturity and mastery of that grievous experience. Assisted too by the mastery gained in writing and in publishing *In Memoriam*, Tennyson was able in *Maud* to change the loved one from a man to a girl without any sense of strain, evasion or disguise.

All these experiences, which contained much that was rancorous and even rancid, flowed into *Maud*. But the central artery, even more important than Rosa Baring, was Tennyson's blood: that link to his father, the black blood of the Tennysons. The pity and terror which Tennyson had felt for his father's plight (a persecuted man who had persecution mania, a hypochondriac who had ill health) enter the poem as a commiseration which is aware that it must risk the accusation of self-pity since what is at issue is precisely the independence, the free-standing health, of self:

> What! am I raging alone as my father raged in his mood?
> Must *I* too creep to the hollow and dash myself down and die. . .

So large and so total, then, was Tennyson's attempt to make his past come to terms with him, that it is not surprising he gave *Maud* a special place in his heart (and in his readings). "You must always stand up for *Maud* when you hear my pet bantling abused. Perhaps that is why I am sensitive about her. You know mothers always make the most of a child that is abused." Jane Welsh Carlyle observed as much: "He seems strangely excited about *Maud*—as sensitive to criticisms as if they were imputations on his honour." The very fact that such imputations were in no way comic to Tennyson made them slyly comic to bystanders, as in the report given by Rossetti:

> One of his neverended stories was about an anonymous letter running thus (received since *Maud* came out)— "Sir, I used to worship you, but now I hate you. I loathe and detest you. You beast! So you've taken to imitating Longfellow. Yours in aversion,—" and no name, says Alfred, scoring the table with an indignant thumb, and glaring round with suspended pipe, while his auditors look as sympathising as their view of the matter permits.

"Oh! that 'twere possible" had been written in 1833–34; somewhat expanded, hastily and unwillingly, for publication in 1837; but not incorporated into the volumes of 1842. A friend of Tennyson's, Sir John Simeon, deserves credit for having begged Tennyson in 1854 "to weave a story round this poem," but the credit should not be overstated. For Tennyson had already vaguely set about doing something before he met Simeon; indeed, he told Simeon that "Oh! that 'twere possible" "was really intended to be part of a dramatic poem." But what kind of dramatic poem is *Maud?* In 1856, perhaps remembering that R. H. Horne had earlier called "St. Simeon Stylites" a "monodrama," Robert Mann described *Maud* as a monodrama. Alexander Macmillan echoed the term three years later; and in 1875 Tennyson expanded the title to *Maud: A Monodrama.* His original title had been *Maud or the Madness:* the account of the poem which he gave to his son is direct, and conscious of the antagonism which the poem had roused:

> This poem of *Maud or the Madness* is a little *Hamlet*, the history of a morbid, poetic soul, under the blighting influence of a recklessly speculative age. He is the heir of madness, an egoist with the makings of a cynic, raised to a pure and holy love which elevates his whole nature, passing from the height of triumph to the lowest depth of

misery, driven into madness by the loss of her whom he has loved, and, when he has at length passed through the fiery furnace, and has recovered his reason, giving himself up to work for the good of mankind through the unselfishness born of a great passion. The peculiarity of this poem is that different phases of passion in one person take the place of different characters.

To his friend Knowles, Tennyson put the point slightly differently: "No other poem (a monotone with plenty of change and no weariness) has been made into a drama where successive phases of passion in one person take the place of successive persons." Yet the reason why *Maud* works as a monodrama (is something other than a *congeries* of short poems, or a sprawling dramatic monologue, or a mutilated drama) is the essential relationship between those two very different subtitles: "A Monodrama" and "or the Madness." Dr. Allen had written in his *Essay on the Classification of the Insane* (1837) about "the more fixed and serious forms of alternate states of irresistible excitement of the exhilarating and depressing passions, constituting insane cases." The point is not simply that the hero of *Maud* is the sort of person who (fortunately for the poem, unfortunately for him) has splendidly various "successive phases of passion"; rather, that he is so near madness—and does indeed go mad—that it is possible, apt, and compelling for "successive phases of passion in one person [to] take the place of successive persons." The dislocations of self in the hero can be turned with creative appositeness—to something that is lamentably like the company of successive persons.* Hence, in Sir Harold Nicolson's words, "that flickering half-light between the sane and the insane, which, as in *Maud*, constitutes Tennyson's most personal and poignant note." The flickering is there in the opening section, with its lurid glimpse of a society diseased by Mammonism:

> While another is cheating the sick of a few last gasps, as he sits
> To pestle a poisoned poison behind his crimson lights.

On the one hand, "a poisoned poison" sounds like the very lan-

* There are dislocations of self, similar and dissimilar, in the tape-recordings which resemble the company of successive persons in Samuel Beckett's monodrama, *Krapp's Last Tape*.

guage of mania, a breakdown into the glittering insistence of a taut tautology; on the other hand, it is also a compactly precise description of the drug that the chemist wantonly dispenses—a poison but not necessarily poisoned except by the commercialized indifference that is an evil dispensation. The same goes for the "crimson lights," which are both nightmarish and literal—themselves a half-light between the insane and the sane. George Eliot, who loathed *Maud*, had to concede that "these hexameters, weak in logic and grating in sound, are undeniably strong in expression, and eat themselves with phosphoric eagerness into our memory, in spite of our will."

The hero is divided against himself. Even the ghost of Maud is divided into two phantoms, one dreary and one beneficent. But not only does "the incipient stage of madness" give to the hero's utterances a bitter diversity as of a cast of characters, it also—and again with psychological and moral aptness—attenuates into phantasmal unreality, or into pulsations "growing and fading and growing," the other people whom we see only through the eye and brain of madness, through a victim of what Bagehot called "mental malaria." This may sound like a circuitous excuse for Tennyson's lack of straight dramatic power, a lack which his later plays sadly evince; but as with any true poet, creation took the form of turning to legitimate advantage what elsewhere was indeed a lack or imbalance. One remembers T. S. Eliot's praise of Milton for "his inerrancy, conscious or unconscious, in writing so as to make the best display of his talents, and the best concealment of his weaknesses"; but what is at stake is not "display" and "concealment" so much as intelligent and creative resourcefulness. Tennyson's lack of certain kinds of dramatic gift focused his mind and heart upon that tension between stasis and outcome which the dramatic monologue was uniquely fitted to explore and interpret. In *Maud*, his sense of the relationship between madness and monodrama enabled him to create a living representation of the way in which a morbid self-consciousness precludes the consciousness of others' selves.

For those who agree with T. S. Eliot that a morbid self-consciousness, usurping the place of a religious consciousness, is preeminently the modern malaise, there would be point in applying a generalization of Eliot's which certainly could point to one area of *Maud*'s moral concern with the cruelly unreal:

> With the disappearance of the idea of Original Sin, with the disappearance of the idea of intense moral struggle, the human beings presented to us both in poetry and in prose fiction to-day [1934], and more patently among the serious writers than in the underworld of letters, tend to become less and less real.

"Less and less real," and "more and more vaporous": but part of the point of *Maud* is that, through the eyes of a disordered individual within a disordered society, people will seem less and less real. In which case Gladstone's strictures on *Maud* may seize the right matter by the wrong end: "Both Maud and the lover are too nebulous by far; and they remind us of the boneless and pulpy personages by whom, as Dr. Whewell assures us, the planet Jupiter is inhabited, if inhabited at all." That is wittily said, but (as so often with penetratingly hostile criticism) it too quickly moves from its acute sense of what the poem is like, to its assurance that the poem should not be like that. Boneless and pulpy, the hero indeed intermittently is—and so is his vision of other people. The sense, as in madness, that other people are on another planet: that, which Gladstone is in the vicinity of, is a true insight into this poem and its subject, this poem which speaks often and beautifully about the planets and stars.

To say, then, that the heroine of *Maud* never becomes a living breathing individual is not simply to say that *Maud* fails. The failure is that of the hero's love, which begins in uneasy scorn; moves into a rapture which is indeed nothing but right and proper at such a stage of love but which necessarily has little room for the uniquely personal, the known intimacy which asks time, domesticity, the daily affections; and then is irreparably smashed by the duel and then by Maud's death, before there ever can begin that more mature phase of love which would have to recognize, would delight in recognizing, the unvaporous, the unnebulous, in a breathing loved one. Plainly it cannot be denied that the poem offers a deeply pessimistic view of marriage; both sets of parents are pained and painful, and there is a sense in which it seems too clearly, too easily, a mercy that the hero and Maud are excused from having ever to build an enduring love within the society he vividly deplores. But this is not the same as a complaint about Maud's insubstantiality; that insubstantiality she never loses, and such is the poem's peculiar regret. It is a poem about losing someone whom you have never really had. She is at first beautiful, but as a gem, as an epitome of womankind, as a phantasmal pulse, a dreamlike vision:

> Cold and clear-cut face, why come you so cruelly meek,
> Breaking a slumber in which all spleenful folly was drowned,
> Pale with the golden beam of an eyelash dead on the cheek,
> Passionless, pale, cold face, star-sweet on a gloom profound;
> Womanlike, taking revenge too deep for a transient wrong
> Done but in thought to your beauty, and ever as pale as before
> Growing and fading and growing upon me without a sound,
> Luminous, gemlike, ghostlike, deathlike, half the night long,
> Growing and fading and growing, till I could bear it no more. . .

Among the things which he cannot bear about Maud is precisely the dread of her as a unique person; part of him wants her to be a snobbish puppet, part of him tries to divide her as he himself feels divided–

> and adore,
> Not her, who is neither courtly nor kind,
> Not her, not her, but a voice.

His love never becomes perfect, so it never altogether casts out fear; but it replaces fear and masochism by awe: "And dream of her beauty with tender dread . . ."–tender, both as sweetly moved and as touchingly bruisable. Tender dread is never in *Maud* to be succeeded by the sober certainty of waking bliss; but it is an important human advance. For *Maud* is an unprecedented evocation of a deep fear of love. "And most of all would I flee from the cruel madness of love . . .": *Maud* is not a poem which uses the word "madness" lightly; the essential madness is the fear of love, and the hero is not thinking of traditional cheerful pangs, but of the worst psychic cowardice and dismay. What he centrally fears is not that he cannot be loved but that he cannot love.

> Till a morbid hate and horror have grown
> Of a world in which I have hardly mixt,
> And a morbid eating lichen fixt
> On a heart half-turned to stone.

"Hardly" has a sardonic hardness. "O heart of stone, are you flesh, and caught / By that you swore to withstand?" Stone, but without the elegant fiction of statuary, which creates a flickering pun in "Wept over her" in these lines:

She came to the village church,
And sat by a pillar alone;
An angel watching an urn
Wept over her, carved in stone. . .

So that it is not merely a social snub but an emasculating humiliation which is involved in the threatening insouciance of Maud's brother:

But while I past he was humming an air,
Stopt, and then with a riding-whip
Leisurely tapping a glossy boot,
And curving a contumelious lip,
Gorgonised me from head to foot
With a stony British stare.*

The hideousness of the later débâcle is that it forces the hero back into thinking he cannot love: "Courage, poor heart of stone!," he groans, "Courage, poor stupid heart of stone."

"Then some one else may have much to fear": loving him is dangerous, and so is love. "I hate": that is how *Maud* begins. He does not hate a person, but a place—but then the place has a surrealistic lunacy which suggests a bleeding woman:

I hate the dreadful hollow behind the little wood,
Its lips in the field above are dabbled with blood-red heath,
The red-ribbed ledges drip with a silent horror of blood,
And Echo there, whatever is asked her, answers "Death."

There is a gruesome glimpse of the traditional sense of "horror," (of hair standing on end), so phantasmagorically in relationship with "drip"; and there is a grim equivocation in the phrase "horror of blood." *I hate:* much has to happen before he can say "I love."

Tennyson's profound personal involvement in *Maud*, its act of exorcism, precipitated some of his most central and least idiosyn-

* See Freud, "Medusa's Head."

cratic insights into love, death, and society. But, as was seen from its first appearance, though it "found a pearl," a pearl is a morbid secretion. Tennyson was able neither to endorse nor to repudiate his hero; the accusation that the poet is in collusion with his character is a crucial one. But it is also (as is clear from such very different cases as those of Milton, Swift, Jane Austen, Dickens, and D. H. Lawrence) a very difficult accusation to formulate at once precisely and generally. Nothing but a detailed investigation of each stage of this deliberately (and aptly) fluctuating poem would be of much use. A critic would need to establish distinctions with patient scruple, would contrast these first three lines (too easily self-accusing) with the tautening in the last line, with "sick to the heart" and "sick of life" compacting a heart-felt sickness into "the heart of life":

> And therefore splenetic, personal, base,
> A wounded thing with a rancorous cry,
> At war with myself and a wretched race,
> Sick, sick to the heart of life, am I.

Or where, after crying out for a strong man, the narrator cries out in pain and pathos, a cry that is wrung from him, a cry which sees that a moral rebirth would hurt and would be a sort of suicide:

> And ah for a man to arise in me,
> That the man I am may cease to be!

There is an impressive list of acute readers who have indeed seen this as a nub. Tennyson's friend Dr. Mann referred with some scorn to those who saw *Maud* as "*an aegis covering startling propositions* from too close philosophic scrutiny." But there are testimonies not to be disregarded. That of Gladstone: "We frankly own that our divining rod does not enable us to say whether the poet intends to be in any and what degree sponsor to these sentiments, or whether he has put them forth in the exercise of his undoubted right to make vivid and suggestive representations of even the partial and narrow aspects of some endangered truth." *Make representations:* the phrase would punningly capture the two different concerns. For George Eliot, there was no difficulty, no uncertainty: "In the denunciations we have here of new-made fortunes, new titles, new houses, and new suits of clothes, it is evidently Mr. Tennyson's aversion, and not merely his hero's morbid mood, that speaks." But "evidently" is just what such collusion is usually not. Walter Bagehot more shrewdly played "by no means" against "seemed" in what is a first-rate evocation of a proper unease:

He seemed to sympathize with the feverish railings, the moody nonsense, the very entangled philosophy, which he put into the mouth of his hero. There were some odd invectives against peace, against industry, against making your livelihood, which seemed by no means to be dramatic exhibitions of represented character, but on the contrary, confidential expositions of the poet's own belief. He not only depicted the natural sentiments of an inactive, inexperienced, and neglected young man, but seemed to agree with them. He sympathised with moody longings; he was not severe on melancholy vanity; he rather encouraged a general disaffection to the universe. He appeared not only to have written, but to have accepted the "Gospel according to the Unappreciated." The most charitable reader could scarcely help fancying, that in describing irritable confusion of fancy and a diseased moodiness of feeling, the poet for the time imbibed a certain taint of those defects.

"A neglected young man": for in *Maud*, Tennyson reversed his usual indirection. Instead of the "mask of age," which he had donned for "Ulysses," "Tithonus," "Tiresias," and many other poems, he donned the mask of youth, and in his mid-forties sought the tones of a man's mid-twenties. Most of his best previous poems had dealt with a life which he had not had; they had imagined a uniquely experienced man (Ulysses, St. Simeon, Tithonus) who possessed a past quite other than Tennyson's. But in *Maud* it is only Maud herself who represents a past which Tennyson never had (and was never to have; Emily's good qualities were not Maud's). The rest of the poem is an inexorable grappling with the past that Tennyson had lived through (one can hardly say "enjoyed").

So now I have sworn to bury
All this dead body of hate,
I feel so free and so clear
By the loss of that dead weight. . .

The dead body of the past. Tennyson at this stage of his life was haunted by the feeling that the dead are all too intimidatingly alive; they stalk through *Maud* with a weightier tread than do the shadowy living. He remembers his dead mother—"And that dead man at her heart and mine." His father. It was not to be till the end of his life that he could find such a haunting to be consolatory and kindly, no threat to the livingness of the living: "Peace, let it be! for I loved him, and love him for ever: the dead are not dead but alive."

"Successive phases of passion": some sense of the shape of *Maud* may be gained by selecting the seven sections which most strongly distill its phases. Something has already been said of the first, the opening, "I hate the dreadful hollow behind the little wood. . . ." But such wildness is later succeeded by a simple recognition which is more bleak, a lacerating mildness:

I

O let the solid ground
  Not fail beneath my feet
Before my life has found
  What some have found so sweet;
Then let come what come may,
What matter if I go mad,
I shall have had my day.

II

Let the sweet heavens endure,
  Not close and darken above me
Before I am quite quite sure
  That there is one to love me;
Then let come what come may
To a life that has been so sad,
I shall have had my day.

A deep fear, a wary walking, underlies the rhythm and syntax. "O let the solid ground / Not fail beneath my feet . . .": the verbal mastery which creates such precariousness at the line-brink (as of feeling for a step in the dark) can be seen in the contrast with the manuscript reading, where the note is of the wrong kind of assurance:

Let not the sound earth fail
And open under my feet...

The next phase, of the assurance of loving and being loved and of an inalienable right, crystallizes in the greatest love poem which Tennyson ever wrote. It has the calm of a fulfilled expectation and the surprise of a supple undulation. It holds its good fortune before itself with an inexhaustible amazement; its repetitions are not those of dismay or neurosis, but of a profound wonder:

I

I have led her home, my love, my only friend.
There is none like her, none.
And never yet so warmly ran my blood
And sweetly, on and on
Calming itself to the long-wished-for end,
Full to the banks, close on the promised good.

II

None like her, none.
Just now the dry-tongued laurels' pattering talk
Seemed her light foot along the garden walk,
And shook my heart to think she comes once more;
But even then I heard her close the door,
The gates of Heaven are closed, and she is gone.

III

There is none like her, none...

And so into the exquisite description of the great cedar, and of the night sky. But the extraordinary thing about this section is the way it can incorporate into its delight a mature sense of what still threatens the delight. Mature, in that it is free from self-pity: "my only friend" is a simple statement, not a bid for sympathy, and the hero can say "It seems that I am happy" (a desolating way of putting it) without any exclamatory triumphing but with an awed dignity. The section ends with a brave recognition of vulnerability; it is a poignant moment because the resolution in it is genuine—all along he has been vulnerable but hitherto he has rather liked the idea of being wounded.

Beat, happy stars, timing with things below,
Beat with my heart more blest than heart can tell,

Blest, but for some dark undercurrent woe
That seems to draw—but it shall not be so:
Let all be well, be well.

The next phase of passion creates its climax in "Come into the garden, Maud." Delight has been succeeded by joy; Maud is coming to him from the dance, the dance to which he was not invited. His heart dances; he is giddy, expectation whirls him round. Time is at last his friend and will bring his only friend.

For a breeze of morning moves,
  And the planet of Love is on high,
Beginning to faint in the light that she loves
  On a bed of daffodil sky,
To faint in the light of the sun she loves,
  To faint in his light, and to die.

The death is erotic, ecstatic. The movement circles and returns upon itself, with the joyous intricacy and command of a dance. George Eliot found "very exquisite" the way in which "the music of the verse seems to faint and die like the star"; Ruskin noticed moreover an effect of the stanza-form: "The intense anxiety and agitation of the lover's mind is marked by not one of the lines being exactly similar to another in its prosody." Yet the anxiety and agitation are masterful, not servile, and the lyric ends with an exultant affirmation:

She is coming, my own, my sweet;
  Were it ever so airy a tread,
My heart would hear her and beat,
  Were it earth in an earthy bed;
My dust would hear her and beat,
  Had I lain for a century dead;
Would start and tremble under her feet,
  And blossom in purple and red.*

Thus ends Part I of *Maud*. But the exultation is a bitter irony; the next line of the poem takes us into the disaster of the duel with Maud's brother, and Part II does indeed grimly answer this romantic prophecy of the undying heart: the hero in his madness

* The recording of Tennyson reading this stanza is unforgettably piercing.

believes himself to be dead and buried but racked by the feet overhead.

The next phase is of anguish after the death of Maud.

> O that 'twere possible
> After long grief and pain
> To find the arms of my true love
> Round me once again!

It is an anguish which confronts its worst loneliness in among the crowds of men, rhyming "city" with "without pity." In such a world without pity, self-pity becomes something which we can hardly be brusquely superior to:

> But the broad light glares and beats,
> And the shadow flits and fleets
> And will not let me be;
> And I loathe the squares and streets,
> And the faces that one meets,
> Hearts with no love for me:
> Always I long to creep
> Into some still cavern deep,
> There to weep, and weep, and weep
> My whole soul out to thee.

This is clearly trembling on the brink of madness, with the momentary stiffening in *one* ("I . . . one meets . . . me") having a pathetic fragility, a despairing momentary attempt at the impersonal and formal.

With immediate horror, the next phase succeeds. The "still cavern deep" is deeply macabre, for in madness the speaker now believes himself dead. It is Tennyson's most horrifying vision of a life which is no life, a madness which believes that it is dead and yet longs for death, a suicidal impulse thwarted relentlessly.*

> Dead, long dead,
> Long dead!
> And my heart is a handful of dust,
> And the wheels go over my head,

* There is a suggestion of the crossroad (where the suicide was traditionally buried—Tennyson alluded to this in the last line of "Despair") in: "And the wheels go over my head," etc.

And my bones are shaken with pain,
For into a shallow grave they are thrust,
Only a yard beneath the street,
And the hoofs of the horses beat, beat,
The hoofs of the horses beat,
Beat into my scalp and my brain,
With never an end to the stream of passing feet,
Driving, hurrying, marrying, burying,
Clamour and rumble, and ringing and clatter,
And here beneath it is all as bad,
For I thought the dead had peace, but it is not so;
To have no peace in the grave, is that not sad?
But up and down and to and fro,
Ever about me the dead men go;
And then to hear a dead man chatter
Is enough to drive one mad.

Terror meets pathos, in the piercing combination of a total incomprehension with a patient effort at comprehension and explanation ". . . but it is not so"; and in the withered formality of understatement: ". . . is that not sad?"; and in the honorable recalcitrance which cannot bring itself to face its plight: ". . . is enough to drive one mad." The hopes and consolations which can be woven are so thin against the cold black night of his suffering, a suffering which is heartbreaking just because what it asks for is so humbly minimal, "ever so little":

O me, why have they not buried me deep enough?
Is it kind to have made me a grave so rough,
Me, that was never a quiet sleeper?
Maybe still I am but half-dead;
Then I cannot be wholly dumb;
I will cry to the steps above my head
And somebody, surely, some kind heart will come
To bury me, bury me
Deeper, ever so little deeper.

So ends Part II. Part III constitutes the final "phase of passion," and has always aroused the fiercest of passions. Not that there can be any intrinsic objection to Tennyson's showing us a man recovered from madness (such an objection would be merely an inverted sentimentality); and Tennyson was right to observe that the hero's final ringing affirmations should not be seen in isolation from his earlier ringing denunciations: "Take this with the first where he railed at everything—He is not quite sane—a little shattered." No, the trouble is simply that the hero's moral and spiritual health is offered as residing in his enlisting to fight in the Crimean War.* A just cause, and "The blood-red blossom of war with a heart of fire."

The ending was fierily deplored, and Tennyson respected some specific objections, as when he changed "the long, long canker of peace" (1855) to "the peace, that I deemed no peace" (1856). He was surprised by the rage. George Eliot declared (roundly but anonymously) of *Maud:* "its tone is throughout morbid; it opens to us the self revelations of a morbid mind, and what it presents as the cure for this mental disease is itself only a morbid conception of human relations." She did not share Tennyson's apparent "faith in War as the unique social regenerator." Nor did Gladstone: "What interpretation are we meant to give to all this sound and fury? We would fain have put it down as intended to be the finishing-stroke in the picture of a mania which has reached its zenith."

These objections are real and telling, and they were made with especial acumen by Goldwin Smith. "To wage 'war with a thousand battles and shaking a hundred thrones,' in order to cure a hypochondriac and get rid of the chicory in coffee, is a bathos." But there are four points which should be made, not because they annul but because they set within limits the accusation about *Maud*'s ending.

First, there is a contrariety, or at least an equivocation, within the ending itself.

> And the cobweb woven across the cannon's throat
> Shall shake its threaded tears in the wind no more.

To J. M. Robertson in 1889, these lines "are as entirely admirable in point of poetic art as they are repulsive in their moral intention." But these are not the only lines which convey a pathos, a reluctance, that is at odds with the resonant bloodthirstiness. Such a

* For a strange relationship between the Crimea, delirium and recovery, within the life or imagination of Tennyson's father, see pp. 25–26.

reluctance cannot but temper the moral intention—is, indeed, in a larger sense part of the moral intention.

Second, it would be naïve to assume that the naïveté of *Maud*'s ending renders it simply false. For there have been particular wars which were rightly felt by those who enlisted in them to be honorable, vivifying, and just. It is one thing for a critic or historian to argue that in fact the Crimean War was no such thing; it is another to assume that any poem which sees a patriotic enlistment as an act of personal and national salvation must be lamentably bellicose. Moreover, the general point which Tennyson (in concord with Carlyle) was making is certainly one that can be sympathetically framed, as it was by Dr. Mann:

> sad as open and declared war is, it has in it those touches of moral grandeur which make its horrors tolerable in comparison with the more dreadful social, and domestic hostilities, which seethe continuously in the dense populations of over-crowded lands.

Third, the failure of the ending is partly technical rather than directly moral. (Though the technical failure is related to a failure of Tennyson's imagination, and connects with his unimaginativeness about war.*) What happens is that there is a misguided jump from one phase of passion to the next, from the madhouse of "ever so little deeper" to the fully fledged military affirmation. The ending cost Tennyson much anxiety and effort; he did not make the division into three parts until 1865 (in 1859 he had divided it into two parts), and he retained—with a suggestive anomaly—the numbering of sections, so that Part III does not begin again, as Part II does, with a section I, but begins with section VI. But to leap from straitjacket to military uniform—without any "phase of passion" that was intermediately sane—was to invite misconstruction. George Eliot misrepresents the poem's plot when she says baldly that "From this madness he is recovered by the news that the Allies have declared war against Russia," or when she speaks of "the cure for this mental disease." Yet it is a misrepre-

* "Boädicea" (written 1859–60) is his best poem about war, because it is also about the indurating desensitizing effects of battle-fervor. Tennyson is always imaginatively sensitive to splintering weapons, but not often to splintering skulls.

sentation which the poem invites, by its precipitate unwillingness to conceive that an essential phase of the hero's passion was being shirked.

Last, there is the unmentioned outcome. For the odds are that the hero is going to his death. (Tennyson not only wrote "The Charge of the Light Brigade" at this time, he also published it with *Maud*.) The honorable suicide of a soldier may redeem the dishonorable suicide. The poem ends, not with Maud's embrace, but with God's: "I embrace the purpose of God, and the doom assigned." It was therefore somewhat vengeful of G. W. Foote to insist that "the hero of *Maud* rants about himself until we begin to hope that the Crimea will really settle him." Similarly, it was hasty of Goldwin Smith not to distinguish at this point the poet and the character:

> We do not, like the nations of antiquity to whom Tyrtæus sung, literally *go* to war. We send our hired soldiers to attack a nation which may not be in need of the same regimen as ourselves. To most of us, the self-sacrifice involved in war with an enemy who cannot get at us consists in paying rather more taxes.

A legitimate point against some of Tennyson's patriotic poems, but not a legitimate point against *Maud*. Yet the central perplexing inextricability of the poem is indeed a consequence of Tennyson's tangled feelings. Maud herself (somewhat surprisingly) had sung of men who march "To the death, for their native land." She had sung

> A passionate ballad gallant and gay,
> A martial song like a trumpet's call!

But the poem never brings to light the relation between that passion and the passion of love. It is as if as *Maud* were built upon a gruesome Freudian misprint: "martial," read "marital."

XI

Idylls of the King 1859–1885

In December 1858, Tennyson wrote to his American publishers:

> I wish that you would disabuse your own minds and those of others, as far as you can, of the fancy that I am about an Epic of King Arthur.
> I should be crazed to attempt such a thing in the heart of the 19th Century.

Seven months later, Tennyson published *Idylls of the King*.* True, this was no more than the earliest batch of four ("Enid," "Vivien," "Elaine," and "Guinevere"); true, they did not constitute an "Epic," and perhaps even the completed enterprise never did—though Tennyson's son was to claim mildly that the *Idylls* achieved "Epic unity." Nevertheless, the discrepancy is a revealing one, not because of insincerity but because of vacillation. No other poem of Tennyson's was created with such a central uncertainty as to its shape, style, sequence, and size. Such uncertainty in composition is not in itself any evidence of ultimate uncertainty in achievement. Yet *Idylls of the King* are strikingly uneven, and it is hard not to feel that the strange indecisions of their composition are an index of what went askew.

"Tennyson's Serial Poem": the title which Professor Kathleen Tillotson gave to her important detailed study of the *Idylls* is in danger of overdignifying the compromises and timidities which were engrained in this poetic venture. Tennyson had written his "Morte d'Arthur" in 1833–34, and had published it in 1842.

* Tennyson pronounced "Idyll" with an I as in "idle."

When I was twenty-four I meant to write a whole great poem on it, and began it in the "Morte d'Arthur." I said I should do it in twenty years; but the Reviews stopped me.

More specifically, the *Quarterly Review*, where John Sterling disparaged "Morte d'Arthur" in September 1842. Tennyson told both his son and William Allingham that by this review "he was prevented from doing his Arthur Epic." "I had it all in my mind, could have done it without any trouble." He went on: "But then I thought that a small vessel, built on fine lines, is likely to float further down the stream of Time than a big raft." A good point (though Tennyson unfortunately would not have liked us then to apply the term "a big raft" to the *Idylls*)—but one which already complicates and clouds the initial commitment to "his Arthur Epic," since the point is an independent act of criticism. A more serious complication is that Tennyson had already manifested a public unease about the epic before Sterling ever reviewed him. For he had framed "Morte d'Arthur" with one of those poetic wheedlings, those throwings on your mercy, which Leigh Hunt rightly deplored; preceding and succeeding "Morte d'Arthur" in 1842 was "The Epic" (which Tennyson wrote probably in 1837–38).

> "You know," said Frank, "he burnt
> His epic, his King Arthur, some twelve books"—
> And then to me demanding why? "Oh, sir,
> He thought that nothing new was said, or else
> Something so said 'twas nothing—that a truth
> Looks freshest in the fashion of the day. . ."

"I should be crazed to attempt such a thing in the heart of the 19th Century." In other words, Sterling's doubts had been explicitly anticipated by Tennyson's own doubts; what distressed him in the review, what made it prevent his going ahead, was not its being a shock but its being a telling corroboration of what he had acutely feared. "Morte d'Arthur" was plucked from the hearth; though the lines of "The Epic" had been written and published, the Epic itself had not been written but had been ingeniously burned instead.

In the 1840s, Tennyson "began to study the epical King Arthur in earnest. . . . But it was not till 1855 that he determined upon the final shape of the poem, and not until 1859 that he published the first instalment, 'Enid,' 'Vivien,' 'Elaine,' 'Guinevere.' " Even as an installment, this was far from being in final shape; only the last retained its title, and "Enid"—with more decisiveness than sensitivity of decision—was to be brusquely divided into two idylls, "The Marriage of Geraint" and "Geraint and Enid."

Hallam Tennyson remarks: "In spite of the public applause he did not rush headlong into the other *Idylls of the King*, although he had carried a more or less perfected scheme of them in his head over thirty years." But as Hallam Tennyson then concedes, there were recalcitrances in the scheme. First, Tennyson said "I could hardly light upon a finer close than that ghost-like passing away of the King"; but this passing away was in "Guinevere," which therefore had one kind of claim as an ending, and not in "Morte d'Arthur" which had a conflicting claim. (Moreover, even "Morte d'Arthur" had originally been thought of as the eleventh, not the twelfth, book.) Second, there is his unease in 1862: "I have thought about it, and arranged all the intervening *Idylls*, but I dare not set to work for fear of a failure and time lost." Third, there was his doubt about whether he would ever be able to undertake the Grail story: "I doubt whether such a subject as the San Graal could be handled in these days without incurring a charge of irreverence. It would be too much like playing with sacred things." Yet this last doubt has its own wobble, since Tennyson elsewhere said that he had once made up—in his head and "in as good verse . . . as I ever wrote"—a poem on Lancelot's quest of the Grail.

The "more or less perfected scheme" was fraught with doublings back upon itself. Tennyson's tone in 1868 has something of the haphazard: "I shall write three or four more of the *Idylls*, and link them together as well as I may." But ten years after the first installment there appeared in 1869 the second: "The Coming of Arthur," "The Holy Grail," "Pelleas and Ettarre," and "The Passing of Arthur." This last was "Morte d'Arthur" now preceded by the last great battle (169 lines) and with a concluding 29 lines. Tennyson in 1862 had resisted the idea of using "Morte d'Arthur" as the ending, partly because of the passing away in "Guinevere," and partly because "the 'Morte' is older in style." But others denied that there was any incongruity, and in 1869 "The Passing of Arthur" bore a note: "This last, the earliest written of the Poems, is here connected with the rest in accordance with an early project of the author's." Readers in 1869 were given too a note on how to order the series.

It seemed—and not to the unintelligent—that Tennyson was making up an ordering as he went along when in 1871 he published "The Last Tournament" and in 1872 "Gareth and Lynette." Whereupon, as Hallam Tennyson says, "my father thought that he had completed the cycle of the *Idylls;* but later he felt that some further introduction to 'Merlin and Vivien' was necessary, and so wrote 'Balin and Balan.' " But even here there was wavering. For one thing, Tennyson said in 1873, "I must have two more Idylls at the least to make 'Vivien' come later into the Poem, as it comes in far too soon as it stands." A shrewd criticism, since the earliness of "Merlin and Vivien" has the bad effect of presenting Arthur's court as lamentably corrupted far too early for the moral scheme and for its pathos. Yet far from adding "two more Idylls at the least," Tennyson added only "Balin and Balan"; moreover, he wrote it in 1872–74 and yet did not publish it till 1885, "whether for the sake of purchasers," suggests Kathleen Tillotson, "or because he had not decided whether to make it into one or two." Not that "Balin or Balan" could have been creatively snipped in two. But the composition and publication of *Idylls of the King*, extending over more than fifty years, are not a record of firm creative decision or of an organic responsiveness.

Large-scale attempts have recently been made to reinstate, or rather, instate *Idylls of the King* as a large-scale achievement. But a reader may find himself concurring with the claims that the *Idylls* are intricately patterned; that they show a subtle and erudite mastery of their sources; that they are a complex allegory and that they anticipate Jungian psychology;—without being convinced that they do indeed constitute a poetic whole. Was the title *Idylls* defensively modest or truly so? Gladstone saw a discrepancy between the title and the ambitions:

> We are rather disposed to quarrel with the title of Idylls: for no diminutive (εἰδύλλιον) can be adequate to the breadth, vigour, and maj-

esty which belongs to the subjects, as well as to the execution, of the volume.

R. H. Hutton similarly deplored the title—and then, as has proved so easy to do, he himself stepped up the claims within the title by giving it, not as *Idylls of the King*, but as *The Idylls of the King:* "The great poem called, I think with somewhat unfortunate modesty, *The Idylls of the King*. The title misled the public, and the fragmentary mode in which the poem appeared misled it the more."

It is true that the Victorians were not helped by the fragmentary publication to see such unity as the poem may possess. But they were sensitive to the two crucial disappointments which the poem has long elicited, disappointments so fundamental as to vitiate any ambitious advocacy of the *Idylls* which does not incorporate a stylistic advocacy. Elizabeth Barrett Browning wrote to Tennyson's friend Allingham in 1859:

> But the *Idylls*. Am I forced to admit that after the joy of receiving them, other joys fell short, rather? —That the work, as a whole, produced a feeling of disappointment? —It must be admitted, I fear. Perhaps we had been expecting too long—had made too large an idea to fit a reality. Perhaps the breathing, throbbing life around us in this Italy, where a nation is being new-born, may throw King Arthur too far off and flat. But, whatever the cause, the effect was *so*. The colour, the temperature, the very music, left me cold. Here are exquisite things, but the whole did not affect me as a whole from Tennyson's hands.

Such a criticism cannot be simply dismissed by an insistence that as yet Mrs. Browning had inevitably read only an "instalment," not the whole. For the defects of the *Idylls* are of a kind that no amount of complex cross-patterning or moral concern can compensate for: they are defects of Tennyson's poetic language. Not only is the style of the *Idylls* extraordinarily uneven in quality, but even at its best the style is too often Tennysonian, mannered and extraneous.

There may be some point in a crude list which would indicate where—to one reader at least—the unevenness of achievement is manifest. Of the twelve *Idylls*, three seem to me successful both in style and as wholes: "Merlin and Vivien," "The Holy Grail," and "The Passing of Arthur." Five seem a mixture of the successful and the unsuccessful: "The Coming of Arthur," "Balin and Balan," "Lancelot and Elaine," "The Last Tournament," and "Guinevere." Four seem broadly unsuccessful: "Gareth and Lynette," "The Marriage of Geraint," "Geraint and Enid," and "Pelleas and Ettarre."

"Here are exquisite things." It is for such things that *Idylls of the King* may last. But the staple of the verse is insensitive and awkward. Such a point can hardly be truly substantiated with a long poem, since denigrators and admirers will merely bandy passages which suit their turn. The claim that such-and-such is representative is especially difficult to get established. Yet some sort of anthology of stylistic demerits is called for, since it is such failure of style which renders vacant or academic or wishful the larger claims which the *Idylls* precipitate.

There is, most surprisingly of all, the failure of Tennyson's ear. Of a line like "And thrice the gold for Uther's use thereof," one might say that it should have been spoken not by Arthur but by the battered churl ("Then, sputtering through the hedge of splintered teeth . . ."). Then there are overinsistences, especially in those areas of the poem where Tennyson knew he had failed to create a sense of what the Round Table was in its living vigor:

> And out of bower and casement shyly glanced
> Eyes of *pure* women, *wholesome* stars of love;
> And all about a *healthful* people stept
> As in the presence of a *gracious* king.

There is tautology ("young lads"). There is perilous ambiguity:

> To break her will, and make her wed with him:
> And but delays his purport till thou send
> To do the battle with him, thy chief man
> Sir Lancelot whom he trusts to overthrow,
> Then wed, with glory. . .

There is clumsiness: "A *walk* of roses *ran* from door to door." There is insensitivity to rhythm and line-ending:

> So Sir Lancelot holp
> To raise the Prince, who rising twice or thrice
> Full sharply smote his knees,

–rising twice or thrice? There is meaning unintended and to be ruled out by the reader's sluggish fellowship, as when we good-naturedly agree to supply the word *even* for a line like "He, reverencing king's blood in a bad man." There is vacancy of metaphor: nothing will bring "leavened" into intelligent relationship to "lay at Arthur's feet" in "Merlin and Vivien" lines 138–44. There is vacancy of pomp: "Being mirthful he, but in a stately kind." There is, most sadly, a rotund insensitivity to those delicate sensualities which Tennyson elsewhere masters: "An armlet for the roundest arm on earth" is a line which falls like brawn. There is an aimless shattering of the historical past, as in this gratuitous (and syntactically preposterous) introduction of London:

Now for the central diamond and the last
And largest, Arthur, holding then his court
Hard on the river nigh the place which now
Is this world's hugest, let proclaim a joust. . .

How could Tennyson write a line like "Hard on the river nigh the place which now," with its weak overlap of *hard* and *nigh*, its weak assonance of *nigh* and *now*, its weak rhythm and its weak line-ending? A full-length critique of the *Idylls*' style would be a dispiriting matter; all that may now be said is that to me the faults are endemic, and that they imperil the fine things which are often in their vicinity. Two lines after that gaucherie about "rising twice or thrice," we have a moral vignette which manifests Tennyson's true powers:

But, ever after, the small violence done
Rankled in him and ruffled all his heart,
As the sharp wind that ruffles all day long
A little bitter pool about a stone
On the bare coast.

The central deficiencies of the style are two: that Tennyson has not creatively solved the problem of what the dialogue ought to be in a poem which necessarily embodies archaism; and that he has not creatively solved the problem of accommodating his style (what Arnold called his "curious elaborateness of expression") to the simple exigencies of narrative, of the humble essentials which would permit his story to move. Is it possible to be a disinterested admirer of Tennyson and *not* to notice that in the following sequence the lines about the hern show something of genius, while the lines before and after scarcely show talent?

> ". . . And seeing now thy words are fair, methinks
> There rides no knight, not Lancelot, his great self,
> Hath force to quell me."
> Nigh upon that hour
> When the lone hern forgets his melancholy,
> Lets down his other leg, and stretching, dreams
> Of goodly supper in the distant pool,
> Then turned the noble damsel smiling at him,
> And told him of a cavern hard at hand. . .

Such unevenness suggests that though the feeling of manufacture is indeed strong, there are unequal skills in the manufacturer. "Did you ever read such lines?" asked Meredith about "The Holy Grail": "The Poet rolls them out like half yards of satin." But satin is consistently good stuff. "Why, this stuff is not the Muse, it's Musery."

The question of archaism was, as Tennyson knew, a crucial one.

> Why take the style of those heroic times?
> For nature brings not back the Mastodon. . .

But as the most perceptive Victorians saw, Tennyson did not achieve an imaginative re-creation of the past. Matthew Arnold insisted: "The fault I find with Tennyson in his *Idylls of the King* is that the peculiar charm and aroma of the Middle Age he does not give in them." Walter Bagehot shrewdly noticed the wish of the *Idylls* to have it both ways, as in the matter of love at first sight in "Geraint and Enid":

> It seems hardly fair that a writer should insist on the good side of both species of life; upon being permitted to use the sudden love which arises from not knowing women, and the love-tinged intercourse of

thought and fancy which is the result of knowing them, together and at once.

Gerard Manley Hopkins used the historical tergiversations to launch an attack on the *Idylls* which is perhaps unanswerable and which certainly has never been answered:

But the want of perfect form in the imagination comes damagingly out when he undertakes longer works of fancy, as his Idylls: they are unreal in motive and incorrect, uncanonical so to say, in detail and keepings. He should have called them *Charades from the Middle Ages* (dedicated by permission to H.R.H. etc). The Galahad of one of the later ones is quite a fantastic charade-playing trumpery Galahad, merely playing the fool over Christian heroism. Each scene is a triumph of language and of bright picturesque, but just like a charade—where real lace and good silks and real jewelry are used, because the actors are private persons and wealthy, but it is acting all the same and not only so but the make-up has less pretence of correct keeping than at Drury Lane.

The moral scheme of the *Idylls*, too, has long seemed vulnerable. There is the sense that both Vivien and Modred are scapegoats rather than villains; there is, more importantly, the sense that even Guinevere is too much a scapegoat, in that the doom of the Round Table seems to antedate her adultery. "First mainly through that sullying of our Queen"—but how mainly is mainly? "And all through thee!" cries Arthur to Guinevere, with more fire than cogency. Arthur is himself a demonstration of a root confusion in Tennyson; no critic has ever replied satisfactorily to Swinburne's jibe at "the Morte d'Albert, or Idylls of the Prince Consort"—or to his fervid and detailed argument that "Mr. Tennyson has lowered the note and deformed the outline of the Arthurian story, by reducing Arthur to the level of a wittol, Guenevere to the level of a woman of intrigue, and Launcelot to the level of a 'co-respondent.'" Arthur? "Rather a prig," said Henry James. "Unfit to be an epic-hero," said Henry Crabb Robinson, "a *cocu.*" For the undoubted high-mindedness of the *Idylls* is achieved only by reducing and attenuating the moral considerations to the point where they become low-minded. "The sentiments in these poems," said Bagehot, "are simpler than his sentiments used to be." Offensively inoffensive and simpler. You have only to compare Malory, said T. S. Eliot, "to admire the skill with which Tennyson adapted this great British epic material–in Malory's handling hearty, outspoken and magnificent–to suitable reading for a girls' school: the original ore being so refined that none of the gold is left." A similar resentment was expressed in 1867 by Carlyle:

We read, at first, Tennyson's *Idyls*, with profound recognition of the finely elaborated execution, and also of the inward perfection of *vacancy*, –and, to say truth, with considerable impatience at being treated so very like infants, though the lollipops were so superlative.

The lollipops are indeed superlative, and the more positive point in insisting on the severe limits of the *Idylls*' success is so that one may sincerely admire the innumerable local felicities which the poem offers. The range of Tennyson's rhythmical mimesis and suggestiveness is extraordinary.

First as in fear, step after step, she stole
Down the long tower-stairs, hesitating:
("Lancelot and Elaine")

and Gareth loosed the stone
From off his neck, then in the mere beside
Tumbled it; oilily bubbled up the mere.
("Gareth and Lynette")

And brought his horse to Lancelot where he lay.
He up the side, sweating with agony, got,
("Lancelot and Elaine")

And I rode on and found a mighty hill,
And on the top, a city walled: the spires
Pricked with incredible pinnacles into heaven.
("The Holy Grail")

Then turned, and so returned, and groaning laid
The naked sword athwart their naked throats,
There left it, and them sleeping; and she lay,
The circlet of the tourney round her brows,
And the sword of the tourney across her throat.
("Pelleas and Ettarre")

He spoke: the brawny spearman let his cheek
Bulge with the unswallowed piece, and turning stared;
("Geraint and Enid")

This last, so unexpected an area of virtuosity as to leave Gladstone twice bemusedly praising its "good taste," its "fine taste."

Throughout the *Idylls* there are those peculiar intangibilities which it might seem easy to snatch from the air. The spirits of the hills, "With all their dewy hair blown back like flame." Or the shadowy recesses of memory:

He ended: Arthur knew the voice; the face
Wellnigh was helmet-hidden, and the name
Went wandering somewhere darkling in his mind.
("The Last Tournament")

But it is the similes and the descriptions which are the triumphs within the poem; triumphs which are saddening in that they so seldom relate intimately to the poem's real concerns, but yet manifesting an eye and ear such as few English poets have possessed. Similes that invoke a complexion "Wan-sallow as the plant that feels itself / Root-bitten by white lichen"; or a lake "Round as the red eye of an Eagle-owl"; or (especially rich in the *Idylls*) the power and diversity of the sea. Descriptions that let us glimpse somebody who glimpses "Dust, and the points of lances bicker in it"; or "a shattered archway plumed with fern"; or a spring:

the spring, that down,
From underneath a plume of lady-fern,
Sang, and the sand danced at the bottom of it.

Best of all, the landscapes which mingle with mood: the journey of Tristram through the wood in "The Last Tournament"; the setting of the last battle in "The Passing of Arthur"; or the dream of Guinevere, which draws (as the *Idylls* too seldom do) upon sources of fearful energy from the earlier Tennyson:

for then she seemed to stand
On some vast plain before a setting sun,
And from the sun there swiftly made at her
A ghastly something, and its shadow flew
Before it, till it touched her, and she turned—
When lo! her own, that broadening from her feet,

And blackening, swallowed all the land, and in it
Far cities burnt, and with a cry she woke.
("Guinevere")

John Ruskin admired the first four *Idylls*, and yet: "Nevertheless I am not sure but I feel the art and finish in these poems a little more than I like to feel it."

He looked, and more amazed
Than if seven men had set upon him, saw
The maiden standing in the dewy light.
He had not dreamed she was so beautiful.
Then came on him a sort of sacred fear. . . .
("Lancelot and Elaine")

It is fine, but is there not something inordinate about its needing to enlist those seven men in order to achieve the sweet directness of "He had not dreamed she was so beautiful"? And are not the last two lines, for all their legitimate insinuating, something less than the piercing resilience of such a line from *Maud* as "And dream of her beauty with tender dread"? Yet the *Idylls* have their true poignancies:

Then, when she heard his horse upon the stones,
Unclasping flung the casement back, and looked
Down on his helm, from which her sleeve had gone.
And Lancelot knew the little clinking sound;
And she by tact of love was well aware
That Lancelot knew that she was looking at him.
("Lancelot and Elaine")

The tact, the tenderness, the unmentioned bruises: to me the lines are unforgettable.

With such gifts devoted to *Idylls of the King*, what went wrong? "For narrative Tennyson had no gift at all," said T. S. Eliot (who for narrative had no gift at all): "Tennyson could not tell a story at all." His best poems show the other side of this; his extraordinary powers over situation and mood, played against a known outcome. But *Idylls of the King* could not be simply idylls; they needed to be narratives, epyllia, as well. Tennyson's awed sense of time lent itself not to narrative, not to charting events and outcomes, but to waiting, to suspense. "A doom that ever poised itself to fall": that is what tapped Tennyson's deepest fears and imaginings.* Which is why the finest lines in the *Idylls* are those which show us Merlin suspended in fore-thought: while Vivien chattered seductively,

he was mute:
So dark a forethought rolled about his brain,
As on a dull day in an Ocean cave
The blind wave feeling round his long sea-hall
In silence:

Into the cave of the skull, the forethought reaches, its feeling-round beautifully and tentacularly floating through the rhymes and assonances, *cave* exactly into *wave*, and then (as the wave begins to separate and dissolve its unity) *feeling* into *sea-hall;* fear known in the Cyclopean blindness and the silence; and the delicate creativity of sound in the lines themselves strangely played against "In silence." After such a sense of Merlin's forethought, what actually happens to him—even though it is a dread that haunted Tennyson, a living death, imprisoned forever, conscious but paralyzed, within the hollow oak—cannot but be an anticlimax, a mere story.

A poem which can include such deep felicities cannot be written off, even though its successes must be recognized as sporadic. A critic who is severe about *Idylls of the King* will feel some sympathy with George Eliot, who found that though she could not capitulate, she needed to recapitulate:

I had seemed in the unmanageable current of talk to echo a too slight way of speaking about a great poet. I did not mean to say Amen when "The Idyls of the King" seemed to be judged rather "de haut en bas." I only meant that I should value for my own mind "In Memoriam" as the chief of the larger works, and that while I feel exquisite beauty in passages scattered through the Idyls, I must judge some smaller wholes among the lyrics as the works most decisive of Tennyson's high place among the immortals.

* The terrors in "The Ring" (written 1887) are melodramatic, but one line that rings true evokes this haunting intersection of time and the timeless: "A noise of falling weights that never fell." The same poem, in describing the "creepers crimsoning to the pinnacles," offers the benign version of this paradox: "As if perpetual sunset lingered there."

XII

"Enoch Arden" and "Aylmer's Field" 1864

IN SEPTEMBER 1864, Matthew Arnold—who was no undiscriminating admirer of Tennyson*—wrote to a friend: "I agree with you in thinking 'Enoch Arden' itself very good indeed—perhaps the best thing Tennyson has done." Yet "Enoch Arden" is apparently a narrative poem, and T. S. Eliot with some authority has said that "for narrative Tennyson had no gift at all." What is still alive in "Enoch Arden" (a poem which has its cumbrous upholstery) is a consequence of its equivocal relationship to narrative as such. For providence on the one hand, and *not* acting on the other hand, between them absorb almost all the narrative. The poem's tale is essentially of a tale told only after the event; held back by Enoch, to be released only after he is dead. The poem broods upon some such sentiment as "None the wiser."

The Lotos-Eaters thought that it would be better not to return to Ithaca:

> For surely now our household hearths are cold:
> Our sons inherit us: our looks are strange:
> And we should come like ghosts to trouble joy.

* Tennyson discriminated too. "Matthew Arnold—'Something outside of us that makes for righteousness'—ugh!" (This is a sort of grunt of disgust very usual with T.) "I was asked by some one in London, 'Shall I ask M.A.?' I said I didn't much like dining with Gods!" (Allingham's *Diary*, p. 288, August 8, 1880).

A bitter whisper in *In Memoriam* intimates:

> But if they came who past away,
>   Behold their brides in other hands;
>   The hard heir strides about their lands,
> And will not yield them for a day.
>
> Yea, though their sons were none of these,
>   Not less the yet-loved sire would make
>   Confusion worse than death, and shake
> The pillars of domestic peace.

Enoch Arden returns after more than ten years (he was wrecked on a tropical island), to find his bride in other hands. "Enoch Arden" is Tennyson's most sustained effort at dealing with this lifelong anxiety. Did such an anxiety owe something to the necessarily mixed feelings with which the Tennyson family had received Dr. Tennyson's return in 1825 from the brink of the grave? Certainly the poem broods upon fatherhood. Philip, the rejected suitor in the old days, does gain Annie once she is convinced Enoch is dead; Philip has already become "Father Philip" to the children, and is to be glimpsed by Enoch as their "second father." Such a second father is able to provide a cheerful glow—"so genial was the hearth"—beyond the power of the first father.

The story of "Enoch Arden" was given to Tennyson by his friend Thomas Woolner. Yet it embodies an extraordinary number of Tennyson's preoccupations. There is the prophecy of one's own death; Enoch, like St. Simeon Stylites, and more truly saintly to Tennyson, prophesies when he will die. Then there is the fascinated fear of a kind of life which is no life;* first of all, in Enoch's life on the island. It is not only the injured boy there who "Lay lingering out a five-years' death-in-life"; the boy is released by death, and Enoch serves a longer sentence of such death-in-life. And when he does return to his old life, the hand of providence delivers him only from one kind of nonlife to another: now that Annie has remarried, his *raison d'être* (in the deepest sense) is removed. "Dead or dead to me!" His life would be death

* One of Tennyson's very late poems, written 1888, seeks to triumph over such a fear through Christian love; "Happy: The Leper's Bride" shows the wife choosing death-in-life to be with her husband, "the living-dead."

to her happiness. "Now when the dead man come to life beheld / His wife his wife no more . . .": he "Staggered and shook, holding the branch, and feared / To send abroad a shrill and terrible cry." The moment is a bitterly grim counterpart to the blissfully providential resurrection in "The Lover's Tale": "And there the widower husband and dead wife / Rushed each at each with a cry."

For the part played by providence in "Enoch Arden" is a disconcerting one. Enoch waits on his tropical island—the passage is a fine one even though Hopkins was right to insist that such poetry is "Parnassian": "spoken *on and from the level* of a poet's mind, not, as in the other case, when the inspiration which is the gift of genius, raises him above himself . . . Now it is a mark of Parnassian that one could conceive oneself writing it if one were the poet."

> The mountain wooded to the peak, the lawns
> And winding glades high up like ways to Heaven,
> The slender coco's drooping crown of plumes,
> The lightning flash of insect and of bird,
> The lustre of the long convolvuluses
> That coiled around the stately stems, and ran
> Even to the limit of the land, the glows
> And glories of the broad belt of the world,
> All these he saw; but what he fain had seen
> He could not see, the kindly human face,
> Nor ever hear a kindly voice, but heard
> The myriad shriek of wheeling ocean-fowl,
> The league-long roller thundering on the reef,
> The moving whisper of huge trees that branched
> And blossomed in the zenith, or the sweep
> Of some precipitous rivulet to the wave,
> As down the shore he ranged, or all day long
> Sat often in the seaward-gazing gorge,
> A shipwrecked sailor, waiting for a sail:
> No sail from day to day, but every day
> The sunrise broken into scarlet shafts
> Among the palms and ferns and precipices;
> The blaze upon the waters to the east;
> The blaze upon his island overhead;
> The blaze upon the waters to the west;

> Then the great stars that globed themselves in Heaven,
> The hollower-bellowing ocean, and again
> The scarlet shafts of sunrise—but no sail.

All those vistas of space, and yet solitary confinement. The single inexorable sentence is a prison sentence, with the prison the most grimly open.

Enoch is not the first Tennysonian figure who waits in an unmerciful landscape. But with Mariana, or the southern Mariana, or Fatima, the arrival of the awaited would be a blessing. Yet is the sail that comes to Enoch a blessing? It takes him from one desolation, one isolation, to another. The sail he comes to long for is the ship of death; it comes, and he cries in his last words "A sail! a sail! / I am saved." Saved not from death but from life—or from one of the many forms of death-in-life.

Nowhere is the strange equivocation of providence clearer than in that which convinces Annie that Enoch is dead. She appeals for a sign; puts her finger at random upon a Biblical text, "Under the palm-tree"; and finds "no meaning there." But her ensuing dream shows Enoch under a palm tree, and within her dream she interprets this as meaning he is in Heaven. She wakes, resolves, and marries. But whence the dream? And whence, within the dream, this one interpretation rather than others? Is Annie's subconscious casting about for the go-ahead? Tennyson says nothing, but his silence would seem to have the effect of indicting either providence or Annie. As Ruskin said:

> To my mind, the saddest and strangest thing—yet *so* like human life—but the deepest piece of the tragedy—is the *deceiving* of the wife by the *True* Dream, "Under the Palm Trees." The *Vain* Providence, the Good Spirit becoming a Lying one. Every day the world and its ways get more terrible to me.

An oracle is both a curse and a blessing.

Orphanhood is both a freedom and a deprivation.* Enoch is

* Orphans, without both parents in some cases, figure throughout Tennyson: "Aylmer's Field," "Charity," "Circumstance," "Dora," "Enoch Arden," "Guinevere," "In the Children's Hospital," "Locksley Hall," "Locksley Hall Sixty Years After," *Maud*, "Merlin and Vivien," "Sea Dreams," "Semele," "The Coming of Arthur," "The Last Tournament," "The Lover's Tale," "The Miller's Daughter," "The Mother's Ghost," *The Princess*, "The Voyage of Maeldune." As for the metaphorical uses of orphan, they are legion.

himself an orphan, and when after his return he decides not to intrude upon his family (unaware as they are that he lives), his cry is aptly ambiguous: "No father's kiss for me." Philip had urged Annie to give up hope of Enoch and to marry again: "Why should you kill yourself / And make them orphans quite?" Kill yourself: that preoccupation endured, too. Enoch is lured by a suicidal impulse to look in upon his erstwhile family: the window's blaze (by an irony like that of the lighthouse which both saves and takes lives)

> Allured him, as the beacon-blaze allures
> The bird of passage, till he madly strikes
> Against it, and beats out his weary life.

Enoch does not in the end have to beat out his weary life; his weariness is such that he dies of simply not wanting to live. Tennyson has devoted himself to imagining once more a situation in which suicide is not merely condonable but honorable; Enoch alive (known to be so) "Would shatter all the happiness of the hearth," and his death is the only service he can still render his family. To Tennyson, Enoch was heroic because, like a soldier, he gave his life.

> So past the strong heroic soul away.
> And when they buried him the little port
> Had seldom seen a costlier funeral.*

Those closing lines have been much disliked. If they are to be deplored as Victorianly overrespectful to what money can buy, it should at least be said that there were Victorians who much disliked the tawdriness of the sentiment. Tennyson himself, in saying that the point is that "the costly funeral is all that poor Annie could do for him after he was gone," would seem rather to have meant the costliness as indeed tragically belated and ineffectual even though honorable. A more penetratingly severe criticism of the ending has been made by Martin Dodsworth, who found Enoch neither strong nor heroic: "The trouble with 'Enoch

* Behind the first line we should hear "The little innocent soul flitted away"—the child of Enoch which dies and of which he says at the last: "And now there is but one of all my blood / Who will embrace me in the world-to-be."

Arden' is that it wants to persuade us that very neurotic behaviour is really very good."* The argument would be a complicated one; perhaps it might at least be said that to find Enoch's decision (not to announce himself to his wife) *manifestly* morally wrong, is as overstaunch as finding the decision manifestly a right one (the bigamy of Annie, and the illegitimacy of her baby, are vague but threatening possibilities). Rather, Tennyson was drawn to the story because it does tap a genuinely equivocal moral matter: the nature of martyrdom-suicide. "The dead weight of the dead leaf bore it down."

The wish to die runs deeply into and widely through "Aylmer's Field." Forbidden by her fiercely snobbish father Sir Aylmer Aylmer to see the man she loves, Edith dies of not wishing to live. After "twenty months of silence," she "slowly lost / Nor greatly cared to lose, her hold on life." Her lover Leolin kills himself with a dagger. The funeral sermon for them both is preached by Leolin's brother Averill. "Your house is left unto you desolate"–it excoriates the Aylmers for their hideous pride, and it asks forgiveness for the suicide:

> Friends, this frail bark of ours, when sorely tried,
> May wreck itself without the pilot's guilt,
> Without the captain's knowledge: hope with me.

The mother, shattered by guilt and misery, is left to perform an act of reparation which reenacts her daughter's wish not to live:

> In one month,
> Through weary and yet ever wearier hours,
> The childless mother went to seek her child.

And "Sir Aylmer Aylmer, that almighty man"? If there was to be forgiveness for the suicide of Leolin, the grounds would be that the balance of the mind was disturbed. So Sir Aylmer too has his rending pain of reenactment: the balance of his mind is disturbed. The first line of the poem had shrouded its pun:

* The word "neurotic" was not available to the *Athenaeum* (August 13, 1864), which said: "The poet means that his conduct shall appear brave; in truth, it appears to be that of a dastard."

Dust are our frames; and, gilded dust, our pride
Looks only for a moment whole and sound;
Like that long-buried body of the king,
Found lying with his urns and ornaments,
Which at a touch of light, an air of heaven,
Slipt into ashes, and was found no more.

The last paragraph of the poem unveils the pun on "frames," and offers a somber counterpart to that earlier fragility of death in a hideous death-in-life that always preyed upon Tennyson's mind:

And when he felt the silence of his house
About him, and the change and not the change,
And those fixt eyes of painted ancestors
Staring for ever from their gilded walls
On him their last descendant, his own head
Began to droop, to fall; the man became
Imbecile; his one word was "desolate";
Dead for two years before his death was he...

"Aylmer's Field" is one of the many poems by Tennyson in which a father's tyrannical obstinacy is widely destructive; Edith is "Pale as the Jephtha's daughter," sacrificed to her father's vow. Leolin and Averill, on the other hand, are orphans,* once again both fortunate and deprived. "Till after our good parents past away . . .": Tennyson's poems do rather suggest that the main reason why such parents are good is their having passed away. Averill, as he says himself, was a father to Leolin ("I have loved you more as son / Than brother"); a brother perhaps makes the best kind of father. Unfortunately "Aylmer's Field" does not succeed in converting these personal ruckles into art; as so often when Tennyson is retailing a narrative in a comparatively objective or dramatically free-standing form, he is not less but more at the mercy of the merely personal in pain. He tries to exorcise the essential morbidity of the poem by a strange ritual: the events (which happened in 1793, and are glimpsed against the avenging French Revolution) have been learned of from an old cripple who had "been himself a part of what he told." During the

* They were not so in the outline which Woolner provided for this poem too.

poem, his actual part is revealed (with considerable tact, so that this part of the poem's meaning can easily be overlooked): the crippled boy was caught by Sir Aylmer when bringing the lovers' letters, and is terrified into betraying their letters thereafter:

> Nor let them know themselves betrayed; and then,
> Soul-stricken at their kindness to him, went
> Hating his own lean heart and miserable.

The cripple—now "Old, and a mine of memories"—who divulges the story is another victim of the Aylmer pride; self-hatred was not forgotten, and he too in reparation performs a kind of re-enactment. The informer becomes the informant.

Hallam Tennyson was right to insist that "Aylmer's Field" tapped something deeply personal in Tennyson: "the poet's heart burnt within him while at work on this tale of wrong." To his disillusionment with Rosa Baring—"This filthy marriage-hindering Mammon"—may be added his old and enduring contempt for the contemptuous Tennyson d'Eyncourts. For Arthur Hallam's marriage too had been hindered by Mammon and by family pride. The poem's weaknesses stem from Tennyson's uneasy making of things easy for himself, here where the real difficulties still threatened so much pain. One such easing is the insistence that in any case Leolin Averill was not really Edith Aylmer's social inferior: an equally splendid coat of arms is hinted at, and "There was an Aylmer-Averill marriage once." Like the use of the word "Mammon," which is not altogether apt—is in some ways revealingly inapt—to the landed pride of the Aylmers, this social insistence establishes that Aylmer was preternaturally, even morbidly, snobbish, but establishes this at some cost: the cost of leaving the poem a bit vacant when it comes to snobs who are less than preternatural. Tennyson never really got the Tennyson d'Eyncourts out of his blood, or out of his hair; or rather, not till the triumph of his peerage in 1883. The vigor of his attack upon Sir Aylmer has some trembling and some fumbling in it. The Rectory and the Hall had long been bound in intimacy,

> though to dream
> That Love could bind them closer well had made
> The hoar hair of the Baronet bristle up
> With horror . . .

And Tennyson's hair in slightly other social circumstances? Tennyson here was somewhat afraid (as he had not been in *Maud*), and some of the strenuous squaring-up is shadow-boxing.

The verse too has its narrative and descriptive gaucherie, especially when it gazes on young love: "a laugh / Ringing like proven golden coinage true. . . ." Its felicities do however ring true, even though they do not ring profoundly: the rhythmical sensibility of

> with her dipt
> Against the rush of the air in the prone swing;

or the affectionate scrutiny of a baby's foot:

> Nursing a child, and turning to the warmth
> The tender pink five-beaded baby soles;

or the tender promise of childhood love,

> But where a passion yet unborn perhaps
> Lay hidden as the music of the moon
> Sleeps in the plain eggs of the nightingale.

But it is the end of the poem which elicits from Tennyson the truest perception of what, humanly, the Aylmers had done. The conclusion here is altogether a conclusion; no vista opens out of it, no promise or threat remains; and Tennyson was released into such a finality (permitted himself so resolute a conclusion) because his lines may end with the end of the line. The end of "Aylmer's Field" is the end of the Aylmers—there are hardly any other circumstances in which Tennyson can creatively imagine a poem's arc as concluded.

> Then the great Hall was wholly broken down,
> And the broad woodland parcelled into farms;
> And where the two contrived their daughter's good,
> Lies the hawk's cast, the mole has made his run,
> The hedgehog underneath the plantain bores,
> The rabbit fondles his own harmless face,
> The slow-worm creeps, and the thin weasel there
> Follows the mouse, and all is open field.

How peaceful even the predatory in nature is, compared with the predatory in human life. With what a touch of genius is human narcissism and self-gratification evoked by contrast with that gentle harmlessness of the rabbit: "The rabbit fondles his own harmless face." And how inexorably grave is the emphasis which sets against the title "Aylmer's Field" the stress which establishes the nature of that field, the calmly final equality of stress in "open" and "field": "and all is open field."

XIII

1. The later poems

THE FIRST VOLUME which Tennyson published after *Enoch Arden* (1864) was *The Holy Grail and Other Poems* (1869). But though his mind and talents were indeed much occupied during his later years by *Idylls of the King* (he did not publish its last installment, "Balin and Balan," until 1885), the *Idylls* were only one outlet for the extraordinary fecundity, energy, and variety which characterized the last two decades or so of his life. He was to publish five more volumes: *Ballads and Other Poems* (1880), *Tiresias and Other Poems* (1885), *Locksley Hall Sixty Years After* (1886), *Demeter and Persephone* (1889), and—published posthumously three weeks after he died—*The Death of Œnone, Akbar's Dream, and Other Poems* (1892).

One circumstance of Tennyson's life asks mention here: his elevation to the peerage as a baron in 1883. A baronetcy (not a barony) had been mooted in 1865, but had been declined. The offer was repeated by Gladstone in 1873; but Tennyson's wish was not to enter into the honor himself ("I had rather we should remain plain Mr. and Mrs.") but transmit it during his lifetime to his son Hallam "at any age it may be thought right to fix upon." But he soon reported that Hallam "would not like to wear the honour during my lifetime."* In 1874, Disraeli (in whose hands it

* It suggests another of the family reenactments that Tennyson's grandfather in 1833 had hoped to retain himself the old name of Tennyson and let his son enter upon Tennyson d'Eyncourt.

then was) said that any such thing would be against all precedent. In 1880, Tennyson wrote to Gladstone:

I am still much of the same mind—except that many of my friends having reproached me as for a wrong done to my family in declining the Baronetcy for myself, I feel still more than I did that I would fain see it bestowed on my son Hallam *during my lifetime*, if that could be done without embarrassment to you.

In 1883, the offer arose again, this time in the stronger form of a barony (Frederick Locker had hoped for, and pressed for, a peerage on Tennyson's behalf in 1873). Tennyson accepted, and took his seat in the House of Lords in March 1884. "By Gladstone's advice I have consented to take the peerage, but for my own part I shall regret my simple name all my life." Why then did he agree? Two public matters will have weighed with him: his gratitude to the Queen, and his sense that the honor was a tribute not solely to him but to literature. These considerations come together in the letter he wrote to the Queen:

This public mark of your Majesty's esteem which recognizes in my person the power of literature in this age of the world, cannot however fail to be gratifying to my nearest and dearest.

Yet the mention of "nearest and dearest" is a reminder that there were private considerations too. Near to Tennyson but not dear to him were the Tennyson d'Eyncourts. The attempt by his uncle Charles in 1839–41 to revive their peerage had failed; in 1873 Locker had even used their claims as part of the case for a peerage for Tennyson. At one blow it was possible for Tennyson to avenge—with the utmost imperturbability—the wrong that had been done to his father and to his family. At first the blow looked like taking a crude form. Tennyson pointed out to Gladstone that:

The younger branch of my father's family, who succeeded to the fortune took the name of Tennyson-D'Eyncourt. Would that do? They say they are descended from the old branch of the D'Eyncourts who came in with William and from the later creation of the same name in tempore Charles II.—if they, then I. It is a small matter.

Small, but in danger of being small-minded. Tennyson went so far as to make inquiries of Edwin Tennyson d'Eyncourt; Edwin could not but think that it would be better to keep to the name of Tennyson. Tennyson concurred. Better, one cannot but think, to vindicate the good old name of Tennyson after all these years. Better to point decorously toward the coals of fire than actually to heap them on the Tennyson d'Eyncourts' heads.* How much had happened since 1835 when the young Edwin had rejoiced in the change of name: "Besides which it will keep us in a great measure clear of the Somersby Family who really are quite hogs."

Yet there was another family circumstance which urged Tennyson to accept the peerage. From the start, Alfred and Emily had thought of their son Hallam; and what they wanted for him was not so much the honor as the role, even the employment. For (history within the Tennyson family repeating itself once more) Hallam Tennyson had been called home in 1876 to his family which was in need of him—called home from Trinity College, Cambridge, like his father, without taking a degree. "We are grieved that our absolute need of Hallam at home has prevented him from accomplishing his university career," wrote Tennyson to the Master of Trinity. Hallam was tireless as secretary, agent, and friend, to his father; his services should not be slighted. But his parents were rightly uneasy. The day before Tennyson died, Jowett was to write to Hallam: "There was nothing that he would have desired more than that you should make a name and career for yourself in your own way, worthy of that which he bequeaths to you: he regretted that he had been a drag on you." In 1881, Emily had suggested to Gladstone that Hallam might be his secretary: "it is time he should have a career of his own. . . ." With such potentialities for guilt in the air, it is not surprising that Emily should have said of the peerage: "That Hallam should inherit the duties belonging to this distinction is cause of deep thankfulness to me"; she was thankful "that he should have an honourable career marked out for him when his work for his father has ceased." It would be to underrate Hallam Tennyson to say simply that he owed his becoming Governor-General of Australia to his father's peerage, but presumably it was no hindrance.

* It was after the peerage that Tennyson was able to engage in a manifest forgiveness of Bayons Manor, in "Locksley Hall Sixty Years After" (1886).

T. S. Eliot lamented that "Tennyson, who might unquestionably have been a consummate master of minor forms, took to turning out large patterns on a machine." In his late years, Tennyson showed himself a master of minor forms, but he still essayed ambitious projects, and to any reader who has been fascinated by either Tennyson the poet or Tennyson the man, no such attempts will seem tedious or be simply rendered superfluous by the existence of their more powerful and more profound predecessors within Tennyson's long achievement. Nevertheless, a survey of a career must establish its proportions by the criterion of intrinsic poetic worth, and this means that most of Tennyson's later poems cannot receive more than honorable mentions.

He took to the writing of ballads, with a strong story-line and a ringing verse-line (often both kinds of line have some coarseness of movement). "The Revenge" (1878) turns once more to military self-sacrifice; "Rizpah" (written 1878, published 1880) comprehends the self-sacrifice of a mother who has collected up the unhallowed bones of her criminal son and now hallows them. Then there were the dramatic monologues which seized upon historical injustices received or inflicted: "Columbus" (1880), not far from death and bitterly treasuring the chains in which he was sent back from his West Indies to Spain; "Sir John Oldcastle" (1880), not far from martyrdom by fire, but very far from courting death; "Romney's Remorse" (1889), the painter on his death-bed lamenting the wrong he once did his wife in the name of Art.

Then there were the classical stories. "Demeter and Persephone" (written 1887, published 1889) is the most calmly mastered of these poems; when Hallam Tennyson suggested the subject, the poet said: "I will write it, but when I write an antique like this I must put it into a frame—something modern about it. It is no use giving a mere *réchauffé* of old legends." Christian love and resurrection are the frame for this story of love and resurrection. A more desperate modernity, a glimpse of the world as merely "flaring atom-streams . . . Ruining along the illimitable inane," had animated the powerful dramatic monologue "Lucretius" (written 1865–68, published 1868), a poem which is not without hysteria but which compacts three of Tennyson's horrors: at erotic madness, at a Godless world, and at a juggernaut universe; it ends with Lucretius's suicide and with his bitter injunction "Fare thee well!" Suicide again, but as an honorable martyrdom, a recovery of married love, is the climax of "The Death of Œnone" (written 1889–90, published 1892), where Œnone's supreme act of forgiveness toward Paris is to fling herself upon his funeral pyre.*

There are the dialect poems, of which the best are "Northern Farmer. Old Style" (written 1861, published 1864), and "Northern Farmer. New Style" (written 1865, published 1869). These have the shrewd directness, the gruffness, the grim humor, which were so much a part of Tennyson's character. But it is a gruffness which does not preclude pity and pathos; R. H. Hutton was characteristically perceptive in seeing a link between "Northern Farmer. Old Style" and that poem so very different in style which appeared next to it in the 1864 volume, "Tithonus":

> the feeling expressed in both that there is a price at which life, with its sweetness lost, is not worth purchasing; and though to the Northern Farmer that price is the sacrifice of what he calls "breaking rules" to please the doctor, *i.e.* giving up his accustomed draught of ale, and to Tithonus it is the loss of all that made up the vigour and gladness of life, incurred to save an ever-dwindling consciousness of personality stripped of all command over the old springs of happiness, still there is just enough common to the two thoughts to make the range of dialect and feeling the more startling and effective.

As for "Northern Farmer. New Style," it is perhaps the most telling, because the least literary, of all Tennyson's attacks upon what he more grandiloquently called "marriage-hindering Mammon"—and upon a father's blind and narrow insistences.

> Dosn't thou 'ear my 'erse's legs, as they canters awaäy?
> Proputty, proputty, proputty—that's what I 'ears 'em saäy.

This human directness, unsentimental and unvindictive, characterizes much of the epigrammatic verse which he wrote during his last twenty years. The harshness is not hardness. From 1868

* Paris returns "like the wraith of his dead self"—he returns like Enoch Arden from the dead, but the destructiveness of such a homecoming is healed by Œnone's sacrificial love, as it had differently been by Enoch's.

to 1874, he wrote a great many epigrams, at once blunt and sharp, which he did not publish, and he returned to this unanaemic vein at the very end of his life. A related energy informs "The Dead Prophet" (written 1882–84, published 1885), with its scorn for those who scorn great men, and its contempt for Froude's revelations about Carlyle. The epigrammatic anger is at work at one extreme in a poem like "Locksley Hall Sixty Years After" (1886), which brings Carlylean energy, acumen, and (unfortunately) hysteria to bear upon the naïve progressive complacencies of Victorian England; and at the other extreme in a poem like "Parnassus" (1889), which sees that the mountain of poetry has now been dwarfed by two huge forms who are Muses of terror: "These are Astronomy and Geology, terrible Muses!" There is a brave bleakness in such verses, one victory of Tennyson's old age, and they should not be underrated–see, for instance, "The Christ of Ammergau" (written 1870, not published) in which Tennyson sardonically fuses two items of news: the doctrine of Papal Infallibility, and the fact that the man who played Christ in the Ober Ammergau Passion Play had been conscripted.

There were isolated successes, such as "Battle of Brunanburh" (written 1876–77, published 1880), probably the best verse-translation of any Anglo-Saxon poetry. But there were also some unisolated failures: the historical plays which Tennyson published from 1875 till 1892.* A great deal of industry, concern, and skill went into the making of them, but to little avail. Even the best things in them never rise much above the level of pastiche, for Tennyson's style, temperament, and insights were radically nondramatic. Of *Queen Mary*, Carlyle said: "To me it seems no more stone-dead, ineffectual 'Tragedy' had ever come across my experience." The reasons for this were adumbrated by Henry James, in his fine account of how Tennyson's verse moves, and of how "to produce his drama he has had to cease to

* *Queen Mary* (published 1875, produced 1876); *Harold* (published 1876); *The Falcon* (produced 1879, published 1884); *The Cup* (produced 1881, published 1884); *The Promise of May* (prose: produced 1882, published 1886); *Becket* (published 1884, produced 1893); *The Foresters* (produced and published 1892).

be himself." Just what this means was made clear by Bagehot, before Tennyson ever set about these plays, in a discussion of dialogue (which "requires a very changing imagination") as against soliloquy ("steadily accumulating"):

His genius gives the notion of a slow depositing instinct; day by day, as the hours pass, the delicate sand falls into beautiful forms—in stillness, in peace, in brooding.

Not in action or in dramatic outcome; Tennyson's essential genius is exploratory of the human situations for which there seems to be no denouement.

There were two areas where Tennyson's skill was yet at its finest and his sensibility at its most perceptive: his family and friends, and his religion. The epistolary verse which he had offered with such tact and magnanimity in "The Daisy" and "To the Rev. F. D. Maurice" was still at his command—though "command" is exactly what one does not feel in the persuasive kindliness of movement, the generous fluency, of such poems. His late poems to Professor Jebb, to the Master of Balliol, to Mary Boyle,* manifest a self-possession which is fortifying and delicate. The best of them are "To Ulysses" (written 1888, published 1889), which is to F. T. Palgrave's brother; and "To E. FitzGerald" (written 1883, published 1885). Each would ask to be quoted in full. "To E. FitzGerald" comprises a single sentence (fifty-six lines) of such unhurried calm, such imaginative yet unostentatious transitions, such dignity, such affectionate tact, as takes the reader's breath away, while leaving the poet amusedly unflustered. His poem breathes friendship. To be able—without condescension or mock-modesty, without any fatuous attempt at reversing roles and reputations—to praise FitzGerald's *Rubáiyát* with fervor and not with favor: the achievement is as much a moral as a stylistic one. If one may distinguish the favorite from the best, I should say that "To E. FitzGerald" is my favorite among Tennyson's poems.

* A. C. Bradley said that "To Mary Boyle" was "one of the most perfect things he ever wrote, and an example of a kind of verse in which no contemporary approached him."

To his family, too, Tennyson was able to write with an intimacy that never becomes embarrassing or complacent. He can look back upon the serenity which he has long shared with his wife, in the dedication to his last book of poems, "June Bracken and Heather," written a year before he died. Or he can look forward (knowing that the future is no longer his) into the hoped-for happiness of the grandson who shares the name of Alfred Tennyson, in the delightful dedication of his 1880 volume, "To Alfred Tennyson My Grandson." Two family losses moved him to a deeper expression. In 1879, his brother Charles Tennyson Turner died. In commiserating with her sister Louisa (who was also her sister-in-law), Emily Tennyson did not forget the setbacks over which Charles had triumphed:

> this exceeding blessing that through thy help he came out of a state (brought on chiefly by illness) from which scarcely any other human being has been known to be freed into that state of patience and faith and love and hope which has been an example and a delight for all.

A state from which the father of Alfred and of Charles had never been freed. Sixty years ago: "When all my griefs were shared with thee. . . ." In his awed and gentle lines, "Prefatory Poem to My Brother's Sonnets" (1880), Tennyson showed once more that reminiscences need not be casual. In "Frater Ave atque Vale" (written 1880, published 1883), he characteristically combined joy with sadness (once again, "So sad, so fresh, the days that are no more") in mingling two poems of Catullus: his silvery evocation of Sirmio with his elegy for his dead brother.

The death of his brother pained Tennyson deeply, but it did not shock or rack him. Such an anguish struck him in 1886 with the death of his younger son Lionel. Lionel was thirty-two; his work for the India Office took him to India in 1885, where he contracted fever, "hung between life and death for three months and a half," and then died in the Red Sea on his way home. Tennyson was desolated, but he strove to share his wife's Christian fortitude—in her words, "The loss to us is indeed unspeakable but infinite Love and Wisdom have ordained it." Tennyson's first attempt to use his art to fetter his grief was an ineffectual one; he incorporated four fictionalized lines about Lionel in

"Locksley Hall Sixty Years After" (1886), but the lines have neither a distanced freedom nor a personal poignancy. Three years later, Tennyson was able to meet the death of Lionel within his art; neither by confronting it altogether directly, nor by fictionalizing it, but by seeing it through "the lucid interspace" of a tribute to Lord Dufferin, Governor-General of India and Lionel's kindly host. The first half of "To the Marquis of Dufferin and Ava" explains the debt which all England owes to Dufferin; the second half, the personal debt which the Tennysons owe. Lionel's last word was of the Dufferins' kindness:

> And sacred is the latest word;
>   And now the Was, the Might-have-been,
>   And those lone rites I have not seen,
> And one drear sound I have not heard,
>
> Are dreams that scarce will let me be,
>   Not there to bid my boy farewell,
>   When That within the coffin fell,
> Fell—and flashed into the Red Sea,
>
> Beneath a hard Arabian moon
>   And alien stars. To question, why
>   The sons before the fathers die,
>   Not mine! and I may meet him soon;
>
> But while my life's late eve endures,
>   Nor settles into hueless gray,
>   My memories of his briefer day
> Will mix with love for you and yours.

How firmly and how delicately the inversion ("To question, why . . . Not mine!") combines—as the ordinary order would not—an insistence that such a question must inevitably cry out, with the insistence that it can be truly curbed by Christian resignation.

W. B. Yeats was expressing a partial truth, and not just a predilection, when he sketched Tennyson's later years:

> As years passed over him the poet grew not less and the man grew incomparably greater and this growth was accompanied ever by a shedding off of hopes based upon mere mechanical change and mere scien-

tific or political inventiveness, until at the last his soul came near to standing, as the soul of the poet should, naked under the heavens.

In his late years, Tennyson ranged through many kinds of religious exploration in verse. There are the poems which evince the old horror at a Godless universe and how such would eviscerate all human ethics; as "A Voice Spake Out of the Skies" (written 1865, published 1892). There is a new urgency in the indictment of some Christianities for their endorsement of eternal torment*; as in "Despair" (1881) and in its "pendant" poem "Faith," one of his very last poems of 1892. There is the simple evocation and plea, a faith in immortal life; in "Wages" (1867, 1869), and in "Vastness" (1885) with its final moment when another voice speaks with unanswerable finality about Arthur Hallam, whom Tennyson never forgot: "Peace, let it be! for I loved him, and love him for ever: the dead are not dead but alive." There are the poems whose liberalism and unaffected decency owe something to the deliberations of the "Metaphysical Society" to which Tennyson belonged; "The Higher Pantheism" (1867, 1869) was read at the first formal meeting of the Society in 1869. This openness of temper—Tennyson was altogether without religious bigotry—led naturally to the poems

* Here Tennyson honored his father, who "would never read the Athanasian Creed" (Allingham's *Diary*, p. 328, July 27, 1884). Tennyson's religious views remained humane and disconcertingly unorthodox. The *English Review* (September 1850) had said of *In Memoriam:* "We remain undecided as to Mr. Tennyson's faith, though we opine, that, strictly speaking, *he has none*, whether negative or affirmative, and advise him, for his soul's good, to try to get one!" Those who met Tennyson remarked on his beliefs: "Moreover, he was very religious and *Christian* in all his talk about life and politics, &c" (1868, George Grove, in a tone of surprise); "He was not wishful for Turkish rule to be prolonged, but thought 'their religion was a very good religion,'—I suppose, or hope, as compared with other non-Christian religions" (1877, John Bright); "He formulated once and quite deliberately his own religious creed in these words: 'There's a something that watches over us; and our individuality endures: that's my faith, and that's all my faith' " (Knowles). Tennyson was surprised at the "liberality" of Father ———: "When I said I could imagine other revelations than that of Christ he said he saw no reason why there should not be other Christs in other planets. He would have been burnt as a heretic in Galileo's time" (notes at Lincoln).

which ponder whether "All religions are one." "The Ancient Sage," on Lao-tsze (1885); "Akbar's Dream" (1892); "Kapiolani" (1892). There is the mystical autobiography, "Merlin and the Gleam" (1889). Most assured of all, there is "Crossing the Bar" (1889), which Tennson wrote after recovering from a serious illness. Finally, there is the sequence of eight diverse poems, all religious, which were Tennyson's last writings, culminating in "The Dreamer," "the last poem he finished." How characteristic a title, and how characteristic its evocation of the two voices, the despair of the earth and then the hope of the poet's song, ending at last with a serene ending, an outcome arrived at:

And all's well that ends well,
Whirl, and follow the Sun!

2. *"The days that are no more"*

IN 1931 Sir Charles Tennyson drew attention to "one curious characteristic of Tennyson's methods of composition":

I have noted in these early poems a number of lines which the poet used again, often years afterwards, in quite different contexts, in his published work. It is known and has been remarked that Tennyson often stored observations and similes for long periods before finally working them into his poems, and this storage of actual lines from early compositions is a fresh illustration of the same tendency. The remarkable thing is that the lines, when finally taken from storage, fit so naturally and aptly into their new context that they are often among the best passages in the poems in which they are employed.*

Such self-borrowings are relevant to Tennyson's most impassioned subject: Time. "He was," said Humphry House, "an Aeonian poet; one on whom the consciousness of time bore like a burden." It was on the subject of time that Tennyson wrote those lines of his which are most likely to stand against time.

The point is implicit in a famous example of self-borrowing in Wordsworth. His sonnet "Mutability" tells how the outward forms of truth

drop like the tower sublime
Of yesterday, which royally did wear
His crown of weeds, but could not even sustain
Some casual shout that broke the silent air,
Or the unimaginable touch of Time.

* See the account of "Edwin Morris," p. 169.

Why is it moving to learn that the last line, "the unimaginable touch of Time," had been part of a "Fragment of a 'Gothic' Tale" about thirty years earlier? Mainly because of the sureness of Wordsworth's sense of context, the life which here pours into the cliché "the touch of Time." But perhaps we are moved too by the poem's subject, "Mutability," by the fact that despite mutability and the touch of time, for Wordsworth something important endured unchanging and still new: the line of poetry which he had written thirty years before.

Of course, the point is not, strictly, literary criticism; it is a point about biography, or methods of composition—it concerns the question why, of all the good lines which Wordsworth had available from his juvenilia, it should have been this one which later meant so much to him and which he was able to use so beautifully. Again and again Tennyson's self-borrowings explicitly concern time, even the mystical wish to be "Out of the sphere of Time."

Yet there is nothing a poet can use which he cannot also abuse, and *Maud* provides important evidence that Tennyson's self-borrowings can lead to the heart of his failures as well as of his successes. It is not an accident that one reaches for an organic metaphor like "germ" to describe the relationship of "Oh! that 'twere possible" to the completed monodrama. What we find is not the changing but the providing of a context. As originally published, "Oh! that 'twere possible" had no dramatic or psychological setting; itself a cry, it cried out for one. That Tennyson was dissatisfied with it, is clear from his not including it in his volumes of 1842; by 1855, he had created its context.

Maud, then, shows the success of this method of composition, but it also shows us a failure. One section of *Maud* was bitterly ridiculed by many critics on publication, as falling far below the lyrical and psychological force of the rest: the song "Go not, happy day" (I. xvii), which the hero exclaims in his love of Maud:

> Go not, happy day,
>   From the shining fields,
> Go not, happy day,
>   Till the maiden yields....

Pass the happy news,
  Blush it through the West;
Till the red man dance
  By his red cedar-tree,
And the red man's babe
  Leap, beyond the sea.
Blush from West to East,
  Blush from East to West,
Till the West is East,
  Blush it through the West . . .

The objection to this song is not to its happiness but to its being ill written*: the graceless hyperbole which has the red man's babe leaping because of a love-match in England, and the cumbrous repetitions, uncharacteristically devoid of lyrical feeling.

There are indeed true moments of happiness in *Maud*—the section which follows this song ("I have led her home, my love, my only friend") is one of them. But "Go not, happy day" is written in the wrong style; why does the hero fall into this nursery-rhyming? If we ask where we have met such a tone before, the answer is in some of the songs which Tennyson interpolated in the third edition of *The Princess* (1850). "Go not, happy day" was originally one of the songs for *The Princess;* Tennyson found no place for it there, and rather than waste it he made a place for it in *Maud* (made, not found). The tone resembles that of this song from *The Princess:*

And blessings on the falling out
  That all the more endears,
When we fall out with those we love
  And kiss again with tears!

The affinity is evident in the two poems which Tennyson published as "Child-Songs" in 1880, but which he notes were originally for *The Princess:*

Minnie and Winnie
Slept in a shell.

* "Rather a silly outburst," wrote George Eliot (*Westminster Review*, October 1855).

Sleep, little ladies!
And they slept well.

But such a tone was not right for *Maud*—and we can now see why the red man's babe appeared. Not because of any aptness to *Maud* but because of the babe in *The Princess*. But in transferring "Go not, happy day," Tennyson was for once under the ill influence of his habit.*

For the habit at its best, we may turn to some of the finest lines he ever wrote, from "Ulysses":

To follow knowledge like a sinking star,
Beyond the utmost bound of human thought.

In their context as Ulysses speaks (a context soaked in a consciousness of time):

Life piled on life
Were all too little, and of one to me
Little remains: but every hour is saved
From that eternal silence, something more,
A bringer of new things; and vile it were
For some three suns to store and hoard myself,
And this gray spirit yearning in desire
To follow knowledge like a sinking star,
Beyond the utmost bound of human thought.

In a Trinity notebook, these two lines form part of quite a different poem, "Tiresias," which Tennyson did not complete and publish until 1885 but which he had begun at the same time as "Ulysses": October 1833, the month in which he heard the news of Hallam's death. As published, "Tiresias" begins:

I wish I were as in the years of old,
While yet the blessèd daylight made itself
Ruddy through both the roofs of sight, and woke
These eyes, now dull, but then so keen to seek
The meanings ambushed under all they saw....

But a Trinity manuscript begins:

* The unevenness of "The Sailor Boy" (1861) is explained, though not justified, by the fact that it too was originally a song for *The Princess*.

I wish I were as in the days of old,
Ere my smooth cheek darkened with youthful down,
While yet the blessèd daylight made itself
Ruddy within the eaves of sight, before
I looked upon divinity unveiled
And wisdom naked—when my mind was set
To follow knowledge like a sinking star,
Beyond the utmost bound of human thought.

(Again, in "Tiresias," the oppressive sense of time.) It is the context which triumphantly justifies Tennyson's decision as to where to use his resonant lines. What has a star to do with Tiresias? But Ulysses is speaking to his mariners, and mariners do indeed watch and follow stars. And what had Tiresias to do with bounds and horizons? Whereas in his last voyage Ulysses yearns

To sail beyond the sunset, and the baths
Of all the western stars, until I die.

Again, notice how the contrast between Ulysses' aged frame and his burning spirit comes out in a juxtaposition absent from the context in "Tiresias": the play of "this gray spirit" against the "sinking star" (and of the "suns" against the "star"). All these details bind the lines into their context, and so does the echo of Dante in "knowledge." "Ulysses" has as its primary source the speech by Ulysses in Dante's *Inferno*, urging his companions to their last voyage. Tennyson's "knowledge" calls up Dante's *canoscenza*. The difference between the use of those two lines in "Tiresias" and in "Ulysses" is the difference between talent and genius. It is Tennyson's sense of context which releases all the energies of the lines.

The same is true of another of his great lines, again in a context heavy with time: "The phantom circle of a moaning sea." The scene is the last battle in "The Passing of Arthur" (1869)—a scene likely to bring out the best in a poet whose enterprise had shown itself more than forty years earlier in a poem on Armageddon.

Then rose the King and moved his host by night,
And ever pushed Sir Modred, league by league,
Back to the sunset bound of Lyonnesse—

A land of old upheaven from the abyss
By fire, to sink into the abyss again;
Where fragments of forgotten peoples dwelt,
And the long mountains ended in a coast
Of ever-shifting sand, and far away
The phantom circle of a moaning sea.

Could any location be more apt to "this last, dim, weird battle of the west"?—where the fighters are themselves phantoms in the mist, where not only the sea is moaning, and where the life of the king completes its phantom circle?* And yet only a year before (1868), Tennyson had printed, though not published, the line as part of the last section of "The Lover's Tale." In the trial edition, which he suppressed once more, we hear of

A dismal hostel in a dismal land,
A world of reed and rush, and far away
The phantom circle of a moaning sea.

How fortunate that Tennyson somehow knew not to waste the line on such a context. Not, in fact, that he had created the line for "The Lover's Tale" either. More than thirty years before, about 1833, it had formed the climax of his little poem describing Mablethorpe on the Lincolnshire coast. In 1850 he published these "Lines," but without the second stanza which survives in a Trinity manuscript, and which speaks of "The phantom-circle of the moaning main." In the fullness of time, Tennyson ameliorated the alliteration and found for the line the right fullness of context.

For Tennyson, context often meant the fusion of a landscape with a mood. The Harvard manuscript of *The Princess* includes these lines in its Prologue:

Within, the sward
Was kept like any lawn, but all about
Large ivy sucked the joinings of the stones,
Beneath like knots of snakes.

No fusion, because that muscularity, that mood, answers to noth-

* Tennyson frequently used, in symbolic contexts, such words as circle, sphere, orb, and round (all as verbs as well as nouns).

ing in *The Princess*. In "The Marriage of Geraint," Tennyson fuses description and mood, a mood haunted by time:

And high above a piece of turret stair,
Worn by the feet that now were silent, wound
Bare to the sun, and monstrous ivy-stems
Claspt the gray walls with hairy-fibred arms,
And sucked the joining of the stones, and looked
A knot, beneath, of snakes, aloft, a grove.

Sometimes such a gift for placing may crystallize into a discreet pun. The *Memoir* (i. 465) says that the following fragment was jotted down at Torquay:

as the little thrift
Trembles in perilous places o'er the deep.

But this jotting about the plant thrift was not used by Tennyson until he could engage with the other sense of thrift. His poem "Sea Dreams" deals with his disastrous investing of all his funds in Dr. Matthew Allen's wood-carving scheme:

Small were his gains, and hard his work; besides,
Their slender household fortunes (for the man
Had risked his little) like the little thrift,
Trembled in perilous places o'er a deep. . . .

At the other extreme from such a tiny instance of self-borrowing comes the incorporation *en bloc* of a whole passage of blank verse. Context here means pace—Tennyson is a master of pace. Who would have thought that the finest lines in the magnificent closing passage of *The Princess* were originally part of another poem written fifteen years before? The tempo, with its superb rallentando and its tranquil finality, is perfect:

the walls
Blackened about us, bats wheeled, and owls whooped,
And gradually the powers of the night,
That range above the region of the wind,
Deepening the courts of twilight broke them up
Through all the silent spaces of the worlds,
Beyond all thought into the Heaven of Heavens.

Last little Lilia, rising quietly,
Disrobed the glimmering statue of Sir Ralph
From those rich silks, and home well-pleased we went.

Tempo depends here on time as well as timing. "Last," "quietly": the full potentialities of the lines emerge only in this context, as can be seen if we look back at them in "The Lover's Tale" of 1832, which Tennyson suppressed before publication:

When thou and I, Cadrilla, thou and I
Were borne about the bay or sitting gazed
Till gradually the powers of the night
That range above the region of the wind
Deepening the courts of twilight, broke them up
Through all the silent spaces of the worlds
Beyond all thought, into the Heaven of Heavens.
When thou and I, Cadrilla, thou and I
Were moored by some low cavern, while without
Through the long dark. . .

And so on, in a deft passage of Tennysonian verse. But those central lines needed to be something more than merely one among many memories; it was not till the end of *The Princess* that they found the placing which, as it were, they were made for.

Such self-borrowings not only revealed Tennyson's sense of context and his preoccupation with time; they also underline the extreme rashness of the generalizations as to his development, the growth or decline of his powers. The little poem "Poets and Critics" was not published till his posthumous volume of 1892, and its manner suggests that it encapsulates his long battling with the reviewers:

Year will graze the heel of year,
But seldom comes the poet here,
And the Critic's rarer still.

Yet it was written sixty years before, and is Tennyson's reaction, not to a lifetime of reviewing, but to the reviews of his earliest volumes. And for Tennyson, year had indeed grazed the heel of year before he came to publish it.

It is the same with the honeymoon song that introduces the late poem "The Ring," published in 1889, a song which must not be taken as evidence that his lyrical gift had astonishingly survived (or sadly declined) since it in fact dates from 1833.

> Shall not *my* love last,
> Moon, with you,
> For ten thousand years
> Old and new?

Love may last, as the poem itself had lasted—though this could be known to none but the poet and his immediate circle. The "Ode on the Death of the Duke of Wellington" (1852) is imbued with a sense of the passing of an era:

> For though the Giant Ages heave the hill
> And break the shore, and evermore
> Make and break, and work their will . . .

But this vision of time was one which had come to Tennyson far back in time, twenty years before; it is the Soul, in a manuscript of "The Palace of Art," who sees this vision:

> Yet saw she Earth laid open. Furthermore
> How the strong Ages had their will,
> A range of Giants breaking down the shore
> And heaving up the hill.

The convergence for Tennyson of self-borrowings and a preoccupation with time is implicit in two examples furnished by Sir Charles Tennyson. The early unpublished poem "An Idle Rhyme" provided a line for *In Memoriam* (XCV. 40)—the line is "The deep pulsations of the world," which in *In Memoriam* goes on: "Æonian music measuring out / The steps of Time." And the early poem "Sense and Conscience" provided a simile for "The Lover's Tale"—the simile ponders youth and age:

> Even the dull-blooded poppy-stem, "whose flower,
> Hued with the scarlet of a fierce sunrise,
> Like to the wild youth of an evil prince,
> Is without sweetness, but who crowns himself
> Above the naked poisons of his heart
> In his old age."

Yet, as these examples bring out, this is not the case of an artist who has outlived his gift and who is forced to clutch at his unpublished juvenilia—rather as James Thurber, when blind and unable to draw, is said to have devised new captions for his old drawings. In Tennyson the habit was a lifelong one, as is well known from the composition of his first notably successful poem, "Timbuctoo," with which he won the Chancellor's Gold Medal at Cambridge in 1829. For this, "he patched up an old poem on 'The Battle of Armageddon' "; in fact the Trinity manuscript shows that about 120 lines, or roughly half of "Timbuctoo," was lifted whole from "Armageddon." It is characteristic of Tennyson that he went on to borrow from "Timbuctoo" itself; one of its lines turns up in "The Lover's Tale," and two lines in the "Ode to Memory." What is also characteristic is the subject of these further self-borrowings: "A centered glory-circled memory," and "the lordly music flowing from / The illimitable years."

There is no breach between the young Tennyson and the old. His first political pronouncement as a peer was the poem "Freedom," published in, and dated, 1884. Its closing stanza was taken from the poem "Hail Briton" which Tennyson had written but not published fifty years before. And it is not just the closing stanza which was taken over; the Trinity manuscripts make clear that much of "Freedom" was culled from political poems of 1832–33. The political viewpoint is altogether consistent.* Robert Frost wrote:

> I never dared be radical when young
> For fear it would make me conservative when old.

But Tennyson had no need of this "Precaution"; when he wished to speak as a septuagenarian, he simply published at last the words which he had written in his twenties.**

For Tennyson there was never a breach between the political and the personal. Yet when a man's son dies, and he writes a poem

* "England and America in 1782" (published 1872) dates from 1832–34. Even "Riflemen Form" (published 1859) was not a reaction to an immediate crisis, but dates from 1852.

** T. S. Eliot said of Whitman and Tennyson: "Both were conservative, rather than reactionary or revolutionary; that is to say, they believed explicitly in progress, and believed implicitly that progress consists in things remaining much as they are" (*The Nation and Athenaeum*, December 18, 1926).

about the death, one would expect all of that poem at least to be newly created. When Tennyson's son Lionel died on his way home from India in 1886, Tennyson's funeral poem began with a stanza which he had written more than fifty years before in "Hail Briton." "To the Marquis of Dufferin and Ava" thanks the Viceroy for all he had done for Lionel.

At times our Britain cannot rest,
　At times her steps are swift and rash;
　She moving, at her girdle clash
The golden keys of East and West.

Not swift or rash, when late she lent
　The sceptres of her West, her East,
　To one, that ruling has increased
Her greatness and her self-content.

And so through masterly transitions to personal thanks.

But if we look back fifty years, we see that in the earlier context "East and West" was no more than a ringing description of the British Empire; it had none of the personal aptness here found for it. Dufferin had been ambassador in Constantinople and viceroy in India; Lionel Tennyson had died visiting India on his work for the India Office. And once again the lines seem to have risen to Tennyson's mind because of their sense of time, of an era. "Not swift or rash"—the words may, without flippancy, be applied to the habit of composition itself.

For Tennyson, there had never been an era's end so unforgettable as the French Revolution—from his first to his last poems, it preys upon his mind. In "Hail Briton," he has eight lines on revolution and time; these eight lines he transferred to *In Memoriam*, CXIII, where they became some of the noblest lines which he wrote in praise of Hallam, whose death had removed a man of great political promise:

Should licensed boldness gather force,
　Becoming, when the time has birth,
　A lever to uplift the earth
And roll it in another course,

With many shocks that come and go,
　With agonies, with energies,

With overthrowings, and with cries,
And undulations to and fro.

The political and the personal are here truly joined, in the converging of self-borrowing and the sense of time.

The deep biographical roots of his self-borrowing (its being not a convenience but a cast of mind) are evident in the impulse to borrow from similar contexts.* Take these lines about time, from *The Princess:*

all the rich to-come
Reels, as the golden Autumn woodland reels
Athwart the smoke of burning weeds.

Tennyson created these lines from the conclusion to *In Memoriam*, which in the Lincoln manuscript includes this stanza:

We pace the stubble bare of sheaves,
We watch the brimming river steal
And half the golden woodland reel
Athwart the smoke of burning leaves.

When Tennyson's mind went back and rescued those lines he was not simply gleaning natural description, he was reaching to the context of ideal married love (itself golden and autumnal). In *The Princess*, the lines go on to "My bride, / My wife, my life." In the manuscript of *In Memoriam*, they describe how the wedding guests stroll through the countryside after the marriage of Tennyson's sister. The change from "burning leaves" to "burning weeds" is a fine one, in its slight unexpectedness, and in the way in which it transforms "weeds" into part of the golden scene.

It seems important that so many of these self-borrowings have to do with time, but there are three counter-arguments. First, that there are dangers in even speaking of Tennyson's "characteristic" preoccupation with time—everybody is preoccupied with time, and literary critics are always fudging up "characteristics" of an

* Sir Charles Tennyson observes that *In Memoriam,* XCV. 54–55, incorporates two descriptive lines from "In deep and solemn dreams." It may be added that the latter too is an elegiac poem, and that the former is one of Tennyson's greatest evocations of "Æonian music measuring out / The steps of Time."

author or a period which are simply common to humanity. Second, that if most of Tennyson's poems are about time, it is hardly surprising or significant that most of his self-borrowings are also about time. Third, that time is so elastic a concept that it is hard to imagine a poem which couldn't in some sense be claimed as "about" time.

Yet it still seems that Tennyson writes about time with an unusual depth and imagination; that, even so, unexpectedly many of his self-borrowings are concerned with time; and that no far-fetched meaning has to be sought for "time" in order to accommodate them. The habit of self-borrowing manifests both an awareness of, and a means of countering, time. It has the "emotional importance" which Humphry House brilliantly picked out in Tennyson's fascination with description:

> Many of Tennyson's poems—*Maud* most notable among the longer ones—totter on the edge of madness. Constantly the one rallying-point in them as poems is the description of external things. . . . In a number of poems he uses description as if it were in itself the final aim of poetic art. . . . These descriptions . . . had for him a central emotional importance. They stabilised his mind in the contemplation of unending processes, and allayed the restlessness of the searching and journeying involved in his view of what poetry should do.*

Does self-borrowing (a method of composition which became a means of composition) have for Tennyson a comparable function? The dangers of melancholia, even of madness, were not remote from Tennyson; in a world of unending flux, a world where all seemed ephemeral (even the works of the greatest poets), a world where personal identity was a mystery and often a burden, Tennyson found some rallying point in the continuity of his own creativity. What helped to "stabilize his mind" was the reassurance offered by his own past (as in his "Passion of the Past"), and nothing was more reassuring in that past than the surviving, and

* The same might be said of Tennyson's insistence upon accuracy in his poems (accuracy scientific, historical, reminiscential). The insistence seems to me honorable and artistically responsible; in any case, when Nicolson speaks of Tennyson's "maddening accuracy" it should be retorted that it may have maddened Nicolson but it helped to keep Tennyson sane.

still living, evidences of his powers. To revise a published poem was to show that the past was not done with, irrevocable, immutable.* To quarry from his unpublished work was to show that the past was indeed a quarry, its geological obduracy the source of its riches. The threatening melancholia crystallizes in two lines in the poem "Walking to the Mail" about the "morbid devil in his blood":

> He lost the sense that handles daily life—
> That keeps us all in order more or less. . . .

Is it just a coincidence that those lines too had originally been part of another poem ("The Gardener's Daughter")?

Tennyson's self-borrowings, then, seem to have the same emotional importance as his preoccupation with description. Just how important this continuity was to him can be seen from the Tennyson *Concordance*. Self-borrowing needs to be related not only to the word "time" (over 300 times in the *Concordance*) or the favorite adjective "slow," but also to his persistent need for the prefix "re-", itself a signal that the past still lives, can revive. "The blossom that rebloomed"; "Remade the blood and changed the frame"; "Rewaken with the dawning soul"; "Remerging in the general Soul"; "Can I but relive in sadness?"—there are innumerable examples.** For, Tennyson, revision is truly a second vision. "So that, in that I *have* lived, do I live" ("The Lover's Tale").

Tennyson's self-borrowings go to the heart of his poetic skill and of his preoccupation with time. They also bring out the conflict which is often felt in reading Tennyson, the conflict between confidence in his extraordinary expertise and faint uneasiness about the extent to which the expertise is verbal or purely verbal. There is something strange about the predicament of a poet whose wife had continually to urge his friends to provide him with sub-

* Tennyson's detestation of literary piracy and of editions with variant readings has to do with the way in which they threatened his re-creation of the past. The wish to keep his own past alive made him yearn for a past "Before the Love of Letters, overdone / Had swampt the sacred poets with themselves" ("Poets and their Bibliographies").

** Notably: recommenced; regather; re-inspired; reissuing; re-listen; remakes; remodel; re-orient; re-reiterated; re-risen; resmooth; resoldered; retake; retaught; re-told; revisit.

jects or stories for poems.* Yet the end-products are sheer Tennyson.

The oddity of Tennyson's sources is analogous to that of his style: how is it that such apparently dangerous habits so often resulted in something magnificently personal? Certainly the habit of self-borrowing leads to a central point: Tennyson's verbalism. The best criticism of Tennyson is by Walt Whitman:

> To me, Tennyson shows more than any poet I know (perhaps has been a warning to me) how much there is in finest verbalism. There is such a latent charm in mere words, cunning collocutions, and in the voice ringing them, which he has caught and brought out, beyond all others–as in the line, "And hollow, hollow, hollow, all delight," in "The Passing of Arthur."

It comes agreeably to hand that even that line, "And hollow, hollow, hollow, all delight," had originally been fumbled for in a line which Tennyson rejected from "Locksley Hall": "hollow, hollow, hollow comfort."

* Henry Taylor said "He wants a story to treat, being full of poetry with nothing to put it in" (1860; *Autobiography*, 1885, ii.192).

3. "*Crossing the Bar*"

TENNYSON DIED ON October 6, 1892.

His last food was taken at a quarter to four, and he tried to read, but could not. He exclaimed, "I have opened it." Whether this referred to the Shakespeare, opened by him at

> "Hang there like fruit, my soul,
> Till the tree die,"*

which he always called among the tenderest lines in Shakespeare: or whether one of his last poems, of which he was fond, was running through his head I cannot tell:

> Fear not thou the hidden purpose of
> that Power which alone is great,
> Nor the myriad world, His shadow, nor the
> silent Opener of the Gate.

He then spoke his last words, a farewell blessing, to my mother and myself.

"One of his last poems": but it is natural for us to turn rather to that poem which Tennyson had written three years before: "Mind you put my 'Crossing the Bar' at the end of all editions of my poems." Hallam Tennyson had said: "That is the crown of your life's work." This is not to say that it is his greatest poem; but certainly, and without irony, it was a gift reserved for age, to set

* *Cymbeline*, V. v.

a crown upon his lifetime's effort. Its simple dignity is yet consonant with a fine patterning and subtle variety. The third line of each stanza, longer than the preceding line, swells into a release of feeling. But what saves this from self-indulgence, converting it rather to a religious indulgence or remission, is the immediate curbing effect of the stanza's shortened concluding line, reining and subduing the feeling. Two sentences, each two stanzas, each beginning with an exclamation which is vibrant rather than exclamatory and whose vibrations then die away; the poem itself "turns again home." The central stanzas incorporate rhymes which are disyllabic, but not as rhymes with each other; the first and last stanzas maintain only monosyllabic rhymes, and the concluding rhyme (*far* into *bar*) returns us to the first rhyme of the poem (*star* into *bar*). "Face to face": did Tennyson's mind go back to Arthur Hallam and to the manuscript of *In Memoriam*, the final two lines of its final section (CXXXI)?—"And come to look on those we loved / And that which made us, face to face." And did his mind go even further back, moved by the deep reciprocity, to recall that it was Arthur Hallam, in a poem to Tennyson's sister Emily, who had glimpsed this distance: "Till our souls see each other face to face"?

One remembers what Hallam said about rhyme (which he called, with a paradoxical possibility apt to Tennyson, "the recurrence of termination"): "Rhyme has been said to contain in itself a constant appeal to Memory and Hope." *Star: bar / far: bar.* Once again, the poem turns again home, just as its last line returns to its title—to which it has now shown itself entitled. It is a perfect epitome of Tennyson's essential movement: a progress outward which is yet a circling home. In the journey toward death, even the most dignified of adjectives will need to fall away; from the many tender adjectives of the first two stanzas, the poem moves through the third stanza, where there is only the ghostly adjective in "evening bell" (echoing "evening star"), to the last stanza, where there are no adjectives at all. Instead, a final destination which is also home, and a vision that is also a simple sight, without epithets, face to face. Six times it speaks of "I" or "me," and yet no poem was ever less self-absorbed. Its self-possession is a possession of, not by, self, and it is the single occurrence of the word "our" which gently but inexorably claims the poem and which vindicates Tennyson's unclamorous claim to the central humanity of a great poet.

Sunset and evening star,
  And one clear call for me!
And may there be no moaning of the bar,
  When I put out to sea,

But such a tide as moving seems asleep,
  Too full for sound and foam,
When that which drew from out the boundless deep
  Turns again home.

Twilight and evening bell,
  And after that the dark!
And may there be no sadness of farewell,
  When I embark;

For though from out our bourne of Time and Place
  The flood may bear me far,
I hope to see my Pilot face to face
  When I have crost the bar.

Abbreviations

Alfred Tennyson: Sir Charles Tennyson, *Alfred Tennyson* (1949)
Memoir: Hallam Lord Tennyson, *Alfred Lord Tennyson: A Memoir* (1897)
Materials: Hallam Lord Tennyson, *Materials for a Life of A. T.* (privately printed, no date). The early version of the *Memoir*. "*Materials* draft" means Hallam Tennyson's draft, now in the Tennyson Research Centre in Lincoln.
Poems: The Poems of Tennyson, edited by Christopher Ricks (Longman Annotated English Poets, 1969).

The Tennyson d'Eyncourt papers are at the Castle, Lincoln (Lincolnshire Archives Committee). (Indexed there as, for instance, H.61/26.)

Notes

p. 1 "My father": Trinity Notebook 34.
"In no": W. H. Auden, *A Selection from Tennyson* (1947), pp. xv–xvi.
p. 2 "You know": Lincoln; compare *Memoir*, I, 15.
"I hope": Tennyson d'Eyncourt/H.61/26, 19 February 1802.
"the Old Man": H. J. Schonfield, *Letters to Frederick Tennyson* (1930), p. 34; 28 January 1834.
p. 3 "George seems": *Alfred Tennyson*, p. 19; I have not traced this letter, which from Sir Charles's manuscript notes may be dated 20 April 1815.
p. 4 "How I": *Memoir*, I, 7.
"He remembered": *Memoir*, I, 6; also Hallam Tennyson, *Tennyson and His Friends* (1911), p. 213.
"of his": *Memoir*, II, 376.
"I find": H.144/142, 14 August 1820.
p. 6 "Eliza and": H.144/149, 15 April 1822.
"It was": H.144/150, 24 April 1822.
"I did": H.144/159, 21 January 1824.
p. 7 "You speak": H.144/160, 1 February 1824.

"said he": H.144/170, 22 July 1825.

"I found": 2/H.13/1, 24 July 1825.

"It is": H.147/4, 2 August 1825.

p. 8 "Do not": H.97/3, 21 January 1826.

"I fear": H.148/4, 30 October 1827. These important letters, from the Tennyson d'Eyncourt papers, were first quoted by E. F. Shannon, *Times Literary Supplement*, 6 March 1959.

p. 9 "extremely ill": H.148/12, 23 November 1827.

"The day": H.148/12.

"I know": H.148/23, 16 December 1827.

"I have": H.147/6, 5 December 1827.

"Have you": H.148/23.

p. 11 "He mastered": *Tennyson and His Friends*, p. 186.

"fits of": *Memoir*, I, 15.

p. 12 "This reminds": Sir Charles Tennyson, "Tennyson's Conversation," *Twentieth Century*, CLXV (1959), 35.

"who would": *Memoir*, I, 15; Wilfrid Ward, "Talks with Tennyson," *New Review*, XV (1896), 88–89.

"knew her": *Alfred Tennyson*, p. 349. I have not traced this letter to Louis Tennyson d'Eyncourt.

"haunting fear": Sir Charles Tennyson, *Twentieth Century*, CLXV (1959), 35.

"I'm going": *Materials* draft; *Memoir*, I, 17, has "I mean to be famous."

"The Poetry": Sotheby's Catalogue, 14 November 1934.

p. 13 "1. A. Tennyson": Lincoln (Usher Gallery).

"If Alfred": *Memoir*, I, 12.

"There, that": Anne Thackeray Ritchie, *Records of Tennyson* (1892), p. 6; compare *Memoir*, I, 13.

"The first": *Memoir*, II, 93.

p. 14 "Before I": *Memoir*, I, 11.

"When I": Trinity Notebook 34; compare *Memoir*, I, 12.

"I was": *Memoir*, II, 69.

"a day": *Memoir*, I, 4.

"thought everything": Ritchie, *Records of Tennyson*, p. 10; also William Allingham's *Diary* (1907), p. 132, 18 May 1866.

"I have": H.144/160, 1 February 1824.

p. 15 "This passage": *Memoir*, I, 7–8.

p. 17 "I have": Lincoln; 30 October 1825.

p. 20 £20: James Knowles, *Nineteenth Century*, XXXIII (1893), 181. The receipt, signed by Charles and Alfred, is at Trinity. Compare *Memoir*, I, 22.

"omitted from": *Memoir*, I, 23.

"between 15": 1893 reprint of *Poems by Two Brothers*, quoting Tennyson in the preface.

"early rot": *Memoir*, I, 22.

p. 21 "I write": H.147/7, 3 April 1828. *Memoir*, II, 164, misdates and misquotes a letter to Tennyson in 1873, so that instead of "the handsome cook who was burned to death" it has "the handsome cock." See *Materials* draft.

"Last night": *Alfred Tennyson*, p. 58; I have not traced this letter, which from Sir Charles's manuscript notes may be dated 23 September 1828.

"Charles and": 2/H.86/3, 26 January 1829.

p. 22 "It is": 2/H.86/17, 25 February 1829.

"My dear": 2/H.86/19, 27 February 1829. Confirmation of the incident with the constable is in 2/H.86/16.

p. 24 "I think it": 2/H.86/22, 12 March 1829.

"I think things": H.107/19, 7 May 1829.

"I shall": H.147/12, 24 May 1829.

"I have": 2/H.86/71, 31 July 1829.

"Although his": 2/H.86/73, 12 August 1829.

p. 25 thrilling fantasizing: *Memoir*, I, 52, 27 July 1830.

"I hope": 2/H.88/30, 24 or 25 June 1830.

a powerful fantasist: Dr. Tennyson wrote to his father, protesting that "to one person you represented me as 'the greatest liar that ever spoke' " (H.148/1A, 22 January 1827).

good reason: see *Alfred Tennyson*, p. 9.

"Then A.": *Memoir*, II, 147. Knowles, *Nineteenth Century*, XXXIII (1893), 167.

p. 26 "It appears": 2/H.88/36, 5 July 1830.

p. 27 "He is": 2/H.91/5, 3 March 1831.

"All shadow": H.147/3, 15 March 1831.

"His errors": 2/H.91/52, 28 March 1831.

"and though": 2/H.91/17, 9 March 1831.

p. 28 "The house": These interesting letters were published from the Massingberd papers (Lincolnshire Archives Committee) by R. W. Rader, *Notes and Queries*, December 1963. I have modified the spelling.

"Within a": *Materials* draft; *Memoir*, I, 72–73, has "do not generally come . . ."

"The Gardener's Daughter": Trinity Notebook 17.

p. 30 "I am": *Memoir*, I, 34.

"There was": *Memoir*, I, 68.

p. 31 lack of friendship: See Hallam's letters to Gladstone in 1828 and 1829, quoted by Betty Miller, "Camelot at Gambridge," *Twentieth Century*, CLXIII (1958), 136–137.

"Ghosts": *Memoir*, I, 43; I, 497–498. The fragmentary MS is at Harvard.

p. 32 Napoleon's retreat: Trinity Notebook 19; published by the present writer, *Times Literary Supplement*, 21 August 1969.

"I fell": *Tennyson and His Friends*, p. 263.

"You're doing": Lincoln notes; *Materials* draft; *Memoir*, II, 355.
"Have you": C. M. Gaskell, *Records of an Eton Schoolboy* (1883), p. 139.
"I consider": *Memoir*, I, 46, 14 September 1829.
"A noble": "Lines in Answer . . ."; T. H. Vail Motter, *The Writings of Arthur Hallam* (1943), p. 78.
"poor 'Timbuctoo' ": *Memoir*, I, 45.
"poem is": *Poems*, p. 172.

p. 33 "I couldn't": *Tennyson and His Friends*, p. 263; *Memoir*, I, 47.
"two of": H.147/1, 12 July 1829; H.147/2.
"If such": *Memoir*, I, 46.

p. 37 "the poem": Motter, p. 37.
"As I": Hallam's letter is at Lincoln; compare *Memoir*, I, 51.

p. 38 "Hallam either": T. Wemyss Reid, *Monckton Milnes* (1890), I, 146, 24 September 1833.
his father: Hallam, *Remains* (1834).
"They are": *Records of an Eton Schoolboy*, p. 117, 14 April 1828.
"I am sick": *Records*, p. 130, 2 February 1829.
"In my": James Pope-Hennessy, *Monckton Milnes: The Years of Promise* (1949), p. 73, August 1829. *Memoir*, I, 69, gives a letter from J. W. Blakesley to Tennyson, 1830, saying of Hallam: "He was not well while he was in London; moreover, he was submitting himself to the influences of the outer world more than (I think) a man of his genius ought to do." *Materials* draft shows that Hallam Tennyson cut and rewrote this glowering remark, the original form of which is now irrecoverable.
"I am one": *Records of an Eton Schoolboy*, p. 152.

p. 40 "a timid": *Westminster Review*, January 1831; John Jump, *Tennyson: The Critical Heritage* (1967), p. 26.
"The mood": "On Some of the Characteristics of Modern Poetry, and on the Lyrical Poems of Alfred Tennyson" (1831); Motter, p. 196.

p. 46 "that rather": *London Review*, July 1835; Jump, p. 86.
"The poem": Jump, p. 29.

p. 46n "He seems": Jump, p. 26.

p. 49 "If Alfred": James Pope-Hennessy, *Monckton Milnes: The Flight of Youth* (1951), p. 59; Carlyle in Milnes's Commonplace-book, 1855–56.

p. 50 "long, long": *Blackwood's Magazine*, May 1832; Jump, p. 60.
"The nominal": Jump, p. 87.

p. 51 "The questions": Jump, p. 94.

p. 52 "That ultra-": *Church of England Quarterly Review*, October 1842; Jump, p. 129.
"His genius": *Tait's Magazine*, April 1847.

p. 53 "One characteristic": Quoted by E. F. Shannon, *Tennyson and the Reviewers* (1952), pp. 74, 200.

p. 54 "The gold": *Quarterly Review,* September 1842; Jump, p. 116.

p. 55 "I think": *Nineteenth Century,* XXXIII (1893), 182.

p. 55n "At first": Allingham's *Diary,* p. 304, 21 October 1880.

p. 56 "I earnestly": Lincoln.

p. 57 "Alfred went": R. C. Trench, *Letters and Memorials* (1888), I, 84, 2 December 1830.

p. 57 "I hear": Quoted by Carlyle in his vividly humane account of the Torrijos affair, in his *Life of Sterling* (1851), Part I, Chapter XIII.

p. 58 Arthur was forbidden: Hallam to Trench, *Letters and Memorials,* I, 113, 1832. Henry Hallam to T. H. Rawnsley, H.110/15, 22 August 1832.

p. 59 "They promise": 2/H.91/61, 15 April 1831; also 2/H.91/51, March 1831.

"We discussed": 2/H.91/63, 18 May 1831.

p. 60 Dr. Tennyson had left debts: *Alfred Tennyson,* p. 109.

p. 61 egregiously misleading: 2/H.86/10, 4 February 1829, Dr. Tennyson to his father.

"Again if": 2/H.91/83, 10 September 1831.

p. 62 "You inquire": Lincoln, 8 February 1833 (postmark on arrival in Cambridge); *Memoir,* I, 128.

"I am": 2/H.91/72, 12 July 1831.

p. 63 "extremely distressing": H.110/25, 31 October 1832.

"in that condition": H.110/24, draft, 13 November 1832.

"He weeps": H.110/28, 8 November 1832.

"I don't": 2/H.91/66, June 1831.

Years later: *Alfred Tennyson,* p. 199.

Arthur Hallam: Lincoln copy.

p. 64 "I think": H.147/9, received 13 January 1834.

p. 65 "In my youth": Lincoln notebook, "Talks and Walks"; compare *Memoir,* I, 40. As an old man, Tennyson claimed, not without self-delusion, that his youthful "fits of melancholy" had been really "just gout"; H. D. Rawnsley, *Memories of the Tennysons* (1900), pp. 129–130, quoting Tennyson in 1889.

"afraid of": *Memoir,* I, 120.

"I am": Lincoln; the words "a sad . . . prophets old" were quoted without attribution in *Memoir,* I, 79. For a sardonic reference to Tennyson's eyesight in 1831, see Charles Merivale, *Autobiography* (1899), p. 113.

"My blindness": Letter, Lord Boyne; 18 March 1832.

p. 65n "grieved to": Letter, Lord Boyne; 24 March 1854.

p. 66 "Fare thee": Lincoln.

"Alfred is, as": A. M. Brookfield, "Some Letters from Arthur Hallam," *Fortnightly Review,* LXXIV (1903), 173, 4 March 1831.

"Poor Alfred": *Letters to Frederick Tennyson,* p. 23, 8 July 1831.

"Alfred is in": Merivale, *Autobiography,* p. 121, 14 August 1831.

"Alfred I was": Trench, *Letters and Memorials,* I, 111, 20 March 1832.

p. 66n "As to myself": University of Texas; 24 August 1878.

p. 67 "I hope": *Memoir*, I, 101–102.

p. 68 In January 1831: W. R. Nicoll and T. J. Wise, *Literary Anecdotes of the Nineteenth Century*, I (1895), 24.

"He wants": Lincoln; also *Memoir*, I, 81, amended from *Materials* draft.

p. 69 "Meanwhile, perhaps": Merivale, *Autobiography*, pp. 120–121, 14 August 1831.

p. 70 "I have": Trench, *Letters and Memorials*, I, 111, 20 March 1832.

"Have you": Huntington letter (HM 19464); 3 May 1832, to W. H. Brookfield.

p. 71 "One of my": *Poems*, p. 461.

"I was": Lincoln.

Effingham Wilson: *Alfred Tennyson*, p. 130, amending *Memoir*, I, 92.

"Alfred, not": Merivale, *Autobiography*, p. 120, 14 August 1831.

p. 72 "Alfred has": Nicoll and Wise, *Literary Anecdotes*, I, 27, 13 November 1832.

"I felt": Lincoln; also *Memoir*, I, 88–90.

"I scarcely": Letter, Mr. Robert Taylor; 13 October 1832.

"After mature": *Memoir*, I, 90.

"You must": *Alfred Tennyson*, p. 129.

"It can't": Lincoln.

p. 73 "I am oppressed": *Fortnightly Review*, LXXIV (1903), 175, 6 February 1832.

markedly liable: Motter, p. 55; "Yet should sad instinct in my breast / Speak true, and darker chance obtain, / Bless with one tear my final rest." Also Motter, p. 98, "foreboding ill."

"I am now": Trench, *Letters and Memorials*, I, 113, 1832.

"the Blue": *Fortnightly Review*, LXXIV (1903), 177, 2 April 1832.

"very wretched": *Ibid.*, 178, 29 May 1832.

"I am left": Trench, *Letters and Memorials*, I, 118, 6 June 1832.

"When your": *Fortnightly Review*, LXXIV (1903), 179, August 1832.

p. 74 the Rhine: *Memoir*, I, 101.

"except what": H.110/15, 22 August 1832.

Arthur remonstrated: H.110/20; *Letters to Frederick Tennyson*, pp. 27–31; H.110/19.

"A negotiation": *Records of an Eton Schoolboy*, p. 171, 8 September 1832.

"If you": Lincoln; 20 December 1832.

p. 75 "criticism which": *The Speaker*, 22 July 1893; *Uncollected Prose*, ed. J. P. Frayne, I (1970), 277.

p. 79 "tale of ": Hallam Tennyson, *Memoir*, I, 116.

"The 'Lady of Shalott' is": *Literary Gazette*, 8 December 1832 (William Jerdan); quoting the 1832 text.

"has for": "Tennyson," *Literary Essays* (1888); Jump, pp. 353–354.

p. 80 behind the tapestry: Compare "The Devil and the Lady," I, iii, 39–44.

p. 81 "the new-born": *Memoir*, I, 117.
J. W. Croker: *Quarterly Review*, April 1833; Jump, p. 71.
"a 'lame' ": Jump, pp. 88–89.

p. 82 "It is": *Memoir*, I, 500–501.

p. 83 "though more": Jump, p. 130.

p. 85 "a line": Tennyson on Patmore's line, "Her power makes not defeats but pacts," 30 October 1854; B. Champneys, *Coventry Patmore* (1900), I, 165.
"a fine": *A New Spirit of the Age* (1844); Jump, p. 159.

p. 86 "In the place": Jump, p. 74.

p. 88 "After such": Jump, p. 75.

p. 91 "What are": This letter (1831, apparently) was printed in *Notes and Queries*, February 1919, withholding the name of the recipient. The letter says "you Owl o' the turret," which was how Hallam addressed Brookfield.
"to express": *The Alien Vision of Victorian Poetry* (1952), p. 10.

p. 92 "How they": Jump, pp. 78–79. The line which Croker quotes, "Like a dreamy Lotos-eater, a delirious Lotos-eater!", appears in the 1832 but not the 1842 text.

p. 93 "The Spontaneous": *Letters* (1894), II, 60, 11 November 1864.

p. 94 "the meaning": Jump, p. 121.
"the most": Jump, p. 95.

p. 100 "What a": "Mr. Tennyson," *The Poetry of the Period* (1870); Jump, pp. 303–304.

p. 102 "Pierced through with knotted thorns": My text of this manuscript poem has been corrected by the sharp eyes of Mr. John Pettigrew.

p. 103 "When I": *Memoir*, I, 193.
"Next Sir": *Poems*, p. 522. In the Heath MS, "The Two Voices" is likewise entitled "Thoughts of a Suicide."

p. 103n Mary Gladstone, *Diaries* (1930), p. 160, 8 June 1879; Knowles, *Nineteenth Century*, XXXIII (1893), 169; Allingham's *Diary*, p. 62, 28 June 1851.

p. 104 "When thy": Trinity Notebook 15. Published *Times Literary Supplement*, 21 August 1969. The probability is strong that the lines likewise antedate Hallam's death.

p. 105 "The stuttering": "Patterns of Morbidity: Repetition in Tennyson's Poetry," in *The Major Victorian Poets: Reconsiderations*, ed. Isobel Armstrong (1969), p. 25.

p. 107 "The disease": *Edinburgh Review*, April 1843; Jump, pp. 149–150.
In these same months: "St. Simeon Stylites" was written in 1833, by November (*Memoir*, I, 130); it is unlikely to have been written in October, when Tennyson heard of Hallam's death. For an important discussion of the poem as a dramatic monologue, see Robert Langbaum, *The Poetry of Experience* (1957), pp. 87–88.

p. 108 "You ask": *Further Letters*, ed. C. C. Abbott (second ed., 1956), p. 8, 3 September 1862.

p. 109 "powerful monodrama": R. H. Horne; Jump, p. 160.
"The gift": Jump, p. 120.
"faculty of": Jump, pp. 160, 163.

p. 110 "A powerfully": Jump, p. 133.
"Tennyson's sympathy": William E. Fredeman, " 'A Sign Betwixt the Meadow and the Cloud': The Ironic Apotheosis of Tennyson's 'St. Simeon Stylites,' " *University of Toronto Quarterly*, XXXVIII (1968), 79.
"Simeon is": Fredeman, p. 74. Spedding had described the poem's aim as "to shadow forth dramatically the faith, the feelings, and the hopes, which support the man who, being taught that the rewards of another life will be proportioned to the misery voluntarily undergone in this, is bent on qualifying himself for the best place"; Jump, p. 148.

p. 111 a firm ending: Martin Dodsworth has said that "the characteristic Tennysonian conclusion is like that of 'St. Simeon Stylites'—superficially emphatic, actually inconclusive"; *The Major Victorian Poets*, p. 17.
"Tennyson's poem": Fredeman, p. 72.

p. 112 "lay aside": H.113/5, 1 February 1833.
"the name": H.113/9, 9 February 1833.
"They also": H.116A/33, 29 August 1835.

p. 113 "determined to": H.116A/35, 28 September 1835.
"I am": H.116A/31, 1 August 1835.
"Of my Grandfather": Letter, Lord Boyne; 10 March 1833.
"Some of": H.113/62, 28 November 1833.

p. 114 "the great": Lincoln; a different wording is given, unattributed, in *Memoir*, I, 102.
"I feel": *Memoir*, I, 102–103, 31 July 1833.
"The gallery": Lincoln; *Memoir*, I, 104.
"My dear": Lincoln, amending *Memoir*, I, 105. My edition of the *Poems* (like *Memoir* and *Alfred Tennyson*) was in error in saying that Henry Elton's letter arrived 1 October; it was written and posted then.

p. 115 "I beg": Lincoln; 10 October 1833. It may be significant of something in Tennyson's character that he should have sketched three of his semi-comic faces on the outer sheet of this tragic letter.
"We all": H.113/67, 18 December 1833.

p. 116 "came as": *Tennyson and His Friends*, p. 397. Also Trench, *Letters and Memorials*, I, 146–147. On Tennyson's reactions, see *Memoir*, I, 109, 498; and R. W. Rader, *Tennyson's "Maud": The Biographical Genesis* (1963), pp. 11–21.
"a loud": Merivale, *Autobiography*, p. 135, from Henry Alford, 11 November 1833.
"Oh my": From Francis Garden, 14 December 1833. *Materials* draft has a copy of the letter; Hallam Tennyson headed it "Doubtful"

(of inclusion), and deleted "which I have heard you apply to Christianity."

"that bitterness": *Memoir*, I, 498, 26 November 1833.

p. 117 "suffered what": Hope Dyson and Sir Charles Tennyson, *Dear and Honoured Lady* (1969), p. 61, December 1861.

p. 118 "Tennyson has been": *Letters*, I, 25, 25 October 1833.

"will most": H.113/67, 18 December 1833.

"Tennyson has, I": Trench, *Letters and Memorials*, I, 152.

"I could": *Memoir*, I, 96.

p. 119 "I suppose": *Memoir*, I, 12.

p. 122 "It's too": *Nineteenth Century*, XXXIII (1893), 182.

p. 123 "You may": *Saturday Review*, 3 November 1855; Jump, p. 188.

"Most characteristic": *The Poetry of Experience*, pp. 89–90.

p. 124 "It is": *On Translating Homer* (1861), III.

p. 126 Yet one feature: The most scrupulous account of the arguments is by John Pettigrew, *Victorian Poetry*, I (1963), 27–45.

p. 127 "I will": *Poems*, p. 560. "Unfinished" might possibly mean "without final revision"; but Kemble's text, apart from two slips, is that of the Heath MS, and the differences from Tennyson's final text, though of great interest, are few and are matters of detail.

p. 128 "These lines": *Memoir*, I, 214.

"What is": *Memoir*, I, 135.

"Since Hallam's": *Memoir*, I, 500.

"It is a ": Lincoln; 10 April 1859.

p. 129 "Yet oft": See too the sections of *In Memoriam* which Tennyson did not publish, "Young is the grief I entertain," and "Let Death and Memory keep the face." Also Humphry House, "In Memoriam," *All in Due Time* (1955), p. 134.

p. 133 "a purity": *The Galaxy*, September 1875; "Tennyson's Drama," *Views and Reviews* (1908), p. 171. James's sympathetic and acute account of Tennyson's "poised and stationary" style is the counterpart of his wittily malicious description of Tennyson's reading of "Locksley Hall," with James all disingenuous disappointment at how the Laureate would "spout": "With all the resonance of the chant, the whole thing was yet *still*, with all the long swing of its motion it yet remained where it was—heaving doubtless grandly enough up and down and beautiful to watch as through the superposed veils of its long self-consciousness" (*The Middle Years*).

p. 134 Other early poems: "The Devil and the Lady" and "The Grasshopper."

p. 137 "The 'Morte' ": Jump, pp. 119–120.

p. 139 "Not bad": *Memoir*, I, 153.

"Tennyson is": Jump, p. 387.

p. 140 "The uncertain": *The Major Victorian Poets*, p. 18.

"A certain": Jump, pp. 127–128, 132.

p. 141 "Oh! that 'twere possible": The text given at this point is that of 1837.

p. 142n Clough: *Prose Remains* (1888), p. 358.

p. 144 "Observe how": Jump, pp. 359–360.

p. 145 "Life and": Jump, p. 61.

p. 146 "I should": Lincoln; *Memoir,* I, 108. On Henry Hallam's reticence, see Reid, *Milnes,* I, 157.

"I attempted": *Poems,* p. 854; 14 February 1834.

"At that": H.147/10, 1834.

p. 147 "I pity": H.116/22, 27 April 1834.

"I cannot": H.117/54, 14 March 1835.

"Alfred will": Rader, *Tennyson's "Maud,"* pp. 17–18, 127.

Rosa Baring: For a meticulous account, see Rader, *Tennyson's "Maud."*

p. 149 "they want": *Letters to Frederick Tennyson,* pp. 41–42. Rader, *Tennyson's "Maud,"* p. 142, shows that the bonds were not finally discharged till just before *Maud* was written (letter, 25 October 1853).

the Old Man's funeral: H.116A/31, 1 August 1835. See Alfred *Tennyson,* pp. 106–107.

"I hear": H.116A/33, 29 August 1835.

"I know": H.116A/34, 1 September 1835.

"Your letter": H.118/54, 3 September 1835.

p. 151 "John Heath": Yale: *Memoir,* I, 145. *Memoir* wrongly italicizes "I do not . . . at present," which has misled E. F. Shannon (*Tennyson and the Reviewers,* p. 35) and H. C. Merriam (*Edward Moxon,* 1939, p. 170).

p. 152 " 'Dora,' being": *Memoir,* I, 196.

"So true": *On Translating Homer: Last Words* (1862).

"This 'Dora' ": E. L. Griggs, *Coleridge Fille* (1940), p. 202.

p. 155 "a sort": Tennyson to Brookfield, 15 July 1836; Mary Ellmann, *Modern Language Notes,* LXV (1950), 227.

"What has": Trinity, 10 January 1837; *Memoir,* I, 157–160.

p. 157 "His two": *Memoir,* I, 149–150.

"in such": *Memoir,* I, 150, 171; *Materials* draft.

"Next morning": "Written For My Sons"; several drafts are at Lincoln. Compare *Memoir,* I, 148, which removes the sportive humor, leaving only romanticism: "Are you a Dryad or an Oread wandering here?" Fragments of the letters of Emily and Tennyson are in *Memoir,* I, 167–176, and *Alfred Tennyson,* pp. 179–182; some fragments are at Lincoln.

"with one": "Written For My Sons." *Memoir,* I, 108–109, attributed this to "one of her friends" (that is, Tennyson's sister's).

p. 158 "I am": to Brookfield, 15 July 1836; *Modern Language Notes,* LXV (1950), 227.

"But what": C. C. Abbott, *Life and Letters of Darley* (1928), p. 202.

Tennyson's religious beliefs: Rader, *Tennyson's "Maud,"* pp. 69–75, from the Rawnsleys' reminiscences.

p. 159 "I bless": Lincoln, 9 January 1840.
"After this": *Memoir,* I, 176.
" 'Tis true": Lincoln.
"continued unshaken": *Materials,* II, 38.

p. 160 "Do you": Reid, *Milnes,* I, 208, 3 March 1838.
"Tennyson composes": Reid, *Milnes,* I, 220, 1838.
"Do not": *Materials* draft, amending *Memoir,* I, 165–166, which italicizes "careless . . . influence," and which gives "[would be] taken . . . volumes" without attribution.
"I want": F. R. Barton, *Some New Letters of FitzGerald* (1923), pp. 12–13, 27 November 1839.

p. 161 "Wherefore, in these dark ages of the Press": Trinity Notebook 26; published *Times Literary Supplement,* 21 August 1969, with another version of the lines.

p. 163 "His bookseller": Shannon, *Tennyson and the Reviewers,* pp. 35–36, 26 February 1840. Two years later, Tennyson was "disheartened" because he feared (needlessly) that Spedding might not be able to write the review (*Memoir,* I, 180).

p. 165 "the smarting": Jump, p. 360.
"a selfish": *Atheism and Suicide* (1881), p. 3.
"finding fault": "A Word about Tennyson," *The Critic,* 1 January 1887; Jump, p. 348.
"It had": C. C. Abbott, *Correspondence of Hopkins and Dixon* (1935), p. 19, 10 January 1879.

p. 167 "Alfred, whatever": *Letters,* I, 115, 22 May 1842; the particular poem which FitzGerald was deploring, "The Skipping-Rope," is deplorable; Tennyson later suppressed it.

p. 173 "The old": *The Alien Vision of Victorian Poetry,* p. 27.
Tennyson's own predilection: "Tennyson perhaps likes the 'Vision of Sin' best of his own poems" (Allingham's *Diary,* p. 54, 18 August 1849); "one of my poems, which I confess has always been a favourite with myself" (letter, Brotherton Collection).

pp. 173–174 "A Real": H. S. Salt, *Life of James Thomson* ("*B.V.*") (1889), p. 255. As Salt points out, Thomson seems anyway to have mingled "The Vision of Sin" with "The Two Voices."

p. 174 "The word": *A Commentary on "In Memoriam"* (third ed., 1910), p. 164.

p. 175 two small poems: "Conclusion" to "The May Queen," and "The Poet's Song."
"I hate": Allingham's *Diary,* p. 168, 27 December 1867.

p. 176 "You bore": A. M. Terhune, *Life of FitzGerald* (1947), p. 122; *Memoir,* I, 178, omits "Damn!", which makes "curse" vacant.
"What a": Duke University; 22 February 1841.
"I carried": *Some New Letters,* p. 53, 2 March 1842.
"Poor Tennyson": *Some New Letters,* pp. 55–56, 17 March 1842. Also *Letters,* I, 113, 31 March 1842: "Alfred is busy preparing a

new volume for the press: full of doubts, troubles, etc. The reviewers will doubtless be at him: and with justice for many things: but some of the poems will outlive the reviewers."

p. 177 "It is": *More Letters* (1901), p. 17, 1842.

"Don't abuse": *Alfred Tennyson*, p. 192.

p. 178 "When I": *Some New Letters*, p. 19, 17 February 1840.

Dr. Matthew Allen: For Allen's contribution to psychiatry, see Richard Hunter and Ida Macalpine, *Three Hundred Years of Psychiatry 1535–1860* (1963), pp. 855–858. The poet John Clare was a patient of Dr. Allen's from 1837 to 1841.

"He has": *Tennyson and His Friends*, p. 408.

"This philanthropic": *Memoir*, I, 216, 220–221.

p. 179 "I have": *Letters to Frederick Tennyson*, p. 53, 1 November 1841.

"Yesterday it": *Ibid.*, p. 55, 6 November 1841. It is worth noting that Emily Sellwood's father was involved in the legal negotiations.

"I wish": *Materials* draft, amending *Memoir*, I, 212–213, which omits "I feel very crazy."

"Arthur has": Eliza Tennyson to Charles Tennyson d'Eyncourt, H.128/15, March 1843.

"I have done": *Letters to Frederick Tennyson*, pp. 56–57, 4 March 1843.

"So severe": *Memoir*, I, 221.

p. 180 "I feel": C. and F. Brookfield, *Mrs. Brookfield and Her Circle* (1905), I, 103, 7 October 1841. An equally virulent reaction came from Elizabeth Barrett (*Letters to George Barrett*, 1958, p. 99, 8 July 1843). When Emily Jesse died in 1887, Frederick Tennyson wrote a strange poem implying that in heaven it would not be her husband Jesse but Arthur Hallam who would really matter to her (*Tennyson and His Friends*, pp. 54–55.)

"The Tennyson's": *Mrs. Brookfield and Her Circle*, I, 106, 10 October 1841.

"never seen": *Letters*, I, 145, 10 December 1843.

"It is very": Lincoln; 2 February 1844.

p. 181 "I am at": Brotherton Collection; 23 February 1844.

"has since": *Letters to George Barrett*, p. 126, 10 August 1844.

"Old Allen": *Letters to Frederick Tennyson*, p. 58, 11 December 1844.

"Last night": *Some New Letters*, p. 97, 17 January 1845.

p. 182 "the fiery": National Library of Scotland; C. R. Sanders, "Carlyle and Tennyson," *PMLA*, LXXVI (1961), 85, 6 February 1845.

"He was": *Letters*, I, 194, 12 June 1845.

"On my": Wilfrid Ward, *Aubrey de Vere* (1904), p. 87.

p. 183 "It has": *New Letters* (1904), I, 322, 26 October 1844.

in 1843: H. D. Rawnsley, *Memories of the Tennysons*, pp. 88–89.

in 1845: Lincoln; 31 January 1845.

"is considered": C. S. Parker, *Sir Robert Peel*, III (1899), 439–442; throughout this paragraph.

À chaqu'un: New Letters and Memorials of Jane Welsh Carlyle

(1903), I, 180, 5 October 1845. Lady Harriet Baring was related to Rosa Baring.

p. 184 "Mr. Moxon": *Mrs. Brookfield*, I, 200, 5 December 1846.

p. 185 "who, big": Trinity, 10 January 1837; *Memoir*, I, 159, conceals the name with a dash.

"At the very": *Materials* draft, amending *Memoir*, I, 244–245.

"Your father": *Memoir*, II, 216.

Bulwer-Lytton and his son: *Memoir*, II, 28, 1865, on "***'s cork heels," is aimed at Bulwer-Lytton (the Berg Collection letter has "B 's"). Margaret Woods (manuscript reminiscences in the Bodleian Library) reports Tennyson on the heels and the dandyism. Mrs. Bradley quotes Tennyson on Bulwer-Lytton as "hollow and false and loose in principles" (Joanna Richardson, *The Pre-Eminent Victorian*, 1962, p. 94). Lincoln notes by A. D. Coleridge: "Lord Tennyson has a poor opinion of the Bulwers both father and son."

p. 186 "But the": *Letters of Robert Browning and Elizabeth Barrett Barrett*, I, 427, 30 January 1846.

"Alfred looks": National Library of Scotland; Sanders, *PMLA*, LXXVI (1961), 85, 3 May 1846. For Tennyson in November 1846, see *Memoir*, I, 235.

"I was": Lincoln, 12 November 1846, to FitzGerald; amending *Memoir*, I, 233–234.

"Call your": Yale, 1847; amending *Memoir*, I, 236.

p. 187 "They tell": *Memoir*, I, 241.

"A truly": J. Slater, *Correspondence of Emerson and Carlyle* (1964), pp. 436–437, 30 December 1847.

p. 188 "a wretched": *Letters*, I, 237, 4 May 1848.

"very gorgeous": L. and E. Hanson, *Necessary Evil* (1952), p. 361, 26 December 1847.

"self-exculpations": Shannon, *Tennyson and the Reviewers*, pp. 124–132, is particularly shrewd on this.

p. 190 "The grand": *Athenaeum*, 1 January 1848; Jump, pp. 167–168.

p. 195 "He talked": *Memoir*, II, 70–71.

p. 199 "He told": *Memoir*, II, 73.

"It is": *Nineteenth Century*, XXXIII (1893), 170. For Tennyson anc the past, see a notable article by James Kissane, "Tennyson: Th Passion of the Past and the Curse of Time," *ELH*, XXXII (1965).

p. 200 "*Either* the": *English Poetry: A Critical Introduction* (1950), pp. 22 231–232.

p. 203 "Perhaps one": Letter, 3 December 1859; *Works*, XXXVI, 326.

p. 205 "He is": Ward, *Aubrey de Vere*, p. 146.

"moved in": H. D. Rawnsley, quoted by Rader, *Tennyson's "Maud* pp. 78–79.

p. 206 "Tennyson is emerged": *More Letters*, p. 22, November 1848.

In 1849: *Memoir*, I, 255.

"Katie told": Rawnsley, *Memories of the Tennysons*, pp. 123–124.

p. 206n "Poor Charles": Lincoln; 26 March 1859.

p. 207 the publisher Moxon: *Memoir*, I, 328.

"Pray dearest": Trinity; to Lewis Fytche.

"was just": Rader, *Tennyson's "Maud,"* pp. 82–83, throughout this paragraph; quoting Rawnsley, *Tennyson 1809–1909* (1909), pp. 20–21.

tell even his mother: Lincoln; Tennyson to L. Colquhoun, 10 July 1850.

"The bridegroom": Leslie A. Marchand, *Byron: A Biography* (1957), II, 503, quoting Hobhouse.

p. 208 "to the amusement": Written For My Sons"; amending *Memoir*, I, 329.

"Well, all": Rader, *Tennyson's "Maud,"* p. 83, from Rawnsley.

"We seem": Duke University.

"Dear double": Lincoln; 20 June 1850.

"It seemed": Written For My Sons"; *Memoir*, I, 332, unattributed (the words might then as aptly have been Tennyson's). Emily's letter (Lincoln) to Charles and Louisa, 17 June 1850, from Weston super Mare: "You will wonder perhaps what brought us hither. It was my wish to see Clevedon and A.H.H.'s tomb."

"Great was": "Written For My Sons."

"Alfred looks": T. Bliss, *Thomas Carlyle: Letters to His Wife* (1953), p. 271, 3 October 1850.

p. 209 "I should": Vivien Noakes, *Edward Lear* (1968), p. 170, 12 June 1859.

"sunk in": Reid, *Milnes*, II, 264–265, 12 April 1872.

"a Lady": *More Letters*, p. 108, 7 December 1869. Also Terhune, *FitzGerald*, p. 127: "She is a graceful lady, but I think that she and other aesthetic and hysterical Ladies have hurt A.T."

"capable of": R. Stewart, *English Notebooks of Hawthorne* (1941), p. 47, 23 February 1854.

those who think: Harold Nicolson was witty: "The Peace of God," he wrote later, "came into my life before the altar when I wedded her." We may well believe it; but a great many other quite significant things went out of his life from that moment (*Tennyson*, 1923, p. 157).

p. 209n "You know": *Materials* draft, to Dr. and Mrs. Mann. The letters by Emily are at Lincoln.

p. 210 "Her great": Ward, *Aubrey de Vere*, pp. 158–159, 14 October 1850.

p. 211 "the number": *Memoir*, I, 202.

"A.T. has": *Letters*, I, 187, 29 January 1845.

"With respect": *Memoir*, I, 243.

"to *print*": Ward, *Aubrey de Vere*, p. 154.

p. 212 The title: "The title *In Memoriam*, suggested by Emily," *Alfred Tennyson*, p. 247; but the letter, 26 June 1864 (Lincoln), part of which is then quoted in *Alfred Tennyson*, p. 350, does not make it clear whether Emily suggested or preferred the title: " 'Idylls

Chiefly of Seventy Years Ago.' I am anxious about the title, dearest, will this do? 'In Memoriam' has proved a good title so perhaps I may be right in this too. 'Idylls of the King' too."

"It must": *Memoir*, I, 304.

"The sections": *Memoir*, I, 304–305.

"the general": *Nineteenth Century*, XXXIII (1893), 182; see also Gordon N. Ray, *Tennyson Reads "Maud"* (1968), p. 37. A. C. Bradley's *Commentary on "In Memoriam"* is scrupulous and imaginative in its analysis of the poem.

p. 213 "Not that": *Fraser's Magazine*, September 1850; Jump, p. 183.

"It is": *All in Due Time*, pp. 130–131.

p. 214 "We have": to W. B. Donne, 28 February, 1845; C. B. Johnson and N. C. Hannay, *A FitzGerald Friendship* (1932), p. 10.

"from *In Memoriam*": *Memoir*, II, 503. *Memoir*, II, 500: "Between Shakespeare's Sonnets he hardly liked to decide, all were so powerful." Tennyson was collaborating with Palgrave on *The Golden Treasury*.

an important source: There appear to be allusions to *Sonnets* in sections I, LXI, LXVII, LXXII, CXVIII, and the epilogue.

p. 215 "the old": Jump, pp. 183, 185.

"Once again": *Materials*, IV, 460; see *Tennyson and His Friends*, pp. 145, 265.

"It is": *Introduction to the Literature of Europe* (1839), III, 501–504.

"Henry Hallam": *Memoir*, II, 289.

p. 216 "the fact": Brian Reade, *Sexual Heretics* (1970), p. 9.

p. 217 "If anybody": *Nineteenth Century*, XXXIII (1893), 187.

p. 218 "That night": Emily's Journal; amending *Memoir*, I, 335.

"that union": *Memoir*, II, 69.

"Men should": Lincoln notebook.

"Certainly, if": Ward, *Aubrey de Vere*, p. 76.

"More as": *The Princess*, VII, 268; but Tennyson did change this (the 1847–48 text) in 1850: "Nor lose the childlike in the larger mind." For "the double-natured Poet," compare "Wherefore, in these dark ages of the Press," p. 161.

"But six": "Tennyson and Musset," *Miscellanies* (1886); Jump, p. 337. D. H. Lawrence listed Tennyson among those with "a proper proportion between male and female" (*Study of Thomas Hardy*, Chapter VII).

"Ironical sidehits": Lincoln, 8 February 1833 (postmark on arrival in Cambridge); the cut version is *Memoir*, I, 127–128.

p. 219 "The Victorians' conception": *George Eliot: A Biography* (1968), p. 496.

"a female": *Literary Gazette*, 15 June 1850.

"the tone": *The Times*, 28 November 1851. Humphry House (*Times Literary Supplement*, 4 November 1949) showed that Manley Hopkins—Gerard Manley Hopkins's father—wrote either this review, or that of *The Princess* (*The Times*, 12 October 1848), or both. In Kingsley's reference to "the disagreeable review of you in the *Times* some years back," written by a "poetaster parson, ———," the dash (*Memoir*, I, 455) stands for the name Aris Wilmott (Kingsley's letter, 29 November 1859, Lincoln).

p. 220 "It is": Originally the Introduction to *Poems of Tennyson* (Nelson Classics, 1936); as "In Memoriam," in *Essays Ancient and Modern* (1936). *Selected Essays* (third ed., 1951), pp. 333–334.

p. 221 "*In Memoriam* is": Jump, p. 364.

"Whatever was": *Westminster Review*, October 1855; T. Pinney, *Essays of George Eliot* (1963), p. 191. When G. H. Lewes died in 1878, George Eliot read *In Memoriam* repeatedly, and copied sections of it into her diary (Haight, *George Eliot*, p. 516).

"His genius": *Tait's Magazine*, April 1847.

"M. Verlaine": "Verlaine in 1894"; *The Savoy*, April 1896; *Uncollected Prose*, I, 399.

"they are": *Materials*, II, 17.

Teilhard de Chardin: E. R. August, "Tennyson and Teilhard: The Faith of *In Memoriam*," *PMLA*, March 1969.

p. 222 "I do": "Review of a Free Enquiry into the Nature and Origin of Evil" (1757).

"incompatible incoherences": Jump, p. 339.

p. 224 "is full": *Letters*, I, 263, 31 December 1850.

Its language falters: Humphry House is especially perceptive on this (*All in Due Time*, pp. 136–137).

p. 225 "It's too": *Nineteenth Century*, XXXIII (1893), 182.

VII, "Dark house, by which once more I stand": There is a commentary on this section, by the present writer, in the introduction to *Poems and Critics* (1966).

"I should": *Selected Essays*, pp. 332, 336.

"a morbid": *Tennyson*, p. 27.

p. 226 "He is": *Further Letters*, p. 219, 10 September 1864.

p. 227 "a conclusion": E. B. Mattes, *In Memoriam: The Way of a Soul* (1951), p. 98.

p. 228 Tennyson's choice of stanza: A resonant early fragment of *In Memoriam* (later modified as section III) rhymes *abab: Poems*, p. 866. The effect is markedly different, even though the first stanza is close in the lines' wording to Tennyson's final text.

"air of": Jump, p. 365.

"their metre": Jump, p. 183.

p. 229 "as generated": "The Voice of the Shuttle," *Beyond Formalism* (1970), p. 339.

p. 231 "I see": Berg Collection.

"Who is": *Correspondence of Crabb Robinson with the Wordsworth Circle* (1927), I, 536–537.

"his great": *Memoir*, I, 335.

"there are": *Letters of Queen Victoria 1837–1861* (1908), II, 266.

p. 232 "The night": *Nineteenth Century*, XXXIII (1893), 167; *Memoir*, I, 335–336. Tennyson's letter to Forster contradicts Hallam Tennyson on this dream: "my father, as he has assured me, had not any expectation of the Laureateship, or any thought upon the subject: it seemed to him therefore a very curious coincidence . . ."

"I was": Harvard; November 1850; cut from *Memoir*, I, 336.

"Mr. Poelaur": *Memoir*, I, 461.

"A. – 'He' ": Allingham's *Diary*, p. 132, 18 May 1866.

"it is": H.141/10, 5 February 1855.

p. 233 "Horrid rubbish": H.141/13, 11 February 1855.

"The taskwork": "To the Queen," MS. Tennyson was to meet Queen Victoria in 1862; for a study of their relationship, see Hope Dyson and Sir Charles Tennyson, *Dear and Honoured Lady*.

"As for": Duke University; November 1850.

"Dead as": *Memoir*, I, 340.

p. 233n "you must": *Dear and Honoured Lady*, p. 78, 9 May 1863.

p. 234 "great grief": *Memoir*, I, 375, 1854.

"looks thin": Champneys, *Patmore*, II, 307, 3 November 1851.

Hallam Tennyson: Tennyson had at first yielded to Emily's wish to name the child Alfred, and with Hallam as the second name (Letter to Henry Hallam, 16 August 1852). For the name Hallam, see *Memoir*, I, 359, 361; and Merivale, *Autobiography*, p. 324.

"Many thanks": Champneys, *Patmore*, II, 304–305.

p. 235 "is much": Ward, *Aubrey de Vere*, p. 227.

"I'm black-blooded": *Nineteenth Century*, XXXIII (1893), 174.

"hereditary tenderness": FitzGerald; see p. 178.

"I feel": Wellesley College, 14 September 1857.

"God will": *Memoir*, II, 42.

"I have": To Leigh Hunt, about S. C. Hall; British Museum; 13 July 1837.

p. 235n "May God": H.121/39.

p. 236 "Tennyson is": *English Notebooks*, pp. 553–554.

p. 237 "And in": *Autobiography*, II, 190, 192.

p. 238 "Perhaps the": Gordon N. Ray, *Letters of Thackeray*, III (1946), 128, 25 November 1852. *Memoir*, I, 362.

"I send": L. Huxley, *Life and Letters of T. H. Huxley* (1900), I, 102–103, 28 November 1852.

p. 240 "he would": E. T. Cook, *Life of Ruskin* (second ed., 1912), I, 466.

p. 242 "chatting of": Jump, p. 187.

"a poetry": *English Poetry and the English Language* (1934), p. 104.

p. 244 "Not a": *Memoir*, I, 409–410.

"A real": Reid, *Milnes*, I, 512, 16 July 1855.

p. 246 suicide: Tennyson's revision removed the uncertainty as to the father's suicide; and the hero says, later in the poem, that Maud's love may save his "yet young life. . . . Perhaps from a selfish grave."

Tennyson's life: For a perceptive account of *Maud*'s various fusions, see Rader, *Tennyson's "Maud,"* pp. 88–104.

Aunt Russell: *Memoir*, I, 407–408.

Dr. Allen . . . coal: *Letters to Frederick Tennyson*, p. 55.

p. 247 "You must": *Memoir*, I, 468.

p. 248 "He seems": H. Allingham and E. B. Williams, *Letters to William Allingham* (1911), p. 144, 23 February 1856.

"One of": O. Doughty and J. R. Wahl, *Letters*, I (1965), 281–282, 8 January 1856.

"was really": *Works* (1913), ed. Hallam Tennyson, p. xxxix.

"This poem": *Poems*, p. 1039.

p. 249 "No other": Ray, *Tennyson Reads "Maud,"* p. 43.

"that flickering": *Tennyson*, p. 125.

p. 250 "these hexameters": *Essays*, p. 193.

"the incipient": George Brimley, *Cambridge Essays* (1855); Jump, p. 195.

"mental malaria": *National Review*, October 1859; Jump, p. 218.

"his inerrancy": "Milton II" (1947); *On Poetry and Poets* (1957), p. 176.

p. 251 "With the": *After Strange Gods* (1934), p. 42.

"Both Maud": *Quarterly Review*, October 1859; Jump, p. 246.

p. 253 "a bleeding woman": I owe this observation to Mr. Jonathan Wordsworth.

p. 254 *"an aegis": Tennyson's "Maud" Vindicated* (1856); Jump, p. 198.

"We frankly": Jump, pp. 247–248.

"In the": *Essays*, p. 195.

p. 255 "He seemed": Jump, p. 219.

p. 258 "the music": *Essays*, p. 197.

"The intense": *Elements of English Prosody* (1880); *Works*, XXXI, 339–340.

p. 261 "Take this": *Tennyson Reads "Maud,"* p. 45.

"its tone": *Essays*, pp. 192, 197.

"What interpretation": Jump, pp. 246–247. Gladstone was to recant somewhat, *Gleanings of Past Years* (1879), II, 146–147, quoted in *Memoir*, I, 398–399.

"To wage": *Saturday Review*, 3 November 1855; Jump, p. 187. Goldwin Smith's short piece is excellent throughout.

"are as": "The Art of Tennyson," *Essays Towards a Critical Method* (1889); Jump, p. 437.

p. 262 "sad as": Jump, p. 211.

"From this": *Essays*, pp. 192, 197.

p. 263 "the hero": *Atheism and Suicide*, p. 3.

"We do": Jump, p. 187.

p. 264 "I wish": Yale; to Ticknor and Fields, 11 December 1858.

"Tennyson's Serial Poem": *Mid-Victorian Studies* (1965), pp. 80–109.

p. 265 "When I": *Nineteenth Century*, XXXIII (1893), 181–182.

"he was": *Poems*, p. 1460; Allingham's *Diary*, p. 150, 3 February 1867.
"began to": *Memoir*, II, 125. Tennyson had at first intended to publish by themselves the two idylls "Enid" and "Nimuë" ("Vivien").

p. 266 "I could": *Memoir*, II, 126.
"in as": *Memoir*, II, 125. Sir Charles Tennyson noted the discrepancy.
"I shall": *Memoir*, II, 62.

p. 267 "The 'Morte' ": *Memoir*, I, 482–483.
"my father": *Memoir*, II, 121.
"I must": E. A. Horsman, *Diary of Alfred Domett* (1953), p. 79.
"We are": Jump, p. 251.

p. 268 "The great": Jump, p. 374.
"But the": *Letters to Allingham*, p. 104, 9 October 1859.

p. 271 his "curious": *On Translating Homer: Last Words.*
"Did you": C. L. Cline, *Letters of Meredith* (1970), I, 406–407, 19 December 1869.
"The fault": G. W. E. Russell, *Letters of Matthew Arnold* (1895), I, 127, 17 December 1860.
"It seems": Jump, p. 227.

p. 272 "But the": *Correspondence of Hopkins and Dixon*, p. 24, 27 February 1879.
"the Morte": Jump, pp. 339, 319.
"Rather a": *Views and Reviews*, p. 177.
"Unfit to": E. J. Morley, *Henry Crabb Robinson on Books and Their Writers* (1938), II, 792, 7 November 1859.
"The sentiments": Jump, p. 232.

p. 273 "to admire": *The Listener*, 12 February 1942.
"We read": *Correspondence of Emerson and Carlyle*, pp. 552–553, 27 January 1867.

p. 274 "good taste": Jump, p. 262.

p. 275 "Nevertheless I": *Memoir*, I, 453.
"For narrative": *Selected Essays*, p. 331.

p. 276 "I had": Gordon Haight, *The George Eliot Letters*, VI (1956), 415–416, 6 November 1877.

p. 277 "I agree": *Letters*, I, 239, 22 September 1864.

p. 279 "Parnassian": *Further Letters*, pp. 216–217. See also Bagehot, "Wordsworth, Tennyson, and Browning," *National Review*, November 1864 (Jump, pp. 282–293); imaginatively questioned by Martin Dodsworth, *The Major Victorian Poets*, pp. 8–14.

p. 280 "To my": Letter, 19 June 1869; *Works*, XXXVI, 570–571.

p. 281 there were Victorians: For example, J. M. Robertson (Jump, p. 434). Browning's exchanges with Julia Wedgwood on the ending of "Enoch Arden" are vivid and to the point; R. Curle, *Robert Browning and Julia Wedgwood* (1937), pp. 67, 75–77.
"The trouble": *The Major Victorian Poets*, p. 13.

p. 284 "the poet's": *Memoir*, II, 9.

p. 287 *The Holy Grail:* Title-page 1870.

"I had": 30 March 1873. *Memoir*, II, 145, and 145–146.

p. 288 "I am": British Museum; 3 November 1880; cut from *Memoir*, II, 239.
"By Gladstone's": *Memoir*, II, 300.
"This public": *Dear and Honoured Lady*, p. 109; *Memoir*, II, 436.
in 1873: Lincoln; Locker to Emily, 26 March 1873.
"The younger": British Museum; December 1883; *Memoir*, II, 300–301.

p. 289 "We are": Trinity; 29 March 1876.
"There was": E. Abbott and L. Campbell, *Life and Letters of Jowett* (1897), II, 458, 5 October 1892.
"it is": British Museum; 15 December 1881.
"That Hallam": British Museum; 27 September 1883; *Alfred Tennyson*, p. 472.

p. 290 "Tennyson, who": *The Sacred Wood* (1920), p. 62.

p. 291 "the feeling": Jump, p. 362.

p. 292 "Locksley Hall Sixty Years After": For an important reply to Tennyson's onslaught on the age, see Gladstone, *Nineteenth Century*, January 1887.
"To me": National Library of Scotland; 26 October 1875. Sanders, *PMLA*, LXXVI (1961), 95.
"to produce": *Views and Reviews*, p. 166.

p. 293 "His genius": *National Review*, October 1859; Jump, p. 230. See also R. H. Horne (Jump, p. 160); and Elizabeth Barrett's letter to Browning, 13 June 1845 (*Letters*, I, 93–94).

p. 293n "one of": "The Reaction Against Tennyson" (1914); *A Miscellany* (1929), p. 26.

p. 294 "this exceeding": Lincoln; 30 April 1879.
"hung between": *Memoir*, II, 323.
"the loss": Huntington letter (F1 4119); 26 October 1886.

p. 295 "As years": *Bookman*, December 1892, reviewing *The Death of Œnone; Uncollected Prose*, I, 252–253.

p. 296n "Moreover, he": C. L. Graves, *Life and Letters of Sir George Grove* (1903), p. 156.
"He was": John Bright, *Diaries* (1930), p. 390, 26 April 1877.
"He formulated": *Nineteenth Century*, XXXIII (1893), 169.

p. 298 "one curious": *Unpublished Early Poems by Alfred Tennyson* (1931), p. x.
"He was": "Tennyson and the Spirit of the Age," *All in Due Time*, p. 127.

p. 299 "Out of": This phrase occurs in both "Perdidi Diem" and "St. Lawrence."

p. 310 "Many of": *All in Due Time*, p. 129.

p. 312 "To me": "A Word about Tennyson," 1887; Jump, pp. 349–350.

p. 313 "His last": *Memoir*, II, 427–428.

p. 314 "Till our": Hallam's "To Two Sisters" (Motter, p. 90).

INDEX

Index